Systems Theories for Psychotherapists

Systems Theories for Psychotherapists explores three key theories that underpin many of the models of psychotherapy: general systems theory, natural systems theory, and language systems theory. The book presents the aesthetics (how to see and understand what is happening) and the pragmatics (what to do in the therapy room) behind each theory. It also explores how therapists can successfully conceptualize the problems that clients bring to therapy, offering a range of contemporary examples to show how each theory can be applied to practice.

Starting with an introduction to systems theories, the book then delves into cybernetics, interactional systems, natural systems, constructivist theory, and social construction theory. Each chapter uses a distinctive case example to help clinicians to better understand and apply the theories to their own therapeutic setting. Woven throughout the book are three helpful learning tools: "Applying Your Knowledge," "Key Figure," and "Questions for Reflection," providing the reader with the opportunity to critically engage with each concept, consider how their own worldview and preconceptions can inform their work with clients, and challenging them to apply prominent systems theories to their own practice.

Systems Theories for Psychotherapists is a clear and valuable text for undergraduate and graduate students in mental health programs, including counseling, marriage and family therapy, social work and clinical psychology, as well as for all practicing clinicians.

Michael D. Reiter is the author of seven previous books, approved supervisor by the American Association of Marriage and Family Therapy (AAMFT), and a licensed marriage and family therapist. He is professor of Family Therapy at Nova Southeastern University.

Systems Theories for Psychotherapists

From Theory to Practice

Michael D. Reiter

Routledge
Taylor & Francis Group
NEW YORK AND LONDON

First published 2019
by Routledge
52 Vanderbilt Avenue, New York, NY 10017

and by Routledge
2 Park Square, Milton Park, Abingdon, Oxon, OX14 4RN

Routledge is an imprint of the Taylor & Francis Group, an informa business

© 2019 Taylor & Francis

The right of Michael D. Reiter to be identified as author of this work has been asserted by him in accordance with sections 77 and 78 of the Copyright, Designs and Patents Act 1988.

All rights reserved. No part of this book may be reprinted or reproduced or utilised in any form or by any electronic, mechanical, or other means, now known or hereafter invented, including photocopying and recording, or in any information storage or retrieval system, without permission in writing from the publishers.

Trademark notice: Product or corporate names may be trademarks or registered trademarks, and are used only for identification and explanation without intent to infringe.

Library of Congress Cataloging-in-Publication Data
Names: Reiter, Michael D., author.
Title: Systems theories for psychotherapists : from theory to practice / Michael D. Reiter.
Description: New York, NY : Routledge, 2019. | Includes bibliographical references and index.
Identifiers: LCCN 2018034603 (print) | LCCN 2018035270 (ebook) | ISBN 9780429444029 (E-book) | ISBN 9781138335035 (hbk) | ISBN 9781138335042 (pbk) | ISBN 9780429444029 (ebk)
Subjects: | MESH: Psychotherapy—methods | Systems Theory | Models, Psychological | Personal Construct Theory
Classification: LCC RC480.5 (ebook) | LCC RC480.5 (print) | NLM WM 420 | DDC 616.89/14—dc23
LC record available at https://lccn.loc.gov/2018034603

ISBN: 978-1-138-33503-5 (hbk)
ISBN: 978-1-138-33504-2 (pbk)
ISBN: 978-0-429-44402-9 (ebk)

Typeset in Joanna MT & Frutiger
by Apex CoVantage, LLC

This book is dedicated to my wife, Yukari, who keeps me connected to a variety of larger systems.

Contents

Preface		xii
1	**Introduction to Systems Thinking**	**1**
	Case Description	1
	Understanding Your Client	4
	Case Conceptualization	6
	Lineal and Nonlineal Epistemologies	10
	Systems Theory	11
	Bioecological Model of Human Development	13
	Key Figure: Gregory Bateson	14
	Systems	15
	Theory and Practice	18
	Structure of the Book	19
	Questions for Reflection	19
2	**Cybernetics Aesthetics**	**20**
	Case Description	20
	A Brief History of Cybernetics	21
	Key Figure: Norbert Wiener	21
	Feedback	22
	Restraint	25
	Tendencies	27
	Entropy and Negentropy	27
	Homeostasis	28
	Morphostasis/Morphogenesis	31
	Theory of Logical Types	32
	Circularity and Recursion	34
	Double Description	37
	Questions for Reflection	38
3	**Cybernetics Pragmatics**	**39**
	Case Description	39
	Stability and Change	40
	Behavior	40
	Rules	43
	Overt Rules	45
	Key Figure: Don D. Jackson	46

	Covert Rules	47
	Marital Quid Pro Quo	48
	Family Myths	49
	Hypotheses	50
	Roles	51
	Equifinality	53
	Circular Questions	55
	Differences in Perception of Relationships	56
	Differences in Degree	56
	Differences in Temporality	56
	Hypothetical and Future Differences	58
	Questions for Reflection	59
4	**Interactional Aesthetics**	**60**
	Case Description	60
	Difference	61
	Distinctions	62
	Information	63
	Punctuations	63
	Redundancy/Pattern	65
	Symmetrical and Complementary Patterns	66
	Map/Territory	69
	Ecology	70
	Whole/Part	71
	Key Figure: Paul Watzlawick	74
	Open and Closed Systems	74
	Boundaries	75
	Diversity	77
	Family Life Cycle	78
	Questions for Reflection	80
5	**Interactional Pragmatics**	**81**
	Case Description	81
	Axioms of Communication	81
	Axiom 1	82
	Axiom 2	83
	Axiom 3	86
	Verbal and Paralingual Communication	87
	Content/Process	88
	Metacommunication	90
	Axiom 4	90
	Axiom 5	91
	Key Figure: John Weakland	92
	First Order Change	93
	Second Order Change	93
	Paradox	96
	Paradoxes in Therapy	97

	Boundary Making	100
	Questions for Reflection	100
6	**Natural Systems Aesthetics**	**102**
	Case Description	102
	Key Figure: Murray Bowen	104
	The Emotional System	105
	Anxiety	107
	Individuality and Togetherness	109
	Bowen's Eight Concepts	111
	Differentiation of Self	111
	Emotional Triangles	114
	Nuclear Family Emotional Process	116
	Family Projection Process	119
	Multigenerational Transmission Process	120
	Emotional Cutoff	121
	Sibling Position	121
	Societal Regression	122
	Questions for Reflection	123
7	**Natural Systems Pragmatics**	**124**
	Case Description	124
	Genograms	124
	Illustrating Genogram Mechanics	125
	Self of the Therapist in Bowen Family Systems Practice	133
	Detriangulating	135
	Key Figure: Michael Kerr	137
	Therapist as Coach	138
	Effectiveness of Natural Systems Theory	139
	Questions for Reflection	140
8	**Constructivist Aesthetics**	**142**
	Case Description	142
	Constructivism	142
	Realism	144
	Radical Constructivism	145
	Observer	147
	Postpositivism	148
	Reality	149
	Autopoiesis	150
	Key Figure: Humberto Maturana	151
	Structure (Determined and Coupling)	152
	Perturbations	153
	Languaging	154
	Meaning	156
	Coordination	157
	Hermeneutics	158

	Deconstruction	159
	Discourse	160
	Questions for Reflection	161
9	**Constructivist Pragmatics**	**162**
	Case Description	162
	Constructivist Psychotherapy	162
	Focusing on Meanings	164
	Meanings in Therapy	166
	Story/Storyteller	167
	Problem-Determined and Problem-Organizing Systems	170
	Key Figure: Harlene Anderson	172
	Curiosity	176
	Distinguishing Self	176
	Casual Enactments	178
	Scaling Questions	179
	Questions for Reflection	180
10	**Social Construction Aesthetics**	**181**
	Case Description	181
	Modernism Versus Postmodernism	182
	Social Constructionism	183
	Key Figure: Kenneth Gergen	185
	Discourses	185
	Power	186
	Personal Agency	187
	Authenticity	188
	Reality as Multiverse	190
	Systems Stories	191
	Language Games	191
	Misunderstandings of Conversations	191
	The Structure of Narratives	192
	Deconstruction and Reconstruction	193
	Relational Responsibility	194
	Strengths Rather Than Deficits	196
	Questions for Reflection	197
11	**Social Construction Pragmatics**	**198**
	Case Description	198
	Social Constructionist/Postmodern Therapy	198
	Client as Expert	200
	Co-Construction	201
	Re-Authoring Conversations	202
	Externalization	202
	Counter Documents	206
	Outsider Witness Practices	207
	Reflecting Teams	208
	Problem Talk Versus Solution Talk	210

Key Figure: Insoo Kim Berg and Steve de Shazer	213
Either/Or and Both/And	214
Therapy via Questions	215
Resources	216
Questions for Reflection	217
References	218
Index	224

Preface

One of the reasons that I wanted to write this book was because people new to the field of psychotherapy were either not engaging with the main tenets of the various systems theories or were finding that the readings were not written in a way for clear understanding. This book is an attempt to present many of the primary ideas of three of the most influential systems theories in a clear and useful manner.

I want to make evident that we (myself and the various contributors) are therapists, and as such, we are privileging therapists' perspectives of the various ideas of systems theory. We understand that many of the ideas we will be talking about in this book were developed in fields far afield from psychotherapy. However, given that we are psychotherapists who are trying to talk to psychotherapists, we will primarily present these ideas through their use by therapists and about therapy. Further, this presentation will be our understanding and usage of the concepts, which others may understand in their own way. We acknowledge that others may conceptualize the ideas differently.

While we provide many concepts from each of the various systems theories on how to view what is happening for people, we are not providing the full picture. Each of these theories can be explored in much greater depth, and we encourage you to bore into each in more detail. Further, we cannot list every means and method here in what therapists do based on these epistemologies. We have chosen those techniques that we find most useful and most representative. For most of the book, we use a semi-piecemeal approach where we discuss various ways of thinking and behaving that are connected to a specific systems theory. However, due to space limitations, we cannot provide a full-blown therapeutic model that is informed by that theory (except in the case of natural systems theory). We apologize to those therapists operating from these various systems theories who may use them differently in the therapy room. Again, we encourage you, the reader, to continue further explorations into these various landscapes.

We believe that concepts are best understood when contextualized. This is why we decided to provide a case example for every chapter pair so that you can see how the ideas and techniques can be useful in the therapy room. For us, if an idea cannot be applied in your practical dealings with clients, it is not that useful for you and becomes more of an academic exercise. Since therapy is about assisting people to live the lives they desire, hopefully everything in this book can be used to help you understand and work with clients more efficiently and effectively. Further, in order to reduce the awkward use of "his or her" and "himself or herself," we have decided to alter the use of gender pronouns throughout the book. In all odd numbered chapters, the therapist pronoun is "he" and the client pronoun "she." In even numbered chapters the therapist pronoun is "she" and the client pronoun "he."

I want to thank Christopher F. Burnett for contributing the two chapters on natural systems theory as well as the cover artwork for the book, as he has for most of my previous books. My colleague, Jim Hibel, helped ensure that the constructivist chapters represented our construction of those ideas. Clinton Lambert aided in the initial conceptualization of the structure of the book as well as working with me on the cybernetics chapters. My graduate assistant, April Brown, helped me with many of the "Key Figure" features as well as provided significant feedback, which helped the clarity of the chapters. Several of my graduate students read drafts of chapters and provided their feedback, since the book was written for them, and I wanted to ensure that the ideas came across in a manner that was digestible. These students included Rita Cebuc, Brittany Dakota Chabot, Dana Engel, Jessica Popham, Kelsey Railsback, Julie Schwartzberg, Jody Schulz, David Staves, and Boglarka Varga.

I want to thank everyone at Routledge, especially Clare Ashworth, for helping in the production of this book.

CHAPTER ONE
Introduction to Systems Thinking

Michael D. Reiter

We start our exploration of systems theory where it most matters, your contact with a client. Imagine you work for a therapy agency and are meeting with a new self-referred client. The client initially met with an intake specialist who conducted a biopsychosocial assessment. Most agencies, like your hypothetical one, utilize some type of initial assessment to determine the most appropriate services for the client. These might be individual, couple, family, or group therapy. The results of the assessment might also lead the intake specialist to recommend inpatient or outpatient services or perhaps even psychiatric services or hospitalization if the client is at risk of harming self or others. For this case, the intake specialist recommended outpatient individual therapy, and the agency assigned the case to a staff therapist—you. When you get to the office, you are given the write-up of the biopsychosocial, which is presented below.

CASE DESCRIPTION

Presenting Problem

Daniel Martinez is a 32-year-old, married, Hispanic male. He is self-referred for therapy. Daniel explained that he has been depressed for the last three to four months. He is also experiencing anger, mainly at his wife, with whom he says he has been having difficulties getting along with for the last year. While the depressed feelings are causing him great concern, they have not interfered with his ability to work as a music teacher at a local middle school.

History of Presenting Problem

Daniel explained that, while he was never a happy-go-lucky type of person, he never experienced this level of upset and malaise before in his life. There were times in his life he felt very sad, but nothing that he thought was abnormal. Daniel's father died four years ago after getting into a car accident while he was driving drunk. Daniel never had a very close relationship with his father and found himself being more angry at his father than sad. The primary times in his life when he found himself very sad were the deaths of his two cats, one that died when he was 16 and the other that died seven years ago.

Current Medications

Daniel reported that he is currently not on any medications and has never taken any. He has no history of substance use or abuse.

Other Relevant History

Developmental/Medical History

Daniel stated that as far as he knows, his mother's pregnancy with him was normal. Daniel reported that he met all of his developmental milestones such as crawling, walking, talking, and potty training on time. Current medical history is that the client goes regularly for checkups and has had no hospitalizations, medical illnesses, or surgeries.

Psychiatric History

Daniel reported no psychiatric history for himself or in his family. However, he stated his family has an aversion of psychiatry, and no one in his family has ever seen a psychotherapist or psychiatrist. Daniel explains that this is his first time ever going to a psychiatrist or therapist.

Current Family History

Daniel married Johanna 11 years ago. They had met in high school and dated on-and-off through college, as Daniel went for a music degree at a state school that was four hours from their hometown. Once he graduated, he moved back home, and he and Johanna married. Two years later, they had their first child, a son they named Jonathan. Two years after this, they had their second child, a daughter they named Miranda. There are no current financial stressors in the immediate family.

Past Family History

Daniel is the second child of three siblings to Carlos and Lucy. He has an older sister, Carla, and a younger brother, Tico. Daniel was born in Nicaragua, and his early childhood was uneventful. Carlos worked as a carpenter for a furniture manufacturer. Daniel reports that Carlos was "old school" and would discipline with an iron hand. He never felt close or connected to his father. As far as Daniel could remember, Carlos always drank. He was mainly a beer drinker but would drink hard liquor when available. Daniel stated that he does not think his parents had a loving marriage.

When Daniel was 11, his parents moved the family to the United States to have greater opportunities for the children. His father found construction work and was able to support the family, although the family was not well off. Daniel got along well with his sister but seemed to have a competitive relationship with his brother. Currently, he is not that close with either. Carla, his sister, is married with two children and lives in Managua, Nicaragua. Tico is currently working in Europe in the field of finance. Daniel has not seen him in over two years.

Daniel loves his children but states that sometimes he is not sure how to be a good father. He knows that he does not want to raise his children the way his parents raised him.

Educational History

Daniel was an average student through elementary, middle, and high school. When he was 11, his parents moved from Nicaragua to the United States. One year later his mother bought him a guitar for his birthday, and Daniel took to it. At 14, Daniel formed a band that he stayed in throughout high school. He found enjoyment in practicing and playing gigs at local venues. At 13, Daniel's parents divorced. Daniel stated he was not that impacted by this event as his parents had been fighting a lot as long as he can remember. Daniel went to the state university to study music. He graduated with average grades and decided to move back home to be with Johanna, a Caucasian female he had met and began dating in high school. Daniel stated that he did not think he was good enough to be a professional musician but wanted to train the next generation of aspiring musicians. He joined a local band that played cover songs and occasional originals. This is one of his most enjoyable activities; however, that band ended nine months ago. He is currently looking for a new band to join.

Social History

Daniel reported that he gets along well with others but finds that he is a bit on the introverted side. He has never had a large friend base, especially when he first moved to the United States, as he had little facility with the English language. He is currently fluent but still has an accent. During high school, he dated a couple of female classmates, but nothing that he considers to be serious until he met Johanna. Daniel finds that he is able to connect with people around music. For the most part his relationships with bandmates have been positive, but he has had occasional disputes with various bandmates based on differences in musical directions. These disputes were verbal rather than physical. There was no history of relationship violence in any of Daniel's relationships.

Vocational History

Daniel earned a Bachelor's degree in music and began teaching private lessons upon his graduation. At 23, he began teaching music at an elementary school. He held that job for five years and then became the music teacher at a middle school, primarily for the jazz band.

Legal History

Daniel reported no legal history. He is a permanent resident to the United States but still maintains his Nicaraguan passport as well as his US passport.

Assessment of Spirituality and Cultural Concerns

Daniel reported no spiritual or cultural concerns. He was born and raised Catholic and believes in God; however, he mainly attends church for special events such as weddings or holidays. His current family primarily speaks English although he tries to occasionally speak Spanish with his children since his mother is more comfortable speaking in Spanish and he would like the children to have some of his linguistic cultural heritage.

Mental Status Exam and Client Strengths

Daniel is a 32-year-old, married, Hispanic male. He arrived on time to the interview, was dressed casually, and was well groomed. The interview was conducted in English. While he had an accent, the content of his speech was well articulated with no seeming language barrier. He was orientated to place, person, and time, with no evidence of formal thought disturbance. He denied experiencing hallucinations and delusions. Daniel also denied any suicidal or homicidal ideation, plan, or intent. The client's strengths are his affability, commitment to work, and family orientation.

Understanding Your Client

Even before you enter the room with your new client, you have preconceptions about what may be happening for him. These preconceptions come from your therapeutic training and are mainly connected to your theoretical orientation. This is why a social worker, mental health counselor, marriage and family therapist, and clinical psychologist may understand differently what is important to look for when first meeting a client as well as what might happen in therapy. We are trained in our graduate programs what to explore and what to give priority to. These trainings usually become the foundation for our preconceptions. This is one reason why it is important for therapists to engage with ideas outside of their scope of training, to bring in new ideas in order to expand their theoretical basis.

Not only do people have preconceptions for what happens inside the therapy room, they also have them for what happens outside of therapy. All people have views and ideas of why people behave the way they do. They then apply these conceptions to every situation they find themselves in. These views are informed by people's understanding on human functioning they may have learned through classes, religious training, or pieced together on their own. Take a second and remember a time when you talked with your friends or family about a third person's behavior. The person you were talking with had some explanation for why the third person was doing what s/he was doing. Further, the person paid attention to certain actions, statements, or non-actions from the third person and then created an explanation for them. For instance, the person might say, "Amanda must have yelled at me because she was frustrated at work and didn't like that I was trying to encourage her to stand up for herself." Someone else might say, "Amanda yelled because she is jealous of me." Here, we can see that people utilize their own way of understanding self and others. In this book, we hope to provide several frameworks for understanding people that might help clients shift from a problem experience to a more preferred life.

Let's go back to our client, Daniel, and the biopsychosocial assessment you've been given. Besides the therapist's own way of understanding, using a biopsychosocial assessment also has preconceptions about what may be happening for the client. There is a built-in assumption that there are biological, psychological, and social components and that these are connected, but not the same. Further, focusing on each of these areas and their interconnections are important to help the clinician develop a case conceptualization that includes why the person is having the current difficulties and what might be done to help the person reach his goals.

The assumptions that people have as to why people function as they do are not innately bad or good, but they are not neutral either. These starting premises have consequences; they contribute to the experience and effect of a session for the client, therapist, and agency. They impact how the therapist attempts to enter into a relationship with a client, what the therapist expects from self and client, and the direction the therapist wants therapy to go. Thus, a therapist's viewpoints and theoretical assumptions become of primary importance when a therapist begins working with a client.

We are talking about people in general, but we want you, the therapist, to really experience these ideas, so throughout this book, we will ask you to do some self-reflection and self-awareness exercises. You, like all people, have premises, assumptions, and preconceptions that inform how you see the world and how you interact with others. How often have you taken time to explore the frameworks you utilize to help you organize yourself in your contact with the world? For most people, not too often. Take a few moments and think about how you see the world. Why do people do what they do? What is important for you to think about when exploring human functioning? What starting premises do you hold? These are big questions that may be difficult for you to answer at this point, but you will hopefully be able to by the end of this book. To help you in this process, we will zoom in our lens and have you begin to become aware of your preconceptions and assumptions by thinking about our client Daniel.

Applying Your Knowledge

For our client Daniel, answer the following questions.

1. What would you say is the biggest concern that Daniel faces?
2. Why do you think Daniel is having his current problem(s)?
3. What role do you think medication(s) might play for Daniel?
4. How motivated do you think Daniel is to not have this problem?
5. How hopeful are you that Daniel will overcome this issue?
6. How long do you expect therapy to last?
7. Who is the client? Might you conceptualize the client as someone other than or in addition to Daniel? If so, who?
8. Who is involved in the problem/solution? Therapy?
9. What, if anything, does Daniel's context mean for the problem?
10. What patterns do you notice in Daniel's life, especially surrounding the problem?

The answers to the questions presented in the "Applying Your Knowledge" section have serious consequences. They represent how you view and will likely interact with your client as well as what is most likely to happen in the therapy room between the two of you. For instance, if you answered that Daniel is depressed because he has low self-esteem, you are likely to meet with Daniel and focus therapy around ways to increase his self-esteem. If you believe that Daniel is depressed because there is some type of biochemical imbalance happening in his brain, you will likely refer him for a psychiatric consult for the possibility of talk therapy in combination with psychotropic medication. Conversely, if you believe Daniel is experiencing depression because he is involved in a relationship with his wife Johanna that is not in line with his expectations for what it means to be married, then you would be more likely to invite Johanna into therapy with Daniel and discuss the patterns of their relationships. This would allow you to explore how they might change the marital relationship to better fit their hopes and expectations of what they want for their marriage.

If you work in an agency, the agency's answers to these questions also have serious consequences. Agencies often have expectations and requirements of what therapeutic model can be used, whether a psychiatric diagnosis needs to be made, and what must be presented in paperwork, as the agency may need to justify the services they are providing to a third party, such as an insurance company. This paperwork can further influence what kinds of thinking and questions you ask and potentially shape how therapy may go. What if your answers to what is happening for the client and the agency's answers are different? What if your answers differ from your client's? What if your answers, those of the agency, and those of your client each differ? How do you bridge these various viewpoints and expectations?

When using the information from the biopsychosocial, we start to piece together a picture of who our client is. From this picture, we make therapeutic choices. For many therapists in agency settings, they usually end the biopsychosocial with a section about clinical findings, diagnostic impressions, and a possible treatment plan. The sections on clinical findings and diagnostic impressions lead us to fill in the blanks of what is happening for our client and creates a view of "truth" as to what is happening for him. This process is known as a case conceptualization. While not all therapists utilize a biopsychosocial assessment, all therapists do use a case conceptualization, some more overtly than others. Throughout the remainder of this book, we present various ways to conceptualize cases, each of which impacts how you understand what is happening for clients and the possible pathways in therapy.

CASE CONCEPTUALIZATION

As a therapist, it is extremely important to understand what is happening for your clients. In other words, why are they having the problem(s) they currently have. Some therapists believe it is imperative to uncover the etiology of the problem; that is, how did it develop? By exploring the etiology of the problem, the therapist may be able to help the client rectify the situation. For instance, if the etiology of Daniel's depression is because of faulty thinking, the therapist can help him learn how to dispute his thoughts. Or if the etiology is chemically based, psychotropic medications might be used. Other therapists don't focus so much on etiology, but instead on how the problem is being maintained. This would lead them to interrupt the client's actions that keep the problem alive.

The understanding of why and/or how a problem is happening is known as a **case conceptualization**. Case conceptualizations are a core competency in psychotherapy (Sperry & Sperry, 2012). They provide the foundation for therapists in order to understand client difficulties as well as therapeutic pathways. It is very important to have a case conceptualization; otherwise, therapy meanders with therapist and client usually having little direction to travel. Or, traveling in a particular direction may be quite temporary, lasting only a single session. Case conceptualizations provide a map to the territory of psychotherapy. They allow therapists to become competent in knowing what it is they are seeing and what they should be doing.

There are two main viewpoints of case conceptualizations. The first is that they are used to explain how come the client is having difficulties (Berman, 2010). This type of conceptualization explores the *why* of the client problem. With this conceptualization, the therapist would then subsequently develop a **treatment plan** that focuses on change. The second viewpoint of case conceptualization is that it is a combination of the *why* with the *what to do* (the conceptualization and the treatment plan). Reiter (2014) explained that case conceptualizations are a combination of two areas: a theory of problem formation and a theory of problem resolution (see Figure 1.1). These two theories are intricately related. Knowing why a problem formed and/or is maintained usually provides the therapist a guide to how the problem will be resolved. For instance, viewing Daniel's depression as his attempt to cope with the current organization of his family, the therapist would then focus on reorganizing the family in a way that Daniel, and the other members of the family, find more satisfying. A conceptualization of Daniel's problems occurring because he has not yet developed his own sense of self—he has not differentiated himself yet—would lead the therapist to help Daniel develop an "I" position where he can distinguish his own thoughts and processes from other family members.

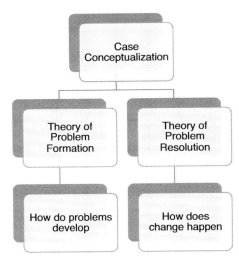

Figure 1.1 The Two Components of Case Conceptualizations: A Theory of Problem Formation and a Theory of Problem Resolution.

One of the most important skills a psychotherapist has at his disposal is the use of a case conceptualization. This is one of the main ways that a therapist is different from a friend. While friends have their own understanding of why people have problems and what they should do, it is usually a quite limited orientation. Therapist conceptualizations are developed over time through advanced learning in many areas including human development, sexuality, individual, family, and group process, mental health issues, and an understanding of systems. Friends tend to be well intentioned yet ineffective in helping the person to change since they quickly attempt to get the person to stop feeling pain. Just think about the last time you or a friend went through a serious breakup of a romantic relationship. Most likely, someone close to you, or that individual, invariably said something to the effect of, "Don't worry, it's going to be okay. You deserve better. You'll find someone better." While these words and sentiments are supportive, they may come at the expense of allowing the person in pain to feel justified in experiencing their pain. The person does not feel validated and safe to have their experience. They are being told to stop feeling and thinking what they currently experience. Therapists, with a case conceptualization that includes a theory of problem formation and a theory of problem resolution, will take a much different tact with the person. Hopefully, the therapist's position will be much more useful and lead to the person achieving the goals she has for herself.

We can look at this in a different language. The case conceptualization is the combination of cognition and action. Keeney (1983) described the combination of cognition and action as demonstrating a therapist's epistemology (see Figure 1.2). **Epistemology** can be defined as how organisms think, know, and decide (Bateson, 1979). Many people are unaware of their epistemology and act without exploring the rationale for their actions—their cognitions. Therapists are trained to connect their thinking and doing. Therapist training and classwork focuses on how to think about what is occurring for self, others, and the interaction between the two and how therapists can use their knowing to decide what to do. Likewise, a therapist's case conceptualization is perhaps the primary way to understand the therapist's epistemology. It is an important clue as to how the person/therapist comes in contact with the world and organizes information. This organization then helps the therapist determine what actions to take.

Applying Your Knowledge

Take a few moments to think about your own therapeutic epistemology. In one paragraph, how would you describe your theory of problem formation? How would you describe your theory of problem resolution? Based on your theory of problem resolution, what therapeutic strategies do/would you tend to utilize? How does exploring these areas help you to understand yourself better as a clinician?

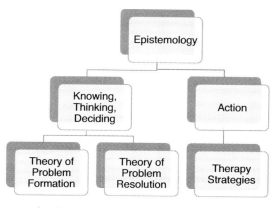

Figure 1.2 The Components of a Therapist's Epistemology.

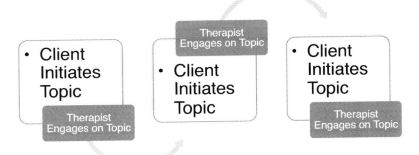

Figure 1.3 The Process of Conversation When a Therapist Follows a Client's Lead.

A therapist's case conceptualization is his conduit to take theory and put it into practice. Without a case conceptualization, therapists would most likely be jumping around and following a client's lead. While, in theory, following a client's lead is not problematic, it is troublesome when it does not come with a way of understanding why following that client's lead is useful. However, there have been times when following the client's lead, even when not understanding why, can prove useful. Yet this occurs more out of luck than skill. Understanding why would potentially offer far more useful opportunities far more often as the therapist would be better able to replicate pathways that were effective toward positive change for the client.

This brings us back into the realm of epistemology. The therapist needs a way of understanding his own process of understanding. Otherwise, therapist and client will most likely have conversations ad infinitum as the client will bring up a new topic, the therapist will engage her about that topic, the client will bring up a new topic, the therapist would follow, etc. (see Figure 1.3).

This process happens every day in most people's conversations, and there is nothing problematic about it. This is what we would consider small talk between people where they chit-chat on various topics such as the recent football game, a movie, or the weather. However, within the context of a therapeutic conversation, just following the client's lead is problematic. It is missing the *therapeutic* component—a component that leads to change. Without the therapeutic component, the therapist is just following the client's train of thought without utilizing his own view of the purpose of the therapy. This is where a case conceptualization becomes quite useful.

The therapist's case conceptualization helps the therapist pay attention to some ideas and actions rather than others. This trained and focused attention provides the basis for guiding the therapeutic conversation into areas that become ripe for change to occur. Keeney (1983) explained the importance of knowing what to look for in the therapeutic situation, "Basic to understanding epistemology is the idea that what one perceives and knows is largely due to the distinctions one draws" (p. 24). Case conceptualizations provide the therapist with ideas of which distinctions to make. This may come in the form of paying attention to a person's thinking, behavior, and/or feelings. Alternatively, case conceptualizations lead to the therapist making a distinction about seeing a client as an individual, a couple, or a family.

Keeney (1983) reasoned that *what* we know is inseparable from *how* we know. This is the difference between content and process. We all have various facts that we can recall. Yet there are unique ways in how we come to gather those facts and how we put them together. What distinctions we draw not only influence what we see happening for the client, therapist, and therapeutic encounter, but they influence what we see happened in the past and is happening in the present and potential future. How we explain the *what we know* and *how we know* demonstrates how we see the world.

Having a means of making distinctions provides the therapist with a lens in which to see what is happening for the client, the therapist, and the therapeutic encounter. Keeney (1983) explained, "The

INTRODUCTION TO SYSTEMS THINKING

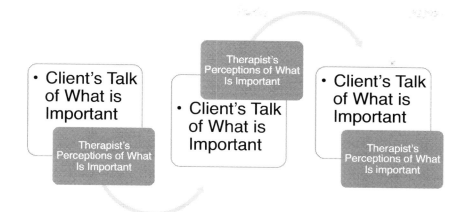

Figure 1.4 The Process of a Conversation When the Therapist Follows the Client's Lead Through His Own Perception of What Talk Is Important.

most basic act of epistemology is the creation of a difference" (p. 18). The therapist will then, based on his premises of what differences are important, guide the therapeutic conversation in particular ways (see Figure 1.4).

Here, the client usually discusses what she believes is important to her and, consequently, what she thinks the therapist should know. The therapist, utilizing a specific case conceptualization, will then respond to that information in a certain way. Perhaps this will be to acknowledge it, ask more questions about it, or ignore it if it does not fit within the framework of what the therapist believes is useful. Keeney and Ross (1983) explained that the therapist serves a function of an "information gatekeeper," determining what gets talked about and what information is not highlighted. This gatekeeping occurs through the therapist filtering the information based on his case conceptualization. Some information the client presents will fit the case conceptualization, and the therapist will remain in that conversational space. Other information will not fit the case conceptualization, and the therapist will not continue talking about it. Likewise, the client will also acknowledge, ask further about, or ignore what the therapist says in relation to how that fits within the client's framework of what is important to discuss in the therapy session.

Let's go back to our client, Daniel. We now know that all therapists who would work with Daniel will display their epistemology through their case conceptualization. Some of these therapists would take a lot of time to scrutinize their thought processes, the philosophy behind their ideas, what it means about how people function, and who they are as a person/therapist. Other therapists working with Daniel would not take much time thinking about what is going on for him and would just act. Both of these extremes demonstrate the epistemology of that therapist. The former extreme may lead to nothing beneficial happening in therapy since the therapist is not trying to intervene. The latter extreme may lead to the therapist saying or doing something rash that may even be harmful for the client. There is also a middle ground where there is a balance between thinking about our understandings and using those to make thoughtful interventions in the therapy room. We present to you now some quick examples of how there is a connection between the thinking and doing of therapy.

A therapist using a Rogerian model may conceptualize this case by seeing that Daniel is currently not living congruently. This may be because he was raised with conditions of worth—he had to be a certain type of child for his father to accept him. He may also be experiencing this with his wife. From the Rogerian perspective of thinking, the therapist's actions are more clearly defined. The therapist would enter the therapeutic conversation with the goal of providing three core conditions to the client: unconditional positive regard, accurate empathic understanding, and transparency (Rogers & Truax,

1967). This would be in the hope that Daniel would begin to live his life in a more congruent manner where his actions are in line with his self-concept.

A therapist using a cognitive-behavioral model would instead make distinctions on what Daniel is telling himself about whatever is happening in his life. When he and his wife argue, the therapist would inquire as to what are Daniel's thoughts and which of these thoughts are irrational beliefs or cognitive errors. Using this way of knowing, the therapist's actions include helping Daniel to identify his thoughts, assess which are useful and which aren't, and then help him to substitute more rational and effective thoughts.

Psychodynamic therapists would explore Daniel's early life to determine the unconscious conflicts Daniel is currently experiencing. This may be that he has not resolved movement through a certain psychosexual stage of development. Based on this way of thinking, the therapist would then utilize distinct strategies for change, such as using interpretations, dream analysis, and exploration of transference.

We have taken time in this introductory chapter to focus on case conceptualizations because they are the conduit for the therapist's epistemology to be useful for the client. As we will explore throughout this book, we cannot look at just the client. We also cannot look just at the therapist. Our understanding of therapy must include the interaction between therapist and client. Further, the understanding has to include the client's context, which may be the family, school, work, religion, etc. We would also need to understand the therapist's context, which may be the location of therapy, aspects of diversity, and the therapist's therapeutic orientation. We would then also need to understand the context in which therapy occurs, as some cultures and social locations privilege the concept of therapy over other cultures. Our aim in this book is to help you to enhance your case conceptualization by utilizing ideas from one or more of the systems theories that will be presented in this book.

LINEAL AND NONLINEAL EPISTEMOLOGIES

There are approximately 400 different psychotherapy models (Kazdin, 1986). While there is overlap between many of them, each has a distinct way of constructing the theory of problem formation and theory of problem resolution. Thus, there are over 400 unique modes of epistemology for therapists. Psychodynamic, Rogerian, and cognitive-behavioral models are just three of many that we could have used as examples. Most of these 400 models utilize a lineal epistemology. A **lineal epistemology** is reductionistic, atomistic, and anticontextual (Keeney, 1983). It used to be called a "linear epistemology" in that it was described like a line segment in geometry. A simple example was A leads to B, which then leads to C, in that order, every time. However, therapists tend to stay far away from all things mathematical, and so they preferred to change the description to "lineal." Therapists who use a lineal epistemology tend to follow a medical model, view psychopathology in a traditional sense, and believe in psychiatric nomenclature (i.e., believe in and use the *Diagnostic and Statistical Manual* (DSM) or the *International Statistical Classification of Diseases and Related Health Problems* (ICD) as guides to what is going wrong for people). While we are not espousing a particular theoretical model in this book, we are promoting a different epistemology than what may be standard.

For our client Daniel, if we were to use a lineal epistemology, we might reduce what is happening to him to a diagnostic label. This might be that he is suffering from Major Depressive Disorder. Given that he currently has this disorder, we would try to treat it, perhaps using medications (a psychiatric consult) or through a theoretical modality, such as cognitive therapy, to help him try to overcome this disorder (see Figure 1.5).

Figure 1.5 Depiction of a Lineal Epistemology.

INTRODUCTION TO SYSTEMS THINKING

In this book, we will focus on a nonlineal epistemology. Therapists who operate from a **nonlineal epistemology** take into consideration complexity, interrelation, and context (Keeney, 1983). Most models of therapy can be viewed with a nonlineal perspective. For instance, in person-centered therapy, the notion of incongruence is housed within a context of relationships. Daniel is not just incongruent; what he is experiencing with his feelings, beliefs, and self-concept is not in line with how he is acting. In essence, while he may see himself as being strong, he experiences himself as weak in that he is not handling his current situation well. The incongruence Daniel experiences is connected to others. Currently it is with his wife Johanna. Daniel may receive messages that he has to be a certain type of husband for Johanna to love him. These conditions of worth may be what Johanna holds or may be Daniel's sense of her expectations. In either case, Daniel's current functioning is interrelational. We can widen the lens of complexity to explore Daniel's family history and the potential conditions of worth that were present while he was growing up. These conditions are not separate from how he has constructed his sense of self. We can widen our lens even further in exploring how Daniel may feel that he is not good enough given that he is an immigrant and does not speak without an accent. This relates to his connection with a larger society.

We hope to show that all therapists, regardless of psychotherapeutic model, could (and should) use a nonlineal epistemology to help them in their work with people. One form of nonlineal epistemology is systems theory. Our aim in this book is to bring in many of the ideas and principles of three different systems theories so that you can first understand and incorporate them into your own way of knowing and then use them to guide your actions as a therapist.

SYSTEMS THEORY

Perhaps the first place we can start in exploring systems theory is to discuss where problems are housed. For many therapists, problems are housed within the person (see Figure 1.6). As a very simplistic explanation, psychoanalytic therapists view problems as being a conflict within people's unconscious processes. Cognitive therapists view problems as people engaging in irrational/illogical beliefs. Person-centered therapists view problems as people being incongruent.

A system's epistemology shifts the location of the problem from within the person to understand the person within her context(s). This notion holds that people's behavior makes sense within the ecology of their context—how the various components come together, such as self, relationships, culture, work, etc. If we only focus on the person, we lose sight of how her problem makes sense given the situation. The context may be a relationship to a person, an organization, or a cultural group. But even the word context is a bit misleading as it seems to be singular rather than plural. For the purposes of this book, we will talk about context with the understanding that within "the context" are multiple contexts. This is where the complexity of a nonlineal epistemology comes into play. As we will explain throughout every chapter, individuals are always involved in a context that has innumerable layers interacting simultaneously.

With this view, we can look at the relationship between context, person, and problem. **Contexts** can be either situational or relational. **Situational contexts** include the *what* or *where* of the action. For instance, some of Daniel's situational contexts include his home, work, band settings, culture, and immigrant status. **Relational contexts** refer to the *who* of the action. For Daniel this could be Johanna, his children, his bandmates, or his students.

Figure 1.6 A Visual Depiction of Problems Being Located Within People.

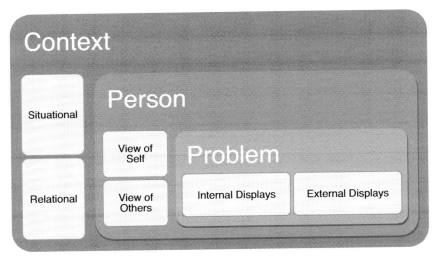

Figure 1.7 The Relationship Between Problems, People, and Context.

Next, we can view the person and the person's view of self and of others. Daniel has a sense of self that includes his self-esteem, self-worth, self-efficacy, etc. He also has a view of others, who they are as a person, what they mean to him, and their importance in his life.

Lastly, we can look at problems and how they display themselves internally or externally. **Internal displays of problems** manifest through negative actions toward the self. For Daniel, these can be seen in his feelings of depression. Other possible internal displays could be feeling unloved, lonely, anxious, and fearful. **External displays of problems** consist of negative actions toward other people or things outside of self. In Daniel's case, this could be, although we have not seen evidence of it, if he physically assaulted Johanna, destroyed bandmates' musical instruments, or was verbally abusive toward his students.

Systems therapists try to understand how the problems, whether internal, external, or both, fit within the person's views of self and other, within a particular context (a combination of situational and relational; see Figure 1.7).

Applying Your Knowledge

Take a moment to think about yourself and a "problem" that you are currently experiencing. This may be a problem you consider individual or relational. Think about the internal displays you have around the problem. When you think of that problem, what feelings come to your awareness? What beliefs do you have around this problem? How does the problem impact your cognitions? Now think about the external displays. How do you act toward others around the problem? How can people see that you are experiencing the problem? Shift up a level to think of your sense of personhood in connection to the problem. What is your view of yourself in dealing with the problem? What is your view of others? Now shift up one more level and think about the context. What are the situational aspects of the problem? When does it occur? Where? Lastly, think about the relational context. What are the relational interactions that impact the problem? Who is involved in the maintenance of the problem? Does looking at the problem as being housed within a context change your understanding of the problem? Does it change your relationship to the problem?

Systems thinking does not suggest you must lose the understandings of individuals and internal/external displays of problems within them. Rather, systems thinking suggests that that understanding is simply incomplete without also understanding the relationships between each layer. It is in describing relationships and how they interact with one another, which defines the thinking as systemic. Therefore, there are plenty of ways that individuals can be described systemically. One way to systemically describe relationships and their interactions is the Bioecological Model of Human Development.

BIOECOLOGICAL MODEL OF HUMAN DEVELOPMENT

We have talked about the nonlineal epistemology, which is based on complexity, interrelation, and context. To explore the notion of complexity and interrelation within contexts, we focus now on how contexts are housed within contexts. One pertinent example of this is **Bronfenbrenner's bioecological model of human development** (Bronfenbrenner & Morris, 2006). This model describes how an individual develops within the various contexts that she interacts with. These include the microsystem, mesosystem, exosystem, and macrosystem. The **microsystem** is the innermost part of the model in which the person actually interacts. This might be the person's family members, friends, neighbors, teachers, etc. The **mesosystem** includes interactions between different parts of the person's microsystem. This would be the person's family interacting with her friends. The **exosystem** is composed of aspects that do not directly impact the person but impact the microsystem. For instance, a change in a spouse's work schedule changes the responsibilities of the partner at home as she now has to fill the void left by the other person. The **macrosystem** is the widest impacting component in which laws, beliefs, and cultures impact the microsystem. Figure 1.8 presents the bioecological model.

If we use Daniel as an example, he is the center of this framework. He has a unique way of viewing the world that leads him to behave in certain ways—which we call his personality. His microsystem includes his wife, children, students, mother, bandmates, acquaintances, etc. Daniel's mesosystem may be the interactions between his wife and his mother, his mother and his children, and his bandmates and his

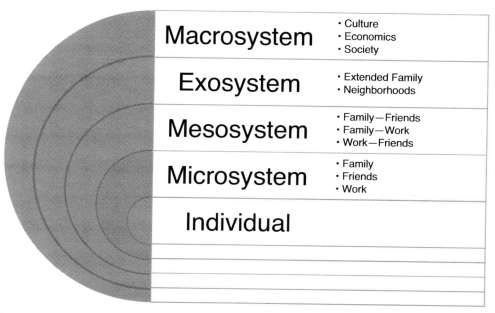

Figure 1.8 Bronfenbrenner's Ecological Systems Theory.

wife. The exosystem includes the school system, the current political system, the economy, etc. Daniel's macrosystem would also include the norms and values of the cultures that inform Daniel on who he is. These may have roots in religion, US values, and Nicaraguan values or cultural views, amongst others. If we only looked at Daniel as someone with specific personality traits, we would miss out on much of the influence on him. We would lose the sense that there is variety in how his personality is displayed, which is based upon the situational and relational contexts Daniel experiences in that moment. In ever expanding layers, we need to look at how his family members' interactions impact him (and how he impacts them); his role in interactions between those close to him (such as being triangulated between his mother and his wife); how his job impacts him as well as his influence on the school system; and how his values were influenced by the main cultures he associates with, which include those from Nicaragua, the United States, and Catholicism.

Bronfenbrenner also discussed the **chronosystem**, which is the impact that time and historic influences have on the interplay of the individual and the various systems impacting her. People may move in and out of the microsystem, as people change contexts, such as graduating from a school and entering into a workplace, and getting married or divorced. The exosystem may change when governments change, such as when the President of the United States and Congress switch from one political party to another. The mesosystem would also change as the connection between the exosystem and microsystem changes because of new ideas, policies, or people. For Daniel, his view of himself has changed from when he was a child growing up in Nicaragua to when he first moved to the United States and had difficulty adjusting because of a language barrier. These views then changed when he became an adolescent, where peers may have played a larger role, to when he was dating as a young adult, to today understanding himself as husband, father, teacher, son, and friend. By understanding the chronosystem, we can see how the person's worldview, behaviors, and personality change based on the interactions between the various systems.

We will not discuss Bronfenbrenner's bioecological model of human development again, but use it here to help you to see how an individual can be viewed as more than just an isolated entity—how individuals are not only a system unto themselves but are connected to a variety of systems. No one functions as an isolate. We all have connections. These connections are to people, organizations, and ideas. For most of this book, we will focus on the individual's connection to those people in her microsystem—primarily her family, but there is always more to the context than we can see and understand.

Key Figure

Gregory Bateson

Gregory Bateson was born May 9, 1904 in Grantchester, just outside of Cambridge, England. His life and work cut across many fields including biology, anthropology, social science, and cybernetics. Bateson's father, William Bateson, was a geneticist, a fellow of St. John's College, and the first director of the John Innes Horticultural Institute. During his childhood, Gregory was exposed to natural history, investigating butterflies, beetles, dragonflies, flowering plants, etc.

Bateson graduated Cambridge University in 1925, studying biology, primarily taxonomy. He engaged in graduate work from 1927 to 1929 and had the opportunity to travel to the Galapagos Islands, where he was able to apply his knowledge about natural history. In 1936, he married Margaret Mead, the famous anthropologist. They had a daughter, Mary Catherine Bateson, who became a prominent voice in cultural anthropology. Bateson and Mead divorced in 1950. In 1951, Bateson married Elizabeth Sumner and had a son, John Sumner Bateson. Gregory and Elizabeth divorced in 1957, and Bateson married for the third time in 1961 to Lois Cammack. They had one child, Nora Bateson.

INTRODUCTION TO SYSTEMS THINKING

> Throughout his career, Bateson engaged in many anthropological explorations. On a trip to New Guinea, he studied the Iatmul peoples. From this research, his book *Naven* (1936/1958) was born. Bateson then spent time in Bali, investigating relationships of the native peoples, which was published in his work, *Balinese Character*. Upon returning to the United States, Bateson, with his then wife Margaret Mead, solicited the aid of Milton Erickson, the world's most prominent hypnotherapist at the time to analyze films of Balinese dance and explore how the dancers were in trance.
>
> After World War II, Bateson was a participant in the Macy Conferences. These multidisciplinary conferences brought together leaders from a variety of fields to interact with one another and expand scientific knowledge. Bateson is most famous for his connection with the Macy Conferences that focused on cybernetics. Bateson was able to take the principles of systems theory and cybernetics and apply them to human beings. These ideas, along with the pragmatic therapy of Milton Erickson, became the foundation for many psychotherapeutic models, such as MRI brief therapy and strategic family therapy.
>
> Bateson received a grant from the Rockefeller Foundation in 1952 to study communication. This research project lasted ten years and became extremely important in the history of family therapy. Bateson initially recruited Jay Haley, John Weakland, and William Fry to explore paradoxes in communication. In 1954, the grant ended, and Bateson then obtained a two-year grant from the Macy Foundation. In that same year, Don D. Jackson, a psychiatrist who had worked with schizophrenics, joined the group as a clinical consultant to help explore paradoxical communication in schizophrenics. In 1956, Bateson and colleagues published one of the most important articles of interactional process, "Towards a Theory of Schizophrenia," which introduced the concept of the double bind. This article helped launch the beginning of the field of family therapy.
>
> Perhaps Bateson's most influential work came in 1972 with the publication of his book, *Steps to an Ecology of Mind*. This book brought together many of Bateson's writings in a variety of areas including anthropology, biology, epistemology, and ecology. In 1979, Bateson published *Mind and Nature*, which further advanced the notion of systems theory.
>
> Gregory Bateson died on July 4, 1980.

SYSTEMS

The remainder of this book will focus on several different systems theories: general systems theory, natural systems theory, and language systems. We will provide an introduction to each of these three primary systems theories. Our exploration will start in Chapters 2 and 3 with general systems theory as it relates to cybernetics and then in Chapters 4 and 5 regarding interactional theory, as many models of psychotherapy, especially family therapy models, utilize these ideas as their base. We will then present, in Chapters 6 and 7, ideas from natural systems and close the book with exploring language systems, with roots in constructivism (Chapters 8 and 9) and social constructionism (Chapters 10 and 11), as they also provide a wider lens to understand problems.

So let us take a second to first introduce what a system is, as we will be frequently coming back to this concept. Bateson (1991) defined a **system** thusly, "A system, after all, is any unit containing feedback structure and therefore competent to process information" (p. 260). This definition demonstrates that a system can range in terms of size. On one end is that of a single person (or even smaller, such as a cell; however, in this book, we are primarily talking about human beings). Each individual takes in feedback from the environment, via the senses, and processes that information to determine how to function. Systems can be even larger, to encompass several people, or even as large as countries or groups of nations. Systems can also be large organizations, schools, and ecological or social systems. This is commonly expressed by our descriptions of school *systems*, eco*systems*, the solar *system* the nervous *system*, or any other common phrase that suggests relationship between parts. The most iconic small group system is the family, and we will often talk about clients and their connections to their families in this book.

What we are presenting is not a foreign phenomenon for you as systems have been part of our whole lives. From the day we are born, we are exposed to many systems. First, most of us are born in a hospital. The hospital you were born into is a system. It is comprised of many units (i.e., nursing, doctors, staff, and patients) who work together to function, taking in information from within and without to adjust their rules to work better. That hospital is also part of a larger ethos, the health care system. Besides the health care system, we are born into many other systems, such as those based on the country of birth. But perhaps the most influential system we come into contact with at birth is the family system. We also are born into a cultural system, one that helps determine the type of name we will have, how people treat us, and the meaning that we have for not only our family but for people in society.

One of the hallmarks of systems is that all parts of the system are interconnected and mutually influence one another. We will get into the intricacies of how this happens in later chapters, but for now, we can provide an overall understanding of how the parts in the system function together. In the previous paragraph, we discussed some of the systems a baby comes in contact with when it is first born. When the child is brought home and placed in the crib, many parents hang a mobile for the child to look at. The mobile provides a good metaphor for understanding how systems function. When all of the hanging components (units) are placed in position, the mobile will come to hang in a certain configuration. When you remove one of the pieces, the mobile will shift and stabilize in a different way. Thus, the removal or addition of a piece causes all of the other pieces to shift into a new interdependent configuration.

Applying Your Knowledge

Think about your family system. Include your parents, siblings, spouse, and children (depending on your particular family). Perhaps other people play a significant role such as grandparents, aunts, uncles, or cousins. How did the family system change when a new member entered the system, either through birth or marriage? What new ways of interacting occurred? How did the family system accommodate when someone exited the family, either through death or divorce? You can even include family pets, such as a dog or a cat, and think about how the family reconfigured and interacted around the inclusion of the animal.

Families change and adjust based on the entry or exit of people into the family. For Daniel, his family reorganized when he was born, as they had with the birth of each of his siblings. When he left the house for college, the family had to reorganize again to accommodate him not being there on a daily basis. In his current nuclear family, the structure and functioning of the family shifted with the birth of each child. However, systems change not only by the amount of people coming into or out of the system, but also the functioning level of each person currently in the system. When one person begins to underfunction, one or more other people in that system have to adjust to compensate and will likely overfunction.

In Figure 1.9, Daniel and Johanna function as a parental whole, being able to work together, perhaps not equally or in a mode of being egalitarian, but functioning in a way to support one another in spousal and parental duties. Perhaps Johanna has primary childcare duties while Daniel works outside of the home to provide money for the family. When he comes home, he may prepare dinner, help with homework, oversee bath time, and engage in nighttime rituals. Johanna does not have to do extra work in the

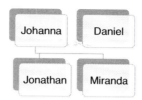

Figure 1.9 Structure of the Martinez Family When Daniel and Johanna Are Functioning Equally.

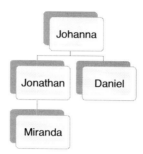

Figure 1.10 Structure of the Martinez Family When Daniel Is Depressed and Underfunctioning and Johanna Is Overfunctioning.

parental realm because Daniel is doing what they have negotiated for him to do, and Johanna is doing what was previously negotiated. Jonathan's and Miranda's behaviors also help maintain this organization.

However, as Daniel begins to decrease his parental engagement as his experience of depression increases, Jonathan and Miranda shift from looking toward him for support to gaining that support from Johanna. Johanna then must increase the time and attention she gives to the children, while also taking care of Daniel as he begins to have difficulties (i.e., becoming more morose, not cleaning up after himself, and not being conscious of household responsibilities). While this caretaking may take a physical form, such as making meals and cleaning house, it is also emotional and psychological. Johanna will have to invest more energy into thinking about Daniel. Through Daniel's underfunctioning and Johanna's overfunctioning, the Martinez family has to reorganize to be able to function in this current crisis (see Figure 1.10).

When one person changes her behavior, it impacts more than the individual. Because people are connected to one another, what we are calling a system, a change in one person will most likely lead to a change in another person. For the Martinez family, a change in any one person impacts a change in all four. As Daniel withdraws from engagement in the family, Johanna increases her engagement and Jonathan and Miranda shift some of their engagement with Daniel to their mother or each other. But a change in any member may lead to a reorganization of how the family functions. For instance, if Jonathan attempts to gain more independence from his family, the other three members would need to accommodate. Perhaps this would be by allowing him more space. This allowance would happen by loosening their proximity to Jonathan with a likely concomitant increasing of proximity to each other. Or they may try to maintain their current functioning, which would also change their interactions as Daniel and Johanna increase behaviors to reduce Jonathan's attempts at independence.

Not only do the people in one system change their interactions and organization when there are changes, but that system's interactions with other systems changes as well. As Daniel begins to underfunction in this family, it is likely he is doing less in his engagement with his family of origin and also at work.

This means that others must compensate for his changed behavior. His mother may look to Johanna for connection to her grandchildren rather than going straight to Daniel. At his work, other teachers may need to cover for him or increase their energy in interacting with him in order that the workplace functions well.

THEORY AND PRACTICE

You may be asking yourself why it is important to understand systems theory (or any framework for psychotherapy). This is because one's theory and one's practice are inextricably linked. As we discussed in the case conceptualization section, whether you know it or not, what you do in the therapy room (theory of problem resolution) is tied to how you view why people have problems (theory of problem formation). Knowing how they are tied together and what your theory of problem resolution/formation is potentially provides more opportunities to make better-informed decisions in therapy.

Every person on earth has problems. This includes your client, your friend, your doctor, your partner, you, and even me! When most people are upset, sad, disappointed, or whatever they may be feeling based on whatever situation they are in, they usually will talk to someone. Mostly they talk to people they are close with, such as a partner, parent, or good friend. The other person is usually caring and will try to provide some type of statement to help the other person out. It may come in the form of an affirmation of the person, "Don't worry so much. You are such a good person and will get through this." While this is nice and supportive, it usually does not lead to change. Understanding change can be quite difficult.

This is where being a psychotherapist is different than being a friend or family member. Like the friend/family member, we want the person to no longer feel the distress she is currently exhibiting. However, how we try to help the person is quite different. The difference comes from the way in which we understand how people develop, maintain, and change problems. This understanding is our theory (of psychotherapy). Usually this theory is one of the therapeutic models that we learned in graduate school (or an integration of models). What we are presenting in this book is one level higher than a specific model of therapy, as we will talk about several overarching theories that many different models operate from.

Based on one's theory, the particulars of what to look for and what to do in therapy become illuminated. Thus, theory is the backbone for practice. Keeney (1983) talked about this connection in terms of aesthetics and pragmatics (see Figure 1.11). **Aesthetics** is the contextual frame. In essence, it is one's overarching theory. The definition of the word aesthetics essentially means "concerned with and appreciation of beauty, especially in art." Descriptions from aesthetics often pertain to the art of therapy or the appreciation of therapy. Another way of explaining aesthetics is that it is the pattern that connects (Bateson, 1979). **Pragmatics** is the practice aspect. Descriptions of pragmatics often pertain to techniques and practical aspects of therapy. Aesthetics without pragmatics does not lead to change. Therapy would be an exploration of what is happening and why it is happening without a sense of where it might go and how it might get there. Pragmatics without aesthetics would not connect to the context in which the problem is housed. It may lead to change, but perhaps not the change the clients, or the therapist, prefers.

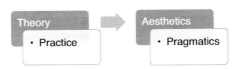

Figure 1.11 The Connection Between Theory/Aesthetics and Practice/Pragmatics.

STRUCTURE OF THE BOOK

This book is structured into chapter pairs that coincide with this notion of the connection between the theory of problem formation and the theory of problem resolution. The first chapter of the pair involves an exploration of the aesthetics of systems theory, focusing on a specific arena from which systems theory originated. In these chapters, we will provide a case example and introduce many systems theory ideas to help you to conceptualize how people function. This first chapter of the pair is the thinking aspect of psychotherapy. The second chapter pair deals with the pragmatics, delving into how therapists utilize the ideas in clinical practice. In these chapters, we continue with the case presented in the aesthetics portion of the chapter pair and provide various techniques that systems therapists might use to help clients. We hope you will see the connection between the aesthetic and pragmatic aspects of psychotherapy, as a therapist understanding what might be happening for people without attempting change does not help the client out of their problematic context. Conversely, attempting change without understanding the client's context might lead to exacerbating the problematic context. We believe that having a grasp of the connection between aesthetics and pragmatics will make you a more influential and effective therapist.

QUESTIONS FOR REFLECTION

1. What do you consider the most important thing to know about your clients? What would be different if something else became more important for you to know about them?

2. How would you describe your current therapeutic epistemology? What would be the opposite epistemology to the one you currently have?

3. Do you prefer learning more about psychotherapy theories or more about techniques and specific questions you can ask or things you can do? Is it okay to prefer both?

4. What is the importance of having a case conceptualization? Is it more important to focus on the theory of problem formation or the theory of problem resolution?

5. What differences would it make if a therapist thinks about clients in larger contexts or smaller contexts? What kinds of questions would be important to each way of thinking?

CHAPTER TWO
Cybernetics Aesthetics

Michael D. Reiter with Clinton Lambert

Chapter 1 introduced us to the idea that every person is a system onto himself, as well as a part in multiple other systems. We now need to explore how a system functions. As we explained previously, there are several different theories of how systems work, such as general systems, natural systems, and language systems. In this chapter, we will be exploring the concept of cybernetics, which is associated with general systems theory, and how that model allows us to see how systems self-regulate. To do so, we will return to our client, Daniel, whom we met in Chapter 1. The following interchange between therapist and client came from the therapeutic discussion of the first session.

CASE DESCRIPTION

Therapist:	What brings you in today?
Daniel:	Well, things haven't quite been going well in my life recently.
Therapist:	What in particular are you most concerned about?
Daniel:	I guess it would be my marriage.
Therapist:	Okay. Your marriage is your biggest concern. Can you tell me something about that?
Daniel:	I've been married for 11 years. For most of the beginning of it, things were fine. We have two children, a boy and girl. They're pretty good kids. They get out of control now and then, but I think it's normal.
Therapist:	You're not that worried about the kids, but about the marriage.
Daniel:	Yes. I can't seem to please my wife. I'm always disappointing her.
Therapist:	How do you know you are disappointing her?
Daniel:	Well, I can see her face sometimes. She also is not as affectionate and fun-loving anymore.
Therapist:	Does she ever tell you that you disappoint her?
Daniel:	Yes. She says things such as, "Are you going to make the bed today?," "You forgot to take the dog on a walk," and "You're not spending enough time with the kids."
Therapist:	What impact do these statements have on you?
Daniel:	I've become depressed recently. You know, a person can only take so much. She'd be mad at me for saying it like this, but she doesn't seem to be able to stop from nagging me so much.

In the previous chapter, we introduced you to the notion of systems. This perspective focuses on how we look at what goes on within a person, between the person and other people, and between the person, other people, and various social contexts. Throughout the remainder of this book we hope to explain how operating from an epistemology of systems theory helps you to help your client. In this chapter, we begin to provide the first level of understanding: through the notion of cybernetics.

Systems theory was first introduced into psychotherapy through the application of ideas from **general systems theory**, which has also sometimes been called cybernetics. However, general systems theory is broader in scope than cybernetics. Bertalanffy (1968, pp. 17, 21) suggested that "cybernetics . . . is but a part of a general theory of systems" but also "should not be identified with 'systems theory' in general." Bateson (1972) described Bertalanffy's general systems work as a context for which to explore cybernetics and where communication takes place. While there are distinctions to be made about general systems theory and cybernetics, the overlap between the two seems to outweigh the differences.

A Brief History of Cybernetics

Cybernetics is a term coined by Norbert Wiener (1948), who defined it as "the science of control and communication in the animal and the machine." Bertalanffy (1968) defined cybernetics as "a theory of control systems based on communication (transfer of information) between system and environment and within the system, and control (feedback) of the system's function in regard to environment" (p. 21). Keeney (1983) defined it more broadly as "part of a general science of pattern and organization" (p. 6). In general, cybernetics explains how a system is self-regulatory, taking in information for possible adaptation or continuation of its current functioning level. Cybernetics could be simply defined as self-correcting systems.

Wiener, and others like him, influenced social scientists and early psychotherapy theorists in promoting machine metaphors to describe human relationships. Perhaps the most common metaphors utilized are the steam engine and the thermostat. The steam engine provides metaphors of analogic feedback, whereas the thermostat describes digital feedback. You may already be familiar with the concepts of "analogic" and "digital" from common clocks and watches. **Analogic communication** means there is a direct correspondence between the "thing" and that which the thing expresses. An analogic clock has hands, which we interpret to tell the time. For therapists, this idea could be loosely translated to nonverbal communication. Some early marriage and family theorists preferred the metaphor "analogic" to "nonverbal" because analogic is also inclusive of the cadence or rhythm of the words as well as how they are sequenced (Watzlawick, Bavelas, & Jackson, 1967). **Digital communication** means that there is not a "thing" used to express another thing. You do not interpret the literal hands of a digital clock; it has none. Digital communication, like digital clocks, is in "words." Words do not have a direct correspondence to that which they describe. For example, the word "long" is not innately longer than the word "short." Digital communication can be loosely interpreted to mean "verbal" communication. Early theorists preferred the metaphor "digital" to "verbal," as it is more inclusive to ideas such as written communication (i.e., letters, texts, emails, etc.). Analogic and digital communication as it relates to therapy will be discussed in Chapter 5.

We can now turn our attention to the second primary metaphor used to discuss how systems are self-regulating, that of the thermostat. An air conditioning system fits the idea of a system from Chapter 1 and describes some basics of cybernetics. The coil or strip expands when the temperature goes up. Once it hits the threshold (i.e., the desired temperature) set by the user, it completes a circuit, turning on the A/C. Once the air cools, the coil or strip contracts, breaking the circuit, thus turning off the A/C. To say it simply, the A/C receives information from the temperature of the room to know when to turn on or off to keep the temperature where it was set. This is a description of a basic cybernetic system as it is self-regulatory.

Key Figure

Norbert Wiener

Norbert Wiener is best known for coining the term "cybernetics." His ability to synthesize mathematics and engineering set the foundations for modern automation, and his ideas continue to influence both the sciences and the arts. He was one of the first to describe "information" as the common language for biology and machines. Gregory Bateson wrote, "I think that cybernetics is the biggest bite out of the fruit of the Tree of Knowledge that mankind has taken in the past 2,000 years" (Bateson, 2000, p. 484).

Norbert Wiener was born on November 26, 1894, in Columbia, Missouri. His father was a professor of Slavic languages and sought to make Wiener a child prodigy. His father's early, rigorous lessons made placing Wiener in school difficult as he was far advanced in some subjects but remedial in others. When Wiener struggled with arithmetic in elementary school, his father decided to put him into algebra instead to offer a greater challenge. Wiener had poor eyesight and coordination, so his doctor prescribed him to quit reading for six months. Therefore, he had to practice mathematics in his head. By age 9, he was taking classes with high school seniors.

After graduating at age 11, Wiener enrolled at Tufts College. As a child, his college days were tough. He was widely acclaimed and often ridiculed for being a prodigy. In 1909, at age 14, he graduated with a degree in Mathematics and enrolled at Harvard for his graduate studies. He graduated Harvard with a Ph.D. at age 18 with his dissertation on mathematical logic, based in part on the ideas of Bertrand Russell. He then left for Cambridge, England, to study directly under Russell who taught him philosophy in addition to mathematics. At 21 years old, just before the start of World War I, he returned to the United States to teach philosophy courses at Harvard.

At 23, he joined the MIT faculty where he was an eccentric professor. He would enthusiastically pick his nose while delivering lectures, snore loudly during faculty meetings, and shake off the ashes of his cigars into his colleagues' chalk trays. He helped create the stereotype of the absent-minded, eccentric, genius professor.

Wiener's idea for cybernetics came to him while he was working on a government contract to build a system that improved the accuracy of anti-aircraft guns. He predicted the plane's location by correlating the measurements of the plane's location with the measurement of the location that immediately preceded it. He weighted the most recent information more than the older information until the measurements had nothing to do with the plane's current location. Each bit of information informed the next bit in real time. This was the basis of feedback. Not only was his development useful for anti-aircraft guns but is still used today in computer vision, vehicle navigation, and many other applications.

At the height of his career, his contributions faded due to his refusal, for ethical reasons, to accept military contracts that wanted to exploit his ideas for profit and war. He was more afraid of the consequences of automation than nuclear weapons, fearing that businesses would use it at the expense of mankind, for the maximization of profits. Norbert Wiener died in 1964, at the age of 69, from a heart attack.

Feedback

Perhaps the most important element of any cybernetic system is the **feedback**. Wiener (1954) defined feedback as "a method of controlling a system by reinserting into it the results of its past performance" (p. 61). Taking the idea of "control" out, feedback is simply when information is being fed back into the system so it can adjust accordingly.

If you have ever been around microphones and speakers, you probably have heard the dreadful consequences of feedback escalating out of control. This feedback sound is an example of **positive feedback** (see Figure 2.1). The microphone picks up sound to be amplified and broadcasts it out of the speaker. If the microphone is too close to the speaker, it will pick up and amplify the sounds of the speaker that in turn feeds back even louder into the microphone. This kind of feedback is unstable and cannot continue to exist as is. Something will eventually give. In this case, the holder of the microphone will probably move away from the speaker upon hearing the cacophony.

We can talk about positive feedback in relation to our client Daniel. In a very simplistic sense, any feedback received by Daniel in which he changes can be considered positive feedback. Imagine Johanna stages an intervention, and family and friends discuss their concern about Daniel's current behavior. If Daniel takes that information in and changes, positive feedback has occurred. In a more subtle way, Daniel may observe that Johanna is less affectionate with him when he is feeling down and she is more attentive when he is feeling up. This may lead him to "act out" more frequently; that is, he would act more "up." Alternatively, Johanna may try to get Daniel to be more active in family life. Her attempts may lead to Daniel feeling more depressed than currently wherein he distances himself from the family. This change would also be considered positive feedback, as there would be a change in the system (even if the change was considered by most people in the system to be "for the worse"). These examples let us know that we don't know whether, in the moment, feedback is positive or negative. Rather, it is the outcome of the feedback wherein we can determine whether the system has remained the same (negative feedback) or has changed (positive feedback).

Negative feedback, conversely to positive feedback, is stabilizing. The air conditioning unit is an example of negative feedback. The hotter it gets in the room, the cooler the air the A/C will blow. The colder it gets in the room, the hotter the furnace will kick on. This feedback serves to keep the room at a fairly consistent temperature, what systems therapists would call homeostasis. For Daniel, if the feedback he gets about his behavior does not lead to him changing, we can consider it negative feedback. This feedback may come in the form of Johanna telling him what he is doing wrong, but doing so in a way that Daniel does not appreciate or recognize as important and thus does not change his behaviors.

The idea behind "positive" and "negative" has to do with the mathematical sign at the end of the formula, not whether it is good or bad. If the formula ends with a positive sign, then it adds more into the equation, giving an even larger positive sign at the end again, which feeds back into an even larger number. In a very simplistic sense, positive feedback highlights a process of change.

If the sign is negative, then the equation cannot spiral outside its limit (see Figure 2.2). Negative feedback describes a process of no change. Negative feedback is a description of the stability of a system. Negative feedback loops are stable and continue to function as they have, where positive feedback loops eventually lead to change of some sort or another.

Figure 2.1 A Visual Depiction of the Positive Feedback Process Where Feedback Leads to a Change in the System.

Figure 2.2 A Visual Depiction of the Negative Feedback Process Where Feedback Does Not Lead to a Change in the System.

One may be tempted to think that therapists are only interested in positive feedback loops, as we often encourage change, but these are descriptions of patterns, not interventions to employ. There are many aspects of people's lives, and of the therapeutic relationship, that therapists want to maintain—or in other words, to focus on negative feedback. In many ways, therapists honor negative feedback more than they do positive feedback. This is usually observed in the therapist credo, "Meet the client where they are at." This demonstrates the thought that the client's current position makes sense in that context. Usually, people will not simply change if you push them. They first want to feel stable and connected and then are more likely to be open to difference.

You have come in contact with feedback for the whole of your life. Some of this feedback has been out of your awareness but still impacts how you function. Other feedback was more obvious. For instance, in school you have most likely written countless papers. Presumably, your teachers have provided you with feedback. This feedback may have been on how well you use the writing style of the field (i.e., APA or MLA format), your grammar, the flow or organization of the paper, as well as the accuracy of the content. Some of the feedback may have stated that you were on track and were doing well in each of these areas. If you received this sort of feedback, you would likely write your paper the same way as you did previously and not change how you functioned. In cybernetics, we would consider this "negative feedback." If the feedback you received explained areas where you could have improved in the way that you constructed the paper and you use that feedback to change how you write your next paper, we would call this "positive feedback." If after each paper you took the instructor's feedback and used it on the next paper, by the end of your schooling, you will most likely be a very good writer as each positive feedback led to a change (one in which you "improved" your process of writing, which "improved" the final output).

Hopefully, you can see that in cybernetics/systems theory, our use of the terms "positive" and "negative" are very different than how we use them in general conversations. If the teacher stated you were on track with your writing style, you would most likely say they gave you "positive feedback" on your paper. However, since the feedback did not lead to change, it was technically negative feedback. If the teacher's comments pointed out your errors, you might generally say it was "negative feedback." However, if that feedback led to you changing how you wrote your next paper, this would technically be positive feedback. Hopefully, this explanation allows you to see that what we commonly view as "positive" and "negative" are not the same when we enter into the world of cybernetics.

Applying Your Knowledge

Think about several areas of your life, such as your roles as student, son/daughter, employee, and partner/spouse. Describe one instance of positive feedback (wherein feedback from someone/each other changed the dynamic between you) and negative feedback (wherein feedback from someone/each other maintained the dynamic between you). Remember that this is not necessarily verbal feedback, but rather, the interaction between you either changed the relationship (positive feedback) or maintained the relationship (negative feedback).

Role of Student

Positive Feedback:
Negative Feedback:

Role of Son/Daughter

Positive Feedback:
Negative Feedback:

Role of Employee

Positive Feedback:
Negative Feedback:

Role of Partner/Spouse

Positive Feedback:
Negative Feedback:

RESTRAINT

Feedback is one aspect of how systems self-regulate. Bateson (1972) explained that cybernetics is also based upon the notion that how things happen is predicated on **restraints**. If there are no restraints on the system, then there is an equal probability of all actions. So then, why is it that some systems function differently than others? It is because each system has a series of restraints that determine an inequality of probability of actions. In that way, restraints work with feedback.

If there were no restraints, all behaviors would have an equal possibility. But as we've seen when we look at people's actions, some behaviors in some situations have a much higher probability than other behaviors. Thus, restraints lead to an inequality of behaviors occurring. People have restraints placed on them, which include their biology, the social ecology, and the myths surrounding who they are and how they are supposed to act. Restraints are the rules of the context, which also include people's presuppositions, premises, and expectations (White, 1986). That is, how people think, what they value, and what they expect limit what options are available for people.

We can look at the relationship between Daniel and Johanna (as well as between them and their children) as being moderated by many different restraints, which lead to a higher probability of some behaviors and lower probability of others. For instance, their relationship occurs in the context of the US culture, which currently has restraints of how husbands and wives are supposed to treat one another. While there are variations in this, we can look at how each person views their own and the other's roles in the marriage. This restraint would be very different in another culture where gender roles are much more pronounced. Another restraint on their relationship may be based on religion. If they come from a religion that does not condone divorce, certain behaviors are not available for them. A third restraint is the physical proximity of their families-of-origin. The closer their families, the more that the couple may engage them and use them as resources for tasks such as babysitting, but also to lean on for emotional support or to help take sides when they have arguments. Figure 2.3 provides a view of how people's behavior is predicated on restraints.

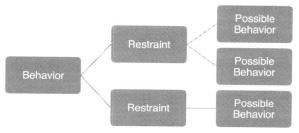

Figure 2.3 The Relationship Between Behavior, Restraint, and the Subsequent Behaviors That Are Possible.

All interactions carry with them some measures of restraints. If a friend were to approach you crying and telling you about a recent death in the family, then that communication most likely restrains responses such as a high five or laughter. Clients come in with certain communications that also carry certain restraints. The therapist's response also carries with it certain restraints; the question asked or the statements made carry with it more restraints, narrowing or adjusting the conversation. Even somewhat similar questions, such as "Did your nagging of Daniel work?" or "Did that way of encouraging Daniel work?" have significant differences in how they restrain the conversation. Subtle differences in restraint between questions such as, "Is there ever a time when the problem isn't happening?" and "When is this problem not happening?" are carefully utilized by some therapists (i.e., solution-focused or strength-based) to minimize restraints on solutions. The former question, being closed-ended and open to "yes" or "no," may lead to the client simply saying, "No, it happens all of the time." Whereas the latter puts a restraint on the answer "no" as it assumes that there are times that the problem isn't happening and the therapist just wants to know when they are.

Here, we can take a closer look at Daniel to explore his behaviors and see them as making greater sense as they are embedded in a sea of restraints that lead to some behaviors being more appropriate to the situation than others. That is, having a wife carries certain restraints on what he does, such as not going out and flirting with women, but rather coming home after work and not going out on his own or with his buddies on the weekend. Having children further carries restraints, as he will watch some shows (perhaps Disney movies) rather than others (perhaps R rated shows, which he might watch, but later at night after the children have gone to sleep). Thus, with the countless restraints on his behavior, we might look at his symptoms of depression and anger through a cybernetic lens, which helps us understand the likely pathways of his behaviors and how they are limited and connected to the context.

We can now also better understand why some people continue engaging in behaviors that maintain the problem, even if the person is actively trying to change. The solutions that people use to try to solve their problems are, in many ways, not unlimited. They are housed within the restraints of the situation. When operating from these restraints, people become limited to alternative ways of trying to handle the problem. Thus, they keep doing the same thing over and over again. This more of the same behavior not only does not work to solve the problem, but leads to an increase in the problem (Watzlawick, Weakland, & Fisch, 1974).

As depicted in Figure 2.3, the same behavior, under different restraints, can lead to different ends. This is called **multifinality**. Its recursive complement is **equifinality**, when different behaviors can lead to the same result. Equifinality may be commonly seen when an alcoholic tries multiple means to quit alcohol, to no effect. When he tries Alcoholics Anonymous (AA), changes roles and behaviors around his home, makes adjustments to schedule, and utilizes an accountability partner, yet still finds himself back to drinking, it can be described as equifinality. If one way isn't working or expedient, then there is always another way.

Applying Your Knowledge

All interactions have some measures of invitation and some measures of restraint. When a therapist nods her head, or says "Mhmm," what does that restrain? What talk from a client would be useful to restrain with a question? What would an example of the talk and the question be? What aspects of a client (i.e., age, race, gender, personality traits, history, etc.) would lead to you having overt restraints, where you knowingly will not explore certain areas with them? What restraints does your work setting have on you as a therapist? What types of behaviors do you not engage in as a therapist because of where you practice, your model of therapy, and the ethical guidelines that you operate from?

TENDENCIES

We have been talking about change, which is what most people think about when they think of psychotherapy. This makes perfect sense since people seek a therapist when things are not going as they would like in their lives and they want something to be different; to feel, think, or behave differently; or to have others they are in relational proximity with to think, feel, or behave differently. Yet many therapists experience clients who come to therapy, and after several change interventions from the therapist, the client has not changed. Most people, and even many psychotherapists, might consider that the client is resistant to change. The resistant client is usually one who is brought to therapy against his will, perhaps by a desperate spouse or ordered from the legal system.

The word "resistance" brings up a lot of mixed feelings and ideas among therapists of all backgrounds. A cybernetic term often used to think of resistance is homeostasis. Resistance and homeostasis certainly do not mean the same thing. **Homeostasis** is the tendency for systems to attempt to remain stable, or not change. "Homeo" simply means "like" or "same," and "stasis" comes from the Greek, meaning "to stand" or "stop." When there seems to be a tendency for the system to stay the same, it may be useful to look at what restraints are preventing other possible outcomes. Perhaps even the same behaviors, under different restraints, can lead to different outcomes (multifinality), or perhaps the same desired goal could be attained from multiple starting points (equifinality). We will talk more about homeostasis below.

ENTROPY AND NEGENTROPY

One of the ways systems maintain continuity involves the tendency to attempt to stay together, which is called **negentropy**. Negentropy comes from thermodynamics (the study of the motion of heat). **Entropy** is the tendency of a system to lose efficiency through heat. Imagine a well-insulated room full of refrigerators with all of their doors open. The opposite, or the negation, of entropy is negentropy. It is the tendency for systems to stay together, or the tendency for order and efficiency. It is not common in mechanical systems but is very common in biological systems. With sufficient stress and hardships, families can come together and become nearly inseparable (negentropy). Under too much stress, that same family may break apart and stay as far away from one another as possible (entropy).

As we have seen, systems are composed of parts that function together as a whole. These parts allow various amounts of information to move between the members as well as between the system and the environment (its ecology). When little information is exchanged between the family and the environment, we would call this a **closed system**. When much information is exchanged, it is considered an **open system**. The openness or closedness of the system helps to determine how well the system functions through its capacity for adaptation.

In systems theory, we see that, when systems are closed, little information comes in, and the system does not function well over time. It thus moves toward a state of imbalance, what we call entropy. Systems need some type of variety in them so they can adapt to the evolving context. Entropy often occurs when a system is not in harmony with the ecology it is housed in. For the Martinez family, it may move toward entropy if the family members did not listen to one another or to others outside of the family. This might happen if Daniel's depression became more severe, yet no one would talk about what was happening. The family functioning would move farther and farther away from how the Martinez members understand who they are as a family.

Open systems, which are more adaptable and thus usually more functional, tend to move towards greater balance. This process is called **negative entropy** or **negentropy** (see Figure 2.4). Here, systems have constraints of patterns and structure (Hoffman, 1981). Negentropy may happen for the Martinez family if friends came to them and suggested that there might be a depression problem. Daniel and Johanna could then adjust their behaviors accordingly so that they maintained their normal interactions.

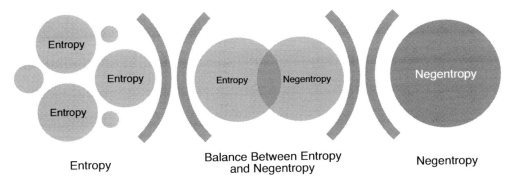

Figure 2.4 The Dynamics Between Entropy and Negentropy. When Systems Experience Entropy, They Tend Toward Breaking Down. Systems Experiencing Negentropy Tend to Stay Stable.

These tendencies are not prescriptive; that is, they do not dictate how families behave. Rather, they are descriptive, since they are just words used to describe what is happening within the system. Cybernetics as a whole is a science of descriptions. How things are described can make a huge difference because it is indicative of how one thinks about the system. If a client were to come in describing his sad moods as a "demon" tormenting him, it would be very different than if he were to describe it as "depression" tormenting him. The description of demon would most likely include the larger system of religious practice whereas describing it as depression would lead to the larger system of therapy practice.

Applying Your Knowledge

- Pick a diagnosis, any diagnosis. How else could that diagnosis be described?
- What difference would it make to you to describe it in that way? To your client?
- Could you understand a client's diagnosis as a way for his family to attempt to stay together (negentropy)? To create distance between them (entropy)?
- When a client is being "resistant" how could understanding the system as attempting to stay the same (homeostasis) be useful? What would you do/ask differently if you saw the family as wanting to stay together and stay stable?
- Can you describe one phenomenon in multiple ways? Such as alcoholism as a means of entropy or negentropy?

Homeostasis

As we explained, systems tend to move toward stability (negentropy) or change (entropy). When entropy happens, the system may disintegrate. For families, this may come in the form of divorce or dissolution of the romantic relationship. Entropy in the Martinez family might begin in the form of them not engaging in their "normal" ways of interacting with one another. Instead, the members of the family would experience chaos, where they would not know how to be with one another. Most likely, the family would destabilize, and divorce would most likely result. Conversely, negentropy maintains the system in balance. The balance that systems maintain is called **homeostasis**. Homeostasis refers to a steady state of functioning.

Figure 2.5 The Relationship Between Stability and Change, Which Are Two Sides of the Same Coin.

The term "family homeostasis" was coined by Don Jackson (1957), referring to the interactions of the family being a closed information system in which the system corrects itself based on feedback. Thus, in order to maintain itself as a family, the family continuously ensures that it is maintaining itself as that particular family. In the Martinez nuclear family of four people, they have a certain way of being. While this way might lead to various members displaying symptoms or not being happy, it is their current established way. Daniel may feel depressed and angry, Johanna frustrated, and Jonathan and Miranda might also experience discord in the household. While people from the outside may easily say, "Just change, you are not happy," it is not that simple, as systems tend to try to remain how they are currently functioning—they have a tendency for stability. The Martinez members each act in ways to maintain the status quo—whether they are happy or not with how the family currently is functioning.

Systems maintain their current state through two interlocking and opposed forces: stability and change (see Figure 2.5). In order to be stable, there has to be a component of change, and in order to change, there must be some type of stability. On the surface, this might seem paradoxical, but stability with no change leads to rigidity. If a system is too rigid, it is not able to be flexible and adapt. Eventually that system will not be able to function as the context in which the family functions always changes. For instance, the Martinez family is functioning in a context that includes developmental changes. Jonathan and Miranda are growing up and are now adolescents. If the family continued to function as if the two children were still quite young, as they were when they were perhaps 6 or so, there would most likely be serious problems as the family could not accommodate to the demands of adolescence. Conversely, if the family only changed, there would be no foundation for family members on how to be with one another. One day Jonathan might try to be in charge, the next he might leave the family. Continuity provides the required safety to explore other ways of being.

This idea of change being needed for stability is paradoxical. So let's provide some examples to demonstrate this. Visualize a tight-rope walker. How does the person stay on the rope (which would be stability)? They do so by moving the pole they are holding (which would be change). A second example comes from standing up in a canoe that is in the water. How do you maintain standing and not going into the water (which would be stability)? You do so by doing small rocking movements—change.

Now that we see that homeostasis is the combination of stability and change, we can go back to our explanation of the most common homeostatic process, your air conditioning system (we introduced this concept earlier in the chapter). You set the air conditioner at a certain temperature—let's say 72 degrees Fahrenheit. How does your air conditioner maintain that temperature? It does so through a process of feedback. When air is brought in through the return and is within a small range of the target temperature, your air conditioner does not turn on since it is maintaining stability (this, if you recall, is negative feedback). However, throughout the day, there may be times when the sun shines in through the windows and the air temperature in the house heats up. When the HVAC detects the heat increase, it then activates (change) until the point that it detects the air temperature to be back within the small range of the initial target temperature.

Families function in many of the same ways. Families have a way of being that is idiosyncratic. That is, systems theory views families from a non-normative perspective where there is not a certain way that a family must be. Some families are loud, which works well for them. For others, they tend to be quiet. Some families are overtly loving, while others do not readily show affection. Some families have members who are very involved in one another's lives, while others tend to not be so enmeshed. These ways of being may be based upon culture, religion, socioeconomic status, or other such factors. None of these ways of being are good, bad, right, or wrong. They just are ways of being, and families that operate from any of them tend to continue to function within that way of being. The Martinez family functions in a way where there is greater closeness between the children and one parent rather than both parents. They have organized along more traditional gender roles and continue to engage in behaviors that maintain this, even though the various members may be unhappy with this organization.

We can usually see the difficulty in change and the tendency for stability when a new family is formed. Each partner is coming from a family of origin that had its own idiosyncratic way of being. The partners need to then adapt to a potentially different functioning style. For instance, someone who was raised in a family that showed little affection may have difficulty entering into a relationship with someone who came from a very affectionate family, and vice versa. The person from the little affection family (where that was the homeostasis) would most likely not show that much affection to his partner (or his partner's family, who is also used to showing a lot of affection). The partner (and family) will likely be quite upset she is not being shown affection. She would then try to engage in ways which would lead to positive feedback, such as telling the other that she prefers him to be more affectionate or being overly affectionate in hopes of modeling. Over time, the two partners will have shifted from the homeostasis of their respective family of origins to develop their own way of being (what we might call a third culture). This would then become the new family's homeostasis (although homeostasis changes over the course of the family life span, as new people, such as children, enter and others leave, such as in divorce or death).

We have explained that negative feedback maintains stability (see Figure 2.6). But perhaps we are being too technical here with terms like negative, feedback, and stability. So let's simplify the idea. People tend to act in ways to keep the status quo. We do so in what we think, what we say, and what we do (and don't do). My (MR) family tends to be a "low drama" family. Given this, if my 13-year-old daughter starts to engage myself and my wife "with attitude," my wife and I may tell her to talk to us again in a calmer manner or for her to go cool off for a bit. What we wouldn't do is to engage back "with attitude" and escalate into a screaming match. These behaviors, which we can think about in terms of patterns, maintain the low drama in our family. If my daughter calms down, the family is back to its normal functioning, and negative feedback occurred.

In the Martinez family, negative feedback occurs when Daniel, Johanna, Jonathan, and Miranda act in ways to keep themselves functioning like they always do. These actions are both conscious and unconscious (overt and covert). When Daniel and Johanna continue to engage in the distancing/nagging back-and-forth, they are engaging in negative feedback. When Jonathan and Miranda go to Johanna for emotional support instead of Daniel, they are engaging in negative feedback.

Thus, negative feedback leads to stability. On the other hand, positive feedback leads to change. This change is in how the family is organized and functions. Positive feedback leads to a new homeostasis, which maintains itself for some time until further positive feedback leads to a newer homeostasis

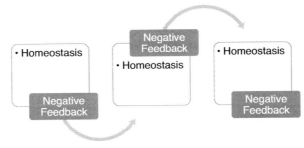

Figure 2.6 A Visual Representation of How Negative Feedback Maintains the Current Homeostasis Level.

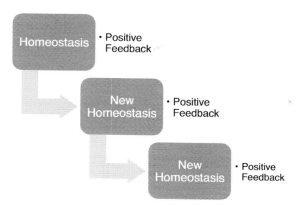

Figure 2.7 A Visual Representation of How Positive Feedback Leads to a New Homeostasis Level.

(see Figure 2.7). For many families, positive feedback occurs around significant transitions in family organization, such as births, marriages, and deaths.

In the Martinez family, positive feedback most likely occurred when Daniel and Johanna married, as both had to adapt from their previous homeostatic functioning (most likely developed in their families-of-origin). Their pre-child way of being is likely quite different than when Jonathan was born. The birth of Miranda most likely led to information coming into the family that they needed to adapt even more to accommodate the inclusion of this fourth member.

The notion of homeostasis is not connected to a view of normal and abnormal. There is not a correct, good, or normal homeostatic level. Systems theorists view the functioning of a family rather than try to make a valuation of the family. However, those outside the system will likely have a view of whether how that system operates is good or bad. This might come in terms of whether the system is "functional" or "dysfunctional." When the system operates in ways that do not adhere to the expectations of the larger group, the system's way of being is usually termed as being dysfunctional. Conversely, when the system operates within the prescribed rules of the larger system (society), it is called functional. We hope you realize that, more important than functional/dysfunctional assessments, is the notion that systems operate based on the restraints placed upon them in that specific context. For instance, when the Martinez family goes to Daniel's mother's house wherein open affection is not common, that restrains how much public display of affection Daniel and Johanna engage in. At Johanna's family's house, where people tend to engage each other through sarcasm and debate, there are restraints that lead to Daniel and Johanna being more sarcastic and more willing to disagree with those they are in conversation with.

Jackson (1977a) stated that "human beings possess a variety of potentialities, that the achievement of certain potentialities may entail certain limitations, and that achievement and limitation vary with conditions" (p. 161). The family's homeostasis is predicated on many restraints. These restraints curtail how the members of the family might be while also encouraging other behaviors. A family's homeostasis will change many times through the family's life cycle. Thus, the restraints on the system will change, and the potentialities and limitations of the people in the system will change. This allows us to pay attention to how people accommodate the new restraints of the system and how they change.

Morphostasis/Morphogenesis

As we just explained, a system does not maintain the same homeostasis for the duration of that system's existence. There are many small changes in the stable state, and there are times when there are significant changes, such as when there is a divorce, death, or remarriage. In the Martinez family, Daniel and Johanna

Figure 2.8 Morphostasis Is the System's Ability to Maintain Stability Within the Context of Change, a Process That Can Be Considered Homeostasis.

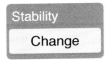

Figure 2.9 Morphostasis Is the System's Ability to Enact Change Within the Context of Stability.

had to accommodate to one another when they first became a couple. Then, with the introduction of each of their children, they needed to change the rules of interaction to adjust from a two-person nuclear family to a three- and then a four-person family. However, once these transitions occurred the family found a stable functioning level—a homeostatic level.

The technical terms for a system maintaining stability or moving toward change are morphostasis and morphogenesis. **Morphostasis** is the system's tendency toward staying the same, that is, holding stability within the context of change (see Figure 2.8). This occurs through the incorporation of negative feedback. Whatever may happen in the environment, morphostasis leads the system to maintain its current structure and functioning. Conversely, **morphogenesis** is the system's ability to change—that is, being adaptable within the context of stability (see Figure 2.9). This occurs through positive feedback where the system engages in amplifying deviation—that is, it changes.

Applying Your Knowledge

Take a few minutes to evaluate your own family and how your family's homeostasis changed over time. What were those critical points where the system changed? Most likely, these were at family life cycle changes, such as births, deaths, going to college, divorce, etc. How would you describe the family homeostasis at each of these pivotal points in time?

THEORY OF LOGICAL TYPES

Whitehead and Russell (1910), in their monumental work, *Principia Mathematica*, attempted to clarify mathematic ideas so as to avoid paradoxes. They did not succeed in avoiding paradoxes, but they did come up with some special ways of thinking about the world. One of their most useful distinctions is their **theory of logical types**. Logical types have to do with categories and members of the categories. Sometimes these categories are called groups or classes. For example, the category "books" has this book as a member, as well as cookbooks, math books, the Bible, and books written by Dr. Seuss. In fact, it has all books as members. The context determines if the item is a class or member. "Books" can be a class, as in the example above, or it can be a member of another larger category. The category "Media" contains books as well as TV, Internet, radio, magazines, etc. as members. A page in a book is of a smaller logical type than a book, a book is of a smaller logical type than the category of books, and the category of books

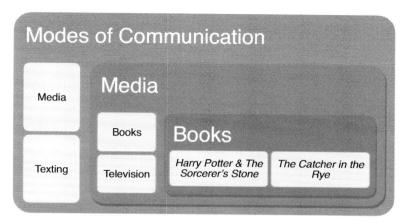

Figure 2.10 Relationship Between Member and Class. In This Figure, There Are Two Members to the Class of Books. Books Then become One of Two Members to the Class of Media, and Media Becomes One of Two Members to the Class of Modes of Communication.

is of a smaller logical type than media. There are potentially endless levels of logical type depending on what is being discussed. Figure 2.10 depicts the relationship between class and member and shows how a member of a class can also be a class.

Whitehead and Russell asserted that, whenever a member was confused with the category for which it is a part, paradox arises. That is, a situation arises that cannot be. Sometimes this sounds silly and obvious, such as Dr. Seuss' *The Cat in the Hat* is not the same thing as "category of book." Other times, it is less obvious. A dog barking, baring its teeth, and running quickly towards you could be interpreted in the category of either aggression or play. The consequences of guessing wrong can have quite a bite to it. However, to then say the dog is barking, baring his teeth, and running *because* it is playing can also be described as an error. "Play" and "aggression" are not tangible physical things, nor are they precise behaviors that always look the same. They are common descriptions that help us organize behaviors that commonly occur together. "Play" doesn't innately exist apart from someone's categorization of those behaviors. If we look at the Martinez family, we can see this in Daniel's viewpoint that Johanna "is on my case." Johanna's behaviors can be seen in a variety of categories, two of which are "care" and "nagging." Johanna's actual behaviors are of a different logical type than the classification that Daniel gives them. For instance, her asking him, "Where have you been tonight?" is a member of a class. Depending on how she says it, where, when, and who else present, it may be of the class of "care" or of "nagging." Depending on which category Daniel places those actions, the interactions between the two will be impacted.

Let's take another example. If a client were to complain of feeling sad most of the time, a loss of interest in things, inability to sleep well, lethargy, or lack of concentration, one therapist may quickly assign this client in the category of "depression." Another therapist may describe the category of "mourning the loss of a relationship" or some other aspect of the client's life. What category gets assigned can make a large difference in how the therapist, client, agency, and therapy process operate. If the therapist asserts that since the client is depressed she is displaying depressive behaviors, the therapist has made an error of logical types. This can be considered a dormitive principle. **Dormitive principles** are when one mistakenly asserts that the category caused the behaviors that created the category.

Let's take a closer look at our client Daniel and his wife Johanna with logical types in mind:

Therapist: Does she ever tell you that you disappoint her?
Daniel: Yes. She says things such as, "Are you going to make the bed today?" "You forgot to walk the dog," and "You're not spending enough time with the kids."

Therapist: What impact do these statements have on you?

Daniel: I've become depressed recently. You know, a person can only take so much. She would be mad at me at for saying it like this, but she doesn't seem to be able to stop from nagging me so much.

The therapist starts by asking about the category of "disappoint" where Daniel answers with certain members of that class as he sees it. Daniel did not answer, "Yes, she said 'you disappoint me.'" He answered by describing members of the category "Disappointing Johanna." He then gave another class to these members: "Nagging." Johanna may have an alternate name for this class of behaviors, such as "Prompting." The therapist may attempt to give a further alternate name to this class of behaviors, redefining what they mean to the clients. This technique is called **reframing**. Literally understood, a class could be understood as a frame, and the members of that class could be understood as the picture in the frame. If the frame is changed, the way the picture on the inside is then understood differently. A picture of a smiling young man in a picture frame on a table in the living room has meaning, while the exact same picture in the frame of a police mug shot has a different meaning. The same picture in a frame with a wreath around it in front of a coffin likely has a third meaning. The above set of questions from Johanna could be framed as "Nagging," or framed as a failed attempt to reconcile the relationship by "Caring too much" or any other description.

Applying Your Knowledge

How else could you frame "depression?" What difference would this new frame make in the therapist? In the client? How else could you frame "resistance"? What difference does that make? Can a frame be reframed? Can it be moved into a broader/larger class? Smaller?

CIRCULARITY AND RECURSION

In Chapter 1, we began to distinguish between lineal and nonlineal epistemologies. Lineal epistemologies function on a premise of cause and effect (see Figure 2.11). As Bateson (1979) explained, a lineal sequence of actions does not go back to the starting point. Most people, unbeknownst to them, believe in and function from a lineal viewpoint. This comes in many forms.

- If my child misbehaves and I punish her, she will not do that misbehavior again.
- I am mad because my partner talked meanly to me.
- If I study hard, I will do well on the exam.
- I became sad because my father recently died.

These beliefs are endemic to how we see the world, which was repeatedly told to us throughout our lives. The scientific method is based on the cause/effect model. Basic experiments are devised to test if there is an effect on the dependent variable (what you are measuring) based on the level of the independent variable (what you are manipulating). We'll give you an example of this.

Figure 2.11 A Visual Representation of the Relationship Between Cause and Effect.

Imagine you want to know if people do better with an exercise regime if they have a personal trainer with them while they are at the gym. We would need to get two equal groups (utilizing random assignment) and have one group exercise with a personal trainer and the other do the same exercise for the same amount of time and repetitions without the trainer. After some time (perhaps two weeks), we would measure the people on some scale (perhaps a fitness test) to see which group did better. In essence, we are trying to see if having a personal trainer *causes* improvement in health.

Experiments like this are based on an empirical model that comes from a quantitative perspective. Quantitative science is the primary mode of research exploration in science—it is the basis of the scientific method. However, there is another research methodology that operates more from a nonlinear perspective—qualitative research. Quantitative research tends to focus on the what, when, where, and who while qualitative research explores the why and how. Further, qualitative research attempts to take into consideration the impact that the researcher has on the research while quantitative research tries to negate any influence the researcher might have on the study. For the personal trainer research study, qualitative researchers might explore how personal trainers and/or their clients understand the usefulness and significance of having a personal trainer. Instead of trying to determine fact, the study would explore the meaning that people place on the event.

The influence of the qualitative researcher may come in the form of **recursion**—the simultaneous mutual influence that people have on one another. Many qualitative research methodologies utilize interviewing, where the interviewer understands that her questions and the presentation of those questions influence the interviewee whose responses and the presentation of those responses influences the interviewer, ad infinitum. In generalizing these understandings to the therapy milieu, therapists pay attention to the recursion that happens between therapist and client, with each person mutually influencing the other.

Let's go back to our client, Daniel, to help us understand these ideas. From a lineal perspective, Daniel's wife nags him, with the effect of Daniel becoming depressed. Daniel is a passive recipient in this process and does not have a relationship to the nagging. Based on this, we would either attempt to get Johanna to stop nagging so Daniel doesn't become depressed, or to get Daniel to better cope with the nagging.

Hopefully, however, you are realizing that there is a major problem here; we are only getting Daniel's perspective of what is happening. If Johanna were to come to therapy, the conversation may go something like this:

Therapist: What concerns bring you to therapy?
Johanna: My husband, Daniel, is very distant and disengaged.
Therapist: Can you describe what he does?
Johanna: He might not come home from work right away, or when he is home, he will go in his music room and play guitar.
Therapist: What is that like for you when he is disengaged?
Johanna: It is very frustrating. I want him engaged. I want him connected to his children. I want him connected to me.

In looking at Daniel's experience, it leads to quite a different story than Johanna's experience. For Daniel, the *cause* is Johanna's attempts to get him to be engaged, and the *effect* is his backing off. While we might view the rationale for Johanna's behavior to be "good" (she is trying to connect a father to his children and a husband to his wife), Daniel experiences her actions as blame that he is wrong and doing something bad. In essence, to him, it comes across as nagging. For Johanna, the *cause* is Daniel's disengagement, which has the *effect* of getting her to try to engage him. Daniel's behavior comes across as disinterest. Figure 2.12 presents the lineal view experience of Johanna and Daniel. Based on the lineal view, neither Daniel nor Johanna are seeing the vicious cycle they are both connected in and which loops itself over and over (what is called circularity and recursion). They are not realizing there is an invisible connection between them where the more Daniel distances, the more Johanna tries to get him to engage, and the more Johanna tries to get him to engage, the more he distances.

If we use a lineal perspective where people behave based on simple cause-and-effect processes, it is easy to lead us to view one person as the problem. It is clear to Daniel that Johanna is the problem (at least her

Figure 2.12 A Lineal Perspective of Cause and Effect Where One Behavior Causes the Next Behavior.

Figure 2.13 Nonlineal Perspective Where People Mutually Influence One Another.

actions). And it is clear to Johanna that Daniel is the problem. This is why, when families come to therapy, they usually come with an identified patient. The **identified patient** is the person the family states is the cause of their current difficulties. We could also call this person the scapegoat or the black sheep. Most families have a black sheep. Think in your family: who would just about everyone agree would be the most problematic person? There may be someone who has gone to jail, has been to a rehabilitation center (perhaps for some type of substance abuse), or, even if doing well, not doing as well as the other people in the family. We can then think about why this person "is" the problem. Most people assume that it stems from something rooted in their personality. They were just always defiant, they didn't get the brains in the family, or they are just "bad news." What is missing in any of these explanations is the impact that the context the person was raised in or is currently experiencing had on their behavior.

Nonlineal epistemologies operate from a notion of recursion. **Recursion** is an understanding that there is mutual influence present in all relationships (see Figure 2.13). Thus, we abandon the notion of an identified patient and look to see what is happening in interactions that allow the symptom or presenting problem to continue. In exploring Johanna's influence on Daniel, we need to also pay attention to Daniel's influence on Johanna. Her behaviors do not happen in a vacuum. They are part of a sequence that involves Daniel's actions to her. And Daniel's actions happen as part of the same sequence.

When we have an eye towards recursion, we cannot understand Person A's behaviors outside of his relation to Person B. Consequently, we cannot understand Person B's behaviors outside of her relation to Person A. Thus, we would need to understand what Daniel is doing that is connected to Johanna's nagging. This is where having multiple people in the therapy room is very useful. It is not only easier to understand these interconnections when both parties are describing their experience, but by having multiple people in the therapy room, the therapist has an opportunity to actually see these interactions in play.

However, we can still operate from these ideas with only one client in the therapy room since one change in the system will lead to system-wide change. This is because people interact based on patterns. If one person changes their actions in the pattern, most likely a new pattern will develop. We also know that one member's actions do not always change the system. Watzlawick et al. (1974) explained, "a member may act without making a difference" (p. 5). Daniel and Johanna may behave in ways, intentional or not, to change their partner and that behavior may be ineffective in enacting any change.

Recursion can also be seen in terms of circularity. We can use these terms fairly interchangeably. By thinking in terms of recursion or circularity, we bypass the notion of lineal direction where we do not come back to the starting point. However, please keep in mind that what someone says is a starting point is an arbitrary demarcation. We will discuss this more in terms of punctuation in Chapter 4. Figure 2.14

CYBERNETICS AESTHETICS

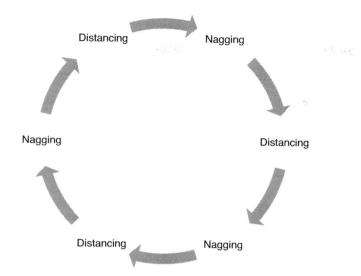

Figure 2.14 Circular Process of Mutual Influence Where There Is No Starting Point.

presents a circular presentation of what is occurring for Daniel and Johanna. As you can see from this visual, there is no starting or ending point. We do not know whether Daniel distanced first, which led to Johanna nagging or Johanna nagged, which led to Daniel distancing. What we do know is that there is a pattern where Daniel and Johanna are influencing and being influenced by the other.

Here, we see that distancing and nagging are inextricably connected with one another. Daniel's distancing does not happen without being connected to Johanna's nagging. And Johanna's nagging does not happen without being connected to Daniel's distancing. Each person is creating the other based on his or her own actions. When we see the circularity of this process, there is not a singular cause or an effect. We don't know which happened first, the nagging or the distancing. What we do know is that the two are connected to one another in a process. In this case, we would call this a vicious cycle, as both Daniel and Johanna find this sequence of interactions to be problematic.

DOUBLE DESCRIPTION

As we have just seen, two people can view the world very differently. We know the old adage, "There is his view, her view, and the truth." However, cyberneticians would view this a bit differently. Instead, they would understand that the two viewpoints come together to provide a richer depth, known as **double description** (Bateson, 1979). This can also be called binocular vision (see Figure 2.15).

Double description allows us to view the relationship. As Keeney (1983) explained, "For the observer, this means that the simultaneous combination of their punctuations yields a glimpse of the whole relationship" (p. 37). If we go back to Daniel and Johanna, we would only have a monocular view if we just heard from Daniel what was happening. This limited view would be that Johanna nags and he distances. The problem with this view is that we might attribute the nagging to something internal to Johanna—that she is a nagger. If so, then treatment would be for Johanna to get her to stop being a nagger. However, the binocular view of nag/distance and distance/nag allows us to see the complementarity of their relationship. Without a second member of the system in the therapy room, it would be the responsibility of the therapist to gain a circular understanding in order to recognize that there is more depth to the story even though they are being presented with a monocular view.

Figure 2.15 Double Description Leads to an Understanding of Relationship and Pattern. Two Different Viewpoints Lead to the Possibility of Seeing Interconnections.

Double description is not only useful to understand what is happening for clients, but also what is happening between client and therapist. This is because double descriptions allow us to view pattern and relationship (Keeney, 1983). If we only used the therapist's view, what would likely happen would be an incomplete picture where we could easily label the client: "He is being resistant" or "He is not responding to me because he is depressed." How we better understand the therapeutic process is to have a binocular view—double description—where we look at the patterns and relationships that occur between therapist and client.

Questions for Reflection

1. Name an item. What category could that item belong to? What category could that category belong to (such as our page, book, and media example)?

2. Think of a client that you have worked with. How is that client a member of a category? How is that category a member of a larger category?

3. What is the importance of viewing families as functioning based on homeostasis? How does that impact what you do in therapy? The types of interventions you might use?

4. A nagging and distancing spouse is a classic example of recursion. Can you think of a few other common examples where one feeds into the other?

5. What are some other examples of positive and negative feedback?

CHAPTER THREE
Cybernetics Pragmatics

Michael D. Reiter with Clinton Lambert

CASE DESCRIPTION

In this chapter, we continue with our client, Daniel, whom we met in Chapters 1 and 2. Daniel came to therapy because of feelings of depression and anger. As discussed, Daniel's feelings do not occur in isolation but are intimately connected to the various contexts he is embedded in—primarily his interpersonal relationships, such as with his wife Johanna—as well as the dominant cultural ideologies he is located in (i.e., Western ideals of gender and marriage). In Chapters 1 and 2, we introduced you to some initial ideas of systems theory and more specifically cybernetics, demonstrating how Daniel's behaviors are connected to Johanna's. However, please keep in mind that it is extremely difficult to separate a person from the multiple interconnections that he is involved with. For Daniel, it is difficult to understand how his behaviors are based only on his relationship with Johanna. More than likely, there is an overlapping of contexts as his behaviors are housed within his connection to his wife, his children, his parents, his work, his friends, his culture, his gender, etc. (see Figure 3.1).

In this chapter, we continue expanding our scope of understanding by providing possibilities on how a therapist might utilize these cybernetically based concepts to help enact change.

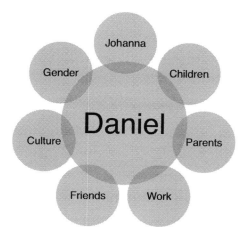

Figure 3.1 The Interconnections Between Daniel and Some of the Various Influential Contexts in His Life.

Figure 3.2 Therapeutic Change Is the Movement of Stability/Change From One Dynamic to Another Dynamic, Always Including Both Operations.

STABILITY AND CHANGE

We begin our continued exploration of cybernetics by focusing on the dynamics that occur between people. In the previous chapter, we explored how two (or more) people are interconnected and mutually influence one another through the processes of circularity and recursion (see Figure 3.2). This circularity leads the system to establish a level of homeostasis. In this homeostasis is the complementarity between stability and change. Cybernetic therapists understand that change involves stability and stability involves change. Thus, every intervention a therapist makes does not only focus only on change or only on stability. Rather, therapeutic change is a change of the dynamics of stability/change (Keeney & Ross, 1985).

Cybernetic therapists make interventions to shift the system from one level of homeostasis (the inclusion of stability and change) to a second level of homeostasis. This second homeostatic level is an approximation closer to how the members of the system want their lives to be. In looking at this therapeutic change process, the intervention can be discussed in terms of **meaningful noise** (Keeney & Ross, 1985). The "noise" is something that is new or different to the system, while also holding meaning to the members.

Working from this mindset with the Martinez family, the therapist will be mindful of holding on to many aspects of their current functioning. Therapy is likely not an overhaul of how they are, but change in certain areas. It is not for the therapist to decide which aspects of their lives they want as stability and which as change—that is for the family to determine.

While we may talk in the rest of this chapter with a focus on one side of this complementarity—primarily change—, please remember that the other part of the complementarity is still operational. We can now zoom our focus in to explore how those interpersonal connections are connected with one another and function to form a stable process.

BEHAVIOR

Using a cybernetic lens shifts us from looking at the internal workings of people to the interpersonal realm. This shift can be seen in a movement away from some of the psychodynamic approaches that try to understand intrapsychic and unconscious processes to much more observable behaviors; primarily behaviors that happen between people. Further, therapists operating from a cybernetic perspective usually place more focus on the present rather than the past, as it is current behaviors, or the verbal labeling of those behaviors, of the client (and those that she interacts with) that are maintaining the problem (Weakland, Fisch, Watzlawick, & Bodin, 1974). Thus, there is usually more focus on the *what* and *how* and less on the *why*. This leads to a therapy more about action rather than on insight.

The behaviors regarded as a symptom play a role in the organization of the system. That is, while there are disadvantages to having the symptom, there are also advantages. This may seem contradictory at first, but upon closer inspection, there is usually some pay-off to the symptomatic behavior, usually in the area of controlling and maintaining relationships (Weakland et al., 1974). Thus, the identified patient, the person who exhibits the symptom, can be seen in many ways as having a lot of influence on how the system functions (Reiter, 2016a). This is especially the case when one member of the system is underfunctioning, which requires one or more other members of that system to overfunction. Symptoms can then be seen not as pathology but as means of communication, which maintains the behaviors of those involved in the symptomatic sequence (Ray & Simms, 2016).

If we look at the Martinez family, we see that Daniel's depression and anger shift the functioning of the family as the rest of the family members have to accommodate to his "problematic" behaviors. While he does not have unilateral control, his behaviors are influential—as are Johanna's and the two children. Each person is behaving in ways that for them is logical and the right response to the situation. Thus, telling them to do something different might not be the most effective therapeutic ploy. Instead, the therapist might provide guidelines for behavior change that are more indirect (Weakland et al., 1974). The Martinez's therapist might suggest a different behavior rather than demand it, such as

> I don't know if this will make sense for you all, or will be useful for you, but it might be interesting to see what would happen the next time that you are starting to feel depressed to make it be known rather than leave the house.

Applying Your Knowledge

As you just read, symptoms/problems make sense within a context and have both advantages and disadvantages. Think about a recent problem that you had. You will probably be able to list many disadvantages that came from experiencing that problem. But what about the advantages? Make a list of three advantages and three disadvantages of experiencing a symptom/problem. Try to ensure that these advantages/disadvantages are interpersonally based.

Problem 1

Advantage 1:
Advantage 2:
Advantage 3:
Disadvantage 1:
Disadvantage 2:
Disadvantage 3:

Problem 2

Advantage 1:
Advantage 2:
Advantage 3:
Disadvantage 1:
Disadvantage 2:
Disadvantage 3:

> **Problem 3**
>
> Advantage 1:
> Advantage 2:
> Advantage 3:
> Disadvantage 1:
> Disadvantage 2:
> Disadvantage 3:

A cybernetically based therapist might make a behavioral intervention without the client recognizing that a change request has been made (see Figure 3.3). For instance, asking a client to continue to have the problem but to just record where they were, what they were doing, and/or what they were thinking when the problem behavior occurs honors both stability and change. While it seems that no change is being requested by the intervention (i.e., "do not do anything different in trying to stop/reduce the problem"), the act of recording when, where, how, or with whom the problem happened is doing something different (i.e., change). In essence, this intervention interrupts the problem pattern while seeming to focus on stability. For Daniel, the therapist might pose this intervention as such,

> Daniel, to get a better sense of what is happening for you when you are feeling depressed, I'd like you not to try to do anything different. Not to try to feel better. Instead, any time that you feel depressed, just record it in a journal. Where were you? What time of day was it? Who were you with? How long did it last? This way, we will have clearer information to work with for the next time we meet.

However, upon gathering this information for the therapist, Daniel has added one more step in the problem sequence—that of recording it. This will lead to the possibility of him experiencing the symptom differently.

> ## Applying Your Knowledge
>
> Take one of the problems that you wrote about in the previous "Applying Your Knowledge" activity. Without doing anything differently around the problem, just record the when, where, how long, and with whom the problem happened. After doing this activity for one week, see if there is any difference in your experience of the problem. How did journaling change your reaction to the problem? What do you now notice that is different than your previous understanding?

Figure 3.3 Stability Is Maintained by Asking Clients to Continue Experiencing the Problem, While Change Is Introduced by Having Them Record the Problem Occurrence.

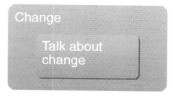

Figure 3.4 Change Is at a Higher Logical Level Than Talk About Change.

Most therapists know that clients come to therapy saying they want change to happen. Perhaps this change is with someone else (i.e., "I wish Johanna would lay off of me" or "Daniel needs to be a bigger part of this family"); the situation (i.e., "If only we had more money, we would be able to handle this better"); or the self (i.e., "I don't want to be depressed anymore" or "I want to be happier"). However, cybernetically based therapists understand that talk about change is not change (see Figure 3.4). These two things are at different logical levels. One ("I want to change") is a subset of the other (changing). Thus, therapists need to do more than just have the client talk about wanting change. They must get change to happen.

The first place we can start in examining change is through an exploration of interpersonal rules.

Rules

Rules are a pragmatic way to understand restraints. Cybernetic thinking prefers to look at why didn't something else happen, instead of why it happened. One way to answer the question "Why didn't they do something else instead?" could be found in the family's rules. These can be one way for describing why one set of behaviors happened in one context while another set of behaviors happened in a different context. Each context comes with its own regimen of restraints.

Let us explore a few contexts that you are likely to have experienced many times in your life. We can start with the family dinner. A few questions we might ask would help us understand the restraints of your family's dinner. What are the cultural rules surrounding gender that hold who can and who cannot participate in the cooking, serving, and cleaning aspects of the dinner? What topics of conversation are and aren't allowed to be discussed at the dinner table? Who is allowed to eat first? Does someone get different access to food?

Another example of a context in which there are restraints is school. What are the cultural rules surrounding gender of who can say what to whom and when? What are students allowed and not allowed to say to teachers? Teachers to students? Teachers to parents? What type of physical contact is allowed or not allowed to occur between teacher and student? How does age and gender play a role in touch between teacher and student? Student and student?

We can also look at the rules of a restaurant. How are people allowed to dress? What types of communication are accepted or not accepted between waitperson and customer? How are customers allowed to communicate their pleasure or displeasure about the meal? How much influence does the customer have in customizing their meal? Can they make special requests? The answers to all of these questions are context specific as some restaurants are open to special requests while others list on the menu that all dishes come as specified.

As just discussed, people behave based on the rules of the interaction they are in and the context in which that interaction occurs. While we can sometimes understand that rules play a role in our behavior (i.e., that we are supposed to talk quietly in a library), we have a tendency to attribute cause for someone's actions based on what we perceive as their innate personality rather than the rules of the context. Think for a minute of your own behaviors and those of others. We tend to provide different attributions for the same actions based on whether we are the actor or the perceiver. This is based on what social psychology calls the **fundamental attribution error** (FAE). People make the fundamental attribution error when they inaccurately attribute cause of behavior to someone's personality (internal attributes) rather than to the situation (external attributes). When looking at our own behaviors we focus on the external conditions rather than internal. For instance, if someone is giving a speech and is quite nervous, we might explain that he is an anxious person. However, when we have to give a speech and feel anxiety, we understand that the situation of having a lot of people in the audience looking at us is leading to the feelings of anxiety.

So, what might the fundamental attribution error have to do with rules? When we are incorrectly attributing cause to the internal attributes of people, it is because we are losing sight of the situation and the rules that impact people's behaviors. When we view ourselves as the actor, we more clearly recognize the dynamics of the situation and the rules we are following. Let's explore this a bit more. Think of your actions in the following two situations: you are at the library and you are at a bar. How are your behaviors different? We would suspect that, while you are at the library, you behave in a more reserved manner, keeping your voice down, not laughing, being fairly somber, and most likely not flirting with the person sitting next to you. Conversely, at the bar, you are probably lively, talking loudly (to compete with whatever music and other conversations are occurring), and being flirty and personal with the person at the next stool. Why would you act so differently when you are the same person? It is because the rules of the situation demand different actions on your part. Or, put another way, there are restraints on your behavior in different contexts that make some behaviors more available than other behaviors in each of the contexts (see Figure 3.5).

Think of any context that you are in and what the rules of that context might be. There are rules of conduct (i.e., stand in line or wait for the green light) as well as rules of interaction (i.e., the volume you can use or what you are allowed to talk about). We usually are not aware of how much our actions are based on the rules until we are in that different situation. For instance, there are distinct rules of interaction between a witness and a judge. If you were the witness in a courtroom, you would know that you should not speak until spoken to, that you should not ask personal questions, and that you should show respect through answers such as, "Yes, your Honor." If these actions are not your normal ways of behaving, you understand that you are engaging the judge in this manner because of the rules of the courtroom context.

Families also have rules of how people can and should interact with one another. Many times, we do not think about these rules since we are so ingrained within the family that behaving like we do just seems to be natural. But these rules have occurred for a lengthy period of time and demarcate one family from another. Jackson (1965) stated, "The observation of family interaction makes obvious certain redundancies, typical and repetitive patterns of interaction which characterize the family as a supraindividual entity" (p. 590). These patterns cannot exist unless there are rules on how people should act and the family members abide by these rules. Some of the rules are very clear to us (overt rules) while others influence us without us being aware of them (covert rules). We'll explore each of these forms of rules in a bit more depth.

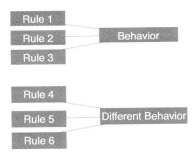

Figure 3.5 Different Rules Restrain Some Behaviors and Increase the Likelihood of Other Behaviors.

Applying Your Knowledge

Your behavior is inextricably tied to the rules of the situation. Take three different situational contexts and think about what the rules are that guide your behavior. How might people view you internally different based on how you act in these three different situations? How might others, but not yourself, be making the fundamental attribution error?

Situation 1

Rule 1:
Rule 2:
Rule 3:
Other FAE:

Situation 2

Rule 1:
Rule 2:
Rule 3:
Other FAE:

Situation 3

Rule 1:
Rule 2:
Rule 3:
Other FAE:

OVERT RULES

All people experience thousands of rules, which restrain their behavior. There are many that are **overt rules**, being known and direct. When you are driving, all of the signs you encounter are overt rules. There are signs that tell you the rules that prevent you from parking in certain areas, how fast you can drive, how many people must be in the car for you to drive in a specific lane, or which direction you can go on that street. In your family, you may have had rules that no one was allowed to curse, you had to respond to an elder with either, "Yes, sir" or "Yes, ma'am," and you must be home for dinner and eat at the dinner table with the rest of the family. Overt rules are very easy to follow as they have been explicitly stated.

In the Martinez family, some of their overt rules might include that Johanna is the primary caretaker for the children, that Daniel be the primary person from the family to interact with his mother, and that husband and wife are the authority figures in the house. Having these overt rules helps each member to function in a way that is in line with the expectations of self and others as to how to be part of the Martinez family, which maintains their homeostasis. Many therapists help clients to be clear on what their overt rules are and how people are able to abide by those rules—as long as those are the rules that people still want in their family. This is because some rules become outdated, based on the developmental stage of the family. For instance, an overt rule might be that a child has to ask permission to leave the house. This rule could have been very useful when the children were quite young but may hamper individual functioning when the child becomes an adult. We will discuss more about the family life cycle in Chapter 4.

We can also help people to develop overt rules of interaction with one another, especially when people fight and have conflict with each other in ways that both deem problematic. A therapist working with Daniel and Johanna might help them by focusing on the rules of their fights. Currently, they seem to be avoiding having overt conflict with one another. Further, their disagreements seem to keep occurring without any resolution. One possibility might be using the **structured fight task** developed by de Shazer (1985). This technique is as follows:

(1) Toss a coin to decide who goes first.
(2) The winner gets to bitch for 10 uninterrupted minutes.
(3) Then the other person gets a 10-minute turn.
(4) Then there needs to be 10 minutes of silence before another round is started with a coin toss.

(p. 122)

This technique would help the couple so that their arguments follow overt rules. This would then interrupt the pattern of their current fights, which do not quite have overt rules. This interruption could then shift this pattern for a new way of being with each other. While all interactional partners and families have overt rules that they follow, it may be the covert rules that have more impact on interactional functioning.

Key Figure

Don D. Jackson

Don D. Jackson was born on January 28, 1920. Jackson earned his medical degree from Stanford University and became a psychiatrist. From 1947 to 1951, he studied with Harry Stack Sullivan, one of the most influential psychiatrists of all time.

In 1953, Gregory Bateson recruited Jackson to join his communicational research project. The group was studying paradoxical communication in schizophrenia. Given that none of the existing team members had any clinical training, Jackson was brought in for his work as a psychiatrist with schizophrenics. This group, in 1956, wrote one of the most influential articles in family therapy history, "Towards a Theory of Schizophrenia," in which they introduced the notion of the double bind.

In 1958, Jackson was the founder and first director of the Mental Research Institute (MRI), which was initially designed as an institute for teaching, research, and outpatient facilities. Within the MRI, the Brief Therapy Center was developed by Dick Fisch, John Weakland, and Paul Watzlawick. The model utilized at the Brief Therapy Center was one of the first brief models of psychotherapy and became a foundation for other models of therapy, such as strategic family therapy, Milan systemic family therapy, and solution-focused brief therapy.

Jackson, along with Jay Haley and Nathan Ackerman, co-founded the journal *Family Process*. Jackson is one of the most important figures in the development of brief therapy, interactional therapy, and marriage and family therapy. His 1957 article, "The Question of Family Homeostasis" has been viewed as one of the foundational papers of family therapy. In his short career, he authored a considerable number of articles, book chapters, and books. One of his most influential books was *Pragmatics of Human Communication* (Watzlawick et al., 1967), which highlighted many of the communicational ideas that had originally been developed during the Bateson project.

Don D. Jackson died on January 29, 1968, at the age of 48.

Covert Rules

Covert rules are the rules that impact behavior that are not formally stated (see Figure 3.6). These unwritten rules are discovered by observing interactions. If we go back to exploring the rules involved with driving, there are covert rules as to how you should interact with other drivers, such as lifting your hand or waving if someone lets you into a lane or flashing your lights if someone does not have their lights on at night.

The covert rules may play into the hierarchy and structure of the family. This can be the case in families dealing with alcoholism where the family learns to avoid the alcoholic when he is drunk or no one talks about the drinking because it inevitably blows up into a fight. However, there was never a conversation that this is how people should respond.

In our case family, no one had to tell the children, Miranda and Jonathan, that if they want something it is better to go to mother than to father as father is stricter. These covert rules were learned through trial and error. No one in the Martinez family would be likely to write them down in a manual of how their family functions. However, these covert rules play a significant role in how members act and react to one another. Daniel knows to stay away from Johanna when she begins yelling at the children, as she has yelled at him in the past when he has tried to engage her while she yelled at the children previously.

One tactic to alter the family rules is to make the covert rules overt (Watzlawick et al., 1974). These therapists often came up with paradoxical and sometimes fantastic interventions and tactics to make rules overt. For instance, with the Martinez family, the therapist might give them a behavior prescription that the children always have to go to Johanna instead of Daniel when they have a question or are making a request. By making their covert rule overt, the family members may then decide to change this rule.

However, even describing and asking about covert family rules can make them overt. Watzlawick et al. (1974) write, "Once the 'game' is overt, it becomes impossible to go on playing it blindly" (p. 123). These therapists often then combine "making the covert overt" tactic with a reframe as the therapist is often the first one to describe a rule in an overt way. The way the therapist describes the formerly covert rule is not neutral; it may make a big difference in how the family then describes and understands the rules. They suggest reframing in a way that is both gentle and aesthetic.

For example, perhaps, as the therapist, you notice that whenever the parents argue the child cries, to which one parent stops the argument to care for the child while scolding the spouse. What rules do you see there? Stop fighting when the child cries? The "winning" spouse is the first one to calm the child? Children should cry to stop their parents fighting? It is okay to scold the other spouse when the child is on your "side"? For this hypothetical family, one or more of these may be true. The rules are covert in that neither spouse sat down with one another and their children and said, "We will fight until/unless a child cries . . . agreed?" These rules just "naturally" happened based on previous restraints of behaviors, past rules for interactions, as well as other contextual implications. However, the current rule is covert to

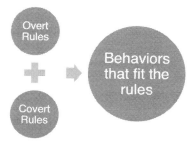

Figure 3.6 Both Overt and Covert Rules Restrain Behavior.

them. What might change if these rules became overt? It may not end the fighting, but almost certainly there would be a thought of, "Hey wait a minute, I see what you did there" from the "losing" spouse. Occasionally, children will laugh when covert rules are made overt, almost as if they already "know." For instance, if Johanna told Miranda that she didn't have to listen to Daniel's rules, Miranda might laugh and say, "Of course." At minimum, it will be difficult for these parents to continue with their same rules and interactions after they become known.

Applying Your Knowledge

A husband comes home and watches TV; his wife yells at him for not helping around the house. He leaves the house to drink till late, comes home drunk, and passes out on the couch. This happens until special events such as friends coming over to watch a sporting event, holidays, and family visits where the husband insists the house be cleaner and the wife leaves home to shop leaving the husband to get it spotless.

What rules could you describe from this scenario? Which rules are more overt? Of the rules you thought of, can you think of another way to name/describe them? Are there any strengths or resources you can utilize in the way you name the covert rules?

MARITAL QUID PRO QUO

The rules of interaction lead people to mainly behave in prescribed ways.

Jackson (1965) described a certain type of family rule that occurs between spouses—the **marital quid pro quo**. Quid pro quo stands for "something for something," and it is a give and take between the two parties. Each person in the relationship gives something to the other, which helps to define what the relationship is. A famous quid pro quo occurs in sexual harassment situations between a boss and an employee. The boss might state that s/he will provide a promotion, raise, or more favorable working condition for something from the employee—perhaps some type of sexual act. Another famous quid pro quo was portrayed in the movie *The Silence of the Lambs*. Hannibal Lecter and Clarice Starling enter into a quid pro quo where Lecter provides insights into the serial killer case that Starling is investigating, and Starling provides details about her childhood to Lecter. In the former example, the quid pro quo might be overt or covert. In the latter example, it was most definitively overt. However, in romantic relationships, usually the quid pro quo is based on covert rules, where the partners have not formally negotiated their dynamic but have developed the unwritten contract.

There are many forms that this bargain can take. In the Martinez family, Johanna agreed to be the primary caregiver while Daniel agreed to take care of the financials. If this was part of a negotiation when they were talking about having children, this would be an overt quid pro quo. However, many couples do not fully talk about role responsibilities. They then find themselves in their current situation, thinking the other person did something to them, rather than understanding how they were complicit in the arrangement. We might view the quid pro quo as a form of **complementarity**, where partners engage in alternative behaviors.

Changing the marital quid pro quo in therapy may be difficult. Watzlawick et al. (1974) explained, "In general, the problems encountered in marriage therapy more often than not have to do with the almost insurmountable difficulty of changing the *quid pro quo* on which the relationship was originally based" (p. 73, italics in original). What is needed in therapy is a second order change, which is a change in the rules of the system rather than a first order change, which would be a change that occurs within the original system rules. A segment of therapy from Salvador Minuchin, one of the most influential family therapists, can help us to see this in practice (Minuchin, Reiter, & Borda, 2014, pp. 91–93).

Minuchin:	My dear, this is your function in your family. You are the sheriff, you are the overseer, you are the one that needs to help. You are an overworked lady.
Mother:	Well, how can I get out of it then?
Minuchin:	You will have to ask Benjamin that, not me.
Mother:	[Turning to husband] How do I get out of it? I am overworked.
Father:	By cutting off some of the extra tactics.
Mother:	Elaborate. I don't understand.
Father:	When you speak of something to any of the children, you speak of it once. And then back off and give it time to implement itself.
Mother:	What if it is something that has to be done right away and they do not do it?
Father:	Then there will be consequences.
Minuchin:	See, he is your foreman. That is not a way in which you will work less. He is giving you instructions of how to work differently.
Mother:	But I have to work just the same.
Minuchin:	Yes, absolutely. That was not a change. That was, keep doing it, but do it in the way I am telling you. He became your foreman just now.

For this couple, they had a marital quid pro quo that placed the wife in a position of primary caretaking and the husband as the primary breadwinner. The change proposed by the husband fit within their existing quid pro quo contract, where the wife still had to be the primary when dealing with the children. Minuchin made this covert contract overt and challenged the couple to change their contract. This intervention of making covert rules overt will most likely lead to second order change as the rules of the rules might change.

Applying Your Knowledge

Based on what you know about Daniel and Johanna (although you might have to extrapolate based on what has been presented), describe their marital quid pro quos. How might they have developed these contracts? What might be a therapeutic change in their quid pro quo?

Family Myths

Based on the rules developed in a family, both overt and covert, families develop beliefs to as who they are and what the roles in the family are. These beliefs are known as **family myths**. Ferreira (1977) explained, "The notion of family myth refers here to a number of well-systematized beliefs, shared by all family members, about their mutual roles in the family, and the nature of their relationship" (p. 51). Family myths are predicated on the rules that have developed over time in a family and that lead to limited response options for individuals.

In Chapter 2, we explained that behaviors are based on restraints. These restraints determine what rules were developed, the roles that people adopt, and the view that people take about who/what their family is. Families develop myths to ensure that they are maintaining themselves. In essence, myths serve to regulate homeostasis (Palazzoli, Boscolo, Cecchin, & Prata, 1981).

Family myths develop over time, perhaps over several generations. The myth is related to the repeated patterns of the family and thus is related to circularity (Gelcer, McCabe, & Smith-Resnick, 1990). Many times, the myth becomes recursively restrictive. In some families, myths develop when a child is viewed as being similar to someone from a previous generation, such as, "Jonathan is just like his grandfather." The child is then imbued with the characteristics of that other person, with that view following him around for his life in that family. These interactions then coalesce into overt and covert rules of interaction that become habituated into the family's homeostasis.

We can also look at these myths developing based on the restraints of the family (White, 1986). There is a network of presuppositions between each family member. These presuppositions serve as restraints, holding some information as not being different and other information as **news**—information about difference. When information does not fit with the family myth, which is based on the connections of presuppositions of system members, it does not become news and may be forgotten. Thus, the family's myths help members to select certain information to pay attention to and other information to disregard. These then become restraints on how people define themselves, their relationships, and which behaviors make sense in that context.

The Martinez family may have developed a myth that conflict is not to be openly and publicly expressed. Based on this underlying mandate, the children may experience the tension between the parents and not feel comfortable saying anything about it. This might lead them to try to appease their mother, who spends more time with them. A cross-generational coalition of mother and children against the father could develop—however, one in which no one overtly engages in serious conflict. Instead, Johanna may see her actions as encouragement of Daniel rather than as scrutiny. Daniel may then internalize his frustrations and anger over his interpersonal relationship with his wife and instead of being able to hash it out, thinking that conflict is wrong, may internalize his feelings so that they demonstrate as depression and anxiety. If we knew more about Daniel and Johanna's families-of-origin, we might be able to see whether this myth was intergenerational, where one or both lived in a family whose myths included presenting themselves as a loving and conflict-free family.

As with covert rules, therapists can help to make the family myths overt. This can come through asking questions about how the family operates and perhaps comparing themselves to other families.

- Does your family deal with conflict like other families?
- Where did people learn to engage one another like this?
- How is it that your family came to learn that conflict was not to be openly expressed?
- How is it that Jonathan is viewed similarly to his grandfather? In what ways is he different?

Once the myth is overt, the therapist can help the family to develop myths that are more accurate to their current functioning. The change in myth would then lead to a change in the rules of the system. These rule changes would then produce a new homeostasis for the family.

Applying Your Knowledge

What family myths are present in your family? Based on those myths, what are the overt and covert rules of interaction? If you were to change one of those myths, what rules would then change?

Hypotheses

All therapists make hypotheses about what is occurring for clients. These hypotheses come from our preferred orientation/model of therapy. There may be many hypotheses developed, which when taken together form the case conceptualization. However, a systemic hypothesis does not happen without a connection to the context. **Systemic hypotheses** rest on two assumptions. First, the therapist understands that the client's behavior is interconnected to the context, which will include people the client is in relationship with as well as larger systems. The second assumption is that the therapist's hypothesis

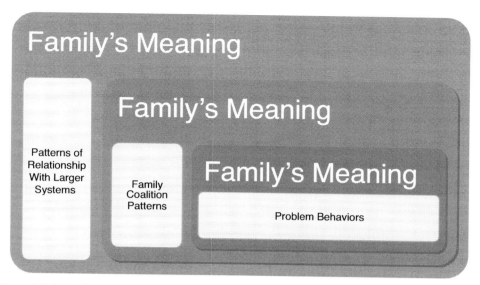

Figure 3.7 A Family's Meanings Are Housed Within Larger Levels of Understanding.

is interconnected to the continuing introduction of information about the client. That is, a systemic hypothesis is developed and continually altered based upon feedback.

The Milan associates have been one of the most influential therapists to highlight the importance of the systemic hypothesis (Palazzoli, Boscolo, Cecchin, & Prata, 1980). The systemic hypothesis has three components (Boscolo, Cecchin, Hoffman, & Penn, 1987). First, the therapist attempts to understand what the family thinks the problem is and how that problem involves the various people in the family. Second, the therapist explores how the family is connected to the larger social systems, such as extended family or the culture. Third, the therapist conceptualizes how the family is connected to the therapeutic system. Taking all of these together leads to the systemic hypothesis.

As explained, the therapist's hypothesis is intertwined with what occurs in the therapy room and modified based on feedback from the information garnered in the therapeutic transactions. This circular and recursive process keeps the hypothesis updated, which then informs what happens next in the therapy interchange. Keeney and Ross (1985) explained that utilizing hypotheses in this way cybernetically organizes the therapy. That is, the therapist's hypothesis informs his questions, which impacts the client's response that the therapist then uses to adjust his hypothesis, etc.

In working with the Martinez family, the therapist may develop a hypothesis that there is a cross-generational coalition of mother and children against the father. This may lead to a question about to whom Jonathan or Miranda is closer. If the response from one or more family members is that Jonathan is closest with Daniel, the therapist would then need to adjust his hypothesis accordingly. The therapist's hypothesis also impacts the meanings that each family member has as to their own family and what is happening between them. This information may then be a difference that makes a difference and leads to change (see Figure 3.7).

ROLES

People have different functions in a family—what we can call **roles**. These roles are determined by what people do. For some, the role is caretaking, which is usually given to one or both of the parents. However, that role may also be taken on by a grandparent, aunt, or older sibling. Another role may be as a challenger.

This person may likely be the identified patient. Others may be the White Knight, the dutiful husband, or the selfless wife. Family roles tend to be consistent since people have developed overt and covert rules of interaction that maintain those roles. These roles thus become part of the family's homeostasis.

Roles can be understood as a pragmatic description of logical types. Roles are a class that is determined by the behaviors within the role. Someone identified as a "black sheep" is a class that has members different than the members of the rest of the family's class. As in, a family that defines itself as "Southern Baptist Christian" probably has certain roles that they understand within their larger context. If a child from this family joins another religion or participates in a group or activity that is against their family rules, they may label that child as the "black sheep." As with all logical types, they are simply descriptive, not prescriptive. Just because someone is in a particular role doesn't mean that they must, or necessarily will, do any particular behavior, the roles are simply restraints as a way of understanding how one set of behavior happened over another. Another way of understanding this is questioning, "Does the role define the behaviors, or do the behaviors define the role?" "Can one change without the other? If so, which must change first?" To say that "he only uses drugs because he is the black sheep" is to mix up these logical types, also called invoking the dormitive principle.

Applying Your Knowledge

What role(s) do you hold in your family? When and how did this role develop? What other people endorsed this role? What behaviors of theirs help to maintain your role? Have you ever tried to take on a different role? If so, how did the people who tended to maintain your role react?

Since roles are based upon the rules of the family, one way to change the rules is to change the roles that people have overtly or covertly agreed upon. Roles are always interpersonal and mutual. One person cannot be controlling unless someone else agrees to be controlled. A person cannot be the peacemaker unless others agree to allow them to intercede in a conflict. Like family rules, these family roles can be overt or covert. This goes to the systems notion of **complementarity** where people are connected in mutual and interdependent ways. Thus, roles change when the rules of connection change—the family's homeostasis will then have changed as well.

Therapists can challenge the roles that people have mutually developed. Whitaker tended to engage the family in role confusion (Whitaker & Bumberry, 1988). He might say to a parentified child, "It's interesting. If you are mothering your mother, that means you are your own grandmother." With our case family, if Daniel was experiencing depression to the point of underfunctioning and Johanna had to overfunction, the therapist might say, "Johanna, how do you know when you are Daniel's wife rather than his mother?" This playing around in role confusion can be silly and fun in session, yet is quite powerful to family members when they decide they want to get out of one (or more) of the roles they find themselves in. To get out of the role, the rules that bind two or more people must be changed. Like family rules, another tactic can be to ask about covert family roles so as to make them overt. Once family roles are discussed overtly, it can be difficult for the family to return to behaving as if they are solely covert.

Roles can also be viewed as **identity**. Minuchin held that families believe that the identity of their members is unique and unchangeable (Minuchin et al., 2014). However, this is a myth. Families believe this myth because the rules of their interactions that have maintained these identities have most likely occurred for many years. One of the therapist's jobs then is to demonstrate to the family that identity is both interpersonal and multiple. This occurs through **unwrapping family member identities**. Someone in the family can be the peacemaker, the planner, the alarm clock, and the sounding board. When the therapist introduces the idea that each family member has multiple identities, new interactional patterns are likely to emerge.

A therapist working with the Martinez family may help to expand each person's identities in various ways. Below is a hypothetical therapeutic interchange to demonstrate how this might occur:

Therapist: Daniel, how did you become the outcast in this family?
Daniel: I don't know. Johanna doesn't include me. It is not fair.
Therapist: Johanna, that is a strange thing that Daniel says. He talks as if you are a jailer and he a prisoner where he has no freedom and everything is restricted for him. How did that happen?
Johanna: He did it to himself. He stays out, drinks, and when he comes home, he goes straight to the television to play video games.
Therapist: So he puts himself in solitary confinement?
Johanna: Yes.
Therapist: So he is his own jailer. Then why don't you set him free?
Johanna: I've tried.
Therapist: Daniel, is she your jailer or parole board?

Here, the therapist explores the patterns of interaction based around the roles the family members have adopted with one another. The covert way of being with one another comes to the surface to become more overt. Further, the therapist unwraps alternative identities, which may lead to new roles and thus new rules of interaction.

Equifinality

We introduced the notions of multifinality and equifinality in Chapter 2. **Multifinality** holds that from the same starting point there are many possible outcomes. From their current way of being with one another, the Martinez family has multiple future configurations. Daniel and Johanna may decide to divorce one another, Daniel might choose to have an affair, they might choose to have another child, or they could become more united. The family is not destined, based on its current organization, to be a specific way.

Equifinality is a related concept to multifinality (see Figure 3.8). In **equifinality**, the same end point (outcome) can be reached through a multitude of means. Many times clients will come to therapy saying, "I tried everything." While it is a nice phrase of speech, we know that it is not correct. There is always something else that someone could have done. It may be more correct for the family to have said, "I have tried everything that makes sense within my family rules and context." But that would be too overt for them to actually say. Understanding these principles helps therapists see, hear, and learn more than simply the content of what clients say.

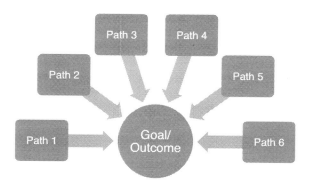

Figure 3.8 Equifinality Is the Concept That Multiple Paths Lead to the Same Outcome.

Daniel may believe that he has tried everything to get Johanna to treat him better. He could think, and has thought, of trying to ignore it, telling Johanna he doesn't appreciate her disrespecting him, and staying out at the pub so they don't get into fights (along with a host of other attempts to fix the problem). Yet, he didn't try therapy yet (individual, couple, or family); he didn't try to work things out through drawing what he wants to say instead of using words; and he didn't try to have the serious conversation about their relationship while they were both naked with him sitting in the bathtub and Johanna sitting on the toilet.

Reiter (2018) explained equifinality in terms of the various ways an offensive player in baseball can get to first base. Being on first base would be the same outcome, while how the player got there is the means. Do you know what the six ways are for the offensive player to get to first base? (Take a second to try to think about it before reading on.)

Here are the six ways an offensive player can get to first base:

1. The batter hits the ball (and either gets a single, there is a defensive error, a fielder's choice, or fielder's interference)
2. Walk
3. Hit by pitch
4. Uncaught third strike
5. Pinch runner
6. Catcher's interference

Applying Your Knowledge

Take a moment to think about a goal that you have. What are five possible pathways that can help you to achieve that goal?

Goal:
Pathway 1:
Pathway 2:
Pathway 3:
Pathway 4:
Pathway 5:

Believing in the concept of equifinality allows the therapist a plethora of options to attempt to reach the client's goals. It is a way to counter the client's belief that, "The only way for me to make it through this is x." There are millions of possible pathways that will move the client from their current state to one that is more pleasant and desired. What they all have in common is that they are something different than the solution attempts the client has already tried. This difference may be based on what the person does or how the person perceives the situation (O'Hanlon, 1999). However, just because something is different does not mean it will necessarily help the client get to where he wants to go, but it increases the possibilities of doing so.

de Shazer (1985) understood this notion of multiple pathways when he developed the **do something different task**. It was utilized for cases in which "one person is complaining about the behavior of another person and, having tried 'everything,' has become stuck reacting in the same way over and over while the troublesome behavior continues" (pp. 122–123). While it is a form of pattern interruption, which all therapy is based on, the do something different task operates based upon equifinality. The therapist does not tell the client what to do differently. That is left ambiguous so that the client has to decide. The wording for the do something different task, in relation to the Martinez family, might go something like the following:

> Between now and the next time we meet, I would like each of you, Daniel and Johanna, when you experience a disagreement between you, no matter how weird or strange, to do something different. It can be anything, no matter how crazy it might seem, as long as it is something you haven't done before. The important thing is that it is different than what you have done in the past.

Daniel might choose (instead of getting frustrated at Johanna and walking away, going to the pub or isolating himself in his music room) to kiss Johanna on the cheek and apologize. Another option is for him to go to the kitchen and put some peanuts in his mouth and then continue the conversation while chewing the peanuts. Or he might do a handstand against the wall and ask Johanna to tell him about her concerns. Johanna could do any of these or might decide to have a conversation with Daniel while they remain back-to-back. She could, once an argument starts, only reply in three-letter words. Or she could answer Daniel with lyrics from some of their favorite songs. We know that these possibilities are a bit on the silly side, and they could also do things that are more serious. Daniel, instead of trying to defend himself when Johanna says something he finds accusatory, could find areas that he agrees with what she is saying. Johanna could say whatever she wants to say to Daniel, but do so sitting or standing in front of him, holding his hands.

Perhaps none of these new response options will be enough to shift the dynamics of the couple. However, in all likelihood, if the couple continues to engage each other in the same non-effective ways that they have up to this point, there will not be change. That is, the couple will maintain their current homeostasis. The do something different task provides the client with additional pathways that have the possibility for them achieving their goals.

As described, therapy is about pattern interruption. Doing something different potentially changes the existing interactional patterns. With the understanding of equifinality, therapists try to get some type of novelty to occur, either in the therapy room or wherever the client experiences the problem.

Circular Questions

Based upon the notion of double description, therapists are able to ask multiple people their perspectives on the same issue. This happens through the use of **circular questions** (see Figure 3.9). Circular questions are based on the notion that living systems function through loop formations rather than linear sequences (Boscolo et al., 1987; Palazzoli et al., 1980). Thus, instead of exploring cause-and-effect relationships, we

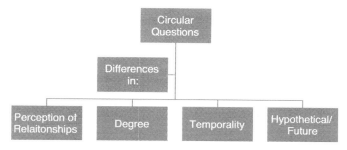

Figure 3.9 Circular Questions Focus on Differences, Which Has the Potential to Bring Information Into the System.

look at mutuality, circularity, and recursion. Initially, circular questions were viewed as triadic questions. **Triadic questions** are when a family member is asked about the relationship between two or more other members of the family.

- Daniel, who is Jonathan closer to? Miranda or Johanna?
- Johanna, when Daniel is feeling down, who shows more anxiety? Jonathan or Miranda?
- Jonathan, who is Miranda closer to, mother or father?

Circular questions are predicated on the concept of difference (see Chapter 4). Penn (1982) explained, "The information sought by circular questions are the differences in relationships the family has experienced before and after the problem began" (p. 272). These differences may be in perception of relationships, degree, temporality, and hypothetical/future (Boscolo et al., 1987). By exploring difference, the therapist attempts to bring information into the session, something that is new to the family members, which may lead to a change in the way people understand what is happening in their lives and, thus, to behavioral change. Let's slow down a bit and explore each of these categories.

Differences in Perception of Relationships

This category usually asks one person about her perception of the differences between two or more other people. Difference in perception questions might be called triadic questions.

- Who is closest to grandmother? Johanna or Miranda?
- Who would be the first to notice that Daniel is upset? Jonathan or Miranda?
- Who does Miranda go to when she needs to talk to someone? Johanna or Daniel?

Differences in Degree

Circular questions in the category of differences in degree ask someone to rank a situation. One form of differences in degree questions is **scaling questions**, which ask clients to place an abstract construct onto a more concrete base. Anyone who has gone into an emergency room has experienced a scaling question when the admitting nurse asks, "On a scale of 1 to 10, how much pain are you in right now?"

Scaling questions are intended to be relational and explore differences in how people might rank whatever is being talked about. Berg and de Shazer (1993) stated, "Scaling questions are used to discuss the individual client's perspective, the client's view of others, and the client's impression of others' view of him or her" (p. 10). Scaling questions can be used in a circular manner, asking about difference in perception between two or more people on the difference of degree (Reiter & Shilts, 1998).

- On a scale of 1 to 10, how motivated are you for change right now?
- If we were to scale your commitment to the marriage, where 1 is low and 10 is the highest, where would you put yourself? Where do you think your partner is?
- In thinking about your level of happiness, where would you say you are on a scale of 1 to 10?
- You said that you are at a 7. Where do you think your wife would put you on that scale? Where would she put herself?

Differences in Temporality

Temporality regards time, which can be used to explore how ideas, behaviors, and symptoms have changed from the past to the present. These types of questions are quite important as they signal to the client that

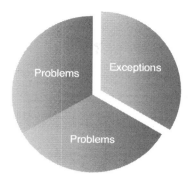

Figure 3.10 The Difference Between Problems and Exceptions.

the problem has not always been present or has not been as severe as it currently is. This then provides hope for change and difference.

- Did the fighting become more serious before or after Miranda left for college?
- Thinking back to the first time you experienced this feeling, what was different in your life?
- When your parents divorced, how was your relationship with each compared to now?

One form of differences in temporality questions is called exception questions (see Figure 3.10). **Exceptions** are times when the problem the client is experiencing did not happen or did not happen to the same degree they are happening now (Berg, 1994). **Exception questions** ask the client about differences in the who, what, where, when, and how, or when the problem was not as problematic for him as it currently is.

- When you two were getting along better, what was different?
- Who were you close to when you were feeling more motivated?
- You mentioned feeling happier in the past. Where did you go when you were happier?

Exception questions are often utilized with assumptions built into the questions. "When you two were getting along better" assumes within it that the couple was getting along better at one point or another, the question is simply "what was different" (during those times). Therapists that utilize exception questions often start with the assumption that no problem happens all of the time and are able to build questions off of that assumption.

Applying Your Knowledge

What other kinds of assumptions do you, or other therapists, hold? What kinds of questions can be asked while holding that assumption? Is it a useful assumption to hold? What other kinds of questions might you ask that assumes that the problem isn't happening all of the time? Look at the questions asked above in this chapter, what assumptions are held by the therapist as he asks them, and what difference does holding those assumptions make?

Hypothetical and Future Differences

Hypothetical differences explore how the client perceives what life would be like if certain events that did happen did not actually happen—or vice versa, that events that did not happen did.

- If you had never met, how do you think your life would be?
- If you were to divorce right now, how do you think the relationship with the children would be?
- If Daniel wasn't symptomatic, how do you think the family would be?

Future differences focus on how clients perceive life would be like in the future, especially if something in their lives were to change. Penn (1985) talked about future questions in terms of **"feed-forward"** where families are asked to imagine how the patterns of relationships would be in the future. One of the benefits of the feed-forward question is that it suggests that how the family currently is not static; change can and will happen.

- Let's say that mom and dad were to divorce. Where would you go to live?
- Take a second and imagine that Miranda and Jonathan graduate high school and move away to college. What does your marriage look like?
- What does the future look like for you two if there wasn't all of this fighting?

Applying Your Knowledge

For the following scenario, develop at least two questions in each of the categories of circular questions.

Cruz and Annabelle have been dating for five years. Cruz has two children from a previous marriage who live with them on the weekends. Annabelle has one child from a previous marriage who lives with them full-time. When all the children are together in the house, Cruz and Annabelle find it to be chaotic. Annabelle thinks Cruz does not discipline his children and that he lets them do what they want. Cruz wants to make sure that the children enjoy coming over to the house and spending time with him, especially since he and his ex-wife do not get along.

Triadic questions:

1.
2.

Differences in perception of relationships:

1.
2.

Differences in degree:

1.
2.

Differences in temporality:

1.
2.

Differences in hypothetical/future:

1.
2.
   Can you think of a triadic question that would illuminate multiple family roles and rules at once?

Questions for Reflection

1. A fundamental idea to cybernetics is the concept of "feedback." How does feedback relate to your understanding of rules? Roles? Hypotheses? Circular questions?
2. How do you make sense of both equifinality and restraints?
3. How does asking circular questions relate to the notion of recursiveness?
4. What is the importance of scaling? How does that relate to the three planes of temporality (past, present, and future)?
5. What role does unwrapping family member identities have in helping families to change their current homeostasis?

CHAPTER FOUR
Interactional Aesthetics

Michael D. Reiter

CASE DESCRIPTION

The Horowitz nuclear family is composed of five members: Joseph (37), Becky (35), Mara (14), Blake (8), and Damon (6). They are a white, Jewish, lower-middle class family who live in an urban area. Joseph and Becky were childhood friends and married when he was 21 and she 19. Two years later, they gave birth to Mara. Becky was very happy to have a child, while Joseph was indifferent. Joseph preferred for Becky to do most of the parenting. He began spending more time away from home, hanging out and going to the track with friends. Becky knew that Joseph was gambling away his earnings but thought that, since he was the primary breadwinner, she should not say anything. She justified not engaging in conflict because it never got to the point where they didn't have enough money to pay the rent or couldn't purchase groceries.

Joseph manages the fabric company that his father started. He completed college and considered going to medical school, but with the start of a family, he put that on hold. Becky didn't enjoy school. Once she graduated from high school, she quickly got a job as a paralegal. Mara is doing well at school. She is interested in dating boys, but her parents have told her she cannot date until she is 16. At home, Mara tends to caretake for her younger brothers, as both Joseph and Becky work until 5:00 p.m. and do not arrive home until at least 5:30 p.m. Blake and Damon spend much of their time together. Blake is also doing well at school. Damon is quite active and occasionally gets in trouble at school for not paying attention. The school psychologist diagnosed him with Attention Deficit Disorder. Damon's rowdy behavior sometimes overwhelms Joseph who, while proud of his children, does not engage with his children as much as Becky would like. However, Becky does not tell him about her concerns as she does not want to fight with him.

Seven months ago, Joseph told Becky that he needed some space. He left the house for five days, and when he returned, he and Becky didn't discuss why he left, where he went, or what their expectations were for the relationship. In the beginning of their relationship, they were sexually active several times per week. After Mara was born, the couple's intimacy reduced to once every couple of weeks, on average. For the last year, they have only been sexually intimate twice.

Becky is closest with Mara, as Mara is very conscientious, helping to clean the house and caretake for the boys. Becky also has help in child raising from a next-door neighbor, who has a daughter the same age as Mara. Becky's family lives in the next town. Her father died the same year that Damon was born. Her mother is retired, and her health is starting to become an issue. Becky brings the children over to see her mother a couple of times a month.

Joseph's father died three years ago. His mother, Ethel, works with him in the fabric company. She was a very strict parent, and while they get along at work, there is not a close relationship between Joseph and his mother. Ethel sees her grandchildren once or twice a month. During these meetings, she tells Becky how she should be raising the children differently, especially around Damon and his hyperactivity. Becky does not show it to Ethel, but she finds these statements extremely insulting and intrusive. Ethel tells Joseph that he could have done better than Becky. Joseph just tries to ignore her when she says things such as this.

In this chapter, we will use the Horowitz family as a guide to help us navigate systems theory concepts with interactional roots. These ideas primarily came through Gregory Bateson's anthropological understandings and the outcome of the Bateson project on paradoxes of communication. That project led to the development of the Mental Research Institute (MRI), where an interactional model of psychotherapy was developed. These interactional ideas are also intimately related to the cybernetic ideas presented in Chapters 2 and 3.

Difference

Throughout this book, we have been talking about how systems are composed of different parts that come together to function as a whole, and that this whole is connected, yet separated from other systems. To distinguish one system from another, we need to look at difference. Difference is a unit of information where there is a distinction between two things (Bateson, 1972).

We do not realize how much of our awareness is based on difference. Think for a second about when you spent a lot of time in your kitchen. There was most likely a certain moment in which you realized that the refrigerator was on. This is because there were many minutes in which the refrigerator was not making noise, and then at a certain point, some mechanism inside the motor made noise. That point, where there was a difference in sound, brought the refrigerator to your awareness. But continue to stay in the room for a while where the refrigerator continues to make the same sound (or no sound), and it leaves your awareness because no difference is occurring.

If we move our view to differences in relationships, we can see that we understand one relationship as not being another relationship. There is a difference between my relationship with my wife and with my child, which makes the two relationships quite distinct. In the Horowitz family, Joseph notices a difference between Blake and Damon based on the boys' behaviors—one more active than the other (although this is not the only difference Joseph notices between them. Other differences include one having blonde hair while the other has brown, one taller than the other, one able to speak more, etc.).

When we explore difference, we make a separation, yet there is still a connection there (Flemons, 1991). Difference denotes a boundary. There is a difference between you and me and, thus, a boundary between us. There is a difference between my family and your family and, thus, a boundary. When we view this boundary, we see two complementary ideas: separation and connection (see Figure 4.1). The boundary separates us—me/you. Yet, the boundary connects us—me and you.

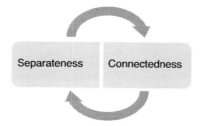

Figure 4.1 The Relationship Between Separateness and Connectedness. While They Are Distinct, They Are Also Interrelated.

In families such as the Horowitz family, there are countless differences. There is the difference between husband/wife, mother/father, parent/child, grandparent/parent, boy/girl, man/woman, old/young, worker/non-worker, etc. These differences help people to contextualize what the relationship is. The rules of interaction are based on these differences. Mara notices a difference between parent and friend and acts differently based on whom she is in contact with (the context). With a friend, she might joke around and say, "You're such a bitch" but will not say the same thing to her mother. Not only is there a difference between parent and friend, but that difference has significance. When Mara marks the difference between herself and her mother, she gains autonomy, yet she also knows that she is connected to her mother.

DISTINCTIONS

In order to experience difference, we need to make distinctions. **Distinctions** happen when we can discern one thing from another. If there are two people in front of you who are standing two feet apart, side by side, you can easily make a distinction between person 1 and person 2. However, if there are two people who are the exact same height, weight, build, etc., and one is standing exactly behind the other, you may not be able to make a distinction between the two.

We can also easily make distinctions between colors when the colors are far apart on the color wheel, such as blue/orange, green/red, or purple/yellow. However, when the two colors are very close on the wheel, it becomes much harder for us to make distinctions between the two. When we cannot make distinctions, we cannot see difference. For instance, most people would not be able to distinguish between royal blue and true blue.

Let's give one last example of making distinctions. Think about the last time you were outside in 95-degree weather for a while and then you walked into a house where the air conditioning was set at 67 degrees. You most likely determined the distinction in temperature at the doorway when you first felt the cold temperature of the house in contrast to the warm weather of outdoors. This was noted as a difference for you. However, let's say you were sitting in the 67-degree room for several hours and I changed the temperature to 68 degrees. Could you make the distinction between the two temperatures? Most likely not. This idea is how the parable of a boiled frog started. A frog will remain in a pot of water that very slowly has the temperature increased to the point of being boiled; the frog was not able to make the distinction that the water was getting hotter.

People make distinctions to inform them whether they are maintaining their homeostasis or if something has changed. If the change in functioning is very minor, it is not punctuated as a distinction and goes unnoticed. That minor change then becomes part of the homeostasis. Over time, these very small adjustments in behavior become the accepted way of being. It is only if the person/family is shown how they used to be that a distinction is made between the two ways of being. Given this, one way therapy helps people shift behaviors is to help them to make distinctions.

Applying Your Knowledge

What distinctions do you make in your relationships? How do these distinctions inform you about difference? How does that difference lead you to behave differently than if you hadn't made those distinctions?

In the Horowitz family, Joseph and Becky are making a distinction between how Blake behaves and how Damon behaves; this distinction is a difference (see Figure 4.2). They are then also placing a judgment on this distinction where they believe Blake's behavior is "good" or "acceptable," and Damon's more

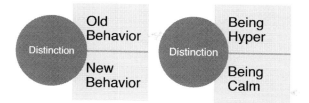

Figure 4.2 People Make Distinctions Between Old Behavior and New Behavior.

active behavior is "problematic." This is just one of millions of distinctions the various members of the Horowitz family are making. Some of the other significant distinctions include Becky (and friends of the family) viewing Joseph in terms of gambling or not gambling, being sexually active and not sexually active, and Ethel making a distinction between Becky as wife for her son and someone else as potentially being wife of her son.

INFORMATION

Systems function based on the use of information. Bateson (1972) famously stated that **information** is the difference that makes a difference. We do not know what difference will be significant enough that it changes the system. If we thought that we could assess the system and then make a specific intervention that would have a specific outcome, we would be operating from a lineal epistemology. However, since systems theory is based on a nonlineal epistemology, one that is based on mutuality and circularity, we know that there is not a predisposed cause and effect.

Instead of the view of cause and effect, systems theorists operate more in the realm of possibility. Here, we can talk about one person's actions toward desired change as **perturbing the system** (we will talk more about perturbations in Chapter 8). In order to do this, a system needs to try to bring in information. If the difference was significant enough to make a difference, the system will then auto-correct; it will change.

For the Horowitz family, the school psychologist drew a distinction when he or she diagnosed Attention Deficit Disorder. This distinction is different than how the Horowitz family previously punctuated Damon's behaviors. Perhaps this new distinction could further alter the way Joseph and Becky mentally and verbally classify Damon. If so, they may feel relieved that it is not their parenting that is causing Damon to be hyper, but an issue with brain chemistry. This new distinction may inform them to bring him to a psychiatrist to put him on some type of hyperactivity medication. This could also change the way they engage him, perhaps by not getting upset so quickly. Damon might then respond differently to them. This is one possibility. However, the ADD diagnosis may not change the way they draw distinctions or the way they punctuate Damon's behaviors. The information would not be "change" as the difference did not persist across time.

PUNCTUATIONS

We've been talking about information and distinctions. If we take these ideas and place them into communicational sequences between people, we can explore how each person punctuates the interaction. **Punctuation** is how the person makes a distinction between the start and end points of the interchange (see Figure 4.3). Just think about two young sisters who are fighting and their parent comes over and asks, "What happened?" One, but most likely both, of the siblings will probably say, "She started it!!" That sibling is punctuating the interaction as the sister did something (i.e., took a toy, made a face, or called them a name). She then responded based on the other's opening gambit.

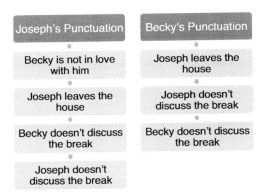

Figure 4.3 The Difference in Punctuations Between Two People. Joseph and Becky Are Each Describing the Same Situation but Have Different Viewpoints on Who Initiated the Situation.

However, the sequence of the interchange is usually much longer than people punctuate (Watzlawick et al., 1967). If we keep to our example of the siblings, they have been engaging one another in a mutual back-and-forth for quite some time. Each of their explanations of who/what started the fight was just an arbitrary starting point for "this" current interchange. In reality, this current interchange cannot be separated from past interchanges between the two.

This sequence of interaction could be described as: . . . 1 2 1 2 1 2 1 2 1 2 1 2 1 2 1 2 1 2 1 . . . , where sibling 1 says that sibling 2 started it and sibling 2 says that sibling 1 started it. The history of interaction often becomes untraceable, and what is left is the pattern. Family therapists following interactional ideas become more interested in these patterns and inviting difference within the sequence.

If we just look at the period of time in the Horowitz family when Joseph left for five days, we would suspect that he and Becky (as well as anyone else in the family) would punctuate it differently. For Joseph, the punctuation might be that he did not feel that Becky was really engaged in the marriage and that she was not demonstrating to him that she was really in love with him, and thus, he spent five days away from home. He would then say that, when he came home, Becky didn't really bring it up so he did not either. Becky's punctuation would likely be quite different. For her, the sequence would likely start with Joseph leaving the house for five days and then coming home and saying nothing about it so she then said nothing about it. Neither person's punctuation is wrong, but neither is correct either. Further, we can keep adding to the sequence of what came before the first item in the sequence. We could ask Joseph what happened before he made a distinction that Becky was acting in a way he didn't consider to be loving. If we continue this process, we can add forward or backward in the sequence, which would help to demonstrate that each person has a limited view of the interactional sequence.

Applying Your Knowledge

Throughout your life, you have had thousands of experiences of two people having different punctuations of the same event. For three situations, list your punctuation and the punctuation of the other person. Then think about the notion of double description presented in Chapter 2 and note what these two punctuations add to the understanding of the relationship.

INTERACTIONAL AESTHETICS

Situation 1

Your Punctuation:
Other's Punctuation:
Relational Understanding:

Situation 2

Your Punctuation:
Other's Punctuation:
Relational Understanding:

Situation 3

Your Punctuation:
Other's Punctuation:
Relational Understanding:

REDUNDANCY/PATTERN

The interactions between people in relationships are not separate but are connected to one another in long sequences that tend to have the same shape. That is, people's interactions with one another tend to be redundant—they maintain a pattern and way of being. These patterns are shaped by the rules of the family as well as shape the rules of the family (see Figure 4.4). Here, we can look at the recursiveness between rules and patterns as they both feed off of, and feed, the other.

Having relationships that are based on patterns is quite useful and comforting. Imagine that every time you went home you didn't know how your partner (or someone else living in the house) was going to react to you. It would be very disorienting. You wouldn't know when entering your house if your partner was going to greet you with a kiss, a meal, a curse, or a slap. But I suspect that you can predict with pretty good accuracy what will happen when you (or your partner) get home today. That is because you have developed a pattern of being with one another. Now, we want to be clear that we are simplifying things as we have multiple patterns with the same person, but usually in different situations. For instance, there is a pattern for when you first come home (i.e., each person says "hello" and gives the other a kiss); a pattern when deciding what to do for vacation (i.e., one person does the planning and the other goes along with it); and a different pattern in the bedroom surrounding lovemaking (i.e., who initiates, how the initiation happens, and what acts occur).

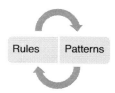

Figure 4.4 The Recursiveness of Rules and Patterns. The Rules of the System Inform What Patterns Are Established While the Established Patterns Inform What the Rules of the System Are.

Patterns are neither good nor bad, they just are. Because relationships are patterned interactions, we can distinguish one relationship from another. We can then make a distinction between when things are going well or not going well. When there is a difference in the pattern, we make a distinction of this pattern versus another action, which then becomes information. Let's say in the Horowitz family there is a typical pattern that, when Becky gets home, Blake and Damon run to the door to hug her and Mara comes to hug her as well. If one day she comes home, no one comes to greet her, and she sees Damon sitting by himself in the corner, something is different. She can probably safely assume that this difference is analogous to something else. And in this case, she would likely use that information to attribute that something was going wrong.

Applying Your Knowledge

To put this notion of what happens when patterns are not followed to the test, do the following. With your romantic partner (if you do not have a romantic partner, you can adapt this exercise with someone else you are close with), you most likely have a pattern of how you watch a favorite television show or movie at home. Likely, you will both sit on the same couch, perhaps quite close to each other. This would be a pattern that both of you enjoy and value. If so, the next time you both agree to watch something on the television, let the other person sit down first. Then, sit in a spot that is not on the same couch and observe what happens. How long does it take them to react? What do they do to let you know they made a distinction between this current way of being and past ways (your patterned relationships)?

It will probably not be too long, perhaps less than a few seconds, before your partner will inquire, perhaps with his or her eyes or vocally, whether everything is okay. They have made a distinction between watching television together this time and past times and detected a difference that has become information. This situation has gone outside of the typical homeostasis of the relationship, and their inquiry is a way to bring it back into alignment.

Symmetrical and Complementary Patterns

As we just discussed, people come together and develop "normal" ways of being with one another. They are normal because they become the norm, the primary way that two or more people tend to interact with one another. They are not normal because they are right but, rather, because they are habituated between the people. These repetitive ways are known as **patterns**. Bateson (1958) discussed two main patterns: symmetrical and complementary.

Symmetrical patterns occur when the two parties engage in similar behavior. There are two subtypes of symmetrical patterns. The first is **competitive symmetrical patterns**. Here, the more that person A does a behavior, the more person B does the behavior. The second subtype is **submissive symmetrical patterns**. This occurs when the less person A does a behavior, the less person B does the behavior. To oversimplify, symmetrical patterns are: More/More (competitive) or Less/Less (submissive).

Let's slow down and really explore these two subtypes. In competitive symmetrical patterns, we might see this as a one-upmanship encounter. The US and Soviet Union nuclear arms race was a competitive symmetrical relationship. The more nuclear weapons the US made, the more the USSR made. And, conversely, the more the USSR made, the more the US made (remember our discussion of punctuation). In most armed conflict situations, we see a competitive symmetrical relationship.

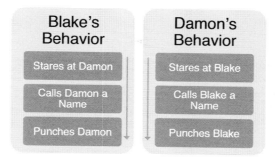

Figure 4.5 Competitive Symmetrical Escalation Between Blake and Damon Where Each Person Attempts to Engage in the Same or One-Up the Behaviors of the Other Person.

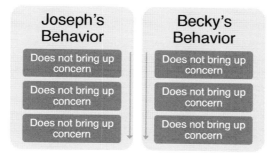

Figure 4.6 Submissive Symmetrical Pattern Between Joseph and Becky Where the Less One Talks About Concerns the Less the Other Talks About Concerns.

We can see a competitive symmetrical relationship (what is also sometimes called a competitive symmetrical escalation) in the Horowitz family if we look at how Blake and Damon engage each other in conflict (see Figure 4.5). Blake may "look funny" at Damon, who gets upset and stares down Blake. Blake follows this challenge with a name call, such as, "You're a dummy," wherein Damon follows in suit and says, "You're a doo-doo head." At a certain point, they will each try to one-up the other until they end in fisticuffs.

For submissive symmetrical patterns, we could view this as one-downsmanship (see Figure 4.6). Here, each person tries to submit to the will of the other. A common occurrence of this pattern happens when two people try to make plans for Saturday night:

Person A: What would you like to do?
Person B: I don't know. You pick.
Person A: No. You pick.
Person B: I'm not sure. What do you want to do?

This process could go on ad infinitum or until one or both parties decides just to stay in and not get together!

Joseph and Becky have implicitly agreed to have a submissive symmetrical pattern when it comes to talking about the status of their relationship. The less that Joseph talks about his concerns in the marriage, the less Becky does. Conversely, the less Becky talks about her concerns, the less Joseph does.

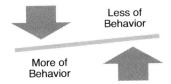

Figure 4.7 Complementary Relationships Involve the Two People in Interaction Engaging in Opposite yet Connected Behaviors.

Complementary patterns occur when the more person A does a behavior the less person B does that behavior. For instance, the more one person talks, the less the partner talks (and vice versa). Or the more one person engages in childcare, the less the other one has to. The common example is that of the pursuer-distancer relationship (see Figure 4.7). Here, we can view the complementarity of the relationship as each person creating the other. Becky has to do more of the childcare because Joseph does not. Conversely, Joseph is able to not do as much childcare because Becky does so. Each is creating who the other is.

Symmetrical and complementary relationships are neither good nor bad. To make a determination of such, we would need to see in what context it occurs. But please note that, even when we understand the context that the relational pattern is housed in, the categorizing of the pattern as either good or bad is quite subjective. This is because, in looking at patterns, therapists from the interactional perspective tend to take a non-normative stance.

There are times when these relationship patterns are "good":

Competitive symmetrical: The more Joseph shows care and concern for Becky, the more care and concern she shows him.
Submissive symmetrical: The less Becky tries to push Joseph's buttons, the less he tries to push hers.
Complementary: The more Joseph deals with Ethel, whom Becky has issues with, the less Becky has to.

There are also times these relationship patterns are "bad":

Competitive symmetrical: The more Joseph shows resentment for Becky, the more resentment she shows him.
Submissive symmetrical: The less Joseph does around the house, the less Becky does around the house (where nothing will get done).
Complementary: The more Becky cleans the house, the less Joseph cleans the house (which will eventually lead to resentment on at least one person's side).

Applying Your Knowledge

You are involved in many different relationships, each patterned in many different ways. Think of three people and list a context in which, with that person, you have primarily a competitive symmetrical pattern, a submissive symmetrical pattern, and a complementary pattern. Describe each of the three patterns.

Relationship 1

Competitive symmetrical pattern:
Submissive symmetrical pattern:
Complementary pattern:

> **Relationship 2**
>
> Competitive symmetrical pattern:
> Submissive symmetrical pattern:
> Complementary pattern:
>
> **Relationship 3**
>
> Competitive symmetrical pattern:
> Submissive symmetrical pattern:
> Complementary pattern:

However, if we just left it like this, we would be presenting a very limited picture. People engage with one another in a variety of patterned relationships, depending on the situation. For instance, in childcare, spouses may engage in a complementary relationship where one person is the primary caregiver. Here, the more Becky oversees the children, the less Joseph does. For that same couple, Joseph may be the primary financial person in the house. That is, the more that Joseph deals with the finances and pays the bills, the less Becky does. This couple would also engage in various symmetrical relationships. When arguing about what to do for vacations, they each might try to take control. The more Joseph tries to organize the vacation, the more Becky does so (competitive symmetrical relationship). Or, when dealing with deciding on home décor, they each might try to default to the other person (submissive symmetrical relationship).

Patterns are just the outcome of two people having an established way of being with one another. They are not set in stone, although they have become the primary and consistent way people interact. This allows therapists to be able to determine what the pattern is and then to change it. Since we know that systems are predicated on interconnected parts, and that one change in the system leads to system-wide change, we only need one person to change his or her part in that pattern and the pattern will most likely change.

Map/Territory

Alfred Korzybski's most famous dictum is "a map is not the territory" (Korzybski, 1933, p. 58). Let us take a minute to figure out what he means by this and what impact this has for us in better understanding systems theory. What we have presented, and will continue to present, in this book is a description of systems theory and how you can use that to understand the clients that you will work with throughout your career. Systems theory, or any other understanding of human functioning, can be viewed as a map. It presents an overview of what is there. However, it is not what is there (the territory). It is a level of abstraction higher than what actually is.

Every psychotherapy model is a map. The territory is the client's life (as well as the interaction between therapist and client), yet each model uses different rules about the various differences in the territory that will be distinguished and will become part of that map. For instance, strictly cognitive models make distinctions about what people think about. Strictly behavioral models do not make distinctions of what people think, but instead, what people do. Thus, unlike other therapists, behavioral psychotherapists' maps contain reinforcement contingencies. Structural family therapists' maps include areas about coalitions, alliances, and hierarchy. Systems theorists' maps, at least the ones that tend to function from a general systems perspective, include areas that focus on patterns, homeostasis, and interpersonal rules (amongst other things).

Ecology

We continue our exploration of systems theory with a focus on ecology. Usually, when people think of ecology, they think of nature. The word ecology can be broken down, where "eco-" refers to the environment and "-ology" denotes the study of. **Ecology** is the study of organisms and their interaction with the environment.

For our purposes, we can view ecology in two ways (see Figure 4.8). The first is that it refers to the connection of people with their environment. Here, we can view the Horowitz family through an ecological perspective. They are a group of dynamically interacting parts (i.e., each family member) that function together. If we expand our view a bit and look at the ecosystem in which the Horowitz family is housed, we see that they interact with many larger systems, such as schools, legal, political, religious, etc.

The family ecology is housed in the connections between individuals in the family as well as the family and the multitude of larger systems, such as school, religion, medical, and culture. Given that the Horowitz family is a lower middle class family, they are intertwined with the economic system, including Joseph's overseeing of the fabric company. The school system plays a significant role in the family's ecology as all three children are currently attending public school. Within that system, Becky has to attend various Individual Education Plans (IEPs) for Damon, given his diagnosis of attention deficit disorder. The extended family impacts the ecology as Becky's mother is having serious health issues that are psychologically and emotionally wearing for Becky. Joseph's mother's intrusiveness also impacts the family's dynamics. We could also explore where in the country the family is living, how urban living impacts them, their Jewish religious beliefs, how their culture informs family functioning, as well as many other larger systems.

The second way that we can view ecology is that it is the interaction of ideas. Bateson (1991) explained, "At the root, it [ecology] is the notion that ideas are interdependent, interacting, that ideas live and die" (p. 265). Here, we can look at some of the main themes from which the Horowitz family comes to know itself. Those themes/ideas shape the rules for their interactions, which become the means for the family to distinguish itself as the Horowitz family. These might be that they are a close family, a good family, a Jewish family, or a family where education is important.

In defining ecology as the interaction of ideas, we can continue to use a zoom lens or wide-angle lens to explore this topic. For a very zoomed in position, the ideas occur within an individual. Here, the varied ideas of the person have come together in a coherent story. Those ideas that do not fit the

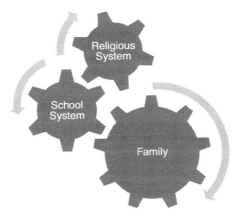

Figure 4.8 The Interaction of a Family Within the Larger Ecology.

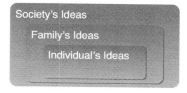

Figure 4.9 Ideas Occur on Multiple Levels and Are Interdependent.

story die and leave our awareness. Ideas that connect with other ideas are woven into our tapestry of understanding.

If we zoom out a bit, we can look at the ecology of the family. This provides us a view that the ideas of individual members are interconnected. In Chapter 3, we discussed the concept of family myths. These myths are based on the family ecology, where individual members have ideas of who they are and how they come together with one another. For instance, there was a period of time in which Joseph left the house and was incommunicado. When he returned, the family decided to ignore this and instead attempted to function as if nothing had happened. The family ecology was about cohesion rather than confrontation.

Taking a wide lens, we see how groups of people's ideas coalesce together to form dominant discourses (see Figure 4.9). **Dominant discourses** are ways of understanding that have been agreed upon, at least tacitly, by a majority of the population of a group. These ideas become "truth" but are not "Truth" (we will talk more about the notion of "truth" in Chapters 8–11). Given that a specific dominant discourse is not a given, they change over time. For instance, the dominant discourse of homosexuality in the United States has changed. The original *Diagnostic and Statistical Manual* listed homosexuality as a mental disorder. It was not until 1973 that it was removed, upon cultural changes in the US coinciding with the social protest movements (i.e., civil rights, women, and gay rights movements). During the mid-20th century, not only was homosexuality viewed as a mental disorder, it was also viewed as a sin by many religious organizations. The perception was that homosexuals were deviants and perverts. Given this, many people who felt attraction to a same-sex person internalized the dominant discourse and felt bad about themselves, thinking that there was something seriously wrong with them. Currently, the dominant discourse on homosexuality has changed (although not for everyone). Homosexuality is now viewed not as a choice but a natural state of who someone is. The media's presentation of homosexuality has also changed, from not presenting a gay character to having shows and movies with one or several gay characters. The dominant discourse is still changing as same-sex marriage has become legalized, yet in various subgroups of the United States (what we can call subcultures or subsystems), there are dominant discourses that differ.

The Horowitz nuclear family has five members, each with their own ideas. Thus, there are five individual ecologies at play. However, through interactions, each member's ideas are influenced by and influence the other family members. Here, the family ecology takes hold, developing various family myths and stories. Yet, the Horowitz family does not live in isolation. They are housed within a culture that has dominant discourses. These ways of understanding what it means to be a man, woman, child, married, family, Jewish, white, etc. impact how they view themselves.

Whole/Part

When trying to understand the ecology of a family, we know that we are always viewing only a partial representation of the family. There are just too many components to conceive of them all at once. However, putting effort into understanding multiple parts and how they come together provides a useful picture, which puts into perspective how actions from one or more of those parts fit into the whole.

Figure 4.10 The Relationship Between Parts That Make Up a Whole.

Systems function as **wholes** (see Figure 4.10). This concept boils down to the interrelationship between the parts, where there is mutuality. As Watzlawick et al. (1967) explained, "Every part of a system is so related to its fellow parts that a change in one part will cause a change in all of them and in the total system" (p. 123). This is why couples or family therapy can be done with only one person present. Given that people are connected through interpersonal patterns, if one person changes his or her actions in that pattern, there is a high likelihood that the dynamics of the relationship will change.

This notion of wholeness is countered by the concept of nonsummativity (Watzlawick et al., 1967). **Nonsummativity** is the idea that the whole is greater than the sum of its parts. If we just add together the pieces of the system, we will not get the whole system as we would be missing the most important ingredient—the manner in which these parts are connected—their relationships.

The most famous equation in systems theory is actually quite basic: $1 + 1 = 3$. At first, this may seem confusing, since most 5 year-olds know that $1 + 1 = 2$. The 5 year-olds are using the principle of **summativity**, where each number is a distinct unit that does not change the other number, but gets lumped together with it. For instance, if you have one apple and add another apple, then you have two apples. The apples, upon being together, do not change the other.

However, the same cannot be said for human beings. How we are depends on who we are with in what context. Thus, the + in our equation of $1 + 1 = 3$ refers to the dynamic relationship that occurs between the two people. Perhaps we can help you understand this concept with a thought experiment. Think of a past romantic relationship (or a very good friend), where the relationship ended. If we were to ask you why the relationship ended, you might have one (or more) of the following responses: the person was too needy or too controlling, cheated, or were lazy and unmotivated. If we believed you, then our equation would revert back to $1 + 1 = 2$, since that individual, and you, are being viewed as isolated. But since that is not the case, we need to continue our thought experiment. After your relationship with the person ended, did the other person enter into a relationship with someone else? The answer is, most likely yes. You may have thought to yourself at the time of the demise of the relationship, "Who would be more stupid than me to have a relationship with this person since s/he is so awful?" Well, someone else did. And for many, it turned into a good relationship. So what was the difference between their relationship with the ex-partner and your relationship with the ex?

The relationship did not end because the other person was too needy. It ended because there was a relationship between someone who was needy with someone who didn't want to be needed (or at least to such a degree). It ended because one partner was controlling and the other didn't want to be controlled. It ended because one person cheated, and the other person didn't want to be cheated on. It ended because one person was unmotivated while the other person wanted a motivated partner. We understand that we are severely simplifying the reasons that a relationship might have ended, but are willingly doing so to help explain this concept.

Systems theory focuses on relationships, and the equation of $1 + 1 = 3$ reminds us to pay special attention to those relationships. While each person is a unique human being, there is also a unique way in which those two people come together. That way is different than how two other people come together. We can help elucidate this by plugging the Horowitz family into our equation. We know that there are five people in this nuclear family. However, there is a lot more going on here. If we just take the parents,

Joseph and Becky, we have one relationship: Joseph + Becky = 3. Joseph is one 1, Becky is another 1, and their unique way of interaction (their relationship) is the third 1. Taken together, we conceive of that as 3.

When Mara was born, the system became more complex. It then became 1 + 1 + 1 = 7. How did we come up with this number? Here, we are looking at individuals, two-person relationships, and three-person relationships. We can view it like this:

1-Joseph
1-Becky
1-Mara
1-Joseph/Becky
1-Joseph/Mara
1-Becky/Mara
1-Joseph/Becky/Mara

When Blake was born our equation changed to 1 + 1 + 1 + 1 = 15. Let's break this down.

- *Individual people*: Joseph, Becky, Mara, Blake
  - Total Number = 4

- *Two-person relationships*: Joseph/Becky, Joseph/Mara, Joseph/Blake, Becky/Mara, Becky/Blake, Mara/Blake
  - Total Number = 6

- *Three-person relationships*: Joseph/Becky/Mara, Joseph/Becky/Blake, Joseph/Mara/Blake, Becky/Mara/Blake
  - Total Number = 4

- *Four-person relationships*: Joseph/Becky/Mara/Blake
  - Total Number = 1

Then Damon was born and our equation changed to 1 + 1 + 1 + 1 + 1 = 30.

- *Individual people*: Joseph, Becky, Mara, Blake, Damon
  - Total Number = 5

- *Two-person relationships*: Joseph/Becky, Joseph/Mara, Joseph/Blake, Joseph/Damon, Becky/Mara, Becky/Blake, Becky/Damon, Mara/Blake, Mara/Damon, Blake/Damon
  - Total Number = 10

- *Three-person relationships*: Joseph/Becky/Mara, Joseph/Becky/Blake, Joseph/Mara/Blake, Joseph/Becky/Damon, Joseph/Mara/Damon, Joseph/Blake/Damon, Becky/Mara/Blake, Becky/Mara/Damon, Becky/Blake/Damon, Mara/Damon/Blake
  - Total Number = 10

- *Four-person relationships*: Joseph/Becky/Mara/Blake, Joseph/Becky/Mara/Damon, Joseph/Mara/Blake/Damon, Becky/Mara/Blake/Damon
  - Total Number = 4

- *Five-person relationships*: Joseph/Becky/Mara/Blake/Damon
  - Total Number = 1

While it may seem that we are just doing an academic numerical exercise, we are laying the groundwork for understanding individuals and families in a more complex fashion. Families are composed of multiple subsystems, and these subsystems function in unique ways. If we just take the spousal subsystem, we can see that Joseph and Becky are its members. However, if we think back to the Martinez family (see Chapters 1–3), there were also two people in the spousal subsystem, but it functioned quite differently. We might also look at a spousal subsystem where very few problems are occurring and the two individuals express much love for one another. There are still two people involved in that subsystem, but because of the + (the relationship), the 3 is very different.

Key Figure

Paul Watzlawick

Paul Watzlawick was born on July 25, 1921, in Villach, Austria. He earned a Doctor of Philosophy degree in 1949 from the University of Venice and then, in 1954, earned a diploma in analytical psychology from the C. G. Jung Institute in Zurich.

In 1960, Watzlawick was invited to the Mental Research Institute (MRI) by Don D. Jackson. At the MRI, Watzlawick worked with members of the Bateson project on communication. This collaboration culminated in the influential book, *Pragmatics of Human Communication* (Watzlawick et al., 1967). These ideas led to a focus on communication that came to be known as the interactional view.

Watzlawick was a founder of and one of the key figures in the ideas coming out of the Brief Therapy Center of the MRI, which developed one of the first brief therapy models of psychotherapy. The book *Change: Principles of Problem Formation and Problem Resolution* was groundbreaking for its time (Watzlawick et al., 1974), highlighting a brief strategic means of helping people to change. The interactional view became the basis of several other models of psychotherapy—most particularly solution-focused brief therapy and Milan systemic family therapy. Watzlawick consulted with the Milan team, helping them shift from a psychodynamic to a strategic/systemic epistemology. Their approach came to be known as Milan systemic family therapy.

Through his interest in Buddhist philosophy, especially Zen philosophy, Watzlawick was able to bridge the philosophies from Asia with a pragmatic scientific rigor. He could speak five languages and, out of all the members of the interactional view of human behavior, was the most influential teacher as he traveled frequently and could explain the ideas in multiple countries to a wide range of audiences.

Watzlawick's voice added to the ideas of radical constructivism. These ideas were presented in many of his books, most notably *The Invented Reality* (Watzlawick, 1984) and *How Real Is Real?* (Watzlawick, 1976). In this area, he stated, "And the most dangerous delusion of all is that there is only one reality" (Watzlawick, 1976, p. xi). Watzlawick also explored the notions of communication and self-fulfilling prophecies. In total, Watzlawick wrote 22 books.

Paul Watzlawick died at home on March 31, 2007, at the age of 85.

OPEN AND CLOSED SYSTEMS

While we have discussed the Horowitz family as a system, we understand that that system is housed within a larger ecology. We might think to ourselves what separates the Horowitz family from the larger world—how do we make a distinction between them and others? In the previous section, we described how the parts of a system interact such that the whole is greater than the sum of its parts. A system is also a part of a larger system. Thus, a family is a part of larger systems, such as extended family, friend networks, neighborhoods, etc.

When we explore the notion of how open or closed a system is, we are looking at how much information is able to be moved in and out of the system. In **open systems**, information can easily move into and out of the system. In **closed systems**, there is a limited amount of information that can move into and out of the system. Realistically, no human system is completely open or completely closed. These are two extreme ends of a continuum. However, we tend to use these two terms to describe which side of

Figure 4.11 How Open or Closed a System Is Can Be Viewed Along a Continuum.

the continuum the system tends to be. We could also use qualifiers, such as "very closed" or "somewhat open" (see Figure 4.11).

As with patterns, the notion of open or closed is neither good nor bad. There are some contexts in which being a bit more closed is more functional for the system, while other contexts being more open is more functional. Yet, when systems operate at an extreme, either too closed or too open, problems are likely to develop. Systems need to bring in new information to function and adapt. If the system is too closed, no information is coming in, and the system may disintegrate. If the system is too open, it will not be able to distinguish itself from other systems.

We can talk about open and closed systems in two fashions. The first is what occurs between a system and its environment. In the Horowitz family, this could be in its relation to school, legal, or religious systems. We can look at the relationship of extended family with the nuclear family. Ethel, Joseph's mother, tries to infuse the system with information, namely on how Joseph and Becky should raise their children. How much Joseph and Becky utilize that information helps us to see how open or closed the system is. It seems as if, at least in the realm of the extended family (in relation to Ethel), the Horowitz system is more on the closed side. If Joseph tries to ignore Ethel, and Becky becomes angry at Ethel's "meddling," they are not taking in and adapting to that new information. If Mara came home to explain that all of the girls her age are dating and Joseph and Becky then change their rule that she cannot date and allow her to, we can surmise that in that regard the system is more on the open side. The system showed its openness when it took in information from the school psychologist about Damon's behavior and incorporated that into how they function, such as going to IEPs and going for a psych consult for possible ADD medication for Damon.

Open and closed systems can also be viewed as to how much information is allowed to flow between members of that system. This openness/closedness helps to distinguish what the boundaries are between people/subsystems. In determining how open or closed the system is, we can look at whether there is any back-and-forth happening between people. This can be discussed in terms of adaptability and rigidity. **Adaptable systems** are able to utilize information from within to make modifications to how they operate. For instance, the Horowitz family could display some type of openness if Mara is able to negotiate with her parents to allow her to start dating since other girls her age have started to date.

If we place this back into our discussion of open and closed systems, families too adaptable would be too open, and those who are not very adaptable would be too closed. When family members are too close (very cohesive), they become too open, while those with little closeness (not cohesive) would be too closed. Very cohesive families tend to become enmeshed with other larger systems, while those with little cohesiveness potentially lead to disengagement.

We can now explore the Horowitz family in terms of cohesion and adaptability. While there is connection between Becky and the children, there is separation between Joseph and Becky and Joseph and the children. The family also tends to maintain their ways of doing things, but it does not seem they do so without any consideration of alternatives.

Boundaries

We have been talking about what separates one system from another—boundaries. **Boundaries** are a demarcation between two things. When people put a fence around their house, they are placing a boundary between their property and not their property. When two opposing sports teams put on

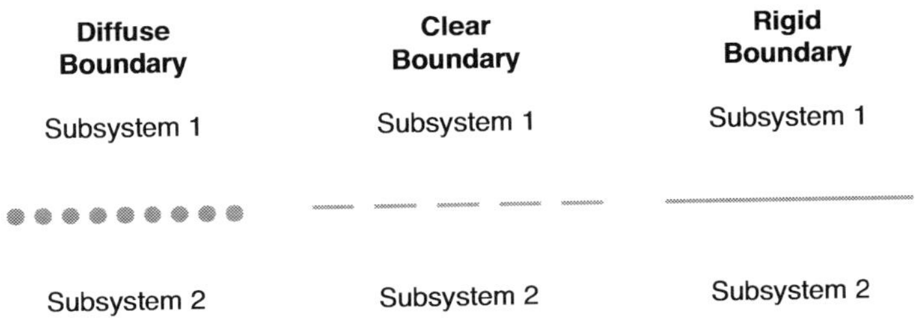

Diffuse Boundary	**Clear Boundary**	**Rigid Boundary**
Subsystem 1	Subsystem 1	Subsystem 1
●●●●●●●●	— — — —	───────────
Subsystem 2	Subsystem 2	Subsystem 2

Figure 4.12 Family Mapping Diagram of the Three Types of Boundaries.

different colored jerseys, they are making a boundary between "our" team and "your" team. However, remember back to our discussion of how there is a relationship between separateness and connectedness, by having those two different team jerseys on, the players are also saying that the two teams are connected—as two teams playing one game.

Minuchin (2012) distinguished three types of boundaries: rigid, diffuse, and clear (see Figure 4.12). Minuchin developed a way of depicting the relationships between family members that he called family mapping. The family map allows the therapist to conceptualize the current organization of the family. From this, the therapist could then map out possible moves to shift the family to a more functional organization.

Rigid boundaries are fairly impermeable. That is, there is little information that is able to pass back-and-forth between the subsystems. The more rigid the boundary, the more closed the system is. When there is a rigid boundary between people, the relationship is usually labeled as disengaged. In the Horowitz family, if Mara tried to talk with Joseph and Becky about changing the rules of her not dating so that she could begin to date like some of her peers, and Joseph and Becky did not listen and told her that they were the parents, they make the rules, and their rules were not to be questioned, we would assess it as a rigid boundary. Joseph not listening to his mother Ethel when Ethel tries to get he and Becky to change their parenting style is also another example of a boundary on the rigid side of the continuum.

Diffuse boundaries are quite permeable; they allow much information to pass back-and-forth between systems. The more diffuse the boundary, the more open the system is. When there is a diffuse boundary between people, the relationships are usually labeled as enmeshed. In the Horowitz family, we would see a diffuse boundary if, when Joseph went out to gamble, Becky was to go to Mara and tell Mara how upset she was with Joseph.

Clear boundaries are semi-permeable. Information is allowed to move back-and-forth between subsystems, but it occurs in a regulated manner. Clear boundaries would be seen if Mara came to her parents wanting to change the rule of her not dating and Joseph and Becky were open to have a discussion about this, took into consideration Mara's viewpoint, and then were open in explaining their decision. Minuchin (2012) believed that clear boundaries tended to be the most functional. However, there are times in families when rigid or diffuse boundaries can be more functional. These times tend to be temporary and specific. For instance, when a child is extremely young, having rigid boundaries is more functional as they help to provide safety for the child.

Applying Your Knowledge

Throughout your life you have experienced each of the different types of boundaries: rigid, diffuse, and clear. For this exercise, for each type of boundary, think about two people that you have experienced that sort of relationship. How could you determine which type of boundary you had with each person?

Rigid Boundary

Person 1:
Person 2:

Diffuse Boundary

Person 1:
Person 2:

Clear Boundary

Person 1:
Person 2:

DIVERSITY

We are able to observe how a family operates based on their cultural and ethnic influences (see McGoldrick, Pearce, & Giordano, 1982). Therapists can learn about how families from various cultures, ethnicities, and racial groups organize and function. It is understood that not all individuals and families from that ethnic group function in the same way, yet there are generalizable ways of operating. These understandings of families, based on ethnicities, are frameworks from which to start to get to know the clients you are working with.

McGoldrick (1982) explained, "Ethnicity describes a sense of commonality transmitted over generations by the family and reinforced by the surrounding community" (p. 4). It informs how we come to understand others and ourselves, providing one lens for people to develop an identity. One's ethnicity contributes to the ecology of the family, providing family meanings on what roles people should take, the rules members interact from, and the various rituals of daily life and special occasion that will organize the family. While it is beyond the scope of this book to explore the various ways that families are organized based on their specific ethnicity, we will take a little time to exemplify this idea through an exploration of the Horowitz family, a Jewish family. These ideas may not hold for families from other ethnicities or even with all Jewish families.

Jewish families tend to hold family as a central tenet, focus on intellectual achievements, financial prosperity, and being able to verbally express one's feelings to others (Herz & Rosen, 1982). The men in Jewish families tend to be the primary earners, thus appreciated for what they do outside of the home. However, they may be underappreciated inside the home. This is because the woman tends to be in charge of what happens inside the home. Joseph and Becky are from a lower middle class, which necessitates both husband and wife working to earn enough income for the family. However, as with many other Jewish families, home life centers around the wife. Becky is the primary person to ensure the family runs as expected, making meals, cleaning, ensuring children are doing homework, arranging for social visits, etc.

Jewish mothers have been stereotyped as being intrusive. This can be seen in Ethel's involvement with the family, where she believes she has the duty and right to comment on how her grandchildren are being parented. This leads to a therapeutic dilemma, as Jewish families tend to have a high degree of family togetherness, what might be called enmeshment. Therapists working with Jewish families may need to develop ways to allow space between members while respecting the interpersonal closeness. For the Horowitz family, the therapist might consider providing space between Becky and Mara to prevent Mara from being a parentified child.

Since Jewish families tend to place a high value on children, they tend to come to therapy because of concerns about the children (Herz & Rosen, 1982). The Horowitz family would most likely say they are coming to therapy for their concern over Damon, rather than something occurring within the marriage. Since children play such an important role in Jewish families, therapists should consider ensuring that there is a strong therapeutic alliance with the children.

Family Life Cycle

Related to diversity and ethnicity is the notion that families experience a life cycle. Families do not stay static but tend to go through standard developmental transitions. This is similar to how individuals go through standard human development transitions from birth, adolescence, young adult, adult, to old age. All people go through these transitions but may handle them quite differently. For instance, someone might experience "the terrible twos" while someone else was quite calm. Others will find adolescence to be a storm, having difficulty individuating, while for others adolescence is a time of peace.

Families also have a life cycle; however, not all families follow the same path. The typical family life cycle includes the following stages: leaving home (single young adult), marriage, families with young children, families with adolescents, launching, and families in later life (Carter & McGoldrick, 1999). With the proliferation of divorce and remarriage, many families are finding that they have additional stages, which impact the organization and functioning of the family. As can be seen in these stages, a family is never going through the life cycle without being connected to other nuclear family systems from a different generation. That is, when one family is in the launching stage, a new family life cycle is started with an individual being a single young adult. For most families, there are three generations of families that are overlapping one another (Figure 4.13).

Given that people are having children at later ages than ever before, many people find themselves in what is known as the **sandwich generation**. The sandwich generation refers to the notion that, while parents are taking care of their young children, they are also taking care of their aging parents, who may have caretaking needs in later life. This can be seen in the Horowitz family as Becky is the primary parent of three children but is also spending a lot of time taking care of her mother, who is starting to have health

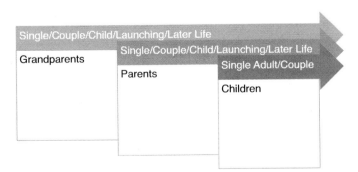

Figure 4.13 |Three Generations of a Family During a Typical Family Life Cycle. One Family Life Cycle Starts at the Launching Stage for the Previous Generation's Life Stage.

issues and is currently a widow. This puts extra strain not only on Becky, but also on her relationship with Joseph who does not seem to be accommodating to these new demands.

At times of transition in a family, the complementary patterns that may have been sufficient for the previous stage are no longer functional. Joseph and Becky have a complementary pattern around childcare where the more Becky caretakes, the less Joseph does. However, with the increased demands on Becky to caretake for her mother, Joseph is maintaining his disengagement and not accommodating to the current situation. This adds stress to a family that already has some increased stressors and challenges because they are a dual-earner family (Piotrkowski & Hughes, 1993). We can see the incorporation of Mara, at times, into the parental subsystem, which places her in a parentified position, where she has to help caretake for her siblings. This is both useful to the family but can also place role strain on members. Joseph and Becky are also having difficulty coming to marital agreement on what their roles should be in terms of parenting and home care.

As a family moves through each life stage, there are various developmental changes that are needed (Carter & McGoldrick, 1999). The single young adult must learn to take on responsibilities that she may not have had previously, such as financial and emotional processes. These include finding employment, a peer network, and beginning to look for a partner. In the couple stage, two individuals must learn how to come together to form a new system. This is sometimes difficult as they are used to the rules from their family of origin and now must negotiate processes with someone who is used to engaging in patterns of interaction that might be quite different. At this stage, each partner has to renegotiate interactions with the extended family. For some families, when a marriage (or serious committed relationship) occurs, they may feel they are losing a son or daughter. Others may experience the addition of a son or daughter-in-law. What is happening at this point is a shift in the boundaries between people and subsystems. When the couple has children, they need to readjust to accommodate the new addition(s) to their family. This requires the couple to potentially change their roles and to negotiate new rules and roles, such as caring for the child, the house, the financials, etc. Further, the couple has to make adjustments with the extended family as their parents are now grandparents and have expectations on how they will be included in the child's life. When the child becomes an adolescent, the family has to again alter their boundaries to allow for more independence for the adolescent—preparing her for the launching stage. Here, the relationship between parent and child shifts to allow the child more say—a move away from a hierarchical position. At this point, the parents are likely to be experiencing middle age and career issues. In the launching stage, parents need to accept various exits from the family as whatever children are in the home leave and begin their adult lives. The couple now does not have the child as a focal point in the home and will have to renegotiate their own relationship. It is at this stage that the couple's parents will likely be experiencing serious illness and death. In the last stage, families in later life, the couple needs to accept that roles are changing and shifting to the next generation. The couple may become grandparents and have likely retired. They will then need to find meaning in new areas as well as accept their growing frailties.

While these are the "typical" stages and "typical" developmental tasks and needs, not all families experience them in these ways. Culture can play a big role in how the family understands what the various tasks are and what family means (Hines, Preto, McGoldrick, Almeida, & Weltman, 1999). The stages/tasks presented may be different depending on whether the family is African American, Latino, Asian, Jewish, or Middle Eastern (as well as many other cultural groups). Further, within each of these cultural groups are subgroups that are based on immigration status, religion, socioeconomic status, etc.

Jewish families tend to have certain life cycle rituals that play a major role in family life (Herz & Rosen, 1982). These include having a bris (circumcision) for newborn boys, Bar or Bat Mitzvah for boys and girls when they reach 13 years old, and sitting shiva when a family member dies. The Horowitz family likely engaged in each of these rituals, which tend to bring extended family closer to one another as well as change the roles that each person has. For instance, at the bris, a couple has just become parents, at a Bar Mitzvah, the child becomes an adult (in the eyes of the religion), and during a shiva, a child may become the matriarch or patriarch of the family, depending on the role of the person who had just died.

The Horowitz family is currently in the stage of families with young children. It seems as if they have still not accommodated to this stage, as Joseph tends to function as if they are still in the couple phase, where he has more freedom of action outside of the house rather than taking care of the children. This puts more of the burden on Becky. Mara also finds herself, because of Joseph and Becky being a dual-income earner family, in the position of part-time parent. The family is also in the early stages of families with an adolescent and will soon need to renegotiate the rules around parental control of Mara. This is starting to come to the forefront with her desire to date and her parents' forbidding it until she is 16.

QUESTIONS FOR REFLECTION

1. What distinctions do you think are important when first meeting with a new client? How do these distinctions help you to understand why the client is coming to therapy?

2. What various types of patterns do you notice in your relationships? How have these patterns changed over time?

3. What importance does focusing on patterns of relationships have in doing psychotherapy? Do you agree with the notion that one change in the system leads to system-wide change? How does that view impact what you do with clients?

4. How important is it to have an understanding of various ethnicities before you meet with clients from that ethnicity?

5. How do patterns of relationship play a role in the various stages of the family life cycle?

CHAPTER FIVE
Interactional Pragmatics

Michael D. Reiter

CASE DESCRIPTION

For this chapter, we continue working with the Horowitz family that we met in Chapter 4. Let's observe a typical exchange around the dinner table.

Becky: Mara, how did things go after school with the boys?
Mara: Fine. They were arguing with each other some.
Becky: What was the argument about?
Mara: Who knows? I think Damon took something of Blake's.
Becky: Blake. What happened?
Blake: He took my GI Joe, and I didn't want him to.
Becky: And what did you do?
Blake: I took it back. He got upset.
Becky: You are older than him and can do different. Joseph, maybe you can have a talk with him.
Joseph: For what? They're boys.
Becky: They shouldn't be fighting with one another.
Joseph: That's what boys do.
Becky: But our boys don't need to do that.
Mara: They can be so annoying sometimes.
Joseph: You both are making too much out of this. Did anyone throw a punch? No. They are always going to have some type of sibling rivalry.

In this chapter, we continue to focus on how therapists utilize concepts such as distinctions, patterns, and communication to help clients to change. The concepts presented in Chapter 4 serve as a backdrop for an interactional understanding of human behavior and how those lead therapists and clients toward possible pathways of change. Many of the principles we will be discussing are based on notions of how people communicate with one another. These ideas were brought into the psychotherapy lexicon through Bateson's project on communication.

AXIOMS OF COMMUNICATION

People are interactional beings. Not only do we communicate with ourselves (i.e., self-talk), but also with others. It used to be that this communication happened when two people were in close proximity with one another so that they could first see and then hear the other person. But with the advent of technology, we're one click away from most anyone anywhere in the world. We don't even have to respond to someone when they send a text, instant message, or post to a social media site. Whether we respond or not is a form of communication. For instance, if Becky asks Joseph where he was for the last few hours, and Joseph doesn't respond, Becky may take his non-response as a communication that he was doing something she would not like and that he prefers not to have a fight. Thus, we are always connected to many people in some form of communication.

Communication occurs through all of our senses. The ability to see, hear, feel, taste, and smell are all conduits for us to be able to send and receive messages to others. Think about going on a date with someone. When you show up at his or her house, you first use your eyes to see the person. Many points of information flood into your mind. What are they wearing? How clean are their clothes? Are they dressed for a romantic night or quite casually? How expensive are their clothes? What does their hair look like? Do they have any tattoos? You then use your ears to listen to them. What is the content of what they are saying? Do they have an accent? Do they sound excited? Nice? Mean? Are they loud or quiet? Perhaps sometime during the date, you are able to touch them. This might be in the form of a hug. Do they slightly touch you or give you a firm hug? How long do they maintain contact with you? Although we tend to communicate less frequently through our senses of taste and smell, these are still channels of communication. For instance, what they smell like provides information that helps you know whether they smoke, wear perfume, and potentially their bathing habits.

We will explore some aspects of communication theory to help us understand the pragmatics of interactions between people. Communication theory in psychotherapy was primarily introduced through the work of Gregory Bateson and the therapeutic work that occurred at the Brief Therapy Center at the Mental Research Institute in Palo Alto, California. Don Jackson, who developed the MRI, began the Brief Therapy Center in 1966 along with Paul Watzlawick and others. Some of the theorists and therapists that contributed to this communicational and interactional work include Don Jackson, Jay Haley, Paul Watzlawick, John Weakland, Richard Fisch, and Virginia Satir. The main focus of their work was in examining how people engage in transactions with one another—through various modes of communication. Watzlawick et al. (1967) provided several axioms of communication. We will briefly discuss each to help you understand interpersonal transactions.

Axiom 1

People are always behaving, which leads to the first axiom: **one cannot not behave**. If you think how you could not behave, you might think that you would not move at all. However, psychologists, psychotherapists, and medical professionals would call this catatonia. Not moving is still a behavior, just one where there is not a lot of movement happening. This can be seen if you go to the mall as some clothing stores occasionally hire people to model clothing in the store windows and be living mannequins. The models are not moving, and sometimes you have to look quite closely to determine whether they are a living person or a mannequin. However, the model's lack of movement is a behavior.

When we think of behavior, we tend to think of it as being conscious and purposeful. While almost all behavior is purposeful, a lot of our behavior is not intentional. If you are sitting next to someone you know well and, without warning, turn and scream in their face, they will automatically flinch from you. They did not have time to consciously think about the situation but behaved based on unconscious processes. If they did consciously think, they would not have flinched as they would have told themselves, "Here is a situation that I am calmly sitting next to my friend who would not try to physically harm me, and thus, there is nothing to be worried about, so I don't need to move."

When Joseph comes home from work and goes into the living room, he is behaving. When Damon runs around the house and screams, he is behaving. When Becky smiles at Ethel when Ethel is telling her how to parent, she is behaving. When Joseph and Becky do not talk to each other about what happened when Joseph left the family for five days, they are behaving. Each person cannot not behave. But what they can do is to behave differently.

Many psychotherapy techniques are designed around getting people to behave but in ways that they currently are not. As explained in Chapter 4, people engage with one another in patterned ways. These patterns are based upon repetitive behaviors that people use to communicate with one another. These communicational

Figure 5.1 The Process of the First Session Formula Task Where Clients Are Asked to Pay Attention to What Is Happening in Their Lives They Want to Have Continue, Which Changes First Their Observational Behaviors and Then Their Outward Behaviors.

behaviors maintain the problem, requiring the therapist to help the client to do something different, to communicate behaviorally in ways that are different than they currently are engaging one another.

Therapists can use **skeleton keys**, or what have come to be called **formula tasks**, to help clients, regardless of most issues, to do something different (de Shazer, 1985). These formula tasks are assignments given to clients that fit a variety of problems and thus do not need to be personalized. We already covered two of them in Chapter 3, the do something different task and the structured fight task. Each of these could be used with Joseph and Becky. For instance, the do something different task sets the stage for at least one member of a problem-maintaining pattern to engage in communicational behavior that is different. Hopefully, it is different enough to be information and change. For Becky and Joseph Horowitz, they have been engaged in a pattern of Joseph doing something Becky doesn't like and Becky not confronting him and holding him accountable to his actions and whereabouts. This leads them to continue doing the same thing over and over (what we would call "more-of-the-same" behavior). Doing something different might change that pattern. This could come in the form of Becky sitting in front of Joseph and holding his hands while asking him where he was or Joseph giving Becky five dollars each time she inquires to his actions outside of the house.

Perhaps the most influential of all the formula tasks is the **first session formula task** (de Shazer & Molnar, 1984). This intervention is worded something like:

> Between now and next time we meet, I would like you to pay attention to all of the things that are happening in your family that you like and want to continue or to have more of. Next session, you can tell me about these observations.

This task shifts people's observational behaviors, where they tend to observe what is going wrong in their lives rather than what is going right (see Figure 5.1). Just paying attention to what is working, rather than what is not, will change the person's behavior. Instead of Joseph looking at and expecting Damon to be hyperactive, he might see Damon act calm and will then interact with him differently.

For families where there is parental strain, where the parents tend to undermine one another, the therapist might utilize the odd days/even days ritual (Palazzoli, Boscolo, Cecchin, & Prata, 1978). This therapeutic assignment consists of the therapist prescribing one parent to be in charge of childcare decisions on odd days (Monday, Wednesday, and Friday). The other parent then is in charge of childcare decisions on even days (Tuesday, Thursday, and Saturday). On Sunday, they are to negotiate between themselves what to do. For the Horowitz family, the therapist might use this ritual to change the patterned relationship of Becky doing almost all of the childcare and Joseph not doing much.

Axiom 2

A second axiom of communication is: **one cannot not communicate**. As we just saw, since we cannot not behave, and behavior is a form of communication, we are always communicating, whether intentional or not. The clothes you wear, how you style your hair, and whether you have tattoos or piercings are all forms of communication, even if you didn't intend to say anything by them.

As we saw with axiom 1, there is no opposite of behavior. The same holds for communication. On a more proximal level, what might not communicating look like on the surface? It would be silence. Yet silence is a very loud communication tool. When Becky is silent to Joseph after they have had an argument, Joseph should know things are not good. Becky is communicating to him that she is still angry and that he should leave her alone. Let us go back to the date we previously described that you had with someone where you used all of your senses to take in information as a form of communication. Let's say that the two of you go for a nice dinner, then afterward go to a play, walk on the beach, or other such activity. At the end of the date, the two of you are driving home. If, on the 30-minute drive back home, the person you are on the date with does not talk, is this not communicating? At the end of that silent 30 minutes, how hopeful are you that there will be a second date? Probably not that much. However, silence isn't always a message of problems. Have you ever spent 30 minutes in the car with someone you know fairly well and didn't speak (and maybe didn't have the radio on) and during that silence you felt very close with the person because you knew you did not have to say anything?

When Joseph comes home and behaves by going into the living room, turning on the television, he is sending a message to leave him alone and/or that he does not want to be, at that moment, that involved with the other family members. When Damon runs around the house and screams, it could be a message that he is upset (or it could be a scream of him having fun!). When Becky smiles at Ethel when Ethel is telling her how to parent, she is sending a message that "I will be nice to you and appease you in this moment, but I am not really listening to you."

Therapists also cannot not behave and cannot not communicate. The question then comes, in what ways does the therapist communicate with the client? One possibility is to talk the client's language. Many traditional psychotherapies operate from the premise that the therapist teaches the client a new language. For instance, cognitive therapists teach clients how to speak in the language of cognitive distortions. These include terms such as polarized thinking, catastrophizing, personalization, and overgeneralization. Brief therapists tend to attempt to learn and speak the client's language (Watzlawick, 1978). This is based on the notion of utilization—that the therapist utilizes whatever the client brings into therapy to help move things forward.

One aspect of what the client has available is the client's language. One of the primary reasons for using the client's language is that it prevents the therapist from entering into an oppositional position to the client (Fisch, Weakland, & Segal, 1982). The more therapists use the client's language, the better chance there is that the client understands and accepts what the therapist is saying—in part, because when learning the client's language, there is a better chance that the therapist will understand what the client understands and accepts.

Besides the therapist thinking of how he can communicate with the client, if there are two or more clients present, the therapist can help them to communicate differently. This can come in many forms. For clients who tend to enter into an escalating competitive symmetrical relationship, where they become loud and aggressive with one another, the therapist can have each person talk to him rather than each other. This is a change in how they normally communicate. One important caveat to doing so is that the therapist needs to be able to maintain **therapist maneuverability** in the pattern of interaction (Fisch et al., 1982). That is, the therapist does not position himself to have only one option. Instead, he has the freedom to make therapeutic choices that he deems best at that moment in time. This can also be explained through natural systems theory (see Chapters 6 and 7) in that the therapist should be a non-reactive party in this triangle.

One technique to help couples communicate differently is called the **Couples Dialogue** (Luquet, 2007; see Figure 5.2). Given that many couples come to therapy with the complaint that they don't communicate well, getting them to communicate differently in session in a way that is more beneficial and desired can be very impactful. The Couples Dialogue helps partners to connect to one another by communicating in a way that one person can express herself in a safe environment while the other person intentionally listens and lets the partner know he understood what was being said. There are three parts to the Couples Dialogue: mirroring, validating, and empathizing. **Mirroring** is when one partner repeats back what the other one has said, without adding anything to the message. Thus, the receiver cannot respond with defensiveness. **Validating** is when the listener allows the speaker to know the she understands, but does

Figure 5.2 The Steps of the Couples Dialogue: Mirroring, Validating, and Empathizing.

not have to agree with, the speaker's point of view. **Empathizing** is when the listener acknowledges the feelings behind the speaker's statements—that she places herself into the shoes of the speaker to sense what the other person thinks, feels, and experiences.

An abbreviated Couples Dialogue with Joseph and Becky might go something like the following:

Joseph: Becky, I would like to talk. Can you get safe?
Becky: Yes.
Joseph: I was a bit frustrated today as I came home, and it seemed that even before I closed the front door I was bombarded with demands. I didn't have a minute to breathe.
Becky: (mirroring) If I got that right, you were frustrated when you came home because it seemed there were demands on you even before you fully got into the house. Did I get that?
Joseph: Yes.
Becky: Is there more?
Joseph: Yes. I was disappointed because I was looking forward to spending some time with the family, but it seemed to just be shoved in my face.
Becky: (mirroring) You had been looking forward to spending time with the family but not when it was shoved in your face right when you walked in. Did I get that?
Joseph: Yes.
Becky: (validating) That makes sense to me since you had been thinking positively about spending time with the family and right when you got in it seemed you were confronted with expectations that you didn't want right then.
Joseph: Right.
Becky: (empathizing) And that left you feeling frustrated and even more so disappointed.

Therapists working with couples in helping them to develop the skills to engage in a Couples Dialogue usually start by having one person practice mirroring in the session with the partner. Once they have been able to mirror without rebuke or defense, the therapist helps the person to validate the other person, accepting that the other person has their own way of thinking. Lastly, the therapist assists the listener in decentering, so that she can empathize and gain an understanding of what the other person is feeling. Each partner would be taught how to listen to the other, providing a safe environment for dialogue that does not become a competitive symmetrical escalation. The Couples Dialogue is but one of many various techniques designed to help people understand that they are always communicating with others and to learn to do so in ways that are more productive.

While we usually think of communication as happening through the words we speak, we also communicate with our bodies. One technique that builds upon the notion of how body position and spatial proximity can be used to help clients communicate is through **sculpting**. Sculpting is a technique that can be used to get around the use of words, allowing people to communicate in a different way to themselves and each other (Satir, Banmen, Gerber, & Gomori, 1991). Clients are asked to place others in the family and then themselves into a physical picture of what their experience is like in the family. Given that perhaps many times they have verbally attempted to express themselves to no avail, expressing themselves physically may be enough to make a difference. There are many ways to engage in a sculpt, such as asking the family members to each take a turn sculpting everyone, or the therapist sculpting his own picture of the family's experience. Clients can then be asked what it is like to be placed by the other into this position. Therapists can also ask clients to do a solution-focused sculpt (Reiter, 2016b). This usually entails two sculpts. In the first, the client sculpts their current problematic experience. This is a way for the therapist to bring forth and acknowledge where the client is at in the moment. The second sculpt is of how the client's experience when the problem was not present or not as significant. This allows them to not only express themselves in the moment, but to take a past positive experience and bring it to life.

Axiom 3

A third axiom of communication is: **communication happens on at least two levels; the report and the command levels** (see Figure 5.3). This can also be talked about in terms of the content and relationship levels of communication or the digital and analog. The **report** of a communication refers to the content that is being conveyed. The **command** of a message refers to how the message is to be taken and thus is about the relationship.

Let's run through three scenarios to help us understand the connection between report and command. Say you are sitting on a park bench, and there are two people sitting on the adjacent bench. One person stands up and then kneels down in front of the other and takes that person's hand. With a soft affected voice he says, "I love you." What is the message he is trying to get across? Most likely it is that the other person is very meaningful to him and he has strong affection for the other (which is why if we heard him say these words, with that tone of voice, along with his behaviors, we might assume a marriage proposal was coming). Okay, now let's alter it a bit. The same two people are sitting on the bench, one person stands up, and in a frustrated voice, where he drops his hands, he says, "I love you." Should the other person be happy? Probably not. The message coming through is, "There, are you happy? I said it. Now shut up and leave me alone." Alright, we'll erase that one and view our final scenario. The same two people are sitting on the park bench, and one person softly and playfully punches the other on the arm and says, "I love you." What is he saying here? Most likely it is saying, "You are my bud. We are in the friend zone." Here, we can see, the report of the message was exactly the same in all three scenarios—"I love you." However, the command was quite different each time.

How do we determine the command of the message? Usually through the nonverbal behaviors and the context in which it is said. The person's tone of voice, facial expression, and body language, etc. help us to properly decipher the report part of the message.

Therapists, knowing that the command of a message is more important than the report of the message, can help clients to gain clarity in their own and the other family members' communications. A therapist working with the Horowitz family may do this through something like the following:

Therapist: Becky, what is it you are hoping Joseph to know?
Becky: That he needs to do more around the house.
Therapist: Joseph, what did you hear Becky say?
Joseph: That I should do more at home.
Therapist: Yes, she said that. But she also said more. What was she telling you about her relationship to you?
Joseph: That she is frustrated with me.
Therapist: Perhaps. But she is also saying that you are important to her and the family. Were you able to hear that?

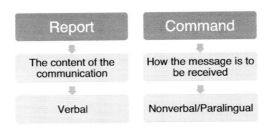

Figure 5.3 The Differences Between the Report and the Command of a Message.

Here, the therapist is able to explore both the report and command of the communication. Since most people, in verbal communication, tend to get stuck in the particulars of the report, the content of the message, they lose sight of the more important aspect, the command. The command of the message can be correlated to the process. It makes communication interactional. The more therapists can help clients to operate based on the command of the communications, relationships can be focused upon and movement in therapy can be made.

> ## Applying Your Knowledge
>
> As you just read, every communication has both a report and command message. For the following client statements, distinguish between the two levels of communication.
>
> *Client 1:* Joseph says to Mara, "Don't even think about dating until you are 16."
> Report:
> Command:
>
> *Client 2:* Becky says to Joseph, "Are you going to sit there and watch television all night?"
> Report:
> Command:
>
> *Client 3:* Blake says to Damon, "Why do you keep annoying me? Leave me alone."
> Report:
> Command:

VERBAL AND PARALINGUAL COMMUNICATION

The words that we use to express our messages come across in two forms: either we speak them or we write them. Either means of expression are referred to as **verbal communication**. The actual words used compose the report of the message. Communicational theorists sometimes call these analogic. Yet, as we've seen, every form of communication has multiple levels (see Figure 5.4).

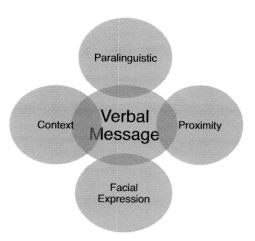

Figure 5.4 The Relationship Between Verbal Messages and Nonverbal and Contextual Clues That Provide Clues to Its Meaning.

The question comes, how does a person understand what the message means? Of course, one aspect of deciphering a message is the words used. However, it is much more complicated than that. The **nonverbal** or **paralingual** aspect of a communication helps us to understand the command of the message, what it says about the relationship. Communicational theorists refer to this as digital.

We get across the command of the message in many ways including our proximity to the other person, our volume, the intonation, and our body language. If I say to my best friend, "You're such a jerk" but say it with a smile and an upbeat voice, it is a very different message than if I say, "You're such a jerk," to a person I dislike, saying it with a scowl.

When Becky says to Blake, "It is getting very late," there are at least two messages. The first seems like it is just a message of information that is letting Blake know that the day is getting later. However, most parents do not say things like this just for the fun of it. There is a more important message, which is that Becky is saying that she wants Blake to begin to get ready to go to bed. Further, Becky is saying that she is higher in the hierarchy and that Blake should listen to her and follow her directives.

Therapists might have people be congruent in their communications so that their words match their tone. An example from a session with the Horowitz might be:

Therapist: Becky, tell Joseph what you want.
Becky: (said softly and not looking at Joseph) I want you to be more available at home.
Therapist: Becky, that didn't sound like you meant it. Turn and face Joseph and look him in the eyes. Now, say the same exact thing, but say it so he knows that you mean it.

Applying Your Knowledge

What are all of the different ways that we can say the same thing to a client? Let's take a general statement such as, "That seems to be very important for you." What are five different ways you can relay this message to a client? How might the client receive a different message from you based on each of these five different presentations of the same statement?

Content/Process

In therapy, we see the different levels of communication play out in our focus on the differences between content and process. Content is what is said while process relays a message of what it says about the relationship. For systems theorists, the process is much more important than the content.

However, this is not discarding that content is important or useful. Sometimes, clarity from each of the members on what they are trying to get across is useful for understanding between members. Further, the content helps the therapist discern the client's way of thinking, which can then be used by the therapist in the therapist's own talk. But for the most part, therapists want to focus on client process. An exploration of content can be the bridge to process. For instance, Minuchin uses talk about the content of a problem to access the process of the family (Minuchin et al., 2014). With the Horowitz family, this use of content to get to process might occur in the following way:

Therapist: Can you tell me about a recent difficulty that you've had?
Becky: Well, the other day Blake and Damon got into a kerfuffle.
Therapist: What was the fight about?
Becky: I'm not fully sure, but I think it was something about whose toys are whose.

Therapist:	How did you find about the fight?
Becky:	Mara told me.
Therapist:	And how did she find out?
Becky:	She was looking after them while I was at work.
Therapist:	And when you came home, what happened?
Becky:	I opened the door, and Mara ran up saying that they were at it again.
Therapist:	What did you do then?
Becky:	I talked with each of the boys to see what happened.
Therapist:	So Mara is the shift foreman, and you are the supervisor?
Becky:	Yeah, I guess you can look at it like that.
Therapist:	Where does Joseph fall into that?
Becky:	When we told him at dinner, he just said it was boy stuff.
Therapist:	So Joseph is the hands-off silent partner?

From first trying to find out the content of what happened, the therapist was able to focus more on process—the interpersonal dynamics around what happened. In systems theory, process is usually more important as people will continue to keep doing how they do something, regardless of the content. For instance, Joseph and Becky, regardless of how long they will be married, will have many fights. If the therapist helps them to problem solve their current fight—let's say about what to do with Damon—they will continue to have problems since they will handle the next fight in the same way. Their content may change, but their process remains the same (see Figure 5.5). Thus, systems therapists try to change the process of interactions, which entails changing the rules of interaction, which will then change the homeostasis of the system.

People tend to come to therapy sessions ready to talk about who did what and how awful it was that they did what they did. Many times clients attempt to explain themselves and focus on a particular issue. For instance, Mara may complain that she should be allowed to wear makeup since others in her class are doing so. Joseph and Becky may then counter with an argument for why she should not wear makeup. The therapist can then try to problem solve by negotiating with the family using the logic of the arguments. This would be a focus on the family's content. However, systems therapists would also be likely to focus on the family's process. How are the members able to engage one another? Are there any alliances? Coalitions? Who sides with whom? Can the daughter stand up for herself, whatever her argument, or is she shot down?

One means of accessing a family's process is through the use of therapeutic enactments. **Enactments** occur when the therapist asks two or more family members to engage one another in session, usually around the problematic situation (Minuchin & Fishman, 1981). As these authors explained, "Enactment is the technique by which the therapist asks the family to dance in his presence" (p. 79). It is getting what happens in the family's home to happen in the therapy office, in the presence of the therapist.

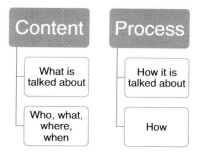

Figure 5.5 The Connection and Differences Between Content and Process.

Figure 5.6 Therapeutic Enactments Allow the Therapist to Have a Distant Position, Which Provides the Opportunity to Observe the Process Between Clients.

Enactments are quite easy to start; the therapist asks one member to converse with another member. However, they are a lot more difficult to do effectively than upon first view (Nichols & Fellenberg, 2000). Some possible statements to begin an enactment include:

- Joseph, turn to your wife and have a discussion about raising your son.
- Becky, talk with your daughter about her school performance.
- Blake, have a conversation with your brother about what you each want.

Once the clients begin to have a conversation, the therapist listens to what they say, but more importantly to how they say it. Does one person talk and the other stay silent? When two people are talking, do they try to bring in a third? Or does a third try to intrude on their conversation?

During the enactment, the therapist is able to take a distant position, sitting back and observing, a luxury that is not always available when the therapist is in the center of the action (Minuchin & Fishman, 1981). When the therapist is engaged in the therapeutic discussion, his lens of what is happening tends to become more zoomed in, and he loses, to some degree, the ability to see process (between family members and between family members and therapist). By having family members talk to one another, the therapist's lens is able to widen, providing the space to really concentrate on the rules of the interactions (see Figure 5.6).

METACOMMUNICATION

We have been explaining how, when people communicate to one another, there are multiple levels of communication. We can now talk about how people talk about their talk. Bateson (1987) defined metacommunication as "communication about communication" (p. 209). This type of communication is at a higher level of abstraction than the content of the initial communication.

Metacommunication includes a focus on codification and relationship that happens in the exchange between people. Weakland, Watzlawick, and Riskin (1995) explained, "There are messages about messages which qualify their meaning" (p. 3). For instance, Joseph and Becky might tell each other, "I am okay," which is not clear until the other codifies the message—meaning that they understand the message in terms of the context. This includes, as we have explored, the nonverbal of how the message is said as well as the situation in which the message is sent.

Therapists can work with clients to explore what they are saying about how they say things to each other. This can come in the form of pointing out their metacommunication to one another or having them have a discussion about what they mean when they converse with one another. For instance, the therapist might say, "Joseph, what are you and Becky really telling each other when you do not discuss the feelings you have with one another?"

Axiom 4

The fourth axiom of communication was discussed in Chapter 4: **members punctuate communication**. That is, they determine the start and stop points of an interchange. Therapists can explore the punctuation each person gives to a transaction. This expansion of their original viewpoint will lead to a focus on interaction. Working with the Horowitz family, this might happen as follows:

Therapist: You mentioned that this past week Blake and Damon had a bit of a situation. Boys, what happened?
Blake: Damon was acting crazy, like usual. He came into my room and took my baseball cards without asking.
Damon: No I didn't. I was just sitting there.
Therapist: Okay. Blake, you saw it that Damon was acting up a bit and went into your room and took some cards without asking.
Blake: Yeah.
Therapist: Damon, you saw it differently. How do you see it?
Damon: He kept on looking at me when he knows I don't like that.
Therapist: That's very interesting. For you, Damon, Blake looking at you in that way was the start and for you Blake, Damon acting up and taking something without asking was the start of the situation. How do the two of you get into these sorts of dances?

The therapist has remained neutral in exploring how each person punctuates the situation. By doing so, the conceptualization of the situation has expanded for each person, and they are better able to see that it is not just the other person doing something but that the two people are connected together. This may lead to possibly viewing the situation differently and/or behaving differently the next time this type of pattern happens in the future.

Axiom 5

The fifth axiom of communication was also presented in Chapter 4: **relationships are based on symmetrical or complementary exchanges**. Given that all psychotherapy models are based upon pattern interruption, viewing communication in terms of patterns of symmetrical or complementary exchanges provides the therapist a view of which pattern to interrupt and how.

For the Horowitz family, there is a complementary pattern between Becky and Joseph around childcare. The more that Becky oversees the children, the less Joseph does. Conversely, the less Joseph oversees the children, the more Becky does. The therapist then has several options available. He might attempt to get Becky to reduce her energy in childcare and increase Joseph's investment in that area. Or he might focus solely on Joseph to have him do more around the house. One way to do this is through unbalancing (Minuchin & Fishman, 1981).

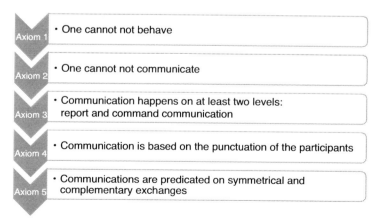

Figure 5.7 The Five Axioms of Communication.

Unbalancing is when the therapist attempts to change the hierarchical arrangement in the family, usually by joining one or more members at the expense of others (Minuchin & Fishman, 1981). Let's look at how this might happen with the Horowitz family:

Therapist: Joseph, I feel for your wife. She is a very overworked lady. What can you do to help her?
Joseph: She just needs to not get that stressed about things. If she just tells them what she expects, that will be sufficient.
Therapist: Becky, when did Joseph become your manager? He didn't talk about change. He is saying that you still need to be the one doing all of the work.
Becky: Did he know he did that?
Therapist: I don't know. But what he did is say, "Keep doing it, but do it like I tell you."
Becky: That's not good. Can you tell him to do it differently?
Therapist: No. You tell him. Tell him that you are overworked and need for him to do more around the house so that you can do less.

In this exchange, the therapist joined with the wife to attempt to change the complementary relationship around childcare so that the wife is doing less and the husband is doing more. Further, the therapist ends with the beginning of an enactment, getting them to interact, to help them to change their interpersonal process (Minuchin, 2012).

Key Figure

John Weakland

John Weakland was born on January 8, 1919, in Charleston, West Virginia. His father was a businessman of Irish ancestry while his mother came from German descent. His older brother graduated from Cornell with a degree in engineering, as did a cousin. This path, of being good at mathematics and physics and thus becoming an engineer, originally made sense to Weakland.

Weakland graduated from Cornell University with a degree in chemical engineering. While working for the DuPont Company, Weakland found the urge to pursue graduate study in the social sciences. He looked into the New School for Social Research at Columbia University and saw some anthropology courses being taught by Gregory Bateson that seemed interesting to him. Before registering, he called Bateson up to talk about the classes; this was the start of a long-lasting and productive collaboration between the two. Bateson encouraged Weakland to pursue anthropology at Columbia University. During his doctoral study, Weakland was able to work on the Cultures at a Distance Project with Margaret Mead (Bateson's first wife) and Ruth Benedict. It was during this time that Bateson offered Weakland a position on his research team in Palo Alto, California.

Weakland joined the Bateson Research Project, focusing on paradoxes of abstraction in human communication. After some time, the team began interviewing hospitalized schizophrenics. This led to one of the most influential articles in the history of family therapy, "Towards a Theory of Schizophrenia" (Bateson, Jackson, Haley, & Weakland, 1956). Most of the members of this research group were involved in the development of the Mental Research Institute (MRI). Weakland also helped to create and was co-director of the Brief Therapy Center at the MRI. He was one of the originators of the use of one-way mirrors in therapeutic settings.

Based on his experiences of studying contemporary cultures, such as Chinese and Navaho, Weakland helped pioneer the use of films and audio in studying families and was one of the first brief therapists. Weakland was involved in many influential texts that espoused the brief therapy model, what came to be known as the interactional view or MRI brief therapy. These works included *Change* (Watzlawick et al., 1974) and *The Tactics of Change* (Fisch et al., 1982).

John Weakland died on July 18, 1995.

First Order Change

When clients come to therapy, they have most likely engaged in countless attempts to change the problem. We assume this since people don't usually go to therapy, let alone make attempts to change something, upon the first presentation of what it is that is concerning them. Once the difficulty they're having becomes of concern, people may do something to try to change it. When that first attempt doesn't lead to resolution, they either try more of it or perhaps change the attempt. However, all of these initial attempts tend to have something in common: they are a change in behavior but not in the structure of the relationship.

We refer to these types of change attempts as first order change. Watzlawick et al. (1974) explained that **first order change** is change that happens within a system that does not change the system. Thus, the rules of the system remain unchanged. However, behavior within the existing rule structure does occur. Most of the change attempts that people make fall within the category of first order change. Sometimes these attempts work, but for people coming to therapy, most likely not.

Joseph and Becky are dealing with several issues, but if we just focus on them trying to deal with Damon's behavior (hyperactivity), we might look at a few of their attempts to get him to calm down. These might have included talking to Damon and asking him to calm down, putting him in time out, taking away toys, or putting him on hyperactivity medication. Each of these attempts is different, but they all fall within the category of first order change because they adhere to the rules of the organization of the family. These rules include Joseph and Becky being the parents and thus responsible in what happens in the house along with having the authority to tell Damon what to do. Given that most clients have attempted many first order change attempts, as well as received advice from friends and family that falls within first order change strategies, therapists can do something different by focusing on second order change.

Second Order Change

While some first order change attempts lead to resolution of the complaint, they are unsuccessful for many of the difficulties that bring people and families to therapy. In these situations, therapists should consider focusing on second order change attempts. **Second order change** occurs when there is a change in the system (Watzlawick et al., 1974). Here, the rules of the system change. Thus, second order change happens at a higher level than first order.

To help understand the difference between first order and second order change, we can explore the 9-dot problem (Watzlawick et al., 1974). This has been frequently used to help visualize the difference between first and second order. Using the nine dots presented in Figure 5.8, connect all nine dots using only four straight lines. Once you put the pen down on the paper, you cannot lift it up again. The solution to the 9-dot problem is presented at the end of the chapter. Please do not read on until you have attempted to solve this puzzle. Once you have either solved the problem or attempted to, please go to the end of the chapter to see the solution.

Figure 5.8 The 9-Dot Problem.

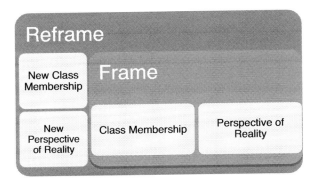

Figure 5.9 The Relationship Between Frame and Reframe.

As you can see from the solution to the 9-dot problem, a change of the rules is needed. Upon first presentation, most people cannot solve the problem since they are using the rules given (i.e., four straight lines, not picking pen up from paper). However, they usually add one extra rule—the lines all have to happen within the confines of what looks like a box. With this rule (which was not given but implied), the problem is unsolvable. However, changing the rule so that the lines can go outside the box, the problem is easily solved. Thus, a change in the rules has led to change.

One of the most frequently used second order change techniques is reframing. Watzlawick et al. (1974) explained, "In its most abstract terms, reframing means changing the emphasis from one class membership of an object to another, equally valid class membership, or, especially, introducing such a new class membership into the conceptualization of all concerned" (p. 98). Thus, a **reframe** is a shifting of the client's perception of reality from one viewpoint to another. Once the person makes that shift, it is very difficult to shift back to the original perception. However, in order to make the shift, the client has to buy into the therapist's alternative viewpoint (see Figure 5.9).

Panichelli (2013) held that reframes are one of the most common techniques in family therapy. One reason for this is that anything can be reframed. When a person believes that her sibling hates her because the sibling is taunting her and picking fights, the therapist can reframe the situation that the sibling is doing all of these behaviors because he is trying to maintain closeness; otherwise, the sibling would just leave her alone.

Based on our case study, a therapist could reframe Damon's ADD as him having a lot of energy. The situation of Joseph leaving the house for a week, if Becky viewed it as him having doubts of being part of the family, could be reframed as Joseph recharging his batteries so that he can be more engaged with the family when he returned. Ethel's "interference" in the family could be reframed as her worry about getting older and no longer being useful to others. Each of these attempts changes the rules of interaction between people by getting people to understand differently what their roles are with one another.

> ## Applying Your Knowledge
>
> Reframes are one of the most utilized and useful tools in the psychotherapist's toolkit. For this exercise, provide at least one reframe for the client's frame of the problem.
>
> *Client 1*: My wife is always on my case and nagging me. She is just an overbearing person.
> Reframe:
>
> *Client 2*: I am so anxious. If I don't do well on this test this could be the end of my academic career. I would be ruined if that happened.
> Reframe:
>
> *Client 3*: Our teen daughter has gotten such an attitude with us recently. It is like she is telling us she doesn't want to be part of this family.
> Reframe:

The Milan team used the reframe in a unique way, where they developed a **positive connotation**, which explained the symptomatic behavior and the behaviors of the other family members around the problem in a way of helping the family (Palazzoli et al., 1978). That is, the therapist takes the client's frame of reference around the problem and provides an alternative frame of reference, wherein the problem behavior is presented as coming from a positive intention.

The therapist working with the Horowitz family, having heard Becky complain that Joseph left the house for one week, can provide a positive connotation that Joseph's leaving was a way of complimenting Becky's parenting skills, as he felt comfortable leaving the children in her care for a week without his support and that he wouldn't do this unless he believed that Becky was capable. Or Damon's behavior can be positively connoted, "It is very good that Damon is being such a whirlwind as he gives husband and wife something to focus on other than their marriage."

A related technique that utilizes second order change as its basis is what is known as **benevolent sabotage** (Watzlawick et al., 1974). This technique is typically used in families where there is discord between parents and child, usually a teenager, where the parents have tried to get the adolescent to obey and the adolescent does not. In these families, the parents have most likely tried first order change techniques, such as having a talk with the child, punishing the child for the undesired behavior, or trying to reward alternative behavior, all to no avail. These attempts all fall within first order change attempts—the parents are the authority in the house, and the child is supposed to listen.

In using benevolent sabotage, the therapist instructs the parents, when the adolescent is not in the therapy room, to switch their attempts from the one-up position they have been using to a one-down position. The parents are instructed to make their request to the adolescent of what behavior they are hoping for, but also state that there is nothing they can do if the child does not follow their directives. The parents are then told to make mistakes surrounding the problem behavior and to apologize for them.

If, in the Horowitz family, Mara is coming home at night past the desired time of her parents, the therapist can ask Joseph and Becky to say to her, "Mara, we would like you to be home by 9pm. However, if you do not, there is nothing we can do about it." Then, they might change the locks on the doors or the alarm code. If Mara stays out past 9pm, she will have to knock on the door to get in. Joseph and Becky can be directed to take a long time to come to the door and apologize to Mara, saying that they were sleeping and didn't hear her.

Benevolent sabotage helps shift the dynamics of parents trying to control a child through force of will to parents showing weakness, a one-down position. This change, from first to second order, may be what is needed to change the rules of interaction that have been leading to the frustrating patterns in the family.

To say this in a different way, first order change may be useful in some situations but does not change the family's homeostasis. In many ways, first order change is related to negative feedback. Second order change is associated with positive feedback and a change to a new level of homeostasis.

Paradox

As we have discussed throughout this chapter, communication happens on multiple levels. When those levels are in agreement with each other, there is understanding, and people can more easily communicate and interact with one another. For instance, when Becky tells Blake, "You need to go clean your room now" in a forceful tone, she is clearly stating that she believes she is the higher authority and that Blake should listen and follow through with the message and thus should immediately clean his room. However, if Becky said this same thing with a softer voice while laughing, Blake may get the message, "I would like you to clean your room, but don't worry about it, you can take your time. Or maybe I will clean it."

When the levels of communication are not in sync, a **paradox** ensues. The person receiving the message now has to make a choice on how he deciphers it. Does he pay more attention to the report level or the relationship level? One of the most famous examples of a paradox is the person who says, "I am a liar." On the report level of this message is that the person is a liar, which is straightforward. However, if we go up one level and hold that the person is a liar, then the content of what he says is a lie and thus the person is not a liar. But if he is not a liar, then the content is a lie, and now we are in a recursive loop (see Figure 5.10).

Couples experience paradoxes in many ways. In the Horowitz family, Becky is frustrated that Joseph does not, on his own volition, clean the house. In her view, he always needs to be prompted to do so. If Becky tells Joseph, "I want you to do it without me telling you" and he does clean the house, Becky doesn't know if it was in response to her demand or was volitional. This is the same case when one partner wants the other to "be spontaneous." If the other person is spontaneous, it came after the command to be spontaneous and thus is not spontaneity!

This notion of paradoxical communication was explored in great detail by the Bateson research group. In 1956, they published one of the most influential, and controversial, articles in all of family therapy, "Towards a Theory of Schizophrenia." In this article, Bateson's group explored schizophrenia through a communicational analysis, specifically using the theory of logical types. In this groundbreaking article, the Bateson team proposed the concept of the **double bind**. This is a situation in which a person receives contradictory messages and will be punished either way they interpret the message.

There are several criteria needed for the occurrence of a double bind (see Figure 5.11). There need to be at least two people who engage each other repeatedly. Double binds, in the technical sense presented here, cannot happen with only one instance. During the interaction, one person gives a primary negative injunction. This is either, "If you do x, I will punish you" or "If you do not do x, I will punish you." There is then a secondary injunction that is contradictory to the primary injunction but also holds that if the person does not follow through on the injunction they will be punished. The secondary injunction is usually nonverbal. The last aspect of a double bind is that there is a tertiary injunction preventing the person from leaving the situation (or talking about their position where they are damned if they do and damned if they don't).

Figure 5.10 Recursiveness of the Report and Command Levels of Communication.

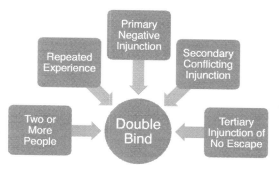

Figure 5.11 Criteria Necessary for a Double Bind.

While it may not be formal, the Horowitz family find themselves in a double bind. They say that they want things to be different, but they do not do anything different. As we learned, homeostasis is the combination of stability and change. Clients coming to therapy usually state that they want change. However, they might not always engage in behaviors to change. Joseph and Becky may say they want a calmer home life, yet they continue engaging one another and their children in the same way, thus leading to no change.

Paradoxes in Therapy

If the family is having difficulties because they find themselves in a paradox in which they want to change but find themselves holding on to stability, the way out of this dilemma is through a **counterparadox** (Palazzoli et al., 1981), otherwise known as a **therapeutic double bind**. Weakland et al. (1974) explained, "Most generally, paradoxical instruction involves prescribing behavior that appears in opposition to the goals being sought, in order actually to move toward them" (p. 8). Regardless of specifics, the goals of therapy are about change, so paradoxical techniques involve not changing (or doing more of the problematic behavior). Since a double bind occurs when a person is punished regardless of their choice of reaction—thus, a lose-lose situation—a therapeutic double bind puts the person in a win-win position. This happens when the therapist shifts the focus from change to no change. This may be done when the therapist wants the clients to go against his directives (Haley, 1987). Thus, if the therapist pushes for change, the clients will go against the therapist by not changing. However, if the therapist pushes for no change, the clients will go against the therapist by changing or not changing and showing compliance with the therapist.

Clients come to therapy seeking change; there is something in their lives that is troublesome to them that they want different. Therapists tend to try to join with this desire for change and will recommend various actions the clients can do to help them get to their goal. Perhaps this comes in the form of a homework assignment. The following week, the clients may inform the therapist that they did not do the homework. The therapist may become extremely frustrated that the clients aren't more actively working for change. However, the change may be too threatening to the family's homeostasis. Thus, the client doesn't change and clings to what they know.

We can switch the use of a few of our words a little bit to "stability" and "change" (see Figure 5.12). When clients say they want to change, the therapist then jumps on board and attempts change. However, the therapist may lose sight of the system's preference for stability. So, if therapeutic work is not leading to change, the therapist can shift his focus to stability—meaning no change. This is the counterparadox.

There are several different types of paradoxical techniques. The two most prominent are restraint and prescribing the symptom. **Restraint** occurs when the therapist encourages the client not to change. This is a therapeutic double bind, where there is a win-win situation because, if the client follows the directive, she is going along with the therapist and there is an increase in the therapeutic alliance. This is good. If the client does not hold to the restraint directive, then she changes, which is what she wants. This is also good.

Figure 5.12 The Relationship Between Stability and Change. The Two Are Intrinsically Connected to One Another Where They Work in Conjunction to Maintain Homeostasis.

We might use restraint with the Horowitz family in working with Joseph and Becky around their verbal conflicts with one another. This could come in the form of what Fisch et al. (1982) call **go slow**. The clients are directed by the therapist not to make change attempts. This is paradoxical since they come in saying they want change. We might say something to the effect of, "This has been a pattern between you two for a long time now. If you really did a serious change, it might be too much for you. So I recommend taking it very slow."

The intention behind restraint and going slow is to disrupt the current patterns that are maintaining the problem. For the interactional therapist, the problem is maintained because of the failed solution attempts surrounding the problem (Fisch et al., 1982; Watzlawick et al., 1974). This is why people from an interactional view tend to say, "The solution is the problem." Failed solution attempts usually happen in three basic ways: 1) people do not take action when needed; 2) change is attempted for something that can't change or is not a problem; and 3) change is attempted at the wrong level—first order change attempts rather than second order change.

For the Horowitz family, they continue to have problems because how they are trying to deal with them are not only not working, but making the problems worse. Joseph and Becky are trying to solve their marital problems by not addressing them. This is the first way of failed solution attempts where they are denying that a problem exists. The more they do this, the more that the distance between them grows. As regarding Damon, they are engaging in the third type of failed solution attempt; they're using first order change attempts rather than second order. Each of their attempts involves the rules of them needing to be good parents who are responsible and in charge of their child. If the therapist was to ask the family to go slow and not engage in change attempts, it would seem to be on the surface that the therapist was asking for no change. However, the go slow technique is designed to change the system, just not the area that is normally expected. Instead of attempting to change what the family says the problem is (i.e., marital difficulties or a hyperactive child), the go slow technique targets how people have tried to deal with the problem (their failed solution attempts).

Applying Your Knowledge

We've all attempted to solve a problem in ways that not only do not solve the problem but actually make it worse. Think about a few situations in which you have experienced each of the ways that people engage in failed solution attempts.

Way 1: Not taking action when action is needed (i.e., ignoring the problem):
Situation 1:
Situation 2:

Way 2: Taking action when action is not needed:
Situation 1:
Situation 2:

Way 3: Taking action at the wrong level (first order rather than second order change attempts):
Situation 1:
Situation 2:

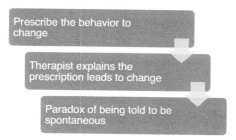

Figure 5.13 The Three Steps for Symptom Prescription.

The second main type of paradoxical technique is **prescribing the symptom**. This happens when the therapist, instead of telling the client not to change, encourages the client to engage in the problem. Watzlawick et al. (1974) stated, "Symptom prescription—or, in the wider, non-clinical sense, second order change through paradox—is undoubtedly the most powerful and most elegant form of problem resolution known to us" (p. 114). Symptom prescriptions have three aspects (Watzlawick, 1990; see Figure 5.13). First, they prescribe the behavior to be changed. This is usually the symptomatic behavior or behavior that the client believes is spontaneous and out of their control. Second, the therapist explains to the client that engaging in this prescription is a pathway toward change. Lastly, a paradox is developed since the client is asked to be spontaneous (but when the therapist has requested it).

Instead of using restraint with the Horowitz family, we might prescribe the symptom. As with most interventions, how they are framed to clients is important, wherein the purpose of the intervention should fit the client's worldview. The therapist might explain to Joseph and Becky:

> I have just met you. It is important for me to really get a sense of how your arguments and disagreements go. Perhaps this week you don't have any, and that would be good, but it wouldn't provide us with any information in order to prevent them in the future. So what I would like you both to do is to choose three times this week and for fifteen minutes engage in your typical argument. That way, next week when we meet, we will have specific data to use to help figure out how to prevent the arguments from occurring in the future.

A related yet alternative paradoxical technique to prescribing the symptom is the **pretend technique** (Madanes, 1981). Many paradoxical techniques are developed with the expectation that the client will resist the restraint and thus will change. Pretend techniques are designed for the client to cooperate. Here, the therapist explicitly states how he wants the client to pretend to have the symptom. One rationale for the pretend technique is that many people believe the problems they are having are spontaneous and out of their control. When people pretend to have the problem, they are able to have more control over the problem and thus will change. Further, what was "real" when they had the problem is now "pretend," and it is more difficult for the person to experience what they believed was real in the same way. When someone is pretending to have a problem, they cannot actually have the problem at that moment.

With the Horowitz family, the therapist might ask Damon to pretend, once the family is home, that he is out of control. He should run around the house and do and say whatever he thinks he should to pretend to be out of control. Joseph, Becky, Mara, and Blake are instructed to deal with this pretend behavior. By doing so, all members will see that they have much more control of the problem whereas before they believed it was automatic.

Haley (1984) explained that one type of paradoxical technique is ordeals. For instance, asking a couple that are having verbal fights to continue to have verbal fights is an ordeal to them. Ordeal therapy is based upon the work of Milton Erickson. **Therapeutic ordeals** occur when the therapist gets the client's commitment that, if the client has the symptom she is complaining about, she would then need to engage in a particular behavior, one that she does not want to do but that is good for her (see Figure 5.14). The

Figure 5.14 Ordeal Therapy Involves Having the Client Engage in Some Type of Non-Desired, but Useful, Behavior Whenever the Symptom Is Present.

rationale is that the person would give up having the symptom to avoid having to go through with the ordeal. As can be expected, to engage in ordeal therapy, the therapist would need to get commitment from the client to follow through. This commitment can come in the form of what is known as **the Devil's Pact** (Watzlawick et al., 1974). Clients are told that the therapist knows what will help her but will not say since he does not believe the client would follow through on it. After a few back-and-forths, the client agrees to do whatever the therapist assigns, thus making a pact with the devil. The therapist can then give the task, in this case an ordeal, with a stronger likelihood that the client will actually do the task.

The Horowitz's therapist could possibly arrange an ordeal around Damon's behavior. If he becomes out of control, the therapist could state that the parents would have to gather the family and together they would need to meticulously clean the house (or do the dishes or some other task) for a specified amount of time (perhaps two hours).

Boundary Making

In Chapter 4, we discussed how subsystems develop boundaries, which impact the rules and roles for family members. Therapists can change the subsystem boundaries to enable a more functional homeostasis. This process is called boundary making. Therapists can help individuals or subsystems to change their interactional process, which will then lead to a change of interpersonal rules and thus interpersonal boundaries. Usually, therapists attempt to help subsystems move from rigid or diffuse boundaries to clear boundaries (Minuchin, 2012). With the Horowitz family, this may come in the form of getting Joseph to tell Ethel that he will listen to her concerns, but the ultimate raising of the children is the responsibility of himself and Becky. This would be a move from a more diffuse boundary to clear boundary. The therapist might also encourage Becky to get Joseph to help her more in childrearing, making a clearer demarcation of the parental subsystem.

One of the most visual hallmarks of boundary making is the physical movement of people in a session. Salvador Minuchin was famous for asking a family member to switch seats with someone else during a session. He did this to engage in boundary making in a metaphorical manner. With the Horowitz family, if Blake was sitting in between Joseph and Becky, the therapist might say, "Blake, switch seats now with your father, as your parents need to discuss some adult business." This action makes a boundary around Joseph and Becky, demarcating them as the adults, separate from the children.

Questions for Reflection

1. How can therapists help clients to communicate differently?
2. What behaviors are useful to change to change how people communicate with one another?
3. What is the importance in focusing on first order versus second order change?
4. How are therapeutic reframes useful in therapy?
5. What are the ethical implications of using therapeutic paradox in therapy?

INTERACTIONAL PRAGMATICS

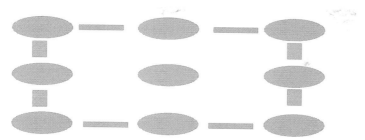

Figure 5.15 The Insolvability of the 9-Dot Problem.

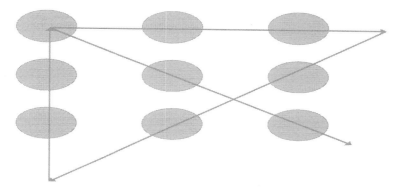

Figure 5.16 Solving the 9-Dot Problem Through Second Order Change.

The 9-dot problem is not solvable if you hold very tightly to the rules given, plus one additional rule. The original rules were that you could only use four straight lines and that once you put your pen down on paper you could not lift it up. If you added the additional rule that you had to stay within the constraints of what looks like a box, then the 9-dot problem is unsolvable (see Figure 5.15).

However, if you do not use the self-added rule of staying within the constraints of what looks like a box, then the 9-dot problem is easily solved (see Figure 5.16).

CHAPTER SIX
Natural Systems Aesthetics

Christopher F. Burnett

CASE DESCRIPTION

Jackie and Liza's decision to seek couples' therapy was initiated by Jackie, around their conflict over the idea of having a baby. They had been together for the past two and a half years, which Jackie reported as being "mostly very good." Jackie said she was feeling the pressure of her age and yearned to have a baby before it was too late. She had explored options for either in vitro fertilization or adoption, but Liza was resistant, not only as she felt she had plenty of time, but also because the idea was calling for her to make a level of commitment she was not comfortable with. She had moved in to Jackie's apartment a little over a year ago, after the lease on her own apartment had expired. She found herself questioning whether she really wanted to stay in this relationship, or any relationship with a woman, long term. Whenever Jackie raised the topic of having a child together, Liza would try to change the subject or leave the conversation altogether. Jackie also reported that Liza had been having problems controlling her drinking lately. She reported that Liza had been going out and getting "really drunk" with her friends with greater frequency over the past few months. Jackie said that Liza's friends and she really didn't get along very well, so she rarely was invited to go herself. She told the therapist that she suspected that Liza had a substance abuse problem that she was refusing to seriously address. Jackie also reported that Liza had resumed having text and phone contact with her last boyfriend and that Liza knew this was upsetting to her.

Jacqulyn (Jackie) is a 38-year-old, middle child in a second generation, Cuban-American family living in Miami. Her father, Ernesto, is 64 years old and has worked as a furniture salesman since his family came to the US in 1980. In his family, Ernesto is the oldest of two brothers. Ernesto met Jackie's mother Maria when she was 16 years old. Maria is 62, and she is the youngest of three sisters. Throughout their marriage, she has mostly been a stay-at-home mother, but she has occasionally worked odd jobs outside of the home. Jackie described them as a very conservative Catholic family. Jackie has an older brother, Luis, age 40, and younger brother, Emilio, age 34. Luis has been married for the past 12 years and has two children, a girl, age 8, and a boy, age 5. Emilio was not married but had been in a committed relationship with Angela for the past six years. They both work full-time, have separate apartments, and no children. Jackie said she grew up with her parents expecting her to fulfill the traditional role of a daughter in a Cuban family. She described this as living at home until she got married, helping to keep the house clean, and maintaining family honor. Her parents found it extremely difficult to come to terms with Jackie's gay identity. She said she went to great lengths to hide it from them, until she was about 17 years old. When she first hinted that she might be gay, they argued with her about it and tried to force her to behave and dress in a more traditionally feminine manner. Eventually the arguing got so bad and heated she wound up getting kicked out of her family home when she turned 18. Her grandfather disowned her when he found out and has since refused to have any contact with her. Now, 20 years later, there has been some grudging acceptance of her and her lifestyle by her parents in private. In the past few years, Jackie has been included in holiday dinners at the house, though her parents never talk about her with anyone outside the immediate family. Jackie's older brother, Luis, remains polite but distant with her. Her younger brother, Emilio, is close to his sister and was a frequent visitor at her home.

Jackie's relationship history and job history can both be described as "off and on." She has worked mostly in "artistic" job settings and mostly in the capacity of an assistant. When she and Liza met, she was working as a DJ in a bar, spinning between sets where a live band was playing. She said she has never been very good around people but described herself still as having a "good heart." She said she has been in only two other serious relationships before she met Liza. One of these lasted two years, and the other one lasted nine months. She describes Liza as "the love of my life" and says that the only reasons she is so critical of her is that she wants Liza to be the best person that she can be.

Liza Brown is 25 years old, and the youngest of five children. Her family has roots in New York City, where she was born, but they have lived in Miami for almost two decades now. Her father, Marvin, is 66 and is a retired bank executive, and her mother, Judy, 65 was until recently a literature professor at a university. They both adored their youngest daughter, who they saw as bright and full of life. Liza conceded it was fair to say they indulged her, as she had been a "late in life" baby who was the apple of her mother's eye. The family home was always filled with people and activity, and Liza had returned to live there for a year after graduating from university with a degree in graphic design. She found enough part time work to allow her to get an apartment with two other roommates. Liza's two older sisters are Lucy, age 42, and Karen, age 40. Both of them are married and each has their own successful careers. Lucy's marriage had always been solid, but Karen's had a history of difficulty and periods of separation. Liza also has two brothers, Kent, age 37, and Rick, age 35. Both of them have followed more or less in their father's footsteps and built successful careers in the world of finance back in New York City. The two older brothers are also married, and Liza has four nephews and two nieces. Liza's parents were surprised when they found out about the relationship with Jackie, as Liza had had many male pursuers and a series of boyfriends throughout high school and college. But they were accepting of it and just wanted Liza to be happy. They suspected this was a phase but were willing to see how things worked out and were openly supportive of her and Jackie in the meantime.

In this chapter, we will look at the work and theory developed by Dr. Murray Bowen, based on the principles of natural systems theory. Thought of broadly, **natural systems theory** assumes that a) there are forces in nature which shape and effect all living things, like the forces found in the theory of evolution and that b) human beings are just another manifestation of these natural forces at work (Kerr & Bowen, 1988). Bowen Family Systems theory (BFST) was developed by Dr. Bowen after years of working with severely mentally ill patients and families in a variety of inpatient psychiatric settings. One of the things that Dr. Bowen's work with schizophrenics led him to believe was that psychiatric symptoms and mental illness were not adequately conceptualized when they were being thought of as "individual" phenomena. From his work, he saw that families and relationship systems played a large role in the maintenance, escalation, and dissipation of individual symptoms and that this influence could extend over multiple generations (Bowen, 1994). In order for him to do this, he drew heavily upon the work of Charles Darwin and was committed to a belief that biological sciences held the key to adequately understanding family and relationship life.

> The scientific facts of evolution have been chosen to replace many of the ideas of Freudian theory. Evolution is a rich body of facts that can be proven and validated. The incorporation of these facts into a new theory required some kind of systems theory to handle the many variables.
> (Kerr & Bowen, 1988, p. 360)

This commitment to biology and related sciences led him to develop a theory grounded in systems thinking as it relates to the natural world.

This is one of the key ways that a Bowen Family Systems approach distinguishes itself from other forms of family therapy. Its reliance on the ideas of natural systems and evolutionary theory sets it apart. Bowen consciously sought to place his work in the context of a scientific framework outside of mere philosophy or conjecture. He wrote:

> My primary effort has gone into making psychotherapy as scientific and predictable as possible. Early in psychiatry I was bothered when "intuition" and "clinical judgment" were used to change

the course of a plan of psychotherapy or other forms of psychiatric treatment. Gross examples occur at times of crisis when the staff, reacting emotionally, needs to plan a change in treatment that is based more on a "feeling" and "clinical hunches" than on scientific knowledge and theoretical principles. It is commonplace for psychotherapists to make changes based more on feeling perceptions and subjectivity than on clinical fact and objectivity.

(Bowen, 1994, p. 470)

In doing so, Bowen was very consciously seeking to place his work and theory outside of what he saw as the mainstream of family therapy practice. He was most interested in developing a theory about how families actually function and what they have in common with all other forms of life. He was consistent in his belief that the bulk of the field of family therapy was much more interested in trying to get people to change than it was in trying to understand what they did and how they did it. This commitment has had profound implications for clinical practice, which will be discussed in Chapter 7.

A key to his understanding was Bowen's belief that human families and human relationship systems had more in common with other forms of life than they were different from them. He believed that far too much emphasis was placed on the unique cognitive abilities of *Homo sapiens* and that far too little attention had been paid to what *Homo sapiens* families had in common with other forms of life. He found this to be especially true when looking at higher functioning mammals and primates. Bowen believed that, using an evolutionary lens, we could see deeply and much more clearly into the parameters of family life and patterns of relational living (Kerr & Bowen, 1988). Taking his cue from Darwin, Bowen believed that there were "forces" at work that helped to shape family and relationship dynamics and that such forces existed beyond simple individual will. This allowed him to develop a number of interesting and explanatory concepts which he employed in order to help families understand the nature of relationship systems in general. In order to fully understand Bowen Family Systems theory, three explanatory concepts that undergird his theory's eight principles must be addressed. These are the constructs of the emotional system, chronic anxiety, and the principle of individuality and togetherness. What follows is an attempt to introduce the reader to each of these integral constructs through the case of Jackie and Liza.

Key Figure

Murray Bowen

Murray Bowen was born on January 31, 1913, in Waverly, Tennessee. He was the oldest of five children. His family lived in the area for generations, and his parents had a family farm. Bowen's early life was spent on the farm helping in the fields and with the livestock. Bowen's father, Jess Sewell Bowen, taught his children about how the land, livestock, crops, and people were interconnected. This was perhaps Murray Bowen's introduction to systems theory and the importance of nature.

   Bowen attended the University of Tennessee, Knoxville, earning a B.S. He then earned an MD from the University of Tennessee, Memphis, medical school in 1937. He completed his residency at the Menninger Clinic in Topeka, Kansas. Based on his experience as a US Army physician during World War II, Bowen became interested in psychiatry. In 1946, he went back to the Menninger Clinic where he explored Freudian theory. However, he quickly began expanding his understanding from the individual psyche to the person's family system.

   After leaving the Menninger Clinic, Bowen worked at The National Institute of Mental Health (NIMH) where he was the first director of the Family Division. He held this position from 1954 to 1960. Bowen's groundbreaking work there led to the development of his famous eight interlocking concepts. These were developed through observation of interactions between schizophrenics and their parents (primarily the mothers) that he had live on the hospital grounds.

> Bowen later became a Clinical Professor in the Department of Psychiatry at the Georgetown University Medical Center. There, he founded the Georgetown Family Center, which later was renamed the Bowen Center for the Study of the Family. The Bowen Center is the primary center for the dissemination of Bowen Theory. Bowen's most influential written works include *Family Evaluation* (1988), co-written with Michael Kerr, and *Family Therapy in Clinical Practice* (1994).
>
> Bowen is famous for proposing eight interlocking concepts that form the basis of natural systems theory. These concepts include triangles, differentiation of self, nuclear family emotional process, family projection process, multigenerational transmission process, emotional cutoff, sibling position, and societal emotional process. These interlocking concepts have made natural systems theory one of the most in-depth systems theories as they describe how any natural system functions, not only families.
>
> Murray Bowen died on October 9, 1990, at the age of 77 in his home in Chevy Chase, Maryland.

The Emotional System

The construct of the **emotional system** is crucial for understanding all of the other related concepts that follow. One of the ways that Bowen Family Systems theory distinguishes itself from other approaches is its belief that human behaviors can be explained, and not merely described, with accuracy. The concept of the emotional system is one of the things that make this kind of assertion possible.

> While Darwin established this physical link between man and the lower forms, Bowen's concept of the emotional system has provided a basis for establishing a behavioral link between the human and other animals. There is a great deal more to be understood about the emotional system, but as further knowledge accumulates this concept is likely to provide extremely important theoretical base for scientific understanding of all animal behavior, including man's.
>
> (Kerr & Bowen, 1988, p. 27)

As Kerr and Bowen admit in the quotation above, the concept of the emotional system is still very loosely defined, even some 30 years later. However, that being the case, it allows us as family therapists to do our work with a particular kind of context always ready at hand. It allows us to assume that Jackie and Liza come into their current relationship from two different, separate "emotional systems," which helped shape each of them as individuals (see Figure 6.1). If we as therapists can go back and gain an understanding of

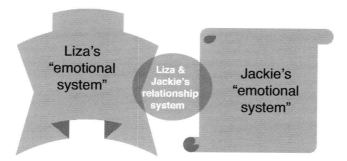

Figure 6.1 The Interconnection Between Two People's Emotional Systems. Each Person Brings Their "Emotional System" into a Relationship.

how each of their respective emotional systems has helped to shape the way that they attempt to create an "emotional system" of their own in relationship to one another, we can go a long way toward explaining certain behaviors that might otherwise not make sense out of such a context.

For example, in this case, it would be very easy for a therapist to focus on Jackie's report of Liza's increased drinking as evidence of the need for Liza to receive substance abuse treatment. However, when understood in the context of the current relationship situation, it becomes much easier to understand Liza's increased drinking as a kind of "distancing mechanism" she is using to maintain emotional distance from what she sees as Jackie's increasingly uncomfortable relationship demands for more closeness.

As an explanatory concept, the idea of the emotional system helps contextualize behavior, functioning, and motivation, at the individual, family, or group level. In this way, it is a cornerstone concept, linking all expressions of life on earth together. It is a concept that allows us to transcend the common, individualistic dichotomies of mind/body and nature/nurture and conveys these ideas to a higher level of systemic abstraction.

When a cybernetic systems or language-based systems approach is used to understand families, these systemic frameworks allow the therapist to only describe those things of immediate, verbalized concern to the therapist or the family members. Therapy has to be oriented around "the problem," and "the problem" has to be stated and verbalized. The concept of an emotional system, believed to be present throughout all living things, allows a Bowen Family Systems therapist to expand the context through which discussions about families and relationships can be held. Using this concept allows a therapist to understand the family as an emotional unit, rooted in biology, and not simply as a collection of relationship problems to be solved. This distinction is not a minor one. In fact, it allows for an entirely different kind of discourse around families, relationships, and interpersonal interactions.

Looking at the situation of Jackie and Liza, we can see from the start that their relationship to one another is the coming together of two branches of very different family of origin. The concept of an emotional system allows us to imagine the kinds of relationships each of them had growing up that helped to shape the kinds of adults that they find themselves being now. For example, it is very easy to imagine that coming into this relationship, Jackie had a history of some difficulty being accepted for who she is in her own family of origin. Her identifying herself as a gay woman has had multiple repercussions throughout her immediate and extended family relations. It has been a source of secrecy and shame in her family, and the reason she was asked to move out from the family when she was 18. On the other hand, it seems that Liza's identification as a gay woman has had far fewer, and much less intense, reactions within her own family of origin. It is an identity that she seems to hold of herself much more loosely, which, in the context of her relationship with Jackie, may also be a source of anxiety for Jackie.

When one thinks about families as an "emotional system" or an emotional "unit," it allows for an expanded, more organic conceptualization of any particular individual's behavior. But we need to be careful here. In any discussion of Bowen's work, the term "emotional" is used in a way far different than what most readers are accustomed. It most certainly does not refer to the things that are most commonly understood as "feelings." Emotional was a default term that Bowen came to use because he was unable to create an alternative that properly conveyed the scope and breath he believed the construct reflected. For him, **emotional** is a catchall term used to describe something about those forces he believed were present in all living things, not just human beings. When these forces express themselves in human families, we can see their effect over time and multiple generations, as well as in the here and now of the presenting complaint. This ability to see the present moment and its historical antecedents simultaneously is made possible through the construct of the emotional system. When conceived of as a property of all living things, the emotional system can be conceptualized as the home of the "life force" that drives all things to seek to survive and reproduce. Kerr and Bowen (1988) write:

> This way of thinking about what "energizes" the phenomenon being described is contained in the concept of the family emotional system. This distinction between "describing" and "accounting for" the phenomenon may seem academic, but it is quite important in the conduct of psychotherapy. The

way a therapist thinks about what energizes or drives the process he observes in a family will govern what he addresses in therapy. . . . The therapy that evolved from Bowen's theory about families was guided by the conceptualization of the family as an "emotional" system.

(p. 11)

Additionally, the concept of the emotional system allows us also to transcend the constructs of health and normality when thinking about family processes. If we imagine that every family's processes and interactions are driven by some internally driven and unseen biological forces, it becomes increasingly difficult, and unnecessary, to apply the standards of health and disease to such processes. Instead, what the concept of emotional system allows us to do as therapists is to try to make sense of both the meaning and the function of all given behaviors simultaneously. In a natural systems view of the world, all behaviors can be understood to be a part of "nature."

Applying Your Knowledge

Are there things you can think about in your family that have been passed down year after year during holidays or other times of family or community gatherings? Particular kinds of rituals your family likes to participate in and teach younger members of the family to perform? Are there heirlooms or other historical items that are treasured by members of your family that you will one day be expected to care for yourself? These are some small but significant ways that membership in an ongoing emotional system are passed down from generation to generation. Participation enlists one as a member of an ongoing relationally based system. Refusal to do so also has relationship consequences that may either be immediate or more long term.

ANXIETY

The second construct necessary for understanding Bowen Family Systems theory is the concept of **anxiety** (see Figure 6.2). We can talk about Jackie and Liza's relationship as containing a high level of anxiety at the moment, but once again, this requires the reader to suspend their usual understandings about the concept. This is not the kind of anxiety that is diagnosed in the *Diagnostic and Statistical Manual* (DSM). In Bowen's own words (1994):

The Bowen theory involves two main variables. One is the degree of anxiety, and the other is the degree of integration of self. There are several variables having to do with anxiety or emotional tension. Among these are intensity, duration, and different kinds of anxiety. . . . All organisms are reasonably adaptable to acute anxiety. The organism has built-in mechanisms to deal with short bursts of anxiety. It is sustained or chronic anxiety that is most useful in determining the differentiation of self. If anxiety is sufficiently low almost any organism can appear normal in the sense that it is symptom free. When anxiety increases and remains chronic for a certain period, the organism develops tension, either within itself or in the relationship systems, and the tension results in symptoms or dysfunction or sickness. The tension may result in physiological symptoms or physical illness, emotional dysfunction, and social illness characterized by impulsiveness or withdrawal, or by social misbehavior. There was also the phenomenon of the infectiousness of anxiety, through which anxiety can spread rapidly through the family, or through society. . . . I shall leave it to the reader to keep in mind there was always the variable of the degree of chronic anxiety which can result in anyone appearing normal at one level of anxiety and abnormal at another higher level.

(p. 360)

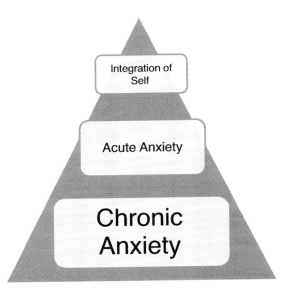

Figure 6.2 The Relationship Between Integration of Self, Acute Anxiety, and Chronic Anxiety. Acute Anxiety Is Usually Temporal and Easier to Adapt to. Chronic Anxiety Is Most Related to the Ability to Integrate Oneself.

Acute anxiety is the anxiety generated by day-to-day and situational problems that pose an imminent threat to wellbeing. The effects of acute anxiety can most easily be seen in the autonomic functions of the body, like the release of adrenaline, increased heart rate, sweating, stomachaches, etc. Generally speaking, the effects of acute anxiety dissipate when the presence of the threat also disappears.

Chronic anxiety is a much more generalized way of anticipating problems and difficulties. It is often associated with situations in the future that are anticipated but don't actually occur. For Jackie, we can hypothesize that proximate source of her chronic anxiety (its most immediate reason) is the stability of her current relationship with Liza. Evidence of this is her concern about Liza's renewed contact with her ex-boyfriend, and Liza's coming home drunk more frequently. It can also be speculated that, given the contentious nature of her relations with her parents, she has a good deal of chronic anxiety invested in the success of any partner relationship she enters into. This is one way to understand how much difficulty she has had maintaining long-term relationships in her life. We can also speculate that she is worried about the ticking of her biological clock, which could be another source of chronic anxiety. This too could well be contributing to the intensity of her current conflicts with Liza. In Bowen's theory, chronic anxiety is something that, once generated, often gets transmitted to other people. Some will hold that Jackie's difficult relationship with her parents has nothing to do with her current situation with Liza. Bowen maintains that one's ability or inability to come to terms with prior relationships, especially with one's parents, has a direct bearing on the nature and quality of one's current relational functioning. In this way, the chronic anxiety generated by Jackie's strained relationship with her parents is transmitted into the intensity we see in the relationship she has with Liza.

For Liza, we can assume that some of the proximate sources of her chronic anxiety in this relationship have to do with her reluctance for the relationship commitment to deepen any further. She may have reservations about the long-term implications of this relationship for her future wellbeing. The more anxious Jackie becomes about the relationship and Liza's commitment to it, the more focal the relationship and its future becomes for both of them. Jackie's efforts to ensure the future includes Liza in it, while Liza's reaction to it is to seek more distance.

One of the ways that I have come to apply the construct of chronic anxiety is to think of it as a kind of "electricity" or energy that sustains relationship systems. Like electricity, it can be both very useful and very dangerous. Like electricity, chronic anxiety's intensity can fluctuate over time, with a variety of consequences to individuals and the emotional systems that they are a part of. In keeping with a natural systems model of the world, chronic anxiety can be seen to exist in all forms of life, especially as regards the irrepressible question of survival. All forms of life expend energy, internally and externally, to manage the challenge of survival. For therapists, it can be very useful to conceptualize this energy as simply a natural product of what is required for living things to stay alive. When viewed in this way, it becomes possible to see anxiety as neither good nor bad in human relationship systems, but simply acknowledge that it "is."

Clinically, the first task of any therapist is reducing client levels of anxiety, both acute and chronic. This requires that the therapist have the capacity to "absorb it." A therapist needs to be able to manage in the face of the anxiety of others in order not to amplify what is already present. Usually this requires thoughtful and reflective practices. Being able to conceptualize the anxiety of others through theory, and in so doing come to understand it thoughtfully, makes anxiety and its manifestations an object of inquiry and in turn a source of therapeutic questioning. This approach has the effect of relieving the therapist from the burden of intervention. Such a stance makes it possible to see the "function" that anxiety plays in the service of the larger family system dynamic. Seeing this allows access to the individual as well as the family's quest for survival. Often this quest is simply the desire to maintain viability across multiple relationship contexts. When chronic anxiety is understood and conceptualized in this way, it expands the context of systems thinking. It adds a dimension of "modulation" to the understanding of how a relationship system is operating. With it, the same people in the same relationships can be understood more accurately when they act very differently in accordance with the level of anxiety/energy/electricity present in the overall emotional system. Such levels clearly change over time, and these changes can then be used to track the intensity and/or duration of certain relationship dynamics. With proper perspective and sufficient distance, these things can be seen to play themselves out generation after generation in any given family system.

Applying Your Knowledge

Have you ever entered into a new romantic relationship vowing not to repeat the same "mistakes" you made in the last one you were in? Have you ever promised yourself that you would not do the things to your children that your parents did to you? Have you ever said to yourself, "If I ever get promoted in this company, I will not do the same things to the employees that my boss is doing to me now"? All of these are examples of how chronic relationship anxiety can color future relationship behaviors. These impacts are not just limited to single generations either, as they can in certain circumstances be carried over generation to generation.

INDIVIDUALITY AND TOGETHERNESS

The third natural systems construct necessary to understand a Bowen Family Systems approach is the construct of **individuality and togetherness** (see Figure 6.3). Again, a natural systems framework allows us to assume that all people, and most animals, have automatic responses to the ebbs and flows that are part of any relationship system. For most people, these responses are understood in terms of "feelings" such as love, hate, longing, happiness, jealousy, anger, etc. Kerr and Bowen (1988) hypothesize that "one function served by emotions and feelings, therefore, is to control the balance between contact and

Figure 6.3 The Connection Between Individuality and Togetherness. The Two Are Said to Be Co-equal Forces of Nature, Which Impact All Relationship Dynamics.

separateness in a relationship" (p. 73, italics in original). It is assumed in every relationship that both parties seek some measure of emotional closeness and some measure of emotional distance from the person and/or group they are in relationship with. Again, here it is important to understand the concepts of emotional closeness and emotional distance doesn't refer simply to the feelings as described above. They refer here to the sense of safety and security provided by being in relationship. For some, closeness equates to safety and security. For others, it is distance and space that translates into that very same sense. Never are these dynamics set once and for all in any relationship context, as they are completely contingent upon the level of anxiety that exists in and around any given relationship system.

For instance, Jackie may say to Liza, "You don't love me like you used to," and in response, Liza may utter, "That's because your jealousy is driving me crazy." Understood from a natural systems point of view, what both of them are saying to the other is that the safety and security of being in this relationship has changed, and I don't feel as close to you as I once did. Jackie is saying that she wants the relationship to get closer in order to feel safe, and Liza is saying that she is trying to put more distance in it for the very same goal.

It is important to keep in mind that individuality and togetherness are contextual "forces" which impact individual behaviors. That is, these two "pulls" exist side by side in any relationship system and exert themselves on it throughout. If we say one partner in a relationship is a "distancer" (in our case Liza) and the other partner (Jackie) is a "pursuer," we are treating each of them as though they are individual actors with specific personality traits. If, however, we understand individuality and togetherness to be forces which occur within and throughout nature, across various forms of life, then we can understand their conflict using a much larger context.

Some would intervene with Jackie and Liza by prescribing that the two of them consciously change roles. The idea being that if the two partners can change roles, where Liza became the pursuer and Jackie the distancer, their entire relationship system would be transformed. Understood through a natural systems lens, however, it becomes almost irrelevant which spouse occupies which role here. The concept of individuality and togetherness allows a clinician to understand that there is a deeper function being played by the couple's movements either toward or away from each other. Jackie's moves to secure greater togetherness with Liza (asking to have a child) and Liza's response (staying out and drinking more) are understood as efforts both of them are making in the context of the emotional system they have created together. In a natural systems framework, the passage of time creates ebbs and flows in any relationship. It is the duration and intensity of the anxiety, as well as the individuality and togetherness forces, that together predict how, as well as if, a relationship system is sustainable. With enough distance and the proper perspective, one can see that the individuals involved, and the roles they play can, and do, transform over time. This is exactly what can be seen using a genogram and why it is so useful as a clinical tool. A genogram is a visual representation of the family system which seeks to make a record of both the factual information about a family's members, as well as an accounting of their emotional processes (much more about this later, in Chapter 7).

In humans, and many other species, danger and threats are often met with increases in the togetherness force, and individual expression is actively suppressed by the pressure of the group (Kerr & Bowen, 1988). The concepts of emotional system, anxiety, and individuality and togetherness are understood to be expressions of the natural processes that seem to operate to some degree or another in all levels of life. Taken together, they all have exerted themselves throughout evolutionary history to help produce human relationship life as we know it today. This leads us to see how there are multiple contexts that must be considered simultaneously in making any assessment about an individual or a family's level of functioning. It is with this kind of "de facto" understanding in mind that Bowen then went on to create his eight concepts that, taken together, we understand as Bowen Family Systems theory. Now that we've undertaken the necessary preparations, let's take a deeper look at some of the crucial constructs of that theory.

> ## Applying Your Knowledge
>
> Have you ever said to your significant other 1) "I'm going to have a girl's night out on Friday night with Amy and Sue"; 2) "Let's plan a getaway weekend for just the two of us at the end of the month"; or 3) "You go ahead and spend Sunday with your family, I am going to stay here and get some things done"? Which of these do you think is an expression of a desire for individuality? Which do you think is an expression of the desire for more togetherness? Which could be seen as an expression of both? The answers are 1), 2), and 3) respectively of course. Bowen's concept of individuality and togetherness should never be seen as a dichotomous variable. These are forces that are always in some kind of relationship relative to one another, and according to Bowen, they are always exerting themselves throughout any relationship system.

Bowen's Eight Concepts

After decades of studying the dynamics of families and relationships in light of serious mental illness, Dr. Bowen articulated what he believed to be eight principles necessary for understanding human families and relationship systems and how they function. Each of these concepts is understood to be interlocking with each of the other constructs, and all of them are grounded in natural systems thinking. While it will be necessary to talk about each of them on its own merits, the reader should understand that none of these concepts can be adequately understood independent of any of the others, which is what makes this a systems theory. The eight concepts Bowen articulated are: 1) differentiation of self, 2) emotional triangles, 3) nuclear family emotional process, 4) family projection process, 5) multigenerational transmission process, 6) emotional cutoff, 7) sibling position, and 8) societal emotional process. What follows below are some introductory remarks to guide the reader regarding these ideas. A dimension many students of the theory report is that the more time you spend with these concepts, the more solidly they reward you as a basis for understanding the complexities of human behaviors and relationship systems.

Differentiation of Self

Likely the most well recognized of all of Bowen's concepts, **differentiation of self** is also probably the most complex, multidimensional, and difficult to grasp of the eight. Papero (1990) writes, "It is difficult, if not impossible, to understand the concept of differentiation of self without seeing the family as an emotional unit" (p. 45). It is a concept that encompasses not only individuals, but family life, both in the present and over generations of time. It even has application in understanding societal development. Thought of in the broadest terms, differentiation can be said to relate to the abilities of individuals or groups of people to be able to distinguish between intellectual processes (thinking) and emotional processes (feelings) as drivers (explanations) of their behavior. There is no adequate single definition of such an encompassing concept. It remains an ever-shifting construct, even for those who use it often. All that can be offered here are some initial guidelines for those seeking to know more about it.

Below are some of Bowen's (1994) early comments on the construct and its relationship to therapy:

> A common mistake is to equate the better differentiated person with a "rugged individualist." I consider rugged individualism to be the exaggerated pretend posture of a person struggling against emotional fusion. The differentiated person is always aware of others in the relationship system around him. There are so many forces and counterforces and details in differentiation that one has to get a broad panoramic view of the total human phenomenon in order to be able to see differentiation. Once it is possible to see the phenomenon, there it is, operating in full view, right in front of our eyes. Once it is possible to see the phenomenon, it is then possible to apply the concept to hundreds of different human situations. To try to apply it without knowing it is an exercise in futility.
>
> (pp. 370–371)

He then goes on further:

> The therapy based on differentiation is no longer therapy in the usual sense. The therapy is as different from the conventional therapy is the theory is different from conventional theory. . . . The goal is to help the motivated family member to take a microscopic step toward a better level of differentiation, in spite of the togetherness forces that oppose. . . . The togetherness forces are so strong in maintaining the status quo that any small step towards differentiation is met with vigorous disapproval of the group. This is the point at which a therapist or guide can be most helpful.
>
> (p. 371)

In the case of Jackie and Liza, from the very little we know at this point, figuring out who between them is the "most motivated" is not at all clear. It sounds like Jackie is the one who wanted them to come into therapy, but it also sounds like her motivation for doing so was to increase their togetherness as a couple, not to increase any mutual sense of autonomy. She may be the motivated "customer" looking for change, but as a therapist, if you were to simply participate in her plan to increase closeness in the relationship, you almost certainly would wind up alienating Liza, whose goal seems to be to maintain, if not increase, the current level of distance in the relationship. Still, for many therapists eager to be of help, it is almost impossible to resist the temptation to immediately start working to get them to be a better, and closer, couple. From Bowen's point of view, this demonstrates a lack of differentiation on the part of the therapist, as their motivation to be of help gets in the way of their being a thoughtful, non-reactive presence for the couple.

Bowen (1994) continues by adding:

> Conventional therapy is designed to resolve, or talk out, conflict. This does accomplish the goal of reducing the conflict of that moment, but it can also rob the individual of his budding efforts to achieve a bit more differentiation from the family togetherness.
>
> (p. 371)

For these and other reasons, the very systemic concept of differentiation of self is hard to accurately summarize through any single definition. However, many are familiar with it through the use of the Differentiation of Self Scale (see Figure 6.4). The **Differentiation of Self Scale** is a theoretical construct that runs on a continuum from 0 to 100, which is said to describe the level to which an individual, or a family system, is able to separate its emotional systems functioning from its intellectual systems functioning over a relatively stable period of time.

Figure 6.4 Bowen Developed a Hypothetical Differentiation of Self Scale. People Higher on the Scale Are Said to Be Able to Differentiate Thoughts From Feeling More Easily Than Those Lower on the Scale.

For Bowen (1994) himself:

> This scale is an effort to classify all levels of human functioning, the lowest possible levels to the highest potential level, on a single dimension. In broad terms it would be similar to an emotional maturity scale, but it deals with factors that are different from "maturity" concepts. The scale eliminates the need for the concept "normal." It has nothing to do with emotional health or illness or pathology. There are people low on the scale who keep their lives in emotional equilibrium without psychological symptoms, and there are some higher on the scale who develop symptoms under severe stress. However, lower skill people are more vulnerable to stress and, for them, recovery from symptoms can be slow or impossible while higher skill people tend to recover rapidly. The scale has no direct correlation with intelligence or socioeconomic levels. There are intellectually brilliant people far down the scale and less bright ones far up the scale.
>
> (p. 472)

Any accurate assessment of where either Jackie or Liza might themselves fall on the differentiation of self-scale will necessarily entail a much more detailed family history taken on both of them, using a genogram. In order to accurately assess the level of differentiation of self in any single individual, one must also have a minimum of three generations of family history in order to make a minimum assessment of overall family functioning.

However, to even get this kind of information from Jackie or Liza, the first efforts of therapy must be directed toward lowering the levels of anxiety that exist in their relationship. Doing this makes it more likely that either one of them (hopefully both of them) can better engage their abilities to think, and not simply react, to one another or the therapist. Once the overall level of anxiety has been lowered, only then is it possible to help Jackie or Liza manage their current relationship with greater thoughtfulness. For a large percentage of people who seek therapy, once the overall level of anxiety lowers, the motivation for continuing evaporates. Feeling better is enough, as for many that was their goal in the first place. When this happens, it can be a test of the level of differentiation of self of the therapist. It can be tempting to tell the client that such a change is only a temporary relief, and for the sake of their own best interests, they should continue in therapy. However, doing so tips one's hand to reveal that they have taken up a "rooting interest" in the outcome of someone else's emotional system. The motivation to continue in therapy must always be the client's; otherwise, any further explorations of family process will be an empty exercise done at the therapist's behest.

In that percentage of individuals, couples, or families who do continue once the initial storm has passed, the role of the therapist becomes one of a coach, mentor, and guide. The job becomes one of educating them to understand the dynamics that underlie all family systems and how to apply such knowledge to their own.

Emotional Triangles

Titleman (2008) makes the case that, through the course of his career, Bowen's focus moved from the individual, to the dyad, to the triangle as the fundamental unit of understanding. In doing so, it seems Bowen paved the way for a very different kind of thinking about the particulars of clinical practice.

> The thinking on which the concept of a triangle is based illustrates the thinking on which the entire family systems theory is based. The theory is an attempt to define *facts of functioning* in human relationships—facts which can be observed to repeat over and over so consistently that they become knowable and predictable. *What* and *how* and *when* and *where* are facts about a relationship that can be observed. Conjecture about *why* something happens is not fact and so the inclusion of such conjecture in the theoretical concepts was avoided as much as possible. While it is a fact that human beings speculate about *why* people do what they do, the content of those speculations is not fact. The triangle describes the what, how, when, and where of relationships, not the why. Triangles are simply a fact of nature. To observe them requires that one stand back and watch the process unfold. Conjecture about why any one person says or does a particular thing immediately takes the observer out of a systems frame of reference. The assignment of motive is necessarily subjective and not verifiable; the assignment of function can be objective and potentially verifiable.
>
> (Kerr & Bowen, 1988, p. 134, italics in original)

The concept of the **emotional triangle** is an attempt to say that all human relationship systems can be described in terms of the structure and function of their component parts. A therapist can do this without the need for speculation about motives. In fact, any effort to discern motive only distracts from the efforts to discern the facts of functioning in a human relationship system.

In the case of Jackie and Liza, we can see this concept take a variety of forms. Jackie's desire to bring a child into the relationship is itself a kind of emotional triangling, signaling the desire for there to be a permanent third member of the relationship. More concretely, we can see that Liza has been actively bringing in both her old boyfriend, and her circle of friends, more actively into her relationship with Jackie, and that doing so has generated a predictable set of responses.

On the concept of emotional triangles, Bowen (1994) writes:

> The theory states that the triangle, a three-person emotional configuration, is the molecule or the basic building block of any emotional system, whether it is in the family or any other group. The triangle is the smallest stable relationship system. A two-person system may be stable as long as it is calm, but when anxiety increases, it immediately involves the most vulnerable other person to become a triangle. When tension in the triangle is too great for the threesome, it involves others to become a series of interlocking triangles.
>
> (p. 373)

Thinking about human relationships through the concept of triangles is an important way to understand how the theory has application (see Figure 6.5). It is through these concepts we see the predictable pathways anxiety takes in human relationships. Once these pathways have been illuminated, variations in the level of anxiety in the system can then be traced over time. Accurately tracking these variations reveals the malleability of functioning of emotional triangles in a relationship system. "A triangle has different characteristics during moderately anxious periods than calm periods" (Kerr & Bowen, 1988, p. 136). It can reasonably be speculated that Jackie's increased talk of wanting a baby is in some ways related to the level of anxiety in her relationship with Liza. In fact, many couples, married or not, often believe that bringing a child into a family will help relieve some of the ongoing tension in their family system. It can also be reasonably speculated that this is not unrelated to Liza's triangulating behaviors of drinking and contacting her old beau. The question for a Bowen clinician is what function does triangulating others serve for the relationship. It is not "How do you stop Liza from going out more?" or "Is it wise for Jackie to want to have a baby at this point in the relationship?".

Figure 6.5 The Three-Person System Is the Smallest Stable Unit. This Figure Depicts the Basic Emotional Triangle. In the Case Used for This Chapter, a Primary Triangle Consists of Liza, Jackie, and a Potential Baby.

Figure 6.6 Systems Consist of Interlocking Triangles, Which Are Means of Binding Anxiety.

In their basic form, emotional triangles act as a regulatory mechanism, keeping the natural anxiety of human relationships within manageable parameters (see Figure 6.6). However, when anxiety rises either due to factors internal, external, or both, it "spreads" out and activates others. Many times, as the anxiety spreads, the triangle where it originated returns back to its original level of functioning. However, there are also many times when the anxiety of the original triangle is such that those affected by it are also unable to manage it sufficiently and, in turn, involve more and more people in the effort to do so. This goes a long way toward helping one to understand the ebb and flow of symptom development in any relationship system.

The shifting alliances of family emotional triangles, the levels, pathways, and history of anxiety in a relationship system, and the development and dissipation of symptoms over time are not things that often openly announce themselves. It takes time, discipline, and patience on the part of the therapist to allow these phenomena to emerge from the everyday descriptions families give as their "explanations" of them. For example, Jackie likely can point to her age as the explanation for "why" she wants to have a child. Liza can say that she is young and just wants to have fun as the reason she is spending more time with her friends and drinking. There may be truth in both claims, but it is the job of the therapist to be able to see beyond such "whys."

The identification of relationship structures and functions in Bowen therapy usually takes the form of an exchange of hypotheses, offered and dismissed, by the client(s) and the therapist in an atmosphere of nonjudgmental and mutual exploration. One of the keys in allowing this to happen is resisting as long as possible the need for intervention on the part of the therapist. Once the function and structure of certain family dynamics and interactions are mutually agreed upon, even if it is only at the level of a basic building block like a single triangle, the process then becomes one of mutual exploring about the range of possible alternate responses.

Bowen (1994) states:

> Knowledge of triangles helps provide the theoretical perspective between individual therapy and this method of family therapy. An emotionally involved relationship is unavoidable in the average two-person patient-therapist relationship. Theoretically, family therapy provides a situation in which intense relationships can remain within the family and the therapist can be relatively outside the emotional complex. This is a good theoretical premise that is hard to achieve in practice. Without some special effort, it is easy for the family to wrap itself around the therapist emotionally, install the therapist in an all-important position, hold the therapist responsible for success or failure, and passively wait for the therapist to change the family. . . . Most important was a long-term effort to attain and maintain emotional neutrality with individual family members. There are many subtleties to this. Beyond this effort it was knowledge of triangles that provided the important breakthrough in the effort to stay outside the emotional complex.
>
> (pp. 374–375)

Applying Your Knowledge

1. Your friend Gail calls you and tells you she has to tell you something urgent. She says that she just saw Mike, Ann's boyfriend, kissing someone in his car, and she doesn't think it was Ann. She asks you what should the two of you now do with this information? What is your immediate reaction? Can that be described as triangulation?
2. You and your partner have an argument over how much you should spend to buy a new car. This isn't the first time the two of you disagree about financial issues. When the weekend comes and you go golfing with your regular foursome, is this something you are likely to discuss with them on the golf course or in the clubhouse afterward? Can this be described as triangulation?
3. At work, your boss has called you in and told you that you are doing an excellent job and that she thinks you are likely to be promoted as soon as the next position opens up. You are so pumped by this news that you can't wait to get home to tell your roommate. Can this be described as a form of triangulation?

NUCLEAR FAMILY EMOTIONAL PROCESS

Nuclear family emotion process refers to the a) patterns of relationship and emotional functioning found in a single generation of a family system and also to the b) predictable ways that symptoms exhibit themselves in family relationship systems (Kerr & Bowen, 1988). In his earlier writings, Bowen described this dimension of family life as the "undifferentiated ego mass," but over time, as his thinking developed, he came to see that "nuclear family emotional process" was a more accurate descriptor of this dynamic (Titleman, 1998). Bowen held that many of the relationship patterns seen between mothers, fathers, and children are replications of the same patterns that occurred in past generations and are likely to be reproduced in the next.

For Jackie, we might see that, throughout her adult life, she has had a hard time sustaining viable relationships. It seems that in her family of origin, she was a great focus of tension and anxiety. As the first-born female in the nuclear family, she may have generated or perpetuated all kinds of issues for her mother or father, or both. Her grandfather eventually "disowned" her, but it is impossible to separate this from a longer history between the grandfather and his offspring, her father. Her parents kicked her out when she turned 18, and again we have to wonder what the ripple effects of doing this were throughout the immediate and larger family systems. We might speculate that in her current relationship with Liza, she too has very high expectations of who and what Liza should be in their relationship. From what we know, it can fairly be inferred that Liza is chafing under those expectations.

For Liza's part, she has always occupied the position of being an indulged youngest who knows how to get others to see things her way. When Jackie demands that she do or be certain things in this relationship, her response is to ask if she really needs to stay in such an arrangement. She has never really felt constraint while growing up, and it would seem has no interest in feeling its effects in the present either.

Understanding nuclear family emotional processes requires an understanding of the relationship between a) levels of anxiety and b) levels of differentiation of self, in the ability to produce symptoms in a relationship system. Kerr and Bowen (1988) stated,

> Where a symptom occurs in a relationship system (in which family member or in which family relationship) is determined by the particular pattern or patterns of emotional functioning that predominate in that family system. If the predominant pattern is parents' externalizing their anxieties into their marital relationship, periods of high anxiety are characterized by marital conflict. If the predominant pattern fosters dysfunction in a spouse or in a child, periods of high anxiety are characterized by symptoms developing in a spouse or child.
>
> (p. 163)

The most common way that spouses or romantic partners manage the anxiety generated by being in relationship to one another is by creating emotional distance from one another. Of emotional distance in marriage, Bowen (1994) says, "It is present in all marriages to some degree, and in a high percentage of marriages to a major degree" (p. 377). When creating emotional distance in the relationship is not sufficient to be able to manage the relational anxiety, Kerr and Bowen (1988) detail the three major areas in which the relationship anxiety present in all such marital relationships manifest in the development of symptoms (see Figure 6.7). The first of these is marital conflict. The second is sickness or dysfunction in one spouse. And the third is projection of the anxiety onto the children.

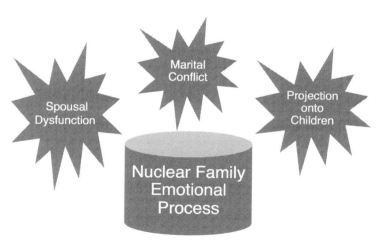

Figure 6.7 The Nuclear Family Emotional Process Is a Way That Couples Bind Anxiety When Emotional Distance Is Not Sufficient and May Consist of Spousal Dysfunction, Marital Conflict, and Projection Onto Children.

From a family systems point of view, the development of symptoms can take the form of physical illness (or more commonly medical disorders), emotional illness (otherwise known as psychiatric or psychological disorders), or social illness (more conventionally understood as conduct or criminal disorders). Kerr and Bowen (1988) then further clarify this schema by adding,

> Family systems theory attempts to bridge this compartmentalization of disorders into categories such as "medical" or "psychiatric" by conceptualizing *all* clinical dysfunctions as linked to the *same* basic patterns of emotional functioning in a nuclear family. The patterns that contribute to the development of physical illness are the same as those that contribute to the development of emotional or social illness.
>
> (pp. 163–164, italics in original)

They go on further to explicate that patterns of emotional functioning do not cause physical, emotional, or social illness, but they are a major influence on an individual's ability to adapt successfully in the face of other factors that do cause illness.

When relationship anxiety manifests itself in marital conflict, what a clinician sees is usually a situation where neither spouse has the interest or capability of giving in or adapting to the needs of the other. Jackie wants to have a child, but Liza has little interest in accommodating her desire. Such relationships are often marked by the very intense level of energy that each spouse brings in terms of their attention to the actions or inactions of the other person. In such relationships, there can be periods of great and even satisfying closeness, but predictably, these are almost always followed by periods of conflict, which then produce much needed distance in the relationship.

When relationship anxiety manifests itself in the dysfunction of one partner or spouse, what presents itself clinically is often described in terms of an "overfunctioning" partner and an "underfunctioning" partner (see Figure 6.8). In this case, it is easy to assume that Jackie is the overfunctioner, and Liza the underfunctioner, but more information would have to be gathered to be sure. Under- and overfunctioner are characterizations that can be ascribed to almost all intimate adult partner relationships; the only question is the duration and intensity of this dynamic. Over a sufficiently long period of time, and with a sufficient degree of emotional intensity, the partner identified as the one who has done the most adapting to the other may develop symptoms as a manner of managing the anxiety associated with doing so.

Lastly, when we see relationship anxiety manifesting itself in the children, the clinical expression of these symptoms again takes either physical, emotional, or social form. Another way to think about the

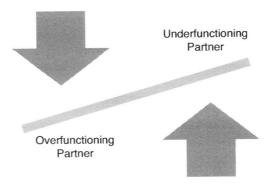

Figure 6.8 When Anxiety Manifests Itself in a Marital Relationship, It Is Often Expressed by Describing One Partner as Overfunctioning and the Other as Underfunctioning.

nuclear family emotional process is to imagine that there is a definite amount of relationship anxiety in the family. The amount absorbed in marital conflict or sickness in a spouse reduces the amount that will be directed onto the children (Bowen, 1994) Kerr and Bowen (1988) further elucidate this point in the following way:

> There is an "emotional atmosphere" in every nuclear family created by each family member's emotional reactions, feeling reactions, subjectively determined attitudes, values, and beliefs, and more objectively determined attitudes, values, and beliefs. The atmosphere determines the level of differentiation and, consequently, the degree of adaptiveness to stress of each child that grows up in the family.
>
> (p. 194)

FAMILY PROJECTION PROCESS

Family projection process can be thought of as the process by which parental relationship anxiety is transmitted onto a child. Clinically, it often reveals itself in the intensity of a relationship between mother and child. Papero (1990) says that neither parent nor child is responsible for this situation, as neither seeks this sort of emotional involvement. Each parent may have some awareness of the intensity present, but each finds themselves unable or unwilling to do anything to alter it. As a process that originates with the parents, the child is simply drawn into it. This occurs to various degrees in any family relationship system, but in some family systems, it becomes a significant part of the system's overall wellbeing. The child then plays an overly significant role in the management and maintenance of the marital relationship.

Using this concept, it becomes possible to imagine that a great deal of the anxiety in Jackie's parents' marriage has been "projected" on to Jackie (see Figure 6.9). Having Jackie to focus on allows both of them not to have to deal with the anxiety generated in their own relationship. The recipient of this kind of projection often is described as being less emotionally "free" than his or her other siblings. Hall (1991) writes: "Oldest, youngest, and only children are frequently recipients of family projections, although children who function in those roles are perhaps more vulnerable to projection than are children chronologically in those positions" (p. 83). In the case of Liza, it seems that her older siblings were much more likely to be recipients of such projection, leaving her a kind of emotional and behavioral freedom that her siblings could complain they themselves never had. Further, the emergence of this kind of projection in a given generation is understood as a cumulative outcome, based on the dynamics of the parental emotional atmosphere(s) experienced by both parents. This assumption goes hand in hand with the next concept of the theory.

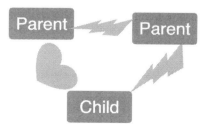

Figure 6.9 The Family Projection Process Happens When the Relationship Anxiety Between Partners Is Transmitted to a Child.

Multigenerational Transmission Process

The concept of **multigenerational transmission process** reflects the idea that in any given family system there is a good deal of divergence in the levels of functioning not only among the individual members, but among nuclear family units as well. This divergence can be seen as something that occurs across generations as well as between members and nuclear family units of the same generation. According to Kerr and Bowen (1988) "Every family, given sufficient generations, tends to produce people at both functional extremes and people at most points on a continuum between these extremes" (p. 221). Every family tree produces different "branches" which helps to foster either functional stability or instability over sufficient periods of time.

Taking Bowen's (1994) own words:

> If we follow the most impaired child through successive generations, we will see one line of descendent producing individuals with lower and lower levels of differentiation. The process may go rapidly a few generations, remain static for a generation or so, then speed up again. Once I said it required at least 3 generations to produce a child so impaired he would collapse in the schizophrenia. That was based on the notion of a starting point with fairly good surface functioning and a process that proceeded at maximum speed through the generations. However, since I now know the process can slow down or stay static a generation or two, I would now say that it would require perhaps eight to ten generations to produce the level of impairment that goes with schizophrenia.
>
> (pp. 384–385)

Kerr and Bowen (1988) say that marked discrepancies in the functioning of members of the same multigenerational family are **facts** about families that are easily observable (see Figure 6.10). The question they raise about such facts is "whether or not they reflect the operation of an orderly and predictable relationship process that connects the functioning of family members across generations" (p. 223) A good deal of the theory seems to rest on the assumption that they do.

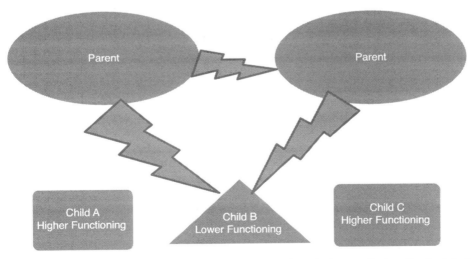

Figure 6.10 Multigenerational Transmission Process Occurs When the Parents Project the Anxiety Generated in Their Own Relationship Onto One of the Children, Whose Functioning Becomes Impaired. The Focus on One Child Allows the Other Children to Be Able to Function at Higher Levels. This Process Happens Across Generations.

In our current case, we can hypothesize that, in her family of origin, Jackie seems to have been the "focused on" child who bore the brunt of her family's projection processes. It would be easy to speculate that, even before the issue of her sexuality emerged as a family crisis, a good deal of the family energy, especially her mother's energy, was focused on her and what they expected her to be. In contrast to that, it can easily be imagined that Liza, in her family of origin, occupied a very different place. As a late in life youngest, with a good ten-year gap between her and her next oldest sibling, the parents most likely already had established a "projected upon" child when she was born, and this was a role she did not fulfill for them. This gave her a great deal more "freedom" than Jackie had ever experienced in her family, and this has allowed her to have relationships outside of the family that are not nearly as burdened with intensity.

EMOTIONAL CUTOFF

Bowen added the concept of **emotional cutoff** to the theory in 1975, as a way to have a concept that addressed emotional process that occurs between generations. An assumption the theory makes about parents and children is that this very special human relationship is never fully emotionally "resolved." All people are assumed to carry with them some degree of unresolved emotional attachment with their parents. Bowen (1994) writes "The degree of unresolved emotional attachment to the parents is equivalent to the degree of undifferentiation that must somehow be handled in the person's own life and in future generations" (p. 382). However, it is also possible to see that some parents "cutoff" from their adult children as well, so the concept needs to be understood in the entirety of its reciprocal dimension. It appears that Jackie and her parents are attempting to repair the cutoff that had occurred in their relationship and that they have taken some steps in this direction. The fact that she is now invited to holiday dinners and that she is welcome back into the house she was kicked out of 20 years ago, all speak to the idea that there is energy being spent by both she and her parents to repair their relationship. In these situations, it is not unusual for the steps to be cautious and tentative, and often there are also setbacks when old wounds get reopened. But from what we know to this point, overtures have been extended and inroads have been made.

In practice the concept has taken on much broader application since its inception. It now is broadly understood to be a descriptive term for understanding the ways, both large and small, that people in relationship systems come to create unresolved distances in them. Cutoff may in fact reduce a certain amount of anxiety in the here and now of difficult relationships. However, one of its hardest to recognize effects is the increased pressure that is then placed on all subsequent relationships. This pressure, more times than not, has just the opposite of its desired effect, and it appears that this is what has happened to Jackie throughout her adult life. Her spotty employment history, and the fact that at age 38, this two and a half year-long romantic relationship is the longest one she has ever been in, would appear to be evidence of her difficulties sustaining ongoing relationships with others. The lack of a viable relationship with her parents makes it likely that all of her subsequent relationships have also been impacted. This absence paradoxically makes future relationships more fraught, for such high levels of intensity often cannot usually be sustained for long periods of time. Like all the other concepts in the theory, emotional cutoff needs to be understood as a matter of degree. It is not possible to imagine a final resolve of one's relationship with one's parents, but all of us struggle to come to some terms nonetheless. The question is just how much energy goes into such an effort, and at what cost to other relationships?

SIBLING POSITION

Bowen based this part of his theory on the work of Walter Toman (1961), whose extensive work focused on the personality profiles associated with fixed **sibling positions**. While Toman did not necessarily work from a systems point of view, Bowen saw how his research easily fit within the parameters of his own thinking. Toman created ten basic sibling profiles with detailed descriptions of the attendant personality profiles that his research revealed about each. Of particular interest to Bowen were the usefulness of such personality predictions and marriage partners. Toman was able to detail things such as the likely dynamics in a marriage between an oldest male and a youngest female, based upon how each of them likely related to other siblings in their respective family of origin. Bowen (1994) incorporated Toman's work into his own ideas about "functional position" within a family system to expand on these concepts and to move them beyond simple birth order. Bowen's understandings of those things that impact a family emotional system allowed him to talk about constructs such as "functional oldest" or "functional youngest" in a family system, based not upon birth order but, rather, upon one's functional position in a family emotional unit.

Liza fits the description of a functional youngest in the classic sense. As the "baby" of the family, she understands all the perks and privileges that position entails. It means she believes that others need to cater to her needs, not the other way around. Jackie is a middle child in birth order only. However, she is also the first-born female and in that capacity may have occupied a certain functional position in her family of origin system. It seems she was anything but the accommodating "go along to get along" personality most closely associated with middle children, which helps us to understand that her birth order and functional position may be two different things. The time at which one is born into an ongoing family system usually speaks to the kinds of emotional forces that likely shaped their experiences in that system. While sibling position can never be taken with any causal certainty as the source of someone's personal style, it can be a good starting place to ask questions about the kinds of impacts and influences that likely shaped ones formative relational experiences.

Applying Your Knowledge

Where are you in the birth order of your own siblings? Typically, first-born children are said to be responsible, high achieving, and natural born leaders. They are comfortable being the center of attention and are often the "leader" of the sibling group. Middle children are often characterized as quiet and peacemakers who have learned to live in the shadow of an older sibling. Youngest children are often characterized as "social butterflies" and are characteristically seen to be the least responsible, especially in financial matters. Of course these are all broad generalizations, and there are always a number of different factors at play in any family dynamic. What a family therapist working from this point of view also often sees is that siblings of different birth orders can occupy different "functional roles" than those assigned by birth. Oldest children can "function" like youngest children in certain families, and vice versa. Do you have the characteristic traits associated with your typical place in the family? Is your functioning in the family different from your place in the birth order? Have changes in your family circumstances led to changes in functioning position among your siblings at any point in time in your family history?

SOCIETAL REGRESSION

The eighth and final concept of the theory is that of **societal regression**. It can safely be said that this is the least well researched of the eight concepts and perhaps the least relevant to direct clinical practice as well. What Bowen saw through this concept was that, in the face of sustained, chronic anxiety, societies, just as families, can begin to lose contact with their intellectually developed principles and resort to more emotionally determined decisions in order to allay the anxieties of the moment. For our purposes, the takeaway of this concept is that as a function of natural systems thinking, those constructs which

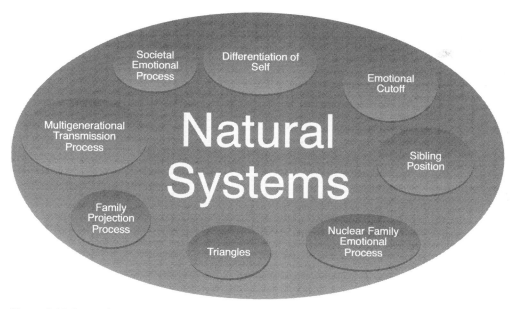

Figure 6.11 Natural Systems Theory Is the Background From Which Bowen's Eight Interlocking Concepts About Family Relationship Systems Emerged.

help us to *understand* and *explain* the dynamics of human family life, can also be successfully applied to the understanding and explanation of larger and larger social groups, up to and including entire societies.

QUESTIONS FOR REFLECTION

1. How does the concept of the emotional system change the way you think about any family, including your own?
2. How does the concept of chronic anxiety impact the way you think about doing family therapy?
3. How does the concept of an emotional triangle change the goals you have as a family therapist?
4. How does the concept of Individuality and Togetherness influence the way you look at conflict in a marriage? In parenting issues involving teenagers? In cases of domestic violence?
5. How would you describe the concept of natural systems to another family therapist who had never heard of the term?

CHAPTER SEVEN
Natural Systems Pragmatics

Christopher F. Burnett

Case Description

In this chapter, we continue with the couple that we met in Chapter 6, Jackie and Liza. The work of therapy, from a natural systems perspective, centers around the process of connecting how relationship dynamics in a person's family system bear on that person's individual functioning in other relationships. The therapist uses her knowledge of Bowen's theoretical concepts to pilot such explorations. Operating from this framework, a therapist seeks to obtain the widest possible perspectives from which to understand each member of the couple. This knowledge furthers the explorations of how they relate to one another currently. Doing this requires obtaining a multigenerational view of their respective family of origin. Collecting such a complex combination of factual and emotional information is achieved by engaging the clients in an activity called a genogram.

Genograms

A Bowen approach is largely lacking in techniques designed to make people and families change and has little interest in such efforts. For Bowen, the work of family therapy is much more about helping others a) reduce their levels of anxiety and b) be better able to adapt to the challenges of effectively living in and among multiple relationship systems. Of course, in order to do this, it is most useful to gather, as best as possible, an organized, easy to access, and comprehensive accounting of those multiple relationship systems. For a Bowen Family Systems therapist, it is also very useful if, as you do this, you can also gather information about the relationship dynamics that hold all the facts of the family together in an ongoing emotional system.

A **genogram** gives both the therapist and the client family a way to visualize the entire network of family relationships, as well as the emotional processes that underlie such relationships. Perhaps the most concrete clinical tool associated with Bowen's work is the genogram, also known to some as the family diagram. A genogram allows a therapist to work with multiple generations of a family system in the therapy room, even if there are members of the family that are not present or even living. Such an exercise allows the therapist, along with the client, to look for larger patterns of relationship behavior over much longer periods of time than any other approach.

For Bowen Family Systems therapists, doing a genogram is standard practice, and it is often begun during the very first session. It can be done on a large sheet of paper, in pencil or in pen. I prefer to do it on a whiteboard I have installed in my office, which allows me an easy way to erase mistakes or misunderstandings when large amounts of complicated, sensitive, personal information are being communicated.

Illustrating Genogram Mechanics

Jackie: We came to therapy because I am afraid that my girlfriend is becoming an alcoholic. It has been going on for a while now, but I thought it was time for us to get some professional help before things really got out of control, and it was too late.

Liza: I don't have a drinking problem. I have a problem being hounded all the time and being told what to do. You are not my mother, but you sure enjoy acting like you are. This is really no way for an equal partner to feel in a relationship, like they are constantly being observed for every little thing that they do. I am here because I want my relationship to work, but our problems have nothing to do with my going out with my friends and having a little fun. As a matter of fact, if I didn't do that once in a while, I think this relationship would be in even worse shape than it is right now.

Therapist: We will get into the specifics of all that in plenty of time. However, in order for me to be of the greatest service to the both of you, it will be important for me to have the complete picture of all the things and people that make up each of your respective family systems, so we can all have a better idea of how both of you got to this place with one another, and what the realistic options are for going forward together.

As Jackie and Liza enter the office, it is clear to me that they are quite agitated with one another. It is quite obvious that they chose not to sit together. Liza instead sought out a single chair, and Jackie stares at her as she settles in the love seat, alone. Jackie begins by announcing that the reason they are both here is because her partner Liza may have a serious drinking problem, and she wants her to get the help she needs before it is too late. Liza quickly responds that the reason they have come for couple's therapy is not because of her drinking but because she and her partner are having a very difficult time getting along lately. She said that she still wants to make the relationship work, but she is tired of feeling smothered every time she wants to go out with friends and have some fun.

I acknowledge both of them and the reasons they give for coming to therapy. I assure them that we will get to each of their complaints about what is going on in their relationship in good course, but that before we get started on those, it will be very helpful to me, and to the process of therapy, if they will allow me a little space and time to gather some information on their respective families and backgrounds before we do this. I assure them that we will get to the complaints that have brought them here, but I also let them know that, due to the way I work as a therapist, it will be important for me to have some understanding of the "entire cast of characters" that make up each of their respective family systems in order for me to do the work that I do best.

I get out of my chair, and I go to the whiteboard that I have installed along an entire wall of my office. I draw two circle figures and connect them with a dotted line to indicate that they are in a committed relationship to one another, but they are not married. I then ask Jackie where in her family system was she born? Is she the oldest? Youngest? She tells me that she is the middle child, but the only girl, with an older and a younger brother. I ask her age and then the ages of her oldest brother and her youngest brother. She tells me she is 38, that her oldest brother is 40, and her youngest brother is 34. I then ask her to give me the names of her brothers, and she tells me that the oldest one is Luis, and the youngest one is Emilio.

Doing a genogram has a number of practical, immediate uses in the situation as described above. First, it is a very effective way for the therapist to communicate nonverbally to the anxious couple just what they should expect from being in this kind of therapy. It communicates through the therapist's actions that this experience will not be one where the therapy is driven by the participants. Despite the fact that these two people are in a state of considerable agitation with one another, the therapist is not simply going to jump into the middle of their complaints. The therapist is doing their very best to communicate their own internalized knowledge that there is more to be understood here than just the immediate complaints of the day. The goal of a Bowen Family Systems therapist is to create an atmosphere where thoughtful conversation and factual information can be exchanged in a safe and nonjudgmental atmosphere. The first step to doing this is for the therapist to communicate to both parties that facts are valued over complaints, and that those facts can and will be collected within an atmosphere free of judgment or blame.

The next set of questions simply follows the family of origin up from Jackie's generation to the next previous generation. This is yet another move away from the immediacy of her complaints about Liza, but if she objects, the therapist can still easily insist that this information is necessary in order to make a full assessment of her family system, and how it relates to her presenting complaint.

Are your parents still married? Do you know what year it was that they got married? Do you know how long it was that they knew each other before they got married? Do you know what place in his family that your father was born? Is he an oldest child? How many brothers does he have? And your grandparents, your father's parents, are they still alive? No? Okay, do you know what year it was that your grandfather passed away? And your grandmother, do you know what year she died? Do you know how many years they were married? What kind of work did your grandfather do? And your grandmother, did she work outside of the house as well?

Can you tell me something about your mother's family? What child in it was she? Does she have siblings? Are they still alive? What are their names? Are they all married? Are there any separations or divorces in this family? And your grandparents on this side, are they still alive? What year was it that your grandfather passed away? What year was it when your grandmother passed away?

In taking in all this information to fill out the genogram of both family systems, the therapist undertakes this task in a calm, thoughtful, and measured tone. In doing so, it communicates to both Jackie as well as Liza that this experience will not be one where the emotional temperature is easily raised. On the contrary, in these very first steps toward developing a relationship between clients and therapist, what is being both valued and demonstrated is a *lessening* of emotional expression through the thoughtful, almost boring, gathering of factual family information. Gathering things such as names, dates, and locations, makes it difficult for either of them to find things to object to. It also conveys the idea that it will be the therapist who sets the tone for all the conversations to come. People who come in upset with one another are not given much oxygen to further fan those flames. This process may even demonstrate to them that through these conversations, a modicum of consensus is possible. In our case, if Jackie is coming into therapy with the idea that Liza is the one who needs to get fixed, taking this kind of factual family information from both of them can have the effect of taking such wind right out of her sails.

Liza, what about you in your family, where were you born? Oh, so you are a youngest. How many brothers and sisters do you have? Let's start with the oldest. Okay, she is 42, and is she married? What is her name? Lucy? Okay. How many children do she and her husband have? Do you know when they were married, what year? Is this the only marriage for both of them? And after her is Karen. And how old is she? Is she married? Do you know what year they were married? Do they have children? How many? Is this the only marriage for the both of them? And who then comes after her? Your brother Kent, how old is he? Is he married? Any children? Do you know what year he was married? Is this the only marriage for each of them? And the last of your siblings is . . . ? Rick? How old is he? Is he married? Do you know when they were married? Any children for them? Is this the only marriage for each of them? And your parents, what are their names? Are they both still alive? What is your father's birth order in his family? How old is your father? How many siblings does he have? Are all of them still alive? How old is your mother? Where was she born in her family of origin? Does she have any siblings? Are they all still living as well? Do you know when your parents were married? Are they still married? Is this the only marriage for each of them? And your grandparents on your mother's side, are they still alive? Do you know what year it was when your grandfather passed away? And your grandmother? Is she living alone now? And how old is she? What about your father's parents? Do you have any ideas about what years it was when they died?

The therapist makes it clear that this information is being gathered for the benefit of both parties (see Figure 7.1). It is being done in order to further their mutual exploration of the family processes that likely helped bring them to this point in their own relationship. The therapist is also making it clear that she will not be pushed into taking sides in the relationship right off the bat. She is insisting that the process will be orderly, fair, and thoughtful if it is to go forward at all. Many people respond positively once they recognize that there is "an adult" in the room to oversee that things do not get out of hand in their usual ways.

A second benefit of the genogram process is often how it helps to untangle confusing and/or contradictory claims. This is not to say that you can always get everyone to agree on what the facts of the family system are. It is to say that the genogram can be an exercise that allows people to express multiple points of view and to have those points of view received calmly, thoughtfully, and factually, even when they are contradictory. Here, the therapist's role should not be that of an arbiter of the truth but simply a recorder of all the information. Doing this helps a therapist to stay out of the inevitable emotional triangling that occurs in these situations. The clinician can note those people

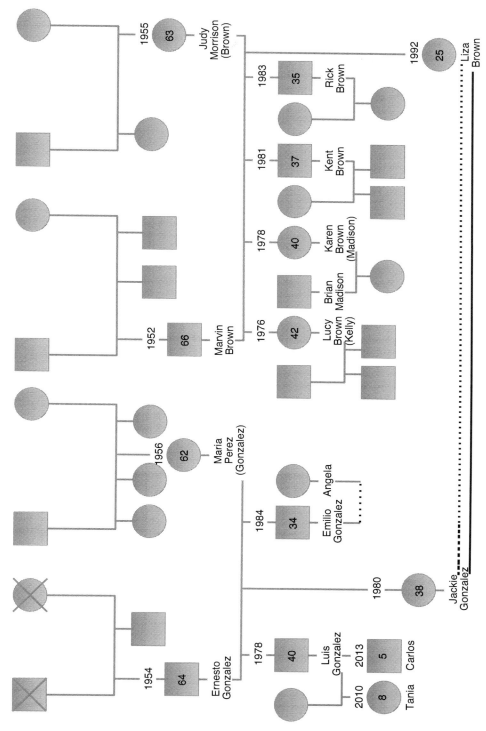

Figure 7.1 Genogram of Jackie and Liza's Family of Origin With Only Basic Facts.

or situations around which conflict seems to coalesce, without the need to "get to the bottom" of such incongruities.

Liza: You are trying to act like my mother all the time. Every time I want to do something fun, you're like, "Don't go out with them again tonight, why can't you stay home and watch a movie with me." I can make my own decisions. I have been doing it for a long time now. I am 25 and can make up my own mind without your help. You know, you always are trying to be all up in my business, and I am really sick and tired of it. I am not a child who needs to be taken care of by you.

Jackie: It's only because I am concerned about you! And I am concerned about us. When you come home all drunk and stuff, you're always in a bad mood. I want you to have fun, but I also don't like having to worry about are you okay and how you're going to be when you come home. When we were first together, we always spent a lot of time together. Now, I only get to see you two or three nights a week. I really don't like Mary and the bad influence she has on you. When she drinks she always wants to get drunk, and you just go along with her, and then both your night and mine wind up ruined.

Simply noting and recording such things, in a calm and openly curious manner, communicates to the clients that there is no need for anything like premature rushes to judgment. All information will be considered in good time and on its own merits. By calmly receiving things that many others in their life may react to emotionally, the therapist is helping to set the overall relationship atmosphere of what happens at least while both of them are in therapy. This helps ensure that information can flow freely. When anyone believes that they and their situation are being accepted without judgment, and their viewpoint is always being respected, it is likely they will continue to share more information about the workings and intricacies of their overall relationship system. If the therapist can avoid being drawn into the preexisting relationship dynamics, it makes it possible that such dynamics may be up for reconsideration by one or the other of them at some later point in the process.

Doing a genogram that focuses strictly on the facts of the respective family systems takes away the focus on the immediate here and now complaining that finger-pointing and pathologizing bring. This first pass at gathering relevant information helps put some basic facts on the table and allows the therapist not to get pulled into taking sides with either Jackie or Liza regarding the demands that each is making of the other to change. It allows that the things each of them is complaining about may be occurring, but that these behaviors on both of their parts can, should, and will be placed into a broader relationship context.

In doing this, the therapist is seeking to understand some of the larger dimensions of the emotional systems that continue to influence how Liza and Jackie navigate relationships. Once the basic facts of the family systems are collected, the therapist can use this baseline of information to begin pressing further. With a skeletal understanding of the different emotional backgrounds, the therapist can then afford to begin to flesh out more specifics. This means subtly, or sometimes not so subtly, inquiring about some of the hot button issues and their history.

Liza, how well did you know Mary before you and she started hanging out together more often? Was she someone you had spent a lot of time with before you met Jackie, or was she someone you had just gotten to know better recently? Did you always go out with your other friends as often, or is Jackie right that it has been happening more often recently than it had been in the past? If it has been happening more often recently, do you recall what changed so that you started making more time for them? Jackie, what had been going on with you around the time Liza started going out more? Was it around the time that the two of you started talking about having a baby, or did that come afterward? Jackie, when Liza comes home intoxicated, what kind of response does that usually get from you? Is that when the arguing between the two of you is worse, or does that stuff happen the next day or so? Jackie, when Liza goes out with her friends, are you ever invited to come along? If not, what do you do while she is out? If so, what is it like when the two of you are out in public with others? Does Liza make you feel comfortable around her friends, or do you feel like you are an outsider in those situations as well?

The genogram, done as a mutual exercise, allows for a wider lens for everyone to look at the current relationship system through. Instead of focusing on how Liza and her drinking are going to be fixed, both partners can be helped to see this is more usefully understood as an outcome of the relationship process between them. By knowing that Jackie is 13 years older than Liza, and that Liza is a youngest child, one can begin making certain assumptions about the likely relationship dynamic between them. By assuming that Jackie functions in the "adult" role in the relationship, the therapist can begin to ask questions to both of them about whether or not this hypothesis holds. Does Jackie feel responsible for Liza's wellbeing? Does she think that Liza isn't capable of making good decisions on her own? Is she trying to protect Liza from what she sees as Mary's bad influence? When it comes to men, does she feel that Liza is vulnerable to them? In each of these questions is contained the larger Bowenian issue of differentiation of self. How much responsibility does someone take for the actions of someone else? Discerning some sense of this is one way to estimate the overall level of anxiety in this, or any relationship system. Putting prior generations of their respective family histories on the table can then deepen the context of this relational understanding. Doing this can lead to questions designed to get at issues such as, "How much time and energy have previous generations spent assuming responsibility for others, and how have these expectations been passed down to your own generation?"

This leads then to the third practical effect of the genogram, which is to give a picture of the family *relationship* system as a multigenerational, ongoing, family *emotional* system. These efforts, aimed at increasing family systems understandings, are also efforts to accurately comprehend individuals as component parts of ongoing and long-standing emotional systems. Kerr and Bowen (1988) write:

> The emotionally determined functioning of the family members generates a family emotional "atmosphere" or "field" that, in turn, influences the emotional functioning of each person. It is analogous to the gravitational field of the solar system, where each planet and the sun, by virtue of their mass, contribute gravity to the field and are, in turn regulated by the field that each help create. One cannot "see" gravity, nor can one "see" the emotional field. The presence of gravity and the emotional field can be inferred, however, by the predictable ways planets and people behave in reaction to one another. The existence of a family emotional field is the product of an emotionally driven relationship process that is present in all families. While the intensity of this process may vary from family to family, and within the same family over time, it is always present to some degree.
>
> (p. 55)

To better understand any single individual, we need to be able to see and understand those emotional system forces that shaped them. To best understand Liza and Jackie's current difficulties, it is very useful to understand how each of them were prepared for this relationship by their experiences in their family of origin (see Figures 7.2 and 7.3). Understanding the emotional atmosphere of their parents, grandparents, siblings, and other extended family members helps bring to light more context regarding the relationship positions each of them occupied growing up, and the relationship functions they served. This information gives larger context to the current state of dynamics not only in their own relationship, but in their respective family of origin as well. In seeking to accurately understand these dimensions, they and the therapist then engage in a process aimed much more at understanding one another, and a lot less at blaming one another.

Looked at from the point of view of conventional psychotherapy or even brief family therapy, the time and effort involved in gathering information with such a broad horizon may seem unnecessarily wasteful. To most observers it seems clear that Jackie and Liza have the problem, not their parents or siblings. In this approach however, a three-generation view is a *minimal* necessity to properly understand any family as an emotional unit and to get a larger sense of the role that each member plays in the maintenance of that system. The therapist needs to be, and to stay, more interested in understanding how these systems operate than in trying to make particular aspects of them "right."

With the basic information gathered about both family systems, our therapist can begin asking about some of the history behind Jackie's relationship to her parents.

How would you describe the relationship you have with your father today? How would you describe it over the past few years since you have known Liza? Have there been any significant changes in that relationship over the past few years? How would you describe your relationship with your mother today? Have there been any changes in that relationship in the past few years? If yes, what might

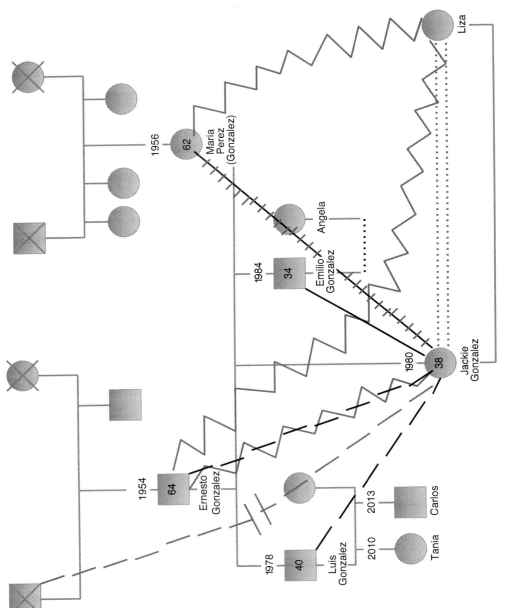

Figure 7.2 Jackie's Family of Origin Genogram With Relational Processes Shown.

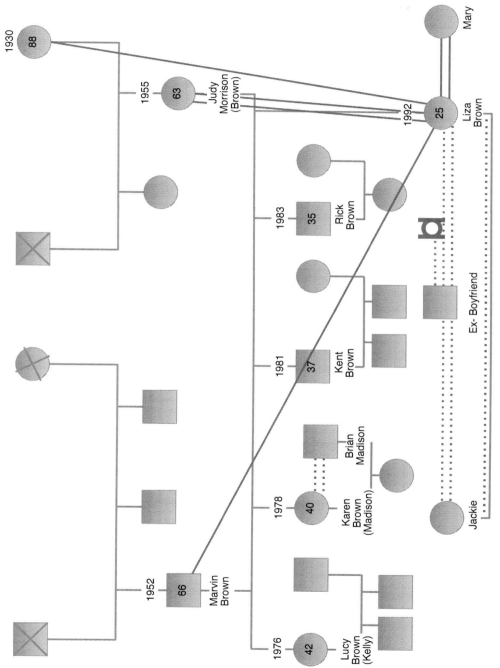

Figure 7.3 Liza's Family of Origin Genogram With Relational Processes Shown.

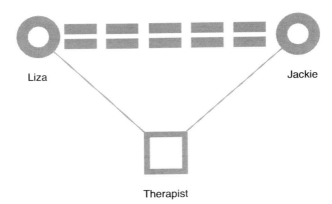

Figure 7.4 The Therapist Needs to Maintain Her Position as Being Connected to the Client's Emotional System but Not a Reactive Member in It.

you attribute those changes to? Which of your two parents would you say you are closer to? Has this always been the case, or has that changed over time? What is your relationship like with Luis? What is it like with Emilio? What do they think of your relationship with Liza? Have they told you this themselves, or is that what you are hearing from other people?

If the therapist were to align solely with Jackie and participate in her idea that what Liza is doing is what needs to be fixed, then the therapist will have been effectively coopted into both their emotional triangle and their larger emotional system (see Figure 7.4). Seeking to fix a drinking problem effectively puts the therapist on Jackie's side and has the effect of making Liza an "outsider." It also has the practical effect of eliminating any further need to explore or understand the larger systems dynamics at play in their relationship. The goal of the Bowen therapist, in this and any other situation, is to maintain a viably flexible position vis-à-vis the participants. That is, the therapist needs to have all parties to believe that they are being understood, if not always readily agreed with. It is only from this relationship position that the therapist is able to maintain her perspective as an observer of, and not a participant in, the emotional system of the clients.

Maintaining this position then means of course that our therapist must also ask Liza about the ways that her family emotional system may have an impact on the way that she is conducting herself with Jackie.

Liza, it sounds like you have a different kind of relationship with your parents than Jackie does. Can you describe your relationship with your father? Have there been any changes in it over the past few years? What does he think of your relationship with Jackie? How did he react when he found out that you were no longer interested in men? How about your mother, how would you describe your relationship with her? Have there been any changes there that you have noticed over the past few years? How did she react when you told her that you were dating Jackie? How did she react when you told her that you were moving in with Jackie? Have either of you talked about your drinking to either your father or your mother? If you didn't, what do you imagine they would say about it? If you did, what did they say about it?

The answers to these questions (and any other questions that these generate) then become a basis for more refined speculation about the actual workings of each of their respective family of origin emotional systems. By focusing on this kind of information, the therapist is seeking to keep herself out of the automatic reactive processes that likely led Liza and Jackie to their current difficulties. It is not unreasonable to infer that Jackie brings to this relationship a good deal more intensity and investment. This supposition is based on both in-room observations as well as the family emotional system that Jackie has described herself coming from. It's a reasonable theory to hold that in her family of origin, Jackie was the projected upon child in the nuclear family emotional process. She, as the only female child, seems to have attracted an extraordinary amount of the family's energy, and likely continues to do so, despite their emotional distance of the past 20 plus years. It also would not be unreasonable to hypothesize that the key relationship for her was the one between herself and her mother. The therapist could ponder (maybe even out loud if the relationship deepened sufficiently) if Jackie's mother had very high hopes and expectations for her first-born daughter (if so, it would seem Jackie has since spent a good deal of her life resisting them). If such a connection was to be made, it then might also be possible that she is operating in the very same way with regard to her expectations of Liza. It is only one among many possible ways to understand their dynamic, but it is probably as good a place as any to start.

As for Liza, it seems that she is able to engage, and then disengage from, relationships with others with a good deal more ease than Jackie. She is used to being the center of other people's attention and is comfortable being in that position. She is used to being pursued romantically and understands the advantages of being so. She seems to have grown up in an atmosphere where there was much more permissiveness and much less investment in who she was than did Jackie. For Jackie, identifying as homosexual and being in a same-sex relationship have many powerful implications throughout her family emotional system, up to and including her cutoff from her grandfather. It seems to have been one of those landmark events in her family's history that impacts people and the ways that they relate to each other forever. For Liza, it would appear that there are far fewer, and far less intense, consequences to this, as the members of her family think that she is just "going through a phase" and are seemingly nonplussed about it. If these guesses are correct (there are a lot more questions, and a great deal more information to be gathered before such assertions can be confirmed, more than we can go into in this limited space), then the therapist has a basis to talk about the *process* of the relationship between the two of them and not simply the *content* of their day-to-day disagreements and complaints.

Applying Your Knowledge

Given what you now know about genograms, create a three-generation genogram of your family. This should include you, your parents, siblings, and grandparents. If you have children, include them as well. The genogram should show ages as well as relationships between people. After you have finished creating the genogram, take some time to consider the major patterns that you can see in the family. You might consider showing the genogram to someone outside of your family to see if an outsider to the emotional system of your family can see patterns that you had not.

SELF OF THE THERAPIST IN BOWEN FAMILY SYSTEMS PRACTICE

Perhaps more than any other therapeutic approach, an enormous emphasis is placed on the role and the discipline of the self of the therapist. Becoming aware of the power of the emotional processes that have shaped one's own family relationships is a first step in helping others do the same. Bowen believed it was that a family therapist be willing to try to understand their place and functioning within their own family system. He detailed his own efforts to understand his place in his own family system (Bowen, 1994). After he talked publicly about his own 12-year effort to become more of a self in his own family, he saw that his students who went back home to visit came to understand his concepts in a much more resonant way. He came to insist that working on one's own system of family relationships was a necessary step to fully appreciate the power of such processes in all families. Bowen (1994) writes:

> I believe and teach that the family therapist usually has the very same problems in his own family that are present in families he sees professionally, and that he has a responsibility to define himself in his own family if he is to function adequately in his professional work.
>
> (p. 468)

The work of understanding yourself in the context of your own family system is important while doing Bowen Family Systems based work for a few different reasons. First, the struggle to define oneself in the face of social and emotional pressures from others is a universal human process. It is one that all human beings participate in in their own particular ways. Bowen believed that the emotional processes he saw in his schizophrenic clients' family systems were the very same emotional processes that existed in every family system, and by extension which exist in many ways throughout all forms of life (Kerr & Bowen, 1988). This made one's own family then the best place to see and learn about these powerful, natural processes.

It is hard to imagine that any therapist working with Jackie and Liza hasn't also occupied their similar relationship positions at some point in life. Most of us have had the experience trying to get the object of our affections to be emotionally closer with us. We likely have also had the experience of trying to create some distance in a relationship that felt like it was closing in uncomfortably. These are relationship positions that anyone seeking intimacy with other human beings inevitably occupy, and then usually emerge out of. If a therapist has not herself reflected on her own relationship history and processes, she could very easily be drawn into one side or the other of Liza and Jackie's relationship conflict without realizing she was doing so. This is how powerful, and how automatic Bowen believed these processes to be.

Like Liza and Jackie, most of us have also had the experience of resisting the well-intentioned suggestions of our friends and relatives about the best thing to do in a romantic relationship. Many of us have likely also ignored the sound advice we were offered by others. Someone with the ability to see the larger picture, and the experience, maturity, and compassion to know that human beings in relationships rarely act logically, can be a welcome, calming addition to any emotional triangle. But this kind of wisdom, patience, and experience doesn't come without its own effortful exploration and reflection on the part of the therapist. Learning about one's own functioning in their own emotional systems is rarely easy or painless, but it is the kind of work that pays off by expanding one's own capacities for empathy and compassion as others seek to do the same.

Clinically, it is important for the therapist to be able to join with the client family *relationship* system at the same time they are able to place themselves outside of the family's *emotional* system. This was how Bowen believed a therapist informed by his theory could best be of service. Doing this makes it possible for families to see their own processes at work. If a therapist fails to maintain a vantage point broader than that of the client, she is likely to be incorporated into the client's ongoing, automatic relationship processes. Once this occurs, rendering an outsider perspective is almost impossible. Seeing these processes at work in one's own family, and working to bring even a small bit of objectivity to them, is a critical step in being able to effectively apply the theory to the family relationship systems of others.

Broadly speaking, education is the overall goal of Bowen's work. Yet, in order for people to be able to understand their situation more clearly, anxiety (reactivity) in the relationship system must be reduced. Jackie and Liza's overall level of anxiety needs to be addressed before either of them can begin to think differently about their current situation. To do this, both of them have to feel that therapy was a safe place to express anxieties about their future with one another. Each of them have to see that the therapist solicited, welcomed, appreciated, and respected their hopes for the future as well as the pain of the past.

This requires the therapist demonstrate an ability to remain emotionally connected to both of them in the face of what may be very intense expressions of fear, anger, hurt, and disappointment, directed at one another and the therapist. It is not enough to simply tell others what they need to do. One must have firsthand familiarity with, and a genuine appreciation of, how difficult changing one's position in a family relationship system is. Commonsense, as well as life experience, tells us there are no clear or simple techniques for doing this. It is, however, generally agreed that the ability to take responsibility for oneself and one's actions is one way to promote an atmosphere of mutual calm and respect with others. With time and training, and a commitment to increasing one's own personal levels of differentiation of self, a Bowen therapist develops greater capacity for this over the course of their career. If the therapist has less of this capacity for thoughtful self-reflection than the client family does, she will likely have little of value to offer them. So, in many important ways, it is the self of the therapist that is the best indicator of success in a Bowen Family Systems approach. It is an asset that is continuously built upon throughout an entire professional career.

> **Applying Your Knowledge**
>
> What sort of self of the therapist research might you do to help you better understand your own place in the emotional system of your family of origin? What kinds of questions do you think you would like to ask other family members? Do you think you could ask these questions in a way that didn't raise other people's anxiety level? Are there any family issues you have always wondered about, but haven't gotten any answers to? What is your birth order? Do you believe it plays any role in how you relate to others? Are you able to make "I" statements in the middle of a heated argument with someone?

DETRIANGULATING

As mentioned in Chapter 6, emotional triangles are a basic building block of all human relationship systems. Human beings are always bouncing between being inside and outside of an entire series of shifting alliances of various intensities at home, work, and play. The concept of detriangulation for Bowen means that in order to be of service, a therapist has to be able to establish and maintain meaningful contact with all parties, while not getting "caught" in any one relationship. Assuming all relationships generate anxiety, and that this anxiety easily entangles others, when Jackie says that Liza needs to change in order for their relationship to continue, the therapist must convey to both of them (but particularly Liza) that this is not the only way that their situation can be understood.

Jackie: Something really has to be done here, as I can't be worried about you all the time, Liza. When you're out with Mary, I get very worried that you're talking to men at the bar and that you might go back to your old ways. It really drives me crazy. So crazy that even when you come home I know that I jump all over your case and make you all upset, but I just can't help myself. I just want us to work out so very badly. That's why this therapy is so important, because I know that if we just get professional help, we will be able to make this relationship work again like it used to.

Liza: Well I want this relationship to work too. I have a lot of investment here as well. But I can't let myself be put down by you all the time. Anytime I want to do something or go somewhere by myself, it becomes this great big production. I need my space. I'm an adult now, and I simply won't let you or anybody treat me any differently. It used to be fun for us to hang out together all the time, but when you keep nagging me about I should do this or I should do that, I just don't have time for it. (Turning to the therapist) Don't you agree? Shouldn't we be talking about ways that Jackie should be treating me more equally, more seriously, as an adult, instead of this being all about trying to get me to stop going out with my friends and drinking?

Making a relationship fix the focus of therapy is not anything out of the ordinary. However, it can also be seen as the therapist doing their part to keep the relationship anxiety manageable. Attempting to fix relationship problems is a way that many therapists manage their own anxiety. In reducing the complexities of a human relationship (like Jackie and Liza's) to a problem to be solved, the therapist is dictating what the parameters of their own involvement in that relationship will be. As the arbiter of what the problem is and how it will (or will not) be talked about, the therapist is limiting the scope of her own involvement. For many, this is an automatic response to the anxiety of others who want you to "do something."

As a contrast, a Bowen Family Systems therapist is constantly aware of this anxiety and the efforts required to manage it. One way of trying to manage it in this case would be by not getting caught up in any single description of the relationship and its dynamics. When Jackie says that Liza is going out too much, or drinking too often, instead of focusing in on one or both of these behaviors as a problem, a

Bowen therapist might instead begin to joke with Liza about how bad it must be at home for her to want to be out of it so often. While at first blush this may seem somewhat caustic or even disrespectful, the intent behind such a comment is to communicate to both parties that the therapist will not be looking for people to blame or problems to solve in these talks together.

Not getting caught up in a definitive description of the problem allows the therapist to then expand the context of the discussion. With a mindset that says neither Jackie nor Liza have a problem, the work of the therapist is to invite them to share this frame of reference for understanding just how their relationship makes sense. Once their initial level of anxiety is reduced, the therapist can engage both of them in conversations designed to help them see their situation through a larger, family systems lens.

The key to this process being successful is how well the therapist is able to stay out of the weeds of the couple's everyday concerns and complaints. Human nature being what it is, it's very difficult for we human beings not to take sides when other people are in disagreement. What Bowen Family Systems theory gives therapists are a set of tools to be able to maintain an observer's stance, even in the face of heated conflict. The process of **detriangulation** is crucial for the success of this kind of work. In almost every case, a client will want the therapist to take their side in any disagreement. A skill that is developed with time and experience is being able to take a client's "side" in a given disagreement and then also being able to talk with them about the other side of that disagreement without judgment or revealing a particular kind of prejudice. For example:

Jackie, I understand your hoping that by coming here I will give you some tools for making things between you and Liza right again. From where I sit, however, it seems to me that there is much more going on here than just Liza's going out with her friends and drinking. What I find to be true is that it takes more than two to tango in any relationship. If we use this time only to talk about things that will get Liza to straighten up and fly right, I am pretty sure she will lose all interest in coming back. It seems to me that she doesn't see anything wrong in what she is doing. One of my beliefs about people and relationships is that people do whatever they think they need to do in order to survive when they are feeling threatened. It makes more sense to me for us to talk about how both of you are feeling threatened by this relationship and where it is going than to try to assign personal blame. Liza, it sounds to me that one of the ways you might be feeling threatened in this relationship is when you feel you are not being trusted to make good decisions on your own? Am I right about that?

Kerr and Bowen (1988) suggest that the process of emotional triangulation has been observed in several species of primates and other animals. By assuming emotional triangles exist outside of human relationship systems, the concept illuminates how structure, function, and nature are amalgamated in this theory. One of the implications of this for clinical practice is that therapists need to be aware of the constant pull clients exert to enlist them in this ongoing, natural process. A good deal of the therapist's work consists in recognizing, then managing, the constant pulls and pushes of these efforts as the therapeutic relationship dynamic plays itself out. Seeing, revealing, and then being able to discuss such structures as they exist in the client's family system help to transform the inherent power of these natural processes. This requires the therapist to strive to always remain thoughtful, at the same time that she also maintains a viable emotional connection with all parties. An effective therapist working in this model would not take Jackie's "side" and insist that Liza stop doing things that put distance in their relationship. Doing this would simply be creating yet another interlocking emotional triangle, and likely just perpetuate the emotional process that they already experience, rendering therapy to be a recapitulation of what happens with significant others in each of their lives.

Trust is a crucial issue in all psychotherapy. It usually takes some time and no small amount of patience before clients give you glimpses into the deeper structures and meanings of their relationships. For someone working from a Bowen point of view, it is key that the therapist "keep their fingerprints off" of those structures and meanings as much as is possible. The discipline and knowledge acquired when someone does their own family of origin work helps them to recognize the ongoing triangling efforts client family members undertake. Not only must a therapist recognize these efforts, she must also tactfully and respectfully deflect them in order to stay in viable contact with those initiating them. Experience and training help you to recognize, and then decline, such entreaties without creating more anxiety in the process.

It is a very human tendency to want to offer advice regarding the affairs of others. Most forms of psychotherapy are built upon this very impulse. But for a Bowenian, the discipline of this work rests on recognizing, and then resisting, the impulse to tell others what to do. As Kerr and Bowen (1998) write:

> In going against the emotional grain, one's emotional autonomy in relationship to a problem between two others is communicated. People recognize immediately when a response to them is not the automatic expected one. One can define a self in this way. Defining a self does not necessarily involve a strong statement of where one stands on a particular issue. A self is sometimes communicated most effectively by what is *not* said or done.
>
> (p. 153, italics in original)

Seeing and understanding the larger, often automatic, forces that underpin the client's relationship system requires the therapist to accept the idea that what happens in that system is not hers to determine. It is only hers to observe or offer commentary on. What the client does with those observations and speculations is clearly understood to be the client's responsibilities. It usually takes a long time for therapists who want to be "helpful" to come to terms with this notion.

Key Figure

Michael Kerr

Michael Kerr was born in 1940. He served in the US Navy for two years and returned to the United States in July 1973. Kerr attended a lecture of Murray Bowen's in 1965 at Georgetown University Medical Center. This was during Kerr's junior year of medical school. The talk, which was about family processes, was particularly relevant for Kerr since he had an older brother who had recently been diagnosed as schizophrenic. Given that Bowen's initial work with families centered around those families where one member was diagnosed as schizophrenic, Kerr related to the processes being discussed. During his medical residency in psychiatry, Kerr decided to explore Bowen's systems ideas rather than the traditional individual approach most other psychiatric residents were pursuing.

In 1972, Kerr became a faculty member at the Georgetown Family Center. In 1990, Kerr succeeded Murray Bowen as Director of the Georgetown Family Center. He had a 20-year collegial relationship with Bowen and became one of the leading voices of natural systems theory. He served as the founding editor of *Family Systems: A Journal of Natural Systems Thinking in Psychiatry and the Sciences*. He held this position from 1994 to 2014. Kerr co-wrote with Bowen the most influential text on natural systems theory, *Family Evaluation: An Approach Based on Bowen Theory* (Kerr & Bowen, 1988). This book still serves as the definitive source of Bowen natural systems theory.

After leaving the Georgetown Family Center, he moved back to his home state of Maine, and there he founded the Bowen Theory Academy. The Bowen Theory Academy is an online venture that is host to a variety of educational materials and activities related to the promotion of Bowen Family Systems theory and thinking, including webcasts and structured lecture series.

Kerr has promoted the ideas of natural systems theory, especially the connection between Bowen theory and evolutionary theory, the notion of differentiation and its application in clinical work, and family emotional process. Recently, he proposed to add the concept of the unidisease to Bowen theory. The unidisease concept is based upon the notion that, regardless of the clinical symptom that the individual/family presents with, there are similar family relationship patterns that can be found in families.

Michael Kerr continues to promote the ideas of Bowen Theory and natural systems theory.

Therapist as Coach

Titleman (2008) writes:

> Eventually Bowen understood that the basic parental–child triangle was embedded or interlocked in triangles involving each spouse/parent in their family of origin, and those triangles were interlocked in still other triangles in the larger extended family making up the multigenerational process. It was at this point that Bowen began describing his efforts as being that of a *coach* rather than a therapist to one or more individuals in a family, undertaking the effort to define or differentiate a self in the family of origin and extended family. Bowen chose the term coach because the focus was no longer mainly on the therapist's staying detriangled from the couple or family. At this time, his focus was to coach an individual to go back to his or her family and make an effort to detriangle from various primary and secondary triangles, in the service of differentiating a self. In other words, the term therapist refers to the therapist's management of self in relation to the family members, and the term coach refers to teaching, supervising, and consulting with a family member in his or her detriangulating efforts, and other aspects of differentiating a self. He or she implements this effort outside the consultation room, in the context of contact with his or her family. . . . The term coaching is most often used when referring to the consultation process with one family member.
>
> (p. 44)

Let's say that in our case the therapist has been successful in getting Liza or Jackie to give up the idea that the other partner needs to be fixed. The theory holds that, if just one of them is able to do this, the overall level of anxiety in the relationship will be significantly reduced. If the overall level of anxiety in the relationship is reduced, it then becomes possible for that person to begin to think about the relationship, and the larger dynamics around it, in new and different ways.

If this happens, the therapist can then move into a different functional role in the system of the relationship triangle. Instead of simply managing the anxiety between the two partners, the therapist can begin moving into a much more thoughtful, reflective, and educational role. Bowen (1994) talked about this as the role of being a "**coach**." In this role, he said it was possible to begin to educate clients about the ways that all family systems function and then help people to apply this knowledge to understanding their own family system and how it functions. Bowen (1994) writes:

> As the system becomes more "open" and he can begin to see the triangles and the part he plays in the family reaction patterns, he can begin the more complex process toward differentiating himself from the myths, images, distortions, and triangles he had not previously seen. This is a big order and a mission that cannot be accomplished quickly. The effort to help or to supervise someone in this effort has been called "coaching" since it is so similar to the relationship of a coach to an athlete who is working to improve his athletic ability. The initial goal is to get the trainee started. Most of learning comes as the trainee works towards his goal. The trainee is aware that progress depends on him. The process is quite different from conventional concepts of therapy.
>
> (pp. 539–540)

One of the first steps in this process of coaching then is helping the client to understand the value of seeking out "**person to person relationships**" with members of their family of origin (Bowen, 1994). When the anxiety between Liza and Jackie is lowered, and Jackie agrees to continue to seek this kind of help in order to understand her history of adult relationships better, one of the first things she might be encouraged to do is to seek to have better person to person relationships with the members of her nuclear family, especially her parents.

Bowen talks about the efforts to seek person to person relationships as the kinds of experiences which help someone to achieve new levels of maturity. He says,

> As a beginning effort, I have suggested to people "If you can get a person to person relationship with each living person in your extended family, it will help you 'grow up' more than anything else you could ever do in life."
>
> (Bowen, 1994, p. 540)

Given the history of Jackie and her parents, this kind of directive might be met with a high degree of resistance at first. However, with the information that was gathered doing the genogram, the "coach" can credibly talk with her about how the high levels of intensity she has experienced in all of her adult relationships might also be related to the intensity of cutoff she has experienced in her relationship to her parents. While recently there have been some movements made toward repairing these relationships, it would still be very important for her to work on having a "person to person" relationship with each of them individually. Bowen cautions that doing this is very different than seeing them together or at holidays, because the intensity of the one on one relationship brings out an entirely different set of dynamics between two people.

> ## Applying Your Knowledge
>
> Where do you think the major emotional triangles exist in your family? How can you tell when the anxiety in one of these triangles gets increased? How do you know when the anxiety level in that triangle is reduced? How would you describe your relationships with each of your biological parents? With any step-parents? With your siblings? What things might you try to do to have even more of a person to person relationship with each of them? What impact do you think making such an effort might have on the other adult relationships in your life?

A second dimension of family dynamics exploration might be what Bowen (1994) called "becoming a better observer and controlling one's own emotional reactiveness" (p. 541). These two *assignments* as he calls them are very closely related to one another. In going back to explore the relationship processes in one's family of origin, developing an ability to become a better observer of familiar things allows a person the same kind of larger, distancing perspective that was important for the therapist as described above. The ability to observe versus just reacting helps a person to move beyond anger and blaming. It allows them to explore different relationship pathways within the system. If someone can operate differently within their system, they might have the experience of controlling their automatic emotional reactiveness to others, even briefly. This in turn can allow for different kinds of interactions, conversations, and explorations.

A third dimension of exploring one's own family of origin is described as "Detriangulating self from emotional situations" (Bowen, 1994). Here Bowen says, "The overall goal is to be constantly in contact with an emotional issue involving two other people and self, and to always have a neutral response. To go silent is perceived by the other as an emotional response" (p. 542). Essentially, this is the same skill the therapist in our case study exhibited when Jackie and Liza first entered therapy. If the therapist provided a good model for how this can be done, by staying out of the automatic triangling processes that the two of them brought into the office, then Jackie and Liza might have a model of how to behave to do the same things when they go back to the members of their family of origin. Genuine, nonjudgmental curiosity about how things in a relationship system actually work, and not predetermined ideas about how they should work, is a key characteristic of this ability. Asking someone to apply this notion in their own family of origin, around issues with long and complicated emotional histories, is no small task and is quite the accomplishment when it occurs.

Effectiveness of Natural Systems Theory

Measuring success in conventional psychotherapy is always a challenge under the best of circumstances. This challenge is heightened exponentially when the overarching goal of your work is to help others to better understand how human relationship systems work. All of the processes and steps described here are aimed at helping people get the distance and perspective necessary to increase their ability to think about their place in the various human relationship systems they are a part of. Clearly, there can never be a definitive end point to such a process. So how can Bowen Family Systems therapists claim that their work is effective?

Many times the effectiveness of this approach is viewed through the lens of the ability of clinicians to effectively navigate difficult, complex relationship situations, where emotional reactivity is high. The ability to look at all sides, and from multiple dimensions, allows practitioners to effectively engage with people across the widest spectrum of human relationship issues possible. The ability to remain committed to the process of better understanding, in the face of constant demands from all involved to align or intervene somehow, is a very rare, but very valuable set of skills. The simplistic way that the question of effectiveness is often answered is to say the goal of this work is to raise others' level of differentiation. This answer is tricky, however, as it implies an investment about how someone else should be on the part of the therapist. "Differentiation is a product of a way of thinking that translates into a way of being. It is not a therapeutic technique" (Kerr & Bowen, 1988, p. 108). Effective therapy from a Bowen Family Systems framework does not produce conventionally measurable changes in behavior; it produces different ways of thinking, which then produce different ways of being in close emotional relationship with others.

I have told my students and supervisees it seems to me that Bowen Family Systems theory is much more immediately useful for the therapist than it is for the client. I find that the more time a person spends in serious company with these ideas and concepts, the better able they are to manage various people and relationship situations, both professionally and at home. Once this is understood, many students report feeling a good deal less pressure to "do" Bowen in the therapy room.

Kerr and Bowen (1988) make the distinction between *basic* and *functional* levels of differentiation. "It is the *basic* level of differentiation that is largely determined by the degree of emotional separation a person achieves from his family of origin" (p. 98, italics in original). Conversely, "Functional level is influenced by the level of chronic anxiety in a person's most important relationship system. . . . It can rise and fall quickly, or be stabilized over long periods, depending largely on the status of central relationships" (p. 99). Thirty plus years of clinical experience has shown me that it is a small percentage of clients who invest the time and energy needed to affect their own family functioning at this basic level.

For the vast majority of those seeking help, once the anxiety around the presenting problem is lowered, the motivation to continue working on oneself diminishes considerably. That is not to say that they don't feel helped or relief. It is just that continuing the efforts to learn more about how their own family systems operate seems beside the point. Effecting functional differentiation in a relationship is not that hard to do, it happens all the time. Therapists of almost any stripe can rightfully claim to be agents of change at this level of relationship. However, changing a family system's basic relationship structure, when it happens, does so only over a period of time. And even then, what is required is a consistent and thoughtful effort on the part of that person seeking to make a change happen. Usually such a person faces considerable resistance or outright opposition from others in this effort. A professional who possesses both knowledge and experience of what this is like can be a very helpful guide to this process. But such a professional also understands that to be transformative, this journey also needs to be personal, and it is often arduous and full of doubt. For many clinicians, this uncertainty around the question of what it means to be effective is the great stumbling block to working from this model. But for those of us who find these ideas fascinating and worthy of lifelong attention, this is their great appeal.

QUESTIONS FOR REFLECTION

1. What do you think the three main reasons for collecting information in the form of a genogram are?
2. List three reasons you think it is important for a therapist to maintain a position of neutrality when working with family systems.

3. In a Bowen Family Systems approach, why is it important for a therapist to work on her own family relationship system?
4. How important is it for a Bowen Family Systems therapist to work to fix the presenting complaint of their clients? Explain.
5. Talk about three reasons you believe that Bowen Family Systems based therapy is effective for use with family systems.

CHAPTER EIGHT
Constructivist Aesthetics

Michael D. Reiter with James Hibel

CASE DESCRIPTION

Frank and Stella, a cisgender, heterosexual, American couple, have been together for nine months. Frank is a 67-year-old black male while Stella is a 64-year-old white female. Both were previously married. Frank's wife of 30 years died of a heart attack four years previously. Stella's husband of 35 years died ten years ago from complications during a surgery. Frank has no children while Stella has three, who are all adult and do not live at home.

The two met at a singles dance and hit it off. Frank was happy to be with Stella because many of the women he had been meeting were, in his words, "not nice" and he felt disrespected by them. Some of the women he had been meeting would give him a phone number, which would not be a correct number when he called. Other women would excuse themselves from their conversation to go to the bathroom and not return. Frank likes that Stella listens to him and is patient.

Stella enjoys the time she spends with Frank, as they do many things together, such as going to music concerts, dances, and various other activities. However, she is hesitant to move forward with the relationship and move in together because she thinks that Frank is too much of a worrier. She senses that he is "different," but she knows that he cares about her, and she is willing to accept what she views as his eccentricities.

Frank and Stella are also having some sexual difficulties. Frank desires sexual contact from Stella, but with her providing physical pleasure to him. He does not touch her breasts and does not try to engage in intercourse. Stella is somewhat frustrated by this and believes it is because Frank has some past problems. She does not want to push the matter with him.

Before we jump into thinking about what one might do if this couple consulted a therapist, in this chapter, we will explore how utilizing a constructivist and biological perspective can help us to view systems, and more specifically **language systems**, including this couple system, in a way that might help a therapist decide what to do.

CONSTRUCTIVISM

A therapist might be inclined to start by describing the couple in terms of what their problems are, possible goals, and what is the truth about them. Alternately, when we are looking at our couple, Frank and Stella, constructivists would encourage us to first ask ourselves whether the understanding that we have of them corresponds to an objective reality. As therapists, we develop a view of how people interact with one another. In the previous chapters, we covered many concepts that help determine what is happening for our client (i.e., how they maintain homeostasis, how they engage in communication on multiple levels, how their level of anxiety impacts their self-differentiation, etc.). In this chapter we explore a very different kind of conceptualization, that of constructivism. This viewpoint highlights the idea that what happens within a person is related to the person's biological and social context as well as our role as observers in describing what is real and true.

Objectivism holds that there is a reality independent from the observer that can be known. A therapist who takes an objectivist position would want to do an assessment of each person and the couple as a whole, in order to determine the "facts" of the case. The therapist would assume that there are objective facts waiting to be discovered and that a well-trained therapist can discover them. An interesting note is that the therapist may not know that they are taking an objectivist position, simply assuming that this is the right way to think. During the assessment, the objectivist-based therapist would attempt to discover if Frank has an anxiety disorder and/or an adjustment disorder, the impact that this potential anxiety disorder has on him, the impact the anxiety disorder has on Stella, the impact that the potential adjustment disorder has on Frank, the impact that the potential adjustment disorder has on Stella, as well as other factors that are present in new relationships between elders. Other objectivist agendas might include assessing the couple's sexual life to determine whether there are problems and the potential of Frank having a sexual dysfunction.

However, in past chapters, we have talked about the map not being the territory. While it can take many forms, **constructivism**, a variation of which has also been called second order cybernetics, generally holds to the notion that the knower creates the known (see Raskin, 2002; Rosen & Kuehlwein, 1996). It is a theory of knowing, not a theory of being (von Glasersfeld, 1995). This shifts the focus of therapy from an assessment of *what is*—which would be an attempt to gain an objective truth of the situation—to an exploration of how the person, in this case the client (and, of course, the therapist), *constructs what they know*.

As constructivists explain it, constructivism is a meta-theory (a theory about theory) that focuses on human knowing (Neimeyer, 1993). Mahoney (1995) clarified:

> Essentially, constructivism is a family of theories and therapies (a) that humans are proactive (and not passively reactive) participants in their own experience—that is, in all perception, memory, and knowing; (b) that the vast majority of the ordering processes organizing human lives operate at tacit (un- or super-conscious) levels of awareness; and (c) that human experience and personal psychological development reflect the ongoing operation of individualized, self-organizing processes that tend to favor the maintenance (over the modification) of experiential patterns.
>
> (pp. 44–45)

In other words, people are organized to make meaning of their experience in ways that are mainly outside of their awareness and that these understandings serve to organize how the person functions. Further, whatever happens within the individual in meaning-construction and self-organization is influenced by, and influences, the social systems the individual is connected to.

Neimeyer (2009) stated that constructivists are "interested in how people use language in a way that shapes and delimits how people appraise themselves, others (especially vulnerable others), and life difficulties in ways that are problematic and disempowering" (p. 17). One of the most important aspects of constructivism is the view of people as active agents rather than passive recipients of information, as they create their understanding of their environment, mental constructs, and behavior. In this sense, knowledge does not objectively represent a single, objective reality. Rather, our constructed knowledge fits the reality that we experience.

From a constructivist perspective, reality is *constructed* by observers through their biology, primarily their perceptual processes (see Figure 8.1). Since the biology and perceptions of each individual are uniquely his or her own, the reality that an individual constructs will be unique. This accounts for the tendency of constructivists to deny the existence of an objective reality beyond that constructed by the observing individual. As von Glasersfeld (1984) stated, "But for constructivists, all communication and all understanding are a matter of interpretive construction on the part of the experiencing subject" (p. 19).

Figure 8.1 Constructivism Is Based on the Notion That the Individual Takes in Outside Events Through Perceptual Processes and Then Makes Interpretations Based on Her Own Unique Perceptions of Contact With the Environment.

Here, importance is placed on how the individual construes experience into meaning. Given that each person has an exclusive biology and perceptual process, we all make unique interpretations as to what is.

von Glasersfeld (1995) further explained the basis of constructivism,

> It starts from the assumption that knowledge, no matter how it be defined, is in the heads of persons, and that the thinking subject has no alternative but to construct what he or she knows on the basis of his or her own experience.
>
> (p. 1)

Thus, most constructivists will usually not deny that there is a reality "out there" but insist that the individual cannot contact it without influencing the way that she understands that contact. A constructivist would need to consider how the therapist is constructing a viewpoint of Frank and Stella and that this viewpoint is not the objective truth of who Frank and Stella are as individuals and a couple, but instead, is a function of how the therapist develops a view of them. Frank and Stella's therapist's viewpoint will most likely be different than other therapists' viewpoints, although there will likely be many overlaps based on how various therapists understand the multitude of personality and therapy theories. Thus, the therapist who states, "This is who Stella and Frank are" will be making a serious omission, as she will not be explaining that this understanding is her own.

While this distinction might seem like a small matter, this is a serious jump for us to make, as most people have been raised in a world in which we are taught that there is a world out there for us to know—a world separate from what we think about it. We have grown up taking and making many assessments to determine who we are. These assessments can seem "accurate" and outside of the influence of the assessor, and summarize the reality of who a person is. We can even look at this in terms of the "quizzes" that people take that are presented in magazines, such as GQ or *Cosmopolitan*. These quizzes usually focus on one's personality or sexuality. When people take them they may view these as objective truth (reality) without realizing that when they are answering each question, they are not—and cannot—answer these questions objectively, but always through their own interpretation of the questions, themselves, the answers, etc.

REALISM

Those adhering to an objectivist position explain that there is an environmental determinism, which is connected to an objective environment. We respond to real stimuli, which have real and predictable effects on us. We can view this as a **realist** position (Rosen, 1996). This is where the behavioral camps fall: that human beings are predicated on behaving based on what the reinforcement and punishment schedules are that are acting upon them. To help exemplify this position, think of what you know of Pavlov's dogs where food got paired with a sound (a bell). This theory of the connection between conditioned and unconditioned stimuli and responses is called classical conditioning. A second major behavior theory is operant conditioning in which what happens after a behavior determines whether the behavior will happen more or less in the future. If some type of reinforcement (positive or negative) occurs after a behavior, there is a higher likelihood for that behavior to happen in the future. If some type of punishment

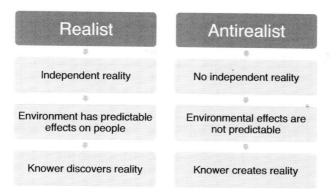

Figure 8.2 The Differences Between a Realist and Antirealist Perspective. Realism Holds That the Knower Can Access an Objective Reality While Antirealism Holds That What We Think We Know Is Created by the Individual.

occurs after a behavior, there is a lower likelihood that the person would engage in this behavior. With all of these behavioral views, the individual does not think about the behavior; it is the environmental consequences that determine the frequency of the behavior. This type of determinism does not allow much space for theories of mental construction (von Glasersfeld, 1995). Bateson (1972/2000) called this way of thinking into question when he thought about what difference it might make to have the same contingencies take place in changing contexts.

We can explore here the distinction between the realist and the antirealist epistemology (see Figure 8.2). Constructivists hold more of an **antirealist position**, where the knower makes reality rather than discovers it (Held, 1995a). The notion of discovering is premised on the idea that there is an objective reality out there, waiting for the right person to discover it, existing before being discovered. From a constructivist perspective, where the observer makes reality, the knower is not able to contact an independent reality, since reality is subjective, based upon the person's knowing process. Realism, then, purports an independent reality that is objective; it is not based on the knower. Constructivists propose the opposite; reality is created in the body of the observer. Thus, for a constructivist, a therapist cannot contact the world, outside of her way of understanding the world.

Radical Constructivism

There is, therefore, a biological component to constructivism, in that constructivists know that we are not contacting the actual objects in the world but, rather, their representations in our body. When Frank looks at Stella, he is not actually seeing Stella. He is seeing light reflections of her that are captured by his retina and transferred into his brain (the process is much more complicated than this, but for simplicity's sake, we will explain it in this manner). Frank also may have eye problems, such as being colorblind or having glaucoma, which then would alter his perception of what Stella looks like. The construction that Frank is making of Stella would also include interpretive processes, which include his cognitive constructs of people, such as his views and feelings on what people should and should not look like, and the ways he would describe this to himself and others through language. The constructivist would still understand that these descriptions are not accurate descriptions of the reality of Stella but, rather, a consequence of Frank's internal processes.

We can also think of these issues in terms of **radical constructivism** where the knower can only know through his own experience, and thus, there is no objective reality (Raskin, 2002; von Glasersfeld, 1984). What each individual knows is based on the structure of each person's perceptual system, which is a closed system to the outside world. We are impacted by events outside the body, which our bodies transform, rather than simply taking it in. While there may be consensus between people of "what is," the experience of contacting that thing is different for each person. This goes to the notion that no thing/event in itself has meaning. Rather, meaning is the outcome of our transformations of input, which allows us to provide a frame to it (and in therapy to engage in reframes).

von Glasersfeld (1984) explained, "Radical constructivism, thus, is *radical* because it breaks with convention and develops a theory of knowledge in which knowledge does not reflect an 'objective' ontological reality, but exclusively an ordering and organization of a world constituted by our experience" (p. 24, italics in original). Thus, radical constructivists place an emphasis on subjectivity rather than objectivity. There is not a denial of events outside of us, but an understanding that what we experience are our own constructed models of what is. von Glasersfeld (1995, p. 51) provided the fundamental principles of radical constructivism:

1.
- Knowledge is not passively received either through the senses or by way of communication.
- Knowledge is actively built up by the cognizing subject.

2.
- The function of cognition is adaptive, in the biological sense of the term, tending towards fit or viability.
- Cognition serves the subject's organization of the experiential world, not the discovery of an objective ontological reality.

The constructivist epistemology shifts our understanding away from the idea that we can objectively view what is happening for our clients, and know the "truth" of the situation. In the field of therapy, much emphasis has been placed on objectivity—that the therapist can understand the world of the client (through empathy) or understand why the client is doing what he is doing (through means such as assessments and diagnoses). Instead, constructivists believe that therapists are constructing a meaning, a construction that is the therapist's rather than the client's, including the idea that objective assessments and diagnoses are the results of the constructions of the test designer or diagnostician. This construction becomes a map upon which the therapist operates (see Figure 8.3). Here is where Korzybski's important statement fits nicely with constructivism: the map is not the territory. Whatever conceptualization the therapist working with Frank and Stella develops, it is the therapist's construction—the therapist's map—and not what actually is.

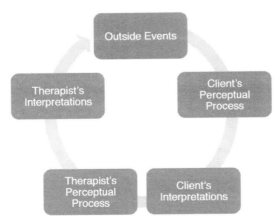

Figure 8.3 In Therapy, Therapists Are Not Able to Access Objective Truth About Their Clients. What They Know Is Based on Their Own Biology and Perceptual Processes.

Observer

From a constructivist perspective, the observer becomes essential, as it is through the observer's experience that knowledge is created. This is knowledge in a very local realm—the individual person. von Foerster (2002) called this Maturana's Theorem Number One: "Anything said is said by an observer" (p. 283). The observer cannot help but first construct meaning in the way of that particular person. Based on this theorem, we can explore some of the conceptions happening in the therapy room with our case couple. When Frank states that before connecting with Stella many women he had tried to talk to were rude, we understand that this is a languaged report of a perception that is coming from him. Other observers, who may have been in contact with these same women, or had been able to view the interactions between Frank and these women, would perhaps have very different perceptions. Stella's view of Frank as "different" comes from her experience with other men that she then compares to Frank. Further, the therapist observes Frank, Stella, and their interaction and sees this from her own biological and perceptual processes, including the influence of her theoretical model, as well as personal experiences. Thus, each of these three individuals' exclamations happen from their own perspective and, perhaps to the consternation of most laypeople, they are equally real from each of their own perspectives.

This leads us into an exploration of the self. From a constructivist perspective, the self is based on an awareness of what one is doing and experiencing (von Glasersfeld, 1995). In explaining this viewpoint, von Glasersfeld altered Descartes' notion of "I think, therefore I am" to "I am aware of thinking, therefore I am" (p. 122). Thinking back to Bateson, on the one hand, the map is not the territory. Rather, the map is an individual's construction of the territory that is out there. At the same time, it could equally be said that the map is the territory, since both map and territory have been constructed by the observer. This places importance on how the individual experiences himself. Life is not about how one conforms to the rigors of the outside world but, rather, how one transforms outside stimuli into a personal construct.

From this perspective, we cannot be objective in our understanding. Our contact with the world is always filtered and transformed. First, a stimulus has to impact one of our sense organs. That stimulus is then transferred into chemical and electrical signals that reach our brain, and then our brain records the data as an experience. Further, based on various characteristics of our experience, we place certain importance and understanding to these stimuli. For instance, a man and woman may understand an interaction differently just based upon their gender, as gender socialization plays a significant role in how people come to make perceptions in general—and then perceptions of who they are in particular. This might also be the case based on someone's racial identity, sexual orientation, age, relationship status, weight, height, etc. When Stella is constructing an understanding of who Frank is and what her relationship with him is, it is based on her mental constructs of being a heterosexual white female. Additionally, she is also developing a perception based on her age, as she would likely understand the relationship with Frank differently than she would have when she was in her 20s. Stella is constructing a "Frank" that fits within her understanding of what is real.

Applying Your Knowledge

Take a second and think about how you understand who you are. Perhaps you can do this simple activity that is often used when helping people to explore their self-concept. Write the phrase: "I am _____" ten times. Then fill in the ten blanks. Now, look at your answers. What might they have in common? How might your answers be based on your age? Your gender? Your race? Your religion? Your family situation (i.e., whether you came from a nuclear family, divorced family, remarried family)? Your sexuality? Transport yourself 20 or 30 years into the future and think about how you might possibly fill in the blanks. What might be different?

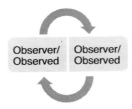

Figure 8.4 The Interpersonal Process Where the Observer Is Also the Observed.

An observer does not exist independent of the observed (see Figure 8.4). When interaction happens, the observed also becomes an observer and an observer an observed. This goes to Heinz von Foerster's Corollary Number One (in connection to Maturana's Theorem Number One): "Anything said is said to an observer" (p. 283). Thus, couples are not one but two units/entities that are having an interaction. By being an observer, the person pays attention to their transformed perceptions of the other and the other's environment. Frank cannot know Stella outside of how he takes in and constructs meaning. When he engages Stella, he takes in his perception of both she and the larger systems she is involved with (such as her children, her work life, or her friends). Throughout this process, he is making distinctions between himself, Stella, and the environment. Maturana explained, "The basic cognitive operation that we perform as observers is the operation of distinction" (Maturana & Varela, 1980, p. xix). As we discussed in Chapter 4, how we distinguish any one thing is through making a distinction between it and what it is not. According to Maturana (1988), observers make distinctions in language. We will be talking a lot more about the importance of language over the next several chapters, as it is the medium in which we come to construct reality.

POSTPOSITIVISM

Science and research have usually centered around the notion of empiricism, where the researcher, separate from what is being studied, can determine the truth. This is often referred to as **positivism**—the idea that objective truth can be discovered by an observer who is neutral. For instance, if a researcher wants to know whether one form of therapy is more effective in garnering positive outcomes than another form (or better than no treatment), the researcher would use the scientific method and randomly assign one group to the treatment condition and one group to the control condition (this is for a simple between subjects experiment). Using an experimental control group to reduce confounding variables and using valid and reliable measures for assessment, the researcher then uses statistics to determine if the difference in outcome scores for the two groups is greater than just by chance. Throughout all of this, the researcher attempts as much as possible to not influence the study—to reduce researcher bias. This then will let the researcher know, with a high degree of confidence, whether one treatment approach is "better" than another. This type of positivist viewpoint is usually associated with a quantitative research epistemology.

However, **postpositivists** understand that the observer inevitably influences what is observed—that the observer is part of the observed, and that detached neutrality is not possible (see Figure 8.5). In our research example, this comes in the form of the researcher's beliefs, hypotheses, knowledge, and own influence, to varying degrees, what is being observed. The researcher decided in advance what model to look at, what to compare it to, what constitutes success, and a myriad of other decisions, most of which are assumed and unexamined. From a constructivist research perspective, the form of a researcher's questions, the affability of the researcher, the response the participant has to the researcher are all part of the equation. Equally important, rather than using statistics, with their assumptions of objectivity, the researcher's understanding of the data leads to a construction of the meaning of the data that is potentially

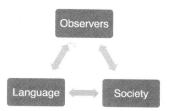

Figure 8.5 The Connection Between Observers, Language, and Society.

different than another researcher engaging in the same study. The researcher is part of the assessment instrument, rather than separate from it. This type of viewpoint is usually associated with a qualitative research epistemology. Thus, in research, positivists tend to engage in quantitative methods while postpositivists may utilize both quantitative and qualitative methods, maintaining a conscious awareness of the consequences of the method they have selected.

Reality

Constructivists, in general, hold that there is not objectivity. Maturana (1988) added clarification by distinguishing between two kinds of objectivity: objectivity-without-parentheses and objectivity-in-parenthesis (see Figure 8.6). **Objectivity-without-parentheses** conforms with traditional ideas of reality where objects exist outside of us, and we can discover that reality objectively. In **objectivity-in-parentheses**, the observer makes distinctions that determine for the observer what is being observed. These distinctions demonstrate that the observer is never knowing reality, but is constructing it—hence the parentheses around anything that is said to be known. This sense of there not being an objective reality holds, no matter how many observers agree about what they are construing (i.e., how they are making distinctions). That is, every person in the world might agree that we live on a planet called Earth, yet they are doing so having each constructed their vision and understanding of Earth.

Within this, there are varying degrees of fit between individuals in how each person is languaging their experience. We can look at objectivity-in-parenthesis as holding existence (of an object/reality) dependent on what the observer does (see Figure 8.7). This goes to von Foerster's (1984) **aesthetical imperative**:

Figure 8.6 Positivist Position of Understanding Reality Where the Observer Accesses Objective Reality.

Figure 8.7 Postpositivist Position and the Aesthetical Imperative Where the Observer Takes Ownership of His Own Constructions of What Is.

"If you desire to see, learn how to act." For the constructivist therapist working with Frank and Stella, this leads to the conceptualization of each of them changing self rather than trying to change the other, since the self of each is the source of their reality. When people accept that they construct their own reality, they are more readily available to accept responsibility for their actions. Instead of Frank saying, "It went wrong because Stella is X type of person" or Stella saying, "We could be happier if it wasn't for Frank being Y," each might change his or her own actions or perceptions in order to "see" themselves, the other, and the relationship differently. Relatedly, Maturana defined **violence** as an act in which one person tries to negate the reality of another, or replace it with his own reality. **Love** becomes defined as the opposite, an acceptance of the reality of the other.

There is also the notion of the **ethical imperative**. von Foerster (1984) explained the ethical imperative in the following way, "Act always so as to increase the number of choices." If Frank and Stella were utilizing the ethical imperative, they would understand that their understanding about the other is not limited to the construction that each of them has currently made. Stella views Frank as being "different." This viewpoint may limit how she perceives what he might do. This may lead to a self-fulfilling prophecy (Watzlawick, 1984). Instead, the more that Stella frames her perceptions of Frank as her perceptions, the more she will be open to new understandings of Frank.

Autopoiesis

We've been talking in this chapter about how people take in information from the outside world and construct knowledge. In previous chapters, we primarily talked about a system in reference to a couple or a family. Yet, as explained in Chapter 1, systems can also be individuals. This is because the individual is a complete unit that is self-contained. In constructivist terms, this notion has come to be called autopoiesis (Maturana & Varela, 1992).

Autopoiesis comes from the Greek, where *auto* means self and *poiesis* means creation. Maturana and Varela (1992) defined autopoiesis:

> An autopoietic machine is a machine organized (defined as a unity) as a network of processes of production (transformation and destruction) of components that produces the components which: (i) through their interactions and transformations continuously regenerate and realize the network of processes (relations) that produced them; and (ii) constitute it (the machine) as a concrete unity in the space in which they (the components) exist by specifying the topological domain of its realization as such a network.
>
> (pp. 78–79)

Said a bit more simply, autopoiesis describes a system that can reproduce and maintain itself. The system self-regulates since it is autonomous and is organized recursively. Maturana explained that autopoiesis can also be considered through terms such as circular organization and self-referential systems (Maturana & Varela, 1980).

The notion of autopoiesis goes against previous notions that the system is determined by the environment in a cause/effect way. When actions, events, and change attempts occur from outside, the system's response is based not on those outside events, separate from the system, but instead on internal structure and organization. Thus, the environment cannot control a certain response from the system since it is the system that determines its response. The actions of the environment are just the situation, which allows the system's response to occur. These actions are called **perturbations**.

Let's focus on Frank and Stella to explain this concept a bit more clearly. All couples and families have universalities to them, such as having a structure, a means of communication, meaning given to their relationships, etc. They also are idiosyncratic in how these universals play out. In this view, the system itself tends to remain stable (self-maintaining) in the face of external events (perturbations). Whether this self-maintenance is to the benefit of the system or not is of great interest to therapists, and the idea of perturbing a system so that it maintains itself by reorganizing in response to a perturbation is crucial to some therapy models. Let's say that Stella's children had an issue with her dating Frank because he is black (or, vice versa). They might engage in overt or covert actions to try to get Stella to end the relationship. This might be through subtle comments, such as, "Are you sure you two are compatible? You've never been with anyone like him" or more straightforward comments, such as, "We don't like it that you are dating a black man. What would your mother think?" Whatever Stella's children do, it will not have a specific outcome on the relationship. Instead, the system's functioning will depend on how that system is organized. In this case, we can look at the system as either the individual (Stella) or the couple (Frank and Stella), or even larger definitions of a system.

Included in the notion of autopoiesis is the concept of **drift**. Systems engage in drift when they are not headed in any particular direction. Since systems are self-referential and self-determining based on their structure, they drift in the way that they can—a concept called **structural drift**. Structural drift happens in the moment based on the interactions between people (Kenny, 1989). One person's structural drift happens based on engagement with another where they develop a coordination of actions. In other words, structural drift is the connection between how a system is organized and the system's connection with the medium (another system).

For Frank and Stella, they engage in structural drift with one another. Frank cannot control how Stella or the relationship will be. Stella cannot control how Frank or the relationship will be. However, the two, by being in connection with one another, function based on their own organization but also change by being involved with one another. This is referred to as **consensual behavior** (Kenny, 1989). Frank and Stella will each display behaviors that would not have existed if it were not for their being in relationship with one another. For each, connection to a different person would lead to different consensual behavior.

Key Figure

Humberto Maturana

Humberto Maturana was born on September 14, 1928, in Santiago, Chile. As a child, he was fascinated with plants and animals, specifically around the topic of life and death. He attended the University of Chile where he first studied medicine and then biology. After studying anatomy and neurophysiology at University College London, he earned his doctorate in biology from Harvard University.

From 1958 to 1960, Maturana was an associate researcher at the Massachusetts Institute of Technology. He then returned in 1960 as a professor in the Department of Biology at the University of Chile. In the 1970s, Maturana, along with his student, Francisco Varela, studied the biological processes of frogs and, from that, brought forth new ideas in cognitive science. Together, they developed the concept of autopoiesis, which explained how living systems are self-generating, self-maintaining structures. Along with these concepts, the duo put forth the notions of structural determinism and structure coupling. These became important concepts in second order cybernetics and constructivist philosophy.

Maturana is viewed as one of the most important minds of the 20th century, especially in regards to constructivism and cybernetics. Leyland (1988) explained,

> Just before Gregory Bateson died, it is said that on being asked who he thought would be most likely to be building upon the work he had been doing in the field of cybernetics, he replied "Humberto Maturana"—a professor of biology at the University of Chile Santiago.
>
> (p. 357)

During the 1980s and 1990s, Maturana began to explore the role of emotions and human origins. This led to his ideas of "love" where a person does not try to control the other.

Structure (Determined and Coupling)

We've been talking about how people construct meaning and their own reality. Our focus shifts from the observed to the observer, as it is the observer who, in a sense, creates the observed. Here, we can explore in more depth how this process happens, as each person is structured in a way to create a certain meaning. **Structural determinism** is the notion that systems (but for this book we will talk about a specific system—people) function in their internal and relational dynamics based on their structure. Maturana and Varela (1980) described that, in examining the organization of a system, one views the component parts not as separate entities but in terms of how they work in relation to the other components of the system (what these authors call the **unity**).

Let's review some of the main ideas we have presented thus far about constructivism and how we can apply Maturana's work to psychotherapy. Efran, Lukens, and Lukens (1990) provided several concepts based on Maturana's structural determinism they believe are useful for psychotherapists:

(a) Living systems are self-creating entities—what Maturana calls "autopoitic."

(b) Science can only study structure-determined entities.

(c) Living systems are informationally closed.

(d) Keeping "objectivity" in quotation marks reminds us that we manufacture that which we think we know.

(e) Fundamentally, life is a purposeless drift.

(f) Survival requires maintaining an adequate structural coupling with the medium.

(g) All our ostensibly rational systems are based on rational starting premises.

(h) Language, biologically speaking, is a specialized form of communal action—it results in the creation of domains of distinction.

(p. 23)

As we've explained, a person is autopoietic in that he is a self-organizing and self-referential system. Further, the person has a structure, which determines how he functions. This functioning changes based on the interactions with various mediums (i.e., other systems). For therapists, perhaps one of the most important concepts is that the medium in which people interact is through language (both verbal and nonverbal).

Efran and Clarfield (1992) explained, "To the structure determinist, the ultimate reference for a human being is himself or herself" (p. 205). This is because not all people are the same since each person is a closed system whose functioning is based on his own organization. While we can look at patterns and tendencies of people (which most quantitative research attempts to do in determining how people, as a group, function), these are explanations in the aggregate, not the specific. For instance, we might review the research on what the experience is for white females being involved in an interracial relationship. We might then be making a mistake for expecting Stella to have those same experiences. While she is in an interracial relationship, how this impacts her can be quite different than the majority of people in the same situation.

This leads to the notion of structural coupling (see Figure 8.8). **Structural coupling** is the connection between the structure of the environment and that of the unity, where each serves as sources of perturbation for the other (Maturana & Varela, 1992). That is, each person acts in a way that is based on their own organization, but also interacting with the other.

During the 1980s and 1990s, some members of the field of psychotherapy adopted many of the ideas of constructivism, specifically those of Maturana. They became a philosophical underpinning as well as a move away from the "therapist as an expert" and instead to "part of the therapeutic system"—what

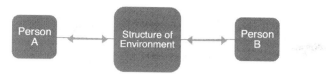

Figure 8.8 Structural Coupling Occurs When Two Individuals (the Unity) Are Impacted by the Other and the Environment While Also Impacting the Other and the Environment.

has been called **second order cybernetics**. Maturana explained the use of these ideas in family therapy, "Their [family therapists] interventions trigger changes in the components which result in the disintegration of a system and the appearance of another because the components cannot reenact their original behavior" (Simon, 1985, p. 42). Maturana was referring to Salvador Minuchin when making this comment. If we look at Minuchin's work, he tends to explore the various subsystems of the family. He issues a series of challenges (perturbations) to that system in an effort to help the system to reorganize. In doing so, a new family organization emerges (Minuchin et al., 2014).

Working with Stella and Frank, the therapist cannot make interventions that will make specific changes for the couple. That is, the therapist could not tell them to do a certain action and know that a specific response would occur. For instance, to tell Frank that he needs to, two times a week, have penile/vaginal intercourse with Stella will not necessary lead to the couple having a more satisfactory sex life. Contrarily, this might actually lead to a larger problem in their sexual encounters. Or, a change in their sexual lives might have unintended consequences in other areas of their relationship. The autopoietic system will respond idiosyncratically and unpredictably to a perturbation. Given that, the therapist cannot make a specific change, since changes are based not on outside influences, but internal organization. The best a therapist can do is to make perturbation attempts, see what happens, and go from there.

Perturbations

Realists assume that cause-and-effect relationships can be predictable, since the cause and the effect can be objectively known in advance. The constructivist view shifts away from the idea that it is possible to make an intervention that has a predictable result. Instead, a more reciprocal view of interaction comes forth, where each person's actions evoke something from the other person, but what that evocation is cannot be determined in advance, since it is determined by the experience of each individual. Constructivists understand that we cannot help but influence the other person (Cecchin, Lane, & Ray, 1994), but we cannot say with certainty what the outcome of this influence will be. These non-predictable influences have come to be called **perturbations**.

Whatever happens to a person (i.e., the perturbations of coming into contact with others or the environment), reorganization of their experience is based upon the perceptions made by the person and not by the other. This reorganization is not determined by the perturbation, and the person often does not have conscious control of it. In essence, it is the system itself that controls the change and reorganization. Maturana (1991) held that perturbations are different from inputs and outputs and described how a system maintains its organization yet engages in a structural change. These perturbations help people and families to change in accord to their social ecology.

However, if the perturbations are too different to have meaning to its organization, the system will not change, or will disintegrate if the system is unable to accommodate to them (Anderson, 1992). For Frank and Stella, they may come in contact with people in their community who do not favor interracial dating. The couple may experience people staring at them, making "rude" comments, or perhaps even physical threats. Conversely, they may also engage with people who are quite in favor of their interracial relationship. However, none of these actions by people outside of the system (the couple) can have a

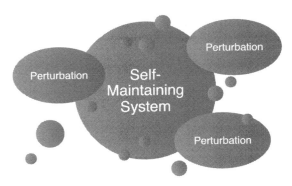

Figure 8.9 Perturbations Are Events From Outside the System, Which Lead to the System Changing, Based on Its Own Self-Organization.

specific, intentional, and predictable result for the couple system. For instance, the person who says, "Black and white do not mix" says so with the intent that Frank and Stella would agree and then would not only break up, but would then, when they choose a new person to date, choose someone from their own race. Yet, how the couple responded to this perturbation, whether they stayed together or broke up, would be determined not by the outside attempt (i.e., the actions of others), but by their own structure—how Stella and Frank are each cognitively organized. However, if, let's say, Stella's children told her they would disown her if she continued to date a black man and she ended her relationship with Frank, this would also be a perturbation to the system. There could be a change in the structure of the system that also maintained the organization of the system, but its nature would still be hard to predict.

Since systems are conservative, that is they tend to repeat their actions, therapy can be seen as a process of perturbing the system; in essence, therapy is a challenge to that conservatism (Efran & Greene, 1996). Some of these perturbations will lead to the system changing itself while others will not (see Figure 8.9).

Since people in relationship are connected to one another through structural drift, one part of a system changing will likely change the consensual behaviors of the couple. This concept is referred to as **orthogonal interaction**. Efran and Greene (1996) explained, "By definition, an *orthogonal interaction* involves a change in a system component that subsequently modifies that component's interaction with other system components" (p. 94, italics in original). This goes back to the idea that has been presented in every chapter of this book; a change in one part of the system can lead to system-wide change. In the case of Frank and Stella, orthogonal interaction might be seen if, in conversation, the therapist and Stella talk about personal identity and autonomy, and Stella may decide that she wants her children to stop telling her what to do. She may then go home and tell her children to mind their own business. The therapist/couple system would then observe the response of the family to this perturbation from the couple, and the family's response back would itself be a perturbation to each individual person system, the couple system, and the therapist/couple system and so on.

LANGUAGING

Human beings are "languaging animals," which means that every explanation or conversation can be defined as the coordination of two people who are both **languaging**: using a shared means of interaction (Maturana, 1991). However, one person's language is not another person's language. We're not talking here about literal language (i.e., Russian, Tagalog, or Hebrew), but how a person understands the words she is using. The words we use help us to create what we are seeing, even as they are intended to carry the meaning of what we are seeing.

From this perspective, language is not just a means of communication, but rather, language is action. It is an event of interaction and fit. Efran and Fauber (1995) stated, "Thus, language is not separate from action, and meanings are fully dependent on the contexts in which words and symbols are used" (p. 277). This has important ramifications for therapy in that constructivist therapists do not focus on getting clients to behave differently (i.e., stop compulsively washing one's hands or engage in deep breathing exercises). Instead, these therapists help clients to language differently. This happens by engaging clients in a unique languaging process that dissolves old meanings and creates new meanings. The idea is that as meanings change, so will actions like languaging and behavior.

The constructivist therapist working with Frank and Stella will pay attention to how each individually, and together as a couple, language their experience. The therapist will have to be cautious to not too quickly put his own meaning on specific words that are used. For instance, if Stella stated, "I find it a little frustrating that Frank does not sexually touch me," the therapist may try to be empathetic and think of his own relationship and what he feels like when his partner does not sexually touch him. However, that is the therapist's conceptualization of what this phrase means. While it might be similar to Stella's, it also may not. This is where greater exploration of the client's language and meanings is a core component of constructivist (and social constructionist—see Chapters 10 and 11) psychotherapy.

One way of exploring the connection between language and reality is that language creates reality; this is what de Shazer (1991, 1994) called "**post-structuralism.**" Drawing from Wittgenstein's (1958) notion of "language games," de Shazer built on the idea that the words people use create an understanding. The words themselves are arbitrary, but how they are used and in what context form our view of what is. In this way, language is reality (de Shazer & Berg, 1993). These authors explained, "Contrary to the commonsense view, change is seen to happen within language: what we talk about and how we talk about it makes a difference, and it is these differences that can be used to make a difference (to the client)" (p. 7).

Given that we cannot ever "know" exactly what someone else is thinking (or feeling), language is our medium of expression to others. My languaging and your languaging will not be the same. For instance, we (MR and JH) had to go back-and-forth to try to distinguish whether the words we were each using when writing this chapter were compatible to how the other was understanding the words (and the ideas and meanings behind those words). Further, we do not know whether these words/ideas/meanings will be internalized by you, the reader, in the way that we intended since how you will understand what is written is based on your unique interpretive and perceptual processes, rather than ours. However, people's language can be compatible or achieve a degree of fit (von Glasersfeld, 1995). My language can be in coordination with your language. von Glasersfeld talked about this interpersonal process as **sharing** (see Figure 8.10). Two or more people come into contact in ways of expressing their experiential reality. The other person attempts to construct the other's experience; however, she can never know an objective reality. von Glasersfeld discussed this in terms of "corroboration by others" and explained that, while

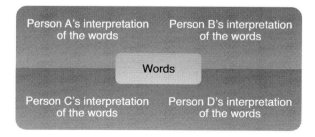

Figure 8.10 The Interpersonal Process of Sharing, Where People Have Their Own Interpretation of Words, Which May Overlap With Other People's Interpretations.

we might use very similar words with people we are in contact with, that does not necessitate that the network of concepts we are each talking about are the same.

Frank and Stella might both say to each other, "I love you." On the surface, we may think that 1) they understand what it is each feels about him/herself to say those words, 2) they understand what it is the other feels about self, 3) they understand what it is the other feels about him/herself, and 4) what this means for their relationship. But when we look deeper, we know that "love" is one of the most talked about concepts for people but also one of the most elusive to agree on. This is why therapists often hear individuals who are involved in a couple relationship say things such as, "If you love me, how could you do *x*?" or "I thought you loved me." The other person usually responds, "I do love you." One major reason that these transactions occur is because "love" is interpreted quite differently by these two people. Frank may believe that doing things, such as going to music concerts and out dancing, is showing love to Stella. For Stella, having love shown to her may be by putting her psychological, emotional, and/or sexual needs first. The couple may find that the other person is not experiencing love, since the word is being used in two very different ways by each, where the meaning of the word is unique for each person. Meanings are based on the organization of the person and form the foundation of the various psychotherapy approaches based on language systems.

Meaning

In the constructivist perspective, life happens in the meaning that people develop about the information they are taking in. By constructing a meaning to information, the observer is making a distinction: they are framing a difference (Neimeyer, 1995a). Thus, we can look at language as the performance of meaning (Raskin & Neimeyer, 2003). Here, we come back to the constructivist perspective that there is not objective absolute truth, but as individuals, we create the truth in the meaning that we give information. No event in itself has meaning; meaning only happens when the individual provides it.

This can be seen in how we give attribution for actions. In social psychology, there are two related effects: the halo effect and the horn effect (Thorndike, 1920). The **halo effect** holds that we attribute positive cause for an action made by someone we have positive feelings for and the **horn effect** holds that we attribute negative cause for an action made by someone we have negative feelings for. Let's provide an example of this: imagine you observed people crossing the street and someone trips. Your very good friend happens to be there and runs over to help the person up and out of harm's way. You would likely say to yourself something like, "Wow, look at Jimmy, he's such a nice person." Okay, let's change the scenario just a bit. You are at the same intersection, and people are crossing the street when someone trips. Someone that you know, but perhaps despise, runs over and helps that person up. In this scenario, you are more likely to say to yourself, "Look at Philip. He's just trying to make himself look good in front of other people." Here, we had two situations that were the same, except for who the protagonist was and what their relationship was to you. However, the meaning of the people's actions was quite different. There was no absolute truth to the event—someone helping someone else up who had tripped. The meaning was constructed by you. If you called this an act of helping, there might be a corroboration-by-others who agree. Others present may have developed their own construction and languaged it differently than you, where perhaps they call it an intrusion.

At the current moment, Stella has positive feelings toward Frank. As such, she makes meaning of his lack of touching her sexually or engaging in intercourse in a way that is more favorable than if she didn't have positive feelings for him. Let's say that the couple broke up acrimoniously. It is much more likely that Stella may, unintentionally, utilize the horn effect where she attributes negative cause of Frank's actions. She might construct a meaning that he is a sick and disturbed individual and that is why he had sexual problems. Attribution theory, such as the halo and horn effects, help us to understand how people can have two very different reactions to the same situation. The situation could have stayed the same, but how the person puts meaning to the situation changes, which alters the individual's experience.

COORDINATION

When examining the connection between systems, we can look at the history of their structural coupling. That is, the systems have ways of interacting with one another that have happened over time. These interactions are a **coordination of action**. Since each system perturbs the other and reacts based on its own structure, Maturana called this process co-ontogenic structural drift. Here, two systems coevolve.

For our purposes, we can view this coordination of action occurring between the client system and the therapist system—what might be called the therapeutic system (see Figure 8.11). To explore this even more, since human beings engage each other primarily through languaging, and languaging is about compatible meaning, we can then talk about how therapy focuses on meaning systems. Goolishian and Winderman (1988) explained this process:

> Given this new vocabulary, therapy might be described as the creation of a network of structurally coupled participant observers interacting within a linguistic domain; each participant observer acting as a reciprocal perturbation for another participant observer, all co-evolving through time, within a relationship network of evolved meanings.
>
> (p. 133)

Therapist and client might then become a language system where each potentially impacts the other without the intention to control the other. What are being changed in therapy are the meanings that each individual puts to the concepts being discussed.

A constructivist perspective assumes that in order to engage in coordination, each person in dialogue needs to accept the legitimacy of the other without any expectation (Maturana & Poerksen, 2004). This is possible since the absence of an objective reality carries the presumption of legitimacy in the perceptions of the other. This brings us back to Maturana's notion of love.

In accepting the legitimacy of the other, they engage in what Maturana calls **love**. This is not the love that we normally think about where romantic partners fall in love with one another or family members "love" one another. Instead, for Maturana, love is a love in the moment that has no conditions attached to it. As Maturana explained, "Whenever we see a person behaving in a relational manner through which another being or him- or herself arises as a legitimate other in coexistence with him- or herself, we say

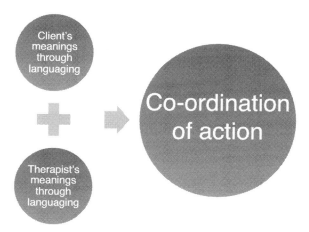

Figure 8.11 The Process of Coordination of Action.

that we see loving behavior in that person" (p. 272). Love happens when a person comes in contact with another person not to change the other, but to be authentic in that moment and allow the other to be authentic. In other words, the two people fit and form a process of structural drift (Kenny, 1989). Each of their interactions triggers an internal change, which leads to the next interaction where each authentically encounters the other, which may trigger a change. Love is what happens when the parties interacting acknowledge the constructed reality of the other, and try, as best they can, to understand and accept the meaning the other makes of their experience. It is the opposite of Maturana's idea of **violence**, in which one tries to negate the constructed experience of the other. Therapists are invited to consider their role in these relationships.

Frank had most likely previously engaged with women not through love, but through expectation, making assumptions of what the women were thinking and what they should be thinking. These assumptions were most likely based on his own desires of what he wanted the other person to be rather than who the person is. It is possible that Frank and Stella's relationship is doing well, for the most part, since they have figured out a way of engaging in coordination of action where they experience more "love" in their interactions than in other relationships. This is probably more so for Frank, as Stella is not trying to change Frank but is more accepting of him for how he is rather than who he might be or who she wants him to be.

This type of engagement with another, where one person does not come into an exchange based on how they want the other to be, can be called **interactional presence** (Keeney, Keeney, & Chenail, 2015). These authors explained, "If you are set to cast pre-formed forms, you are potentially over-bearing (and arguably violent) by the very attachment to a preconceived conscious readiness to steer things your way, even if the latter denies the singularity of your importance" (p. 14). We can view this way of being with others as an I-Thou relationship. This means that the therapist interacts with the other, listening as much as possible without bias or prejudice. Many of the approaches of psychotherapy, such as person-centered, collaborative, and existential therapy, hold to this notion of the therapist developing an I-Thou relationship with the client.

Hermeneutics

We have talked about the notion that people construct individual meaning from the information they take in from the outside world. The millions of pieces of meaning along a person's life are woven together into a narrative. How this text is deciphered falls within the realm of hermeneutics. **Hermeneutics** is the interpretation of texts. While initially used to interpret texts such as biblical and philosophical texts, contemporary hermeneutics interprets both verbal and nonverbal forms of communication. Further, the meaning that an individual makes of their experience serves as a text. A person in relationship with another has the opportunity to make meaning of the text of the other's life.

In therapy, a hermeneutical viewpoint leads the therapist to focus on how clients story their experience. Worsley (2012) explained, "For a therapist to think hermeneutically is to move towards seeing the client's narrative as a sort of text to be understood by both parties as multiple" (p. 306). Hermeneutics is not about interpreting a text to gain the truth of the text, but to bring multiple meanings together and develop a new understanding.

Here, the therapist cannot create a meaning as one cannot force her own understanding on someone else. This is because meaning is created by the individual. However, that meaning may happen through processes of structural coupling—the perturbations and changes involved in relationships. Hermeneutics helps us to understand how the exploration of meaning, and the development of new meaning, occurs between people (see Figure 8.12). Anderson and Goolishian (1992) stated, "In this hermeneutic view, change in therapy is represented by the dialogical creation of new narrative" (p. 29). This can happen through alternative readings of a story (Bruner, 1986). Stories can be reread in many different ways. We can look at them as being truth, morality, allegory, analogy, or lessons learned. Each new reading brings new meaning to the story.

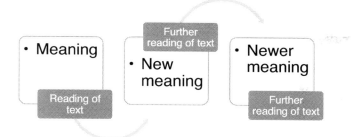

Figure 8.12 The Process of Hermeneutic Analysis of Text (i.e., a Client's Story). The Reading of a Text May Lead to New Meanings of the Text, Which May Lead to a Subsequent Reading Where New Meanings Might Develop.

Deconstruction

Another way to think about the ways in which individuals construct reality, and communicate their understandings through language, is the idea of deconstruction. Since stories are constructed, they can also be **deconstructed**. White (1993), who was influenced by the writings of Jacques Derrida, an influential postmodernist theorist, explained:

> Deconstruction is premised on what is generally referred to as a "critical constructivist" or, as I would prefer, a "constitutionalist" perspective on the world. From this perspective, it is proposed that persons' lives are shaped by the meaning that they ascribe to their experience, by their situation in social structures, and by the language practices and cultural practices of self and of relationship that these lives are recruited into.
>
> (p. 35)

Thus, deconstruction helps people to develop alternate meanings and understandings to their problem-saturated stories, which allow their preferences to come forth.

When operating from a deconstruction perspective, the reader of a text can answer the question of what the text means in two ways (Bruner, 1986). First, deconstruction helps us to see that there is no fixed, objective meaning to a text. Second, from a pragmatic deconstruction lens, the text can have multiple meanings, depending on the perceptions of the author of the text and the reader of the text. What these two ways of viewing the meaning of a text have in common is that there is not only one way to read it; there is a plurality of ways. This opens up possibilities for the storyteller and the receiver of the story to read the text in a way that a new meaning emerges—one that provides new possibilities for those involved in the story.

While many psychotherapists use the term deconstruction, some find that there are too many competing definitions and understandings. For instance, de Shazer (1994) discusses this process of finding alternative meanings in a person's story as **text-focused reading** (see Figure 8.13). Here, the reader keeps engaging the text for deeper levels of interpretation. The reader understands that there can always be hidden meanings, meanings which have not been articulated or thought of before, which require further interpretations. This provides a richness in accessing the text.

We can now look at how Frank and Stella have likely been engaging in a hermeneutic process without even realizing it. Frank has likely told his story of his relationship with women to many people. When he met Stella, he probably told her his romantic past, most notably the death of his wife. When explaining his past connections and disconnections with women, some new understanding or interpretation may

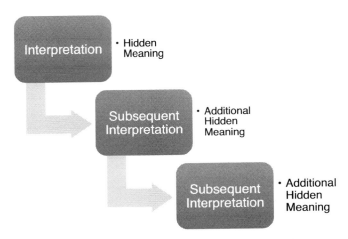

Figure 8.13 The Process of Text-Focused Reading, Where Exploration of a Person's Story Leads to Interpretations That Had Not Been Made Before.

have become present. Through Stella's questions and inquiries into Frank's thoughts about women and his relationship with them, subsequent interpretations were likely to come forth. Frank may then have come in contact with his interpretation of his story in a new way and found some hidden meaning to it; that is, meaning that he did not have previously. This meaning is not "the truth" of his story, but his current construction of the story, which may change upon subsequent tellings of that story. These tellings may happen in the next interchange, the next day, or years later.

Applying Your Knowledge

Think about some aspect of your life. Perhaps it is your romantic relationship, your career path, or your relationship with family members. What interpretation do you have of this aspect of your life? Write that down. Then, tell this story (your current understanding of the aspect you chose) to someone who would be inquisitive and at the end, write down any hidden meanings that emerged and how those might have changed your initial interpretation. Finally, tell this new story to a third inquisitive person and at the end of the conversation write down any new meanings and subsequent interpretations.

Discourse

We end this chapter talking about how a person creates meaning of one's life via the interpretation of one's story. When people tell their story—what can be called their text—to someone else, they engage in a conversation, a **discourse**. Bruner (1986) described the connection between discourse and text (stories or narratives). He explained, "Discourse must make it possible for the reader to 'write' his own virtual text" (p. 25). That is, it is in the process of telling one's story that the story is created. In this process of discourse, there are three features.

First, discourse brings forth **presupposition**. Here, the reader of the text develops implicit meanings rather than explicit meanings. Explicit meanings would suggest that there is an immutable truth to the

CONSTRUCTIVIST AESTHETICS

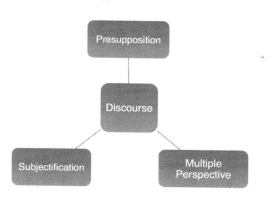

Figure 8.14 The Process of Discourse Involves Presupposition, Subjectification, and Multiple Perspective.

story and the reader's job is to determine what that meaning is. Implicit meanings hold that the reader constructs the meaning of the text. These meanings may have been present in previous readings but are likely to take on a new experience in the current telling.

Second, discourse occurs through **subjectification**. The reader is not reading the text as based in reality but, rather, through the lens of the protagonists in the story. This is related to active listening and empathic responses. When a client is telling you a story of what happened to them the previous night during the family dinner, you are not seeing the dinner as it was but, rather, through how your client, who was only one party of that event, constructed what occurred through their own filters and also through the filters of your own perceptions of listening to the story.

Third, discourse involves the understanding of **multiple perspective**. If there was only one perspective, then the reader would not need to interpret a text; it would be what it is. However, because each person construes the world differently, the reader is more than a reader but is also a writer of that text.

Frank and Stella engage in many discourses throughout their relationship. These might be in face-to-face conversations, email, and text messages. We have been using Frank's story/narrative of his relationship with women as a way to understand many of the constructivist concepts. During the discourse between Frank and Stella, Frank telling Stella of his longing for a relationship triggers a presuppositional process, where he develops a view of the story's meaning rather than coming into the conversation with a viewpoint of what is. While telling his story, Frank and Stella realize that the actions and perceptions are not the truth of the story, but have been filtered through Frank's understandings. This is the process of subjectification. Lastly, as Stella asks questions and makes inquiries into what Frank is telling her, they each may have different interpretations. Further, by considering the other person's perspective, each may come up new interpretations. This process demonstrates the feature of multiple perspective.

QUESTIONS FOR REFLECTION

1. What are the differences between objectivism and constructivism? How do these differences impact the way you might understand what is happening for your clients?

2. How does taking a constructivist position, where nothing is known outside the realm of the observer, fit within a managed care context? How about with DSM diagnosis?

3. How important are the words that we use? What is the connection between languaging and meaning making?

4. What usefulness comes from viewing meaning through story construction?

5. What are the implications of adopting the notion of therapy as a coordination of action?

CHAPTER NINE
Constructivist Pragmatics

Michael D. Reiter with James Hibel

CASE DESCRIPTION

This transcript is from the beginning of Frank and Stella's first therapy session:

Therapist: What brings each of you into therapy, today?
Frank: We just want to make sure that things are going well between us.
Therapist: Okay, Frank, you want to make sure all is well with you both. What about you, Stella?
Stella: Yes, I agree. For the most part everything is fine.
Therapist: For you as well, the relationship is pretty good.
Stella: Yeah. It's just that Frank needs to calm down a bit. He can get anxious when he doesn't need to.
Therapist: Can you give me an example of what you're talking about?
Stella: Well, take the other day. We had plans to go to the movies. However, I got caught up dealing with my daughter and an issue she was having. Frank was calling me every five minutes, "Where are you?" "When are you coming?"—I wasn't late, but he was anxious that I would be.
Therapist: You would like Frank to be a bit less anxious. Frank, what are your thoughts on what Stella is saying?
Frank: I just like everything to be organized and on time and for people to do what they say they're going to do. With my ex-wife, she worked on her own schedule. It frustrated me greatly. If Stella and I agree on something, I just want follow-through on it and that it will happen.
Stella: It will happen. Calm down. Have I ever been late?
Frank: Not that I can remember. Well, there was that one time where there was a car accident on the highway that held you up.
Stella: Right, and I called you when I was stuck in traffic to let you know and you started freaking out on me.
Frank: I just wanted to know where you were.
Stella: No, there is something not quite right. I accept that. I am not judging you. But there is just too much anxiety.

In this chapter, we'll present some ideas of how a constructivist psychotherapist might work with Frank and Stella, based on the theoretical principles of constructivism elucidated in Chapter 8. These understandings and techniques are not set in stone. Constructivist therapists work in many different ways. However, what they all have in common is the notion that the individual constructs her own understanding of her experience.

CONSTRUCTIVIST PSYCHOTHERAPY

In a way, the term "constructivist therapy" is a term without a model. Constructivism is a way of understanding human cognition, and this way of understanding is not limited to therapy. At the same time, there are a number of therapy models that were developed by people whose ways of understanding, and therefore of focusing on human interactions, were influenced by constructivism. So, for the sake of simplicity, we are grouping these therapies under the heading of "Constructivist Psychotherapy."

It is difficult to define constructivist psychotherapy because, as we said, there is not one model or technique. However, as Maturana explained, what they have in common is that none of these models contain the idea that specific techniques will lead to specific and predictable results, as this understanding does not fit with the notion of structure-determined systems (Maturana & Poerksen, 2004). Change happens not from what the therapist does, in essence his interventions, but what the client does with whatever happened in the therapy room. In constructivist psychotherapy, the therapist attempts to pay attention to how the client constructs meanings to see what could change in the ways that the client conceptualizes herself and various aspects of her life. These changes happen based on the client's changing her understanding of her life and relationships, rather than being the result of a planned intervention by the therapist. This may seem confusing now, but we hope to clear this up in the rest of this chapter.

Our clients, Frank and Stella, each understand their relationship similarly—what was referred to as sharing in Chapter 8—but also uniquely since they each construct their own meaning to the relationship. In a very simplified way, Frank may construe meaning of the relationship that those close to him should be respectful of his needs. Stella may understand the relationship as being flawed but acceptable. Each person's construction informs him or her on how to act in the relationship and what to feel when events happen. If Frank's meaning changed, such as people close to you can be connected and not be respectful of his needs, he may not have as much anxiety when people act in ways that go against his expectations. If Stella's meaning changed, where, as she defines, flaws are not quite acceptable, she may push more greatly for change.

So, what is the constructivist therapist's responsibility? The therapist is not responsible for what others do, but for what she says and does in the therapy room. The best a constructivist therapist can do (and this is a lot!) is to listen with self-awareness. As Maturana explained, "To achieve this, one must listen with as many ears as possible, one must not allow one's perception to be blinded by premature judgments, and one must be aware of the emotions coloring what one is hearing" (Maturana & Poerksen, 2004, p. 271). In order to do this, a therapist must operate from love since healing is based upon self-love and self-respect. Remember that "love," as used by Maturana, involves treating the other without expectations and encountering them as a unique person. For therapists, this comes in the form of engaging clients through an I-Thou relationship. Mahoney (2003) discussed this in terms of a **compassionate relationship** being the heart of psychotherapy. He explained, "It [compassion] reflects the essence of our social embeddedness and our symbolic capacities to imagine and honor what someone else may be feeling" (p. 17).

To experience "love," an I-Thou interaction, and a compassionate relationship, the constructivist psychotherapist must view self and client as separate and unique human beings. This can be enhanced by utilizing Carl Rogers three core conditions: genuineness, unconditional positive regard, and accurate empathic understanding (Rogers, 1961). **Genuineness** focuses on the therapist's transparency; in essence, the therapist is being real in the contact. **Unconditional positive regard** highlights how the therapist believes in the client as a person who, given certain conditions, will move toward growth. **Accurate empathic understanding** is the therapist's attempt to discern the client's meanings. In many ways, Maturana's position of love can be equated to Rogers' core conditions.

For instance, Anderson (2012) discussed the notion of genuineness (or what has also been called transparency) as **being public**. She explained:

> It refers to the commitment and activity of not operating from hidden or private ideas, thoughts, questions, but rather being open and making them visible. Though I keep in mind that regardless of what I choose to show other persons, what they see or hear and how they interpret it will be uniquely theirs, not mine.
>
> (p. 68)

This position prevents the therapist from taking a position of certainty and making that idea the center of the therapeutic conversation. Thus, ideas can be challenged by therapist, client, or both. This leads to therapists not privileging their own viewpoints and meanings over the client's.

A constructivist therapist working with Stella and Frank would most likely encompass both "love" and Rogers' core conditions. As Mahoney (2003) stated, "The therapist should be as present as possible and invite a genuine contact with the client as another human being" (p. 16). The therapist will attempt to uncover both Frank and Stella's personal meanings, accepting them each as human beings who have their own way of viewing and understanding the world. This happens through a position of nonjudgmental connection.

Constructivist psychotherapists shift from the "all-knowing expert" on how clients should live their lives to someone who perturbs the system with questions and explorations of meanings. Since people are structure-determined, therapists are not privileged in knowing the world, especially that of the client. The therapist working with Frank and Stella would not have an end goal in mind for them and run roughshod over the couple to get there. Instead, the therapist will attempt to engage them with curiosity in how each has developed their understandings. This exploration may then become perturbations, where Frank and/or Stella develop new meanings, which would likely lead to new thoughts, feelings, and behaviors.

Focusing on Meanings

There are many ways that therapists can operate from a constructivist perspective, all focusing on how people construct meanings. Neimeyer (1995) explained, "From the constructivist vantage point, *psychotherapy* can be defined as the variegated and subtle interchange and negotiation of (inter)personal meanings" (p. 2, italics in original). In other words, constructivist therapies are a mutual exchange of ideas that have the potential to change how therapist and client, not just the client, come to construct their reality. Thus, the focus of therapy is not on relieving unwanted symptoms, but instead on developing new understandings of meaning in clients' lives (Neimeyer, 2009).

The constructivist therapist anticipates that as meanings become understood differently, actions will also change. This happens through continuous reciprocal loops of talk about meaning which impacts the next talk of meaning, etc. (Efran & Greene, 1996; see Figure 9.1). However, what that meaning is or will become is not known or intended by the therapist. This requires the constructivist psychotherapist to be able to live comfortably with ambiguity (Mahoney, 1988).

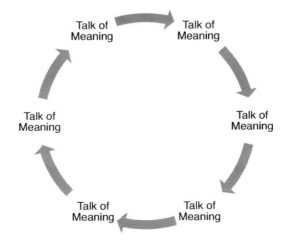

Figure 9.1 Therapy as Talk About Meaning Where Neither Therapist Nor Client Know What Meaning Might Emerge in the Subsequent Conversation.

With our couple, picking up the conversation started at the beginning of the session, this process may take on the following form:

Therapist: Stella, you say that you accept it. Can you discuss that a bit more?
Stella: I know there is something not quite right with Frank. He is a good person. He can have fun. But he's a bit different than others, and that's okay.
Therapist: How do you know he's a bit different?
Stella: You see him here. Most people can handle someone being a few minutes late. Most people don't freak out when things don't go as planned.
Therapist: So for you, you see Frank's reaction when things go off schedule as not being similar to how a lot of other people you know react. Given that, what is it about being with Frank that you accept and is okay for you, since you're still with him?
Stella: I enjoy being around him. I know he cares about me. At our age, you shouldn't be too nitpicky.

Here, each back-and-forth adds to the meaning that Stella is creating. This process can also be done with Frank. However, by being an observer to someone else's talk of meaning the observer may create new meaning for himself.

One way of negotiating meaning in constructivist psychotherapy is through privileging experience over explanation (Neimeyer, 2009). Explanation tends to be an intellectual exercise that keeps focus in the cognitive arena, where most people already maintain their current understanding. Constructivist therapists, operating also in the experiential realm, offer the possibilities of experiencing difference, new awareness, understanding, or meaning. Neimeyer explained it this way, "In this sense, an ultimate goal of constructivist psychotherapies is helping clients become *connoisseurs of their experience*, leaving them better positioned to grasp the entailments of their current self-narratives and to craft and perform new stories" (p. 84, italics in original). To state this differently, we can become experts in the aesthetics and meanings of our own experience, and this appreciation of our own experience can be the first step towards being able to expand on these experiences and create new ones that we like.

Working with Frank and Stella, the conversation around their experiences may take on the following form:

Therapist: Frank, you discussed wanting things to go well between you and Stella. What is that like for you when things are going well?
Frank: There are no fights between us. We're just able to have fun and enjoy each other's company.
Therapist: What do you think it is about being with you that Stella enjoys?
Frank: I don't know. Maybe that we both like music and like to go to concerts. I also like to talk to people.
Therapist: Okay, so your sense is that Stella likes being around you because of a shared enjoyment of music and that you are able to talk with people.
Frank: Yeah. Plus, I think she knows that I will not try to hurt her.
Therapist: What experiences did you have in your life that show that you are a person who would not hurt someone else?

The therapeutic talk is now in the realm of Frank's experiences and the meaning he makes around them. His desire not to hurt someone else can be expanded to explore how that, and other meanings of self, can be utilized to have the relationship that he wants.

Because constructivist psychotherapists operate from a different epistemology than rationalist psychotherapists, constructivist therapists tend to have personal characteristics that differ from other kinds of therapists (Neimeyer, Lee, Aksoy-Toska, & Phillip, 2008). Constructivist psychotherapists scored significantly higher than rationalist psychotherapists did in self-awareness, attending to emotions, tolerance for ambiguity, tolerance for diversity, and openness to experience. Constructivist-based therapists tend to put a greater emphasis on the working alliance in therapy (i.e., acceptance, understanding, and trust) than their rationalist-based colleagues (Lee, Neimeyer, & Rice, 2013).

Psychotherapists who operate from a constructivist perspective tend to be more pluralistic, rather than strictly adhering to one particular model (Neimeyer, 1995b). They focus on people's experiential realities and on how people construct meanings in an ever-changing manner (Bridges & Raskin, 2008). Cecchin et al. (1994) held that an ideal therapist "has a strong personal style with clear beliefs (prejudices) about what works, and what does not work. Simultaneously, this kind of therapist is willing to examine the effect that his or her strong beliefs have on clients" (p. 20).

It is not clear whether people who like to think and relate in this way become constructivist therapists because the ideas fit with how they like to relate to others, or if adopting this epistemology leads people to become therapists who work in this manner. Either way, constructivist therapists tend to operate through a sense of congruence where they are having a human-to-human connection with the people they work with in the therapeutic situation.

The constructivist therapist working with Frank and Stella would likely focus on the therapeutic alliance, attempting to truly listen to both Frank and Stella and hearing how they each understand the self and the situation. Further, the therapist would not come into the session with a preconceived view of how Frank and Stella should be. Instead, he would be open to the various possibilities that are likely to emerge based on the therapeutic conversations—the therapy discourse.

MEANINGS IN THERAPY

As we've seen, constructivist therapists focus on the meanings that clients make around the events in their lives. However, this is done with an understanding that these construed meanings are not "facts" and are not objective realities that have been discovered or uncovered by the therapist. Because of this, there can be multiple meanings about anything. Thus, meanings can be construed differently—in ways that are more desirable by the client. Most constructivist therapists focus on how people view the usefulness of their personal constructions and how new meanings can be developed, that can become more useful. As such, it is not assumed that clients prefer or do not prefer certain interpretations of their experience. In working with Frank and Stella, this may happen by the therapist taking a slower approach:

Therapist: Frank, you stated that the other day Stella called to let you know when she was on the way to your house. Was this an action that you liked or did not like?
Frank: Oh, I liked that.
Therapist: Okay, so that was something you liked. What about it did you like?
Frank: It showed that she was thinking about me and trying to take my thoughts and feelings into consideration.
Therapist: And what is it about her taking your thoughts and feelings into consideration that is something you appreciate?
Frank: I haven't had that too often. It shows that she thinks I am worthwhile.

Instead of just assuming that Frank likes that Stella called him, while it could have been implied, the therapist ensured that the construed meaning was the client's and not the therapist's.

Constructivist therapists continually look for signs that the client has had a change in meaning. Duncan, Solovey, and Rusk (1992) described these signals of change, "Indications include client presentation of new information, heightened self-awareness, improvement of the presenting problem, a change in affect, and/or changes in physical appearance or even seating arrangement" (p. 140). However, the therapist should inquire from the client that these signals indicate a change for the client rather than the therapist's interpretation that change has occurred. Part of this emphasis on change is an exploration on the details.

Since meanings are individually construed, constructivist psychotherapists focus on individual experience, a view called **phenomenology** (Mahoney, 1995). A way to bring out these individual experiences is through rich and thick descriptions. Freedman and Combs (1996) explained that thickening the client's narrative involves repetition and thoroughness. This can be through focusing on details, exploring

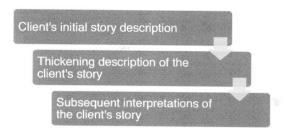

Figure 9.2 Thickening Descriptions of the Client's Story Lead to New Interpretations and Meanings.

how others may view the situation, and increasing the perspectives discussed. We might thicken the therapeutic conversation with our case couple in the following manner:

Therapist: Stella, you described knowing that Frank cares about you and that you enjoy your time with him. Could you talk a bit more about this?

Stella: We do some fun things together. In the time I've been with Frank I've been to more concerts than I had in the previous ten years.

Therapist: When you and he go to a concert, how does that tell you that Frank cares about you?

Stella: He'll ask if I need a drink or if the music is too loud. After our second concert, I told him that it was too loud. The next week he came to my house and gave me a present. It was special earplugs designed for being at concerts.

Therapist: What did Frank giving you the earplugs say to you about the relationship?

Stella: That he is thinking about me. Plus, that he wanted to be with me for a long time. Otherwise, he wouldn't have gotten me them. We've used them a lot.

Therapist: What is your view of Frank's caring for you?

Stella: He's not the typical guy and may not do what others consider romantic. But in his own way he shows that he cares. There hasn't been a day since we met that we haven't talked or he hasn't texted me.

Therapist: What does that tell you that you have spoken or texted every day since you met?

Stella: That I am important to him.

In this interchange, the therapist has tried to enrich the client's initial description to provide fullness to it. There is still a lot of thickening that could occur; however, the client is provided an opportunity to clarify the meanings that she attributes to her experience (see Figure 9.2).

STORY/STORYTELLER

We've been talking about how people have a story or narrative of their experience that is housed in language and is based on the person's internal organization. On further tellings of the story, with thick description, people develop alternative constructions of the meaning of the story. Another way of explaining this is that there is a connection between the storyteller and the story. Maturana (1980) explained the idea that observer and observed are interconnected and that the observer is always making distinctions when observing. In the therapy room, we can view this in terms of the connection between the storyteller (the observer) and the story (the observed). Gonçalves (1995) stated that "psychotherapy is a well-established scenario for storytelling and story making" (p. 199). Therapy, using these constructivist and biological constructs, involves helping the client (the storyteller) tell her story in rich detail. Each time the storyteller tells her story, with the help of the therapist (another observer), she can make new distinctions, and her relationship to the story shifts (Efran et al., 1990).

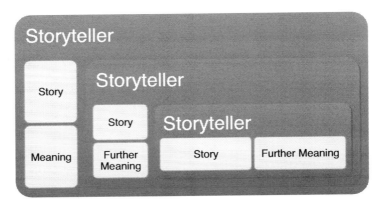

Figure 9.3 The Meaning of the Story to the Storyteller Is Housed Within Previous Tellings of the Story and Past Meanings to the Storyteller.

By making the distinctions in the telling of the story, the storyteller can shift her perspective from one of being swept away by the story, to experiencing the meaning of the story differently. Here, the person makes meaning of what has occurred in her life based on how she decides to frame it. This is especially important since many clients who come to therapy find that they have lost the role of storyteller in their own stories. Rosen (1996) explained, "It is not uncommon for clients to enter therapy at just that point when they realize that they are feeling no sense of self-authorship but, instead, are living roles in others' stories" (p. 24). By exploring the client's current meaning to her story, the story becomes richer, which provides an opportunity for the client to construct new meaning to her experience. This then shifts the subsequent telling of the story and the new meaning attributed to it. Thus, there is an evolvement of story/meaning with each telling where the storyteller has a different relationship to the story/meaning. This recursive process can be seen in Figure 9.3, where each time the storyteller tells the story and accesses her current meaning, a richer understanding of the story/meaning occurs.

When Frank is explaining his position of wanting to be organized and to know when Stella is going to come home and that she not be late, he is constructing a meaning around this. On the first telling of the story, the meaning is related to having not felt respected by others in the past. Through gaining thick description of his experience, Frank may then focus on aspects of the story that he had not articulated or highlighted previously. Perhaps these are times when he felt less anxious of his connection to a significant other. These moments, what might be called unique outcomes, exceptions, or alternative plotlines (see Chapter 11), take on more significant meaning for him. He may begin to view himself as someone who is lovable yet distant. Subsequent iterations of his story lead the newly formed meaning to be understood even more differently, based on how Frank is storying his experience. Concurrently, while in discourse with Stella around this topic, Stella may be telling her own story around being in relationship to someone who is behaving as Frank does. Each iteration of her telling leads to her experiencing herself and her story differently as well.

This recursive process, where the telling of the story leads the storyteller to understand the story differently, which leads to a new telling, which leads to new understandings, etc., is transformative (see Figure 9.4). Anderson (2012) views client change in terms of **transforming**, stating, "Transforming allows me to think of things as continually in motion, continually moving, continually being and becoming" (p. 69). Thus, a person's "story" is not set in stone, but is a living entity that changes upon subsequent tellings.

Therapy then shifts from a focus of what *was* to what one *wants* (Efran et al., 1990). The therapist helps clients distinguish between what they wish to have happen and what they are actively attempting to achieve. Notice that there is a distinction between "wish" and "want." A wish is a desire that seems

Figure 9.4 The Repetitive Telling of a Story Leads the Storyteller to New Understandings of the Story.

far-fetched and unlikely to happen. I (MR) may wish that I was rich and famous or wish I was in a relationship with Jessica Alba (you can choose your fantasy crush here). These wishes are for the most part fantasy. They would be very nice if they happened, but the likelihood of them occurring is very small. Wants, however, are the realistic goals that clients have. I want to have a better relationship with my wife, and I am actively changing how I think about her and what I do with her to make that goal happen. I may hear her complain that I don't do enough around the house, and then I start to wash the dishes, clean the bathrooms, take out the trash, and mop the floors.

Using this line of thought, therapists help clients to develop live goals (Efran et al., 1990). **Live goals** are those wants that people have that they are actively trying to achieve. This is in contrast to goals where people say they want something but do nothing about them. Stella may complain about how Frank does not sexually touch her. However, she doesn't make any change attempts. If she maintains this position, Stella's complaints will likely last. If her desire to have Frank sexually touch her were a live goal, she would be figuring out ways of getting him to be sexually reciprocal and putting these plans into action. Or she would be actively seeking out new ways of perceiving the situation so that it did not concern her any longer. Frank has a live goal of having Stella treat him well. He acts in ways to try to get this goal to happen. While he cannot make Stella treat him well, his actions (such as texting her as to her whereabouts) are perturbation attempts to get the relationship closer to his desired outcome.

Yet, we should keep in mind that people's goals are fluid (Anderson, 2012). They change over time and may do so within the confines of one session. During the course of the therapeutic conversation, Stella may shift her ideas for what she wants, from Frank being less anxious to him being more romantic. However, she may then come to understand her situation differently and shift her want to her being firmer in getting her needs met. Constructivist therapists would likely shift their focus of therapy based on the client's changing wants and goals. This is in contrast to seeing goals as being fixed and something that clients, and therapists, work toward. This may make it difficult for some constructivist therapists to work in agencies or managed care companies where treatment plans based on diagnoses and specific nonmalleable goals are expected.

Based on a constructivist foundation, therapy becomes a way of constructing stories of success that are meaningful to the client and that the client likes better than the story in which they are currently embedded (de Shazer, 1994). The client's initial story is usually that of what is happening in her life that she doesn't like. In therapy, problems are usually the client's first concerns. In constructivist therapies, problems are understood as what clients want and aspects of their lives in which they have engaged in those types of activities. Therapy highlights the client's lived experience and the meanings that they make, rather than the interpretations of the therapist, that become significant for the client.

> ## Applying Your Knowledge
>
> List five goals that you have for yourself. Are any of these goals wishes? Which of them are wants? For those that are wishes, how can you change them into wants? Now that you have made any necessary adjustments to the goals, explore how these are live goals? What are you actively doing to attain each goal? If you are not actively doing something, what could you be doing to potentially reach the goal?

Problem-Determined and Problem-Organizing Systems

If we hold that one party cannot control or change another, then we move into the realm of perturbations, where the most we can do is act and see how the other responds based on their structure. In other words, if you kick a ball, you generally have a pretty good idea where it's going to go; you can make predictions that will likely be fairly accurate. However, you cannot fully take into account the friction between the composition of the ball and the composition of your foot/shoe, the impact of the wind, the non-preciseness of your intended aim, etc. Similarly, you can make a prediction about what will happen if you poke your sleeping cat, but you don't exactly know what it will do next. That depends upon the meaning that the cat makes of the poke. You can intervene to some degree with a ball, but you can only perturb a cat. In constructivist therapies, the therapist does not have the idea of intervening to create a predicate change, since that is not part of constructivist thinking. Rather the therapist provides thoughts or reflections that act as perturbations to the client, leading to an exploration of what meaning the clients make of these perturbations.

In constructivist therapy, we come into a process of coordination where our contact happens through linguistic processes (Maturana & Poerksen, 2004). That is, through "languaging" we contact one another via the world of meaning (Maturana, 1991). This shifts therapy from an occasion where an expert of mental health delivers care to a passive patient, to one where there are two (or more) people who are experts, each on their own meanings. The client is the expert on the meanings she creates, while the therapist is an expert on opening space—a dialogic space—in a conversation for the exploration of those meanings (Anderson, 2005).

Therapy can then be viewed as a linguistic system where meanings are constructed by whoever is in the room having a dialogue together (Anderson & Goolishian, 1988). Given that the context is therapy, usually the dialogue is focused on a problem. Thus, a family or a therapy becomes a **problem-determined system** or a **problem-organizing system**. Goolishian and Winderman (1988) explained this distinction, "Problem Determined Systems are linguistic systems composed of intersecting domains of linguistic experience continually evolving and changing with increasing or decreasing numbers of actors" (p. 135). This view shifts the notion of "problem" from being a distinct entity that is located in a distinct location. Rather, problem, or what can be called a dilemma or life situation (Anderson, 1997), becomes housed within a person's meaning.

This leads to the dilemma being much more malleable as Frank is not an obsessive-compulsive, but Stella makes meaning of her interactions with Frank as those behaviors representing what she knows to be obsessive-compulsive. The therapy dialogue can then focus on how she has come to that meaning and

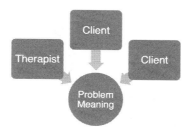

Figure 9.5 The Problem-Determined System Consists of All Individuals Who Are Interested in Talking About a Topic.

what that meaning has for her. This may lead to a newer meaning, one that changes her sense of concern around the dilemma. This dialogue can be between just the therapist and Stella or whoever is interested in conversing around the dilemma. Please keep in mind that there is not just "a problem" as each person in the conversation brings her own meaning for what is a strength and what is a problem. For Frank and Stella, the problem-determined system may change each session:

Session 1: Therapist, Frank, and Stella
Session 2: Therapist and Frank
Session 3: Therapist and Stella
Session 4: Therapist, Stella, and her children
Session 5: Therapist, Frank, and Stella

Each of these configurations would be problem-determined or problem-organizing systems (see Figure 9.5). Each of these systems could generate different meanings of the same problem. Often the problem itself is defined differently, even though events are the same. There are likely to be multiple meanings to each story.

Thus, it is in languaging where problems are created. If we can language a problem into existence, then we can engage in language where alternative possibilities arrive that do not include a problem. This new language happens in a collaborative process between client and therapist in which the main "technique" (which is not a technique but an attitude, philosophy, ideology, and way of being) is a therapeutic conversation—a dialogue—that without knowing the outcome, happens to lead to some type of new meaning or narrative (Anderson, 1993).

Since problems are distinctions people make through the meaning and language they attribute to situations, those distinctions and meanings can be dissolved in conversation. This process leads to the generation of alternative meanings that are likely to promote a sense of agency for the client; the client is in charge of the meaning of the events in her life, rather than the result of those events. To help in bringing out these distinctions and different meanings, the therapist uses three main endeavors: opening space for the client's story, engagement through a "not-knowing" position, and using conversational questions during the dialogue (Anderson, 1993).

Since problems are languaged and therapy is a "collaborative language system" (Goolishian & Anderson, 1987) where meanings are perturbed through conversation, therapists usually start by **opening space** for the client's story. The therapist does not know who wants to be involved in the conversation and does not bring preconceived ideas of who should or should not be present. In these conversations, no one person's perspective is accepted as truth. Rather, each person is viewed to have her own ideas as to what the problem is and the importance of the problem. This is based on the idea that each client is an expert on her own life. The goal in therapy is not to know the other person, but to know as best as one can what they are saying, as well as hearing the "not-yet-said" and ideas that could emerge if given enough space. This perspective helps create a space for a dialogue where meanings change (Anderson & Goolishian, 1988).

Stella is an expert on her life and the meaning that she puts to who she is and how she understands the world. She is an expert on the meaning that she has for Frank's behaviors. However, she is not an expert on Frank. Frank is an expert on Frank—the meanings that he construes for his own experience. The therapist's position is to open space for each person in the therapy room to have the dialogic space to allow their known meanings and their not yet known meanings to come forth.

Key Figure

Harlene Anderson

Harlene Anderson was born on December 1, 1942. Anderson's paternal heritage was Swedish, and her maternal heritage was German. Her parents were self-starters who owned their own business. They would encourage Harlene to be her own person and engage in independent thinking. Through them, she developed a respect for people, which can be seen in her belief that people own their own meanings and are the experts of their lives.

Anderson received Bachelor's and Master's degrees from the University of Houston and a Ph.D. in Psychology with a specialization in Marriage and Family Therapy from Union Institute and University. After graduating with her doctorate, she moved back to Texas, working in community mental health centers where she was perplexed about the differences in clients when they were in the hospital setting rather than their own homes. This led to her beginning to eschew the diagnostic labels that clients had placed upon them by the medical community. As Anderson (1990) explained, "As I developed a bias toward working within or close to the client's reality, I found myself veering away from 'knowing' better than the client" (p. 196).

In 1970, Anderson took a position in the pediatrics department of the University of Texas Medical School in Galveston. This is where she first came across Harry Goolishian, who was the director of the Psychology Division of the Psychiatry Department. Goolishian became a mentor, colleague, and friend. Working with Goolishian, Paul Dell, and George Pulliam, Anderson founded the Galveston Family Institute in 1978. The center has since changed its name to the Houston Galveston Institute.

Goolishian and Anderson may be most known for the concept of "not-knowing," which is a part of their collaborative language systems approach. "Not-knowing" refers to the notion that one person cannot know the understandings of another. On the forefront of the postmodern movement, Anderson and Goolishian helped to shift the notion of the therapist as the expert to the client as the expert (of her own experience and meanings).

In 1997, Harlene Anderson received the Lifetime Achievement Award by the Texas Association for Marriage and Family Therapy. Then in 2000, the American Association for Marriage and Family Therapy presented her with the Outstanding Contributions to Marriage and Family Therapy Award.

Because meanings are created by each individual in the interconnectedness of people languaging with one another, one person's viewpoint is not privileged over another. Thus, a therapist does not know best how things should be for a client. One of the main attitudes a therapist can take to operate within this understanding is that of "**not-knowing**." Anderson (1997) described this position:

> Not-knowing refers to a therapist's position—an attitude and belief—that a therapist does not have access to privileged information, can never fully understand another person, always needs to be in a state of being informed by the other, and always needs to learn more about what has been said or may not have been said.

(p. 134)

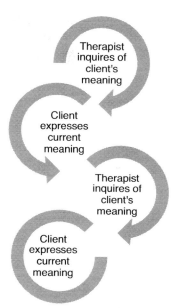

Figure 9.6 The Relationship Between the Therapist's Inquiry of Client Meaning and the Client's Expression of Meaning. Given the Therapist's Attitude of "Not Knowing," Therapy Becomes a Dialogue in Which the Client's Meanings Are Continually Being Explored.

Thus, the therapist is always curious as to how the client understands the situation as well as curious as to how the client's understanding shifts the therapist's understanding (see Figure 9.6).

Therapists who are not-knowing are not ignorant; rather, they know a lot. They are aware of themselves and have conversational skills that allow them to connect with clients and explore the meanings each person places on situations. Maintaining this position of curiosity and desire to understand involves being uncertain and having humility (Anderson, 1997). The not-knowing therapist is uncertain about ultimate objective truth—they are not the purveyors of what is. Thus, they are in a continual state of examination of beliefs. The therapist is also willing to take a risk—a risk of engaging with someone when they do not know what is. However, they are willing to allow the other person the space for the exploration of meaning. Humility comes from wanting more, so as to learn from the client, rather than telling the client the therapist's own beliefs or knowledge.

Since therapy is a dialogical process, where two people come in contact with one another in an I-Thou relationship, without ever truly knowing the meanings of the other, it becomes a process of spontaneous interactions in which neither party knows what will emerge in the subsequent transactions. This dialogical process consists of six overlapping components (Anderson, 1997):

1. A therapist engages in and maintains an internal dialogical space with himself or herself.
2. A therapist initiates and maintains an external dialogue with a client.
3. A client engages in an internal dialogue with himself or herself.
4. Clients engage in external dialogue with each other.
5. A client engages in internal and external dialogue outside the therapy room.
6. A therapist engages in internal and external dialogue outside the therapy room.

(p. 128)

When developing a therapeutic conversation with Frank and Stella, the therapist would begin by accepting that his own viewpoints are not more correct than the client's. This is the beginning of the I-Thou relationship where the therapist views self as a unique person with his own way of thinking and the clients as unique people, each with their own way of thinking. Next, the therapist begins a conversation with Frank and Stella, asking about each of their goals for the meeting. This entails bringing forth their potential similar and different ideas as to the purpose of the conversation. During the session, Frank and Stella each have an internal conversation, most likely regarding what they've been hearing. From this, they then put their thoughts into language and engage the other people in the therapy room in dialogue. The last part of this process is that each person, including the therapist, has both internal and external dialogue once they leave the session while having been impacted by the therapeutic dialogue.

In a collaborative language system dialogue, the therapist comes from the position of not-knowing. This entails the therapist to be curious and attempt to listen to the client's expressions. As Anderson (2007a) explained, "Listening is part of the process of trying to hear and grasp what the other person is saying from their perspective" (p. 36). The therapist does not impose an understanding or interpret the person but asks questions that help elicit the client's meanings and understandings to come forth.

Anderson (2007b) discussed four aspects of the philosophical underpinnings of not-knowing. The first deals with preknowing versus knowing with—coming with set viewpoints or developing viewpoints based on the conversation. In traditional psychiatric and psychological contexts, pre-sessioning is important to begin the assessment process. These would include many of the areas of the biopsychosocial assessment (see Chapter 1). When therapists attempt to understand a client through assessment materials or theoretical constructs, without first engaging with the client, they are coming from a knowing perspective and imposing their own framework on what is happening for the client and what needs to happen for the client for the client to be cured or helped. A second aspect of not-knowing is how therapists think about knowledge. In essence, is one person's knowledge more valued than another person's knowledge? Value here relates to acceptance that people are equal, and knowledge is not determined but, rather, influenced. Thus, perhaps in dialogue a client will change her knowledge, and just as likely, the therapist will change his knowledge based on where the talk of the conversation has led. A third aspect of not-knowing is how the therapist uses his knowledge. Anderson explained that "knowledge cannot be sent (or received) to one person from another, therapists do not have an investment in privileging their knowledge over another's or persuading them of it" (p. 49). In this regard, the therapist does not try to get the client to believe what the therapist believes but instead to inquire into what the client believes. The fourth aspect of not-knowing is how the therapist offers knowledge. It is not provided as "the truth" but done so in a tentative manner, with a sense of possibility rather than definitiveness.

From this perspective, questions are not asked in which the therapist thinks he knows the answer, but questions come from the not-knowing perspective; the therapist knows he does not know the answers. Thus, the question is not diagnostic (i.e., to determine whether someone fits a certain category or criteria that the field might impose on them) but, rather, is asked out of curiosity. These questions are called **conversational questions** (Anderson, 1997). They happen from inside the conversation rather than from outside, meaning that they are a follow-up and enrichment of the client's talk rather than an imposition from the therapist.

Conversational questions allow clients to tell their story and open up exploration of the unsaid in the conversation. They help move the dialogue into a shared inquiry where therapist and client explore the client's meaning together (see Figure 9.7). From this approach, conversational questions are not a set-up for an intervention designed to lead to a change that the therapist thinks would be helpful. Instead, taken together, these questions are perturbations for both the therapist and the client, as one question flows into the next. The task for the therapist then becomes being connected to the conversation, so the next conversational question develops naturally from the therapeutic dialogue.

There is no specific conversational question, but there is a right conversational question. **Right questions** come from the therapist really listening to the client and trying to further explore the client's world (Anderson, 1997). A therapist cannot create these questions ahead of time as clients, and therapists, continually change their understandings. Thus, conversational questions do not lead the interchange to a specific goal or outcome, but are used to continue the dialogical conversation (Anderson & Goolishian, 1988).

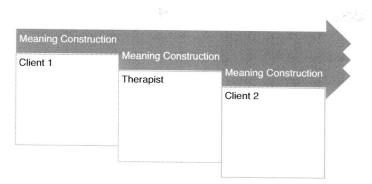

Figure 9.7 Meaning Construction Through Conversational Questioning. Through the Back-and-Forth Dialogue, Each Person Involved Continuously Creates Meaning to Their Own Experience.

When working with multiple people in the linguistic system, conversational questions do not try to gain consensus. The goal is not to have everybody in the room agree. The therapist respects multiple viewpoints, even understanding that her own views may differ than one or more of the other conversational partners. When working with Frank and Stella, the use of conversational questions guided by a not-knowing attitude might take on the following form:

Therapist: Frank, from what you just said, you are concerned about being with Stella and that there is respect in your relationship.
Frank: Yes. Respect is very important to me. I didn't feel respected in my past relationships.
Therapist: You're wanting to be respected. Is that right?
Frank: Yes.
Therapist: How do you know, in your relationship with Stella, that you are being respected?
Frank: When she does what she says she's going to do. Or if there is an issue, to let me know right away and not leave me hanging.
Therapist: Frank, how do you think Stella knows whether she is respecting you or not?

Applying Your Knowledge

For the following client statements, choose which of the two therapist questions is the conversational question:

1. Client: I got an email from a work colleague that just sat wrong with me. I found it to be abrasive and demeaning, and I'm not sure what to do about it.

   a. Therapist Question 1: What was it like to get an email you found abrasive?
   b. Therapist Question 2: What are your thoughts on standing up for yourself?

2. Client: My father just went into the hospital with pneumonia. He is elderly and not doing that great, so this was a huge scare for us.

   a. Therapist Question 1: What have you tried to do to get him healthy again?
   b. Therapist Question 2: How do you understand this feeling for you, with the connection you have for your father?

> 3. Client: It might sound weird, but I found religion. This is really good, but my partner is not there with me. It is bringing a huge wedge between us.
>   a. Therapist Question 1: What do you make of it that this is going on for you right now?
>   b. Therapist Question 2: When do you think you'll make a choice in the relationship?

CURIOSITY

In order to come from a not-knowing position, the therapist must operate from the position of **curiosity**. There are several types of curiosity, some therapeutically beneficial while some are not. If the client says, "You'll never believe this strange sexual position my partner wanted to do last night. I was so disgusted," you as the therapist should be curious but not about what the strange sexual position was. That is more of a voyeuristic curiosity. **Therapeutic curiosity** would be wanting to know how the client made sense of herself that her partner wanted to be sexual in a way the client thought was strange.

Building on the ideas of hypothesizing, circularity, and neutrality (Palazzoli et al., 1980), Cecchin (1987) proposed that neutrality be viewed as a position of curiosity. He explained,

> Curiosity leads to exploration and invention of alternative views and moves, and different moves and views breed curiosity. In this recursive fashion, neutrality and curiosity contextualize one another in a commitment to evolving differences, with a concomitant nonattachment to any particular position.
> (p. 406)

That is, curiosity helps produce new actions and interpretations (Cecchin, 1992).

From this perspective, therapeutic curiosity is not designed to figure out *what is*, but to bring forth explanations of *what might be*. Through conversation, multiple perspectives are brought forth, with no perspective being truth. This polyphony of meanings recursively interact, producing newer meanings. Thus, operating from a position of curiosity restrains the therapist from taking a position of instructive interaction, which would be from an expert position. Instead, the therapist becomes curious as to what new hypotheses he might develop and what new circular ways of viewing will lead to new stories (Cecchin, 1987). By being curious as to the client's meanings, newer meanings for the clients may emerge. This process of therapeutic curiosity might play out with our case couple in the following manner:

Therapist: Stella, how do you understand what Frank is saying about respect?
Stella: I know that he thinks he was treated poorly by his ex-wife. But he needs to know I'm not her. I'm me.
Therapist: Okay, so on the one hand, you understand that he feels disrespected in the past, and on the other hand, you think he needs to understand that you are not the one who has disrespected him.
Stella: Right. I am in this relationship with him now. Not anyone else.
Therapist: You want him to be in relationship with you, not the baggage of past relationships. What is that like for you?

DISTINGUISHING SELF

The constructivist therapist develops a curiosity as to how the other comes to know herself, without placing a template on this (as might be done through personality assessments). Rather, it occurs through the not-knowing stance and exploring how the person comes to distinguish the self. Guidano (1995)

Figure 9.8 Distinguishing Self From Other.

explained that "any knowledge of oneself and the world is always dependent on and relative to knowledge of others" (p. 96). We continually, even unconsciously, make distinctions between ourselves and someone else or multiple others. We can see this principle in action in various models such as natural systems theory's concept of self-differentiation (see Chapter 6), Rogers' person-centered therapy and the I-Thou relationship, and Boszormenyi-Nagy's contextual therapy and the relational dimension of the ontic (Ducommon-Nagy & Reiter, 2014). In the ontic perspective, people come to define themselves by not being the other (see Figure 9.8). Through the use of language, people are able to make the distinction between themselves as subject and as object (Guidano, 1995).

To explain this more clearly, we can look at how Frank and Stella each distinguish themselves. Frank views himself as a male in comparison to his understanding of other males. For instance, he may think about his own father and his thoughts on how his father was treated as well as treated others. Let's say that Frank believes that his mother did not respect his father and that his father just accepted this and was miserable. He may then tell himself, "I will not let the woman I am with disrespect me and be a patsy like my father was." By distinguishing himself as different from his father, the concept of respect becomes a significant factor in how he organizes his construction of meaning for himself in relation to women. Stella might distinguish herself as different from others, such as her sister, Fiona. Let's say that Stella views Fiona in a position of having problematic romantic relationships because she believes Fiona is never satisfied, that Fiona finds little faults in her romantic partner and makes these into something bigger than they are. Consequently, she constructs meaning of being in a romantic relationship in a way that she does not put much focus on aspects of the relationship that might be considered a fault. Instead, she focuses on what she is gaining in the relationship rather than what could be different.

Neimeyer (2009) held that one aspect of constructivist psychotherapy is helping to foster client **reflexivity**, the ability of clients to reflect on their own lives and meanings. He explained, "It is client activity and insight that ultimately produce lasting life adaptations" (p. 83). In traditional psychotherapy, insight—a piece of truth about the client—was provided to the client or generated in the client by the therapist. The therapist gathered data from the client's life and provided interpretations to explain why the client is the way she is and how she got that way. Constructivist therapists flip this script, allowing clients to attribute meaning to their own stories wherein the clients are more likely to develop their own insights that will lead to behavior change.

Therapist: Stella, how do you look back to your parents' marriage compared to your relationship with Frank?
Stella: I thought my mother was way too demanding of my father.
Therapist: You thought mother was too demanding of father. In what ways? (therapist thickening the description of the story)
Stella: She would go after him for any little thing. He didn't make enough money. He wasn't home as much as he should have been. He snored. He smelled the bathroom up. Everything. Anything.
Therapist: How does the perception you have impact how you are in relationship with Frank?
Stella: Well, I didn't think it was fair when my mother did this. I could see how miserable my father was. He was a very beaten man. Growing up, I told myself I would never have a marriage like my parents had.
Therapist: So how similar or different do you think your relationship with Frank is than the one your mother and father had?
Stella: Extremely different. I hardly demand anything from him.
Therapist: Is that how you want it to be?
Stella: I would rather err on the side of letting things go than being demanding, so yeah, it is more how I want it to be.

Here, the therapist did not push his own agenda on the client—an agenda that might be that people should stand up for themselves and have certain expectations of the other. Stella was distinguishing herself from her mother, wanting to be more flexible than demanding. This construction of self was more empowering to her sense of self than being in ways similar to her mother.

Casual Enactments

In Chapter 5, we presented the use of therapeutic enactments to assist the therapist in observing the family's process. We can now talk about another type of enactment, **casual enactments**, that can be used with individual clients to help in the process of exploratory self-reordering. Neimeyer (1995) described that the purpose of these enactments "is to provide for elaboration of the clients' personal worldview while protecting their core role structures from premature invalidation, to buffer them from assault until they are better able to consider abandoning them" (pp. 117–118).

In attempting to help clients, and therapist, explore the client's position, rather than demonstrating what the position should be, casual enactments tend to be brief and informal. They are role-plays where the client is able to take on various perspectives (Neimeyer, 1995). These enactments can be verbal or nonverbal. Working with Frank and Stella, a casual enactment may occur as the following:

Therapist: Stella and Frank, I'd like you to take two minutes and have a conversation with each other, but by taking the other person's position. That is, Stella, talk as if you are Frank, and Frank, talk as if you are Stella.
Stella: Why didn't you call me when you were going to be late today?
Frank: I was only going to be a few minutes late. What was the big deal?
Stella: The big deal was I was worried about you. It would have been respectful for you to call me.
Frank: And it would be respectful of you if you didn't hound me. I need to breathe as well.
Stella: I give you a lot of space. I am not asking you to move in or marry me. Just for you to think how what you do might impact me.
Frank: And what do you think of how your anxiety impacts me?

By engaging in the casual enactment, the person may develop a new construction of understanding. From this interchange, Frank may think about how he does make demands on Stella. This understanding may lead to him changing how he interacts with Stella, perhaps asking more about her and having a more genuine interaction. Conversely, Stella may think that perhaps she can be clearer on what her needs are. This small and quick enactment may bring perturbations to each party, leading them to have new understandings and behave differently in the relationship.

One of the most famous enactments of this type is the **empty chair technique,** which became famous through its use by Gestalt psychotherapists. The empty chair technique is when the therapist asks the client to have a conversation with their construction of another person or with aspects of themselves. For instance, Stella might be asked to talk with her expectancies of self or others, or Frank may be asked to speak with his ex-wife.

Therapist: Frank, you see this empty seat over here. Imagine that your ex-wife is sitting there. What do you want to say to her?
Frank: I would say that. . . .
Therapist: Don't tell me. Tell her, as if she is there.
Frank: It wasn't right the way you treated me. You were disrespectful.
Therapist: What would your ex say?
Frank: She'd say, "I wasn't disrespectful. You were just needy and crazy."
Therapist: Respond to her.
Frank: I wasn't needy. I just wanted someone to love me. You know my parents were very critical of me. I wanted to make sure that everything was right. Why couldn't you accept me?
Therapist: Answer for her.
Frank: Because I was not happy. You were too focused on yourself and didn't fully think about me and my needs. . . .

Therapist: What do you have to say to her?
Frank: I didn't not think about you. It's just I needed some things. I needed. . . . yes, I needed, and maybe you're right. At times, I didn't fully think of you. Perhaps I'm a bit selfish.

Through this enactment, the client is able to make sense of aspects of self he hadn't quite contacted before.

We have presented two examples of verbal enactments. Now we will present a nonverbal enactment. **Family sculpting** is a nonverbal means for people to express their perceptions of their experience (Satir & Baldwin, 1984). Here, clients are asked to put themselves into physical positions that represent their current experience. The therapist can start with either person and ask them to put the partner and then themselves into a physical and spatial position that represents what it is like for them in the relationship. Stella's picture might be with her sitting down on the floor with Frank standing over her with his hands in a fist and his index fingers pointing at her. Frank's sculpt may have Stella facing away from him and looking at her cell phone while he is standing in the corner. These sculpts may lead to Frank and Stella each having a different understanding of what it means to be in this relationship.

The benefit of the client portraying each of these different roles, whether it be the client's perception of real people or the client's perception of aspects of self, is that a contextual shift is likely to happen. However, the therapist cannot predetermine what that shift is going to be. The shift will be based upon the structural determinism of the client.

Scaling Questions

Given that people can never know the objective, real meaning of another, one way of being therapeutic is to utilize the misunderstandings that constitute conversations. de Shazer and Berg (1993) explained, "The therapist's job is to use the misunderstandings inherent in conversation to help the client notice differences so that these noticed differences can be put to work" (p. 19). These differences can come from the client's own rating of where they fall along a scale.

Scaling questions, which were introduced in Chapter 3, are used to help abstract concepts become more concrete so that two or more people can construct a common language with one another—a language predicated on numbers (see Figure 9.9). Numbers become a metaphor for describing problems, successes, and the ways they change. de Shazer and Berg (1993) described the importance of this numerical language,

> Scales allow both therapist and client to use the way language works naturally by agreeing upon terms (i.e., numbers) and a concept (a scale where 10 stands for the goal and zero stands for an absence of progress toward that goal) that is obviously multiple and flexible.
>
> (p. 19)

We caution you to avoid the confusion that the numbers represent a quantity of concern, problem, or feeling that will be resolved through a certain quantity of change. Rather, the scale looks at the meaning of the current situation by comparing it to another, possible future meaning. The numbers never assess an objective

Figure 9.9 Scaling Questions Allow Clients to Experience Their Perceptions in a Different Fashion Than Normal.

quantity of anything. Instead, they help therapist and client to form an understanding of what problems and change mean to the client, giving therapist and client a common language. This changes the scale from a realist, objective assessment of a problem, to a "language game" in which the therapist and client imagine how meaningful a certain change might be through the metaphor of numbers. Thus, a 7 on a certain scale is not good or bad, and the number is not the same for multiple people. This is different than a score on a standardized assessment, such as an IQ test, where two people's scores can be objectively compared.

One of the benefits of scaling questions is that they can be used for any concept. They can be constructed around hopefulness, self-esteem, connection, and a variety of other concepts. The therapist and client construct the scale to highlight differences. These differences might be temporal, such as "right now," "today," or "this past month" (Berg, 1994). The difference might also be based on how various people may perceive the concept and how each might scale it differently (Reiter & Shilts, 1998).

The first answer the client gives to a scaling question provides a baseline. For instance, the therapist could ask Frank and Stella, "On a scale of 1 to 10 where 10 is where you want the relationship to be and 1 is the worst it could be, where would you say you are right now?" Frank might say a 5, while Stella might say a 6. Successive constructions of the client's perception of where they are on the scale help therapist and client explore whether there has been progress. Scaling questions can also be used to help people develop goals. The therapist can ask, "Frank, you were initially at a 5. When you are at a 6, what will be different in your relationship?" This question, with a change in the numerical points, could then be asked to Stella. Their answers then become new meaning constructions and possible pieces of their goals.

The distance between the numbers is not important. What is important is the therapist's belief that change is always happening, conveying the therapist's expectation that change will happen for the client, which helps construct greater hope from the client (Reiter, 2010). The therapist might ask Stella, "You are at a 6 right now. What will you notice that is different when you are at a 6.1?" In this exchange, there is a construction of a vision of a future where there is movement toward the client's goals.

Applying Your Knowledge

Develop five scaling questions that you might ask Frank and Stella.

1.
2.
3.
4.
5.

QUESTIONS FOR REFLECTION

1. What impact does operating from the notion of a problem-determined system have on therapy? What is the focus on? Who comes to the therapy session?

2. What are the pros and cons of operating from a position of not-knowing?

3. In what ways should a therapist be curious? In what ways should a therapist not be curious?

4. How might casual enactments help to shift client's meaning and understandings?

5. How do scaling questions help therapist and client throughout the process of therapy?

CHAPTER TEN
Social Construction Aesthetics

Michael D. Reiter

CASE DESCRIPTION

Xiang is a 34-year-old Asian female. She was born in Thailand, and her family immigrated to the United States when she was 7 years old and her brother, Tam, was 4. In the United States, her father, Malian, was a construction worker who spent a lot of time out of the house playing cards, drinking, and fraternizing with women who were not his wife. Her mother, Chanhira, worked in a local fast-food restaurant. Throughout Xiang's youth, the family did not have much money and lived in a one-bedroom apartment where mother and father slept in one bed and sister and brother slept in the other bed in the same room.

At 18, Xiang received a scholarship to a four-year university for soccer. During her first semester, her parents went through a divorce, and Malian moved back to Thailand. Chanhira took the leaving of her husband very poorly, especially since she was unsure how she was going to pay the bills for the household. Xiang dropped out of college and got a full-time job so that she could help support the family. At night, she slept in the same bed with her mother while her brother slept by himself in the other bed.

When she was 22, Xiang married Edward. She had met him at work and thought that she had found true love. Edward worked at a car dealership and had recently, before meeting Xiang, been involved in an abusive relationship where his girlfriend had gotten a restraining order on him. Xiang did not know about the restraining order until later in their marriage. During the first few years, Xiang found that she was giving up many of her joys so that Edward would be pleased. These included minor things such as where to eat, where to go out for fun, and what they would do with their time. Edward would make statements such as, "You know I don't like Indian or Thai food. Let's go Italian" or "Why do you have to play soccer today? I miss you and want to spend time with you." After five years of marriage, Xiang realized that she had given up much of herself and began to put her foot down. During one of these exchanges, Edward slapped her. There was a huge blowup where Xiang left and stayed at her mother's house for one week. When she returned, Edward was regretful. This lasted several weeks, and then there was another physical incident where he grabbed her. Xiang began divorce proceedings the next day.

Over the next six years, she was in three turbulent romantic relationships. At 34 years old, Xiang met Ben. Over the course of their relationship, she experienced herself again giving up many of her pursuits, joys, and desires so that Ben would be pleased. After going through something similar with Edward, Xiang realized that she was engaging in destructive patterns in many relationships. One of her good friends told her that she was "codependent." Upon looking up the word, she agreed and decided to seek out therapy so that she could have a healthy and productive relationship.

In this chapter, we explore the postmodern notion of social constructionism and how this viewpoint provides psychotherapists with a basis for understanding people. We will use the case of Xiang to help exemplify many of the core philosophical underpinnings of social constructionism.

Modernism Versus Postmodernism

Modernism is the notion that human beings progress and grow through an understanding of legitimate knowledge. It dictates that there is an absolute truth and includes notions of objectivity, individual reason, knowledge, empiricism, scientific truth, and control. Modernism is based on the doctrine that there is an independent reality outside of the observer/knower (Held, 1995b). It developed in the late 19th and early 20th centuries as a move away from ideas prevalent in the Dark Ages, where man believed his actions to be based on religious control to a Western understanding of man having individual reason (Gergen, 2009a).

From a modernist perspective, people can know themselves and their environment and can actively change these through scientific and empirical knowledge. This perspective ascribes to the theory that people can engage in quantitative experiments in an attempt to "prove" what is. **Postmodernism**, in a very simplified explanation, is the movement away from absolute truth (see Figure 10.1). It shifts away from a modernist notion that there is an essential knowable self that has an individual ego at its core to a self based on interpersonal and cultural contexts (Neimeyer, 1998). From a postmodernist perspective, what happens between people and how that interaction creates understanding is valued over the notion of a true reality. People operating from a postmodern position tend to focus on process rather than goals, view self as a narrative rather than a reified entity, conceive of text as an evolving process, and focus on people in social meaning rather than through an intrapsychic realm (Lax, 1992).

From the postmodern position, the individual is not a stable self. Rather, the individual is viewed as more fluid and continuously shifting based on the discourses used to describe and understand self (Pilgrim, 2000). This position is contrary to the view of personality and personality development currently held by mainstream society. Mainstream society views childhood as a formation stage where an individual's personality is not only formed, but is solidified—hence the expression, "You can't teach an old dog new tricks." However, this view that people cannot change, or if so it is very difficult to, after childhood is not a view that psychotherapists should subscribe to; otherwise, what would be the purpose of therapy if people did not change?

Modernists approach a person as a static entity, often using phrases such as, "He's narcissistic," "She's a manipulator," "He's an introvert," and "Xiang is codependent." This approach views the person in a very limited manner with little possibility for change and difference. Postmodernists, on the other hand, would not view someone as an introvert but, rather, that the person or others view her as that. Further, in different contexts, the person might behave in a manner that others might describe as extroverted (or at least not introverted). The more that people talk in a way that creates a different identity, the greater likelihood that the person would live that alternative identity. Xiang, through conversation with her friend and exploration of a medical viewpoint, has developed an identity of being codependent. This has been, for her, reinforced through significant experiences in her life. Xiang is utilizing a modernist position of believing herself to be codependent. The postmodernist would view her as internalizing a social discourse that limits how she views herself and what actions she thinks she can take. In essence, she has created a meaning of who she is that has become reified.

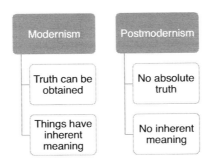

Figure 10.1 The Differences Between Modernist and Postmodernist Views, Mainly Focusing on Whether There Is an Absolute Truth and How Meaning Is Constructed.

Postmodernists believe that no action in itself has meaning. Rather, we create the meaning for what has occurred. This is why, in a conflict, both parties can think they are the "good" and the other side the "bad." Think about all of the wars in human history. Did any side think they were bad and evil? We can use the Star Wars saga as an example. Even though most people who watch Star Wars view the Jedi as good and the Empire as bad, members of the Galactic Empire saw themselves in a positive light and the Jedi in a negative light. The Empire was actually trying to bring peace (based on their construction of what constituted "peace") to the galaxy.

Social Constructionism

In Chapters 8 and 9, we presented a constructivist view of language systems. In Chapters 10 and 11, we will talk about social constructionism. While there are differences between constructivism and social constructionism, they are definitely closely related. In general, constructivists hold that "truth" is created by the individual, while constructionists hold that "truth" is created in the social realm (Gergen, 1994). For the social constructionist, it is the interactive relationships between people rather than how the individual constructs knowledge that becomes central (Rosen, 1996). Thus, the words/descriptions that people use, especially when we are talking about large groups, become a "truth telling" for that cultural group (Gergen, 2009a). Yet, over time, this "truth" might change for a new "truth."

The various constructions that people make become useful in how they are socially utilized (Gergen, 2009a). The distinctions that multiple people make help them to navigate their ecologies (i.e., their social and relational worlds). When we explain "what is" we have to keep in mind that the construct being discussed was socially constructed and is ever-evolving, based on who is in dialogue around the idea (Gergen, 1985). Xiang is attempting to make sense of her life and has "discovered" a "truth" about herself—that she is codependent. This meaning that she has put to her life was not always present and will likely change many more times over the course of her life. How it changes is most likely based on whom she is in contact with as she will come to have one view of herself as codependent when talking with Ben, another with a good friend, and still another when talking with a therapist.

A social constructionist therapist is quite unlikely to attempt to diagnose a client and think that there is a "problem" located within the person. Not only do they tend to not diagnose, they view this process of diagnosing as promoting a cultural discourse of enfeeblement (Gergen, 1994). Given that there is not a problem within a person, the therapist is not needed to develop a cure. This is a major shift from a medical model to a view of meaning being created through cultural linguistics. Symptoms do not come from psychological disorders but, rather, are situated in current living patterns (Efran & Clarfield, 1992; see Figure 10.2). This view helps us, as therapists, to move beyond viewing Xiang as codependent and instead to situate her understanding of herself within the larger discourses of her life: her culture, her gender, her age, her sexuality, and her relational expectations.

In Chapters 8 and 9, we presented how the ideas from constructivism help to inform therapists in the way they view what is happening for clients and what they do in the therapy room. While social

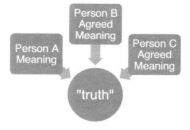

Figure 10.2 People Construct "Truth" Through Social Consensus.

constructionism is similar, it is a distinct way of viewing the notion of knowing and how people construct knowledge. Gergen (1994, pp. 49–53) provided several assumptions for a social constructionist science:

- The terms by which we account for the world and ourselves are not dictated by the stipulated objects of such accounts.
- The terms and forms by which we achieve understanding of the world and ourselves are social artifacts, products of historically and culturally situated interchanges among people.
- The degree to which a given account of world or self is sustained across time is not dependent on the objective validity of the account but on the vicissitudes of social process.
- Language derives its significance in human affairs from the way in which it functions within patterns of relationship.
- To appraise existing forms of discourse is to evaluate patterns of cultural life; such evaluations give voice to other cultural enclaves.

These assumptions are based on a founding that how we come to know something is not the thing itself. Rather, there is joint action between people, in a pattern of relationship that becomes an idea. Essentially, there is an arbitrariness between the person and the object—the signifier and the signified. To use a current phrase, which will likely date this book, we can talk about the recent phrase, "Make America Great Again." What does this phrase really mean? We cannot answer that without situating it within the group that is saying it. On a very general scale, Democrats and Republicans will have very different views of what this phrase means. Within those groups are subgroups who will have their own joint views. We can then move abroad, where other nations (based upon the views of the people living there) will have their own views as to what "Make America Great Again" means. Social constructionists believe that no group's meaning is "right," but each view has significance for those who believe it.

One of the critiques of social constructionism is that it rejects the notion that there is a world beyond the person (Gergen, 1994). Constructionists do not explain what is "in the world" or "in the person." Rather, they hold that, once we start to articulate what is, then we are in the world of discourse. Discourse construction happens in a web of social relationships that are housed within history and culture. Thus, when explaining the world, we are doing so from a specific perspective that is more than the individual. For instance, we can look at what defines a good marriage. The individual's answer to this is not separated from the relational contexts of the individual. These contexts may contain Western versus Eastern philosophies, gender, race, culture, age, and economics. Those individuals connected to traditions of arranged marriage will most likely have very different definitions than those from cultures that value love marriages. These definitions of a "good marriage" will also have changed throughout time, as societies shifted and the role of the spouses in a family changed.

Social constructionists tend to challenge ideas that deal with truth, knowledge, reason, and objectivity (Gergen, 2009a). This leads to the possibility to construct our understandings rather than have them given to us. Here, we can focus on our client, Xiang. Who is she? The answer depends on who is asking/answering. To a religious person, she is a Buddhist. To her boss, a devoted worker. To Edward, an ungrateful bitch. And to a psychotherapist, she may be someone with serious relational issues. All of these views are partial and will likely tell you more about the person making the determination rather than Xiang.

We can now explore the connection between postmodernism and language. As stated previously, postmodernists do not hold to an absolute truth, but rather, truth is a subjective agreement that is made through language. This position makes sense since constructionism was originally a critique and resistance to realism (Gergen, 2001). Thus, we move from the realm of what is to how we talk about what we think is there. Gergen (1982) explained this movement in that "knowledge about social life is not to be viewed as a 'reflection' of what there is, but as a 'transformation' of experience into a linguistic ontology" (p. 202).

Xiang's life does not have to be as it is. This is because she is not a certain type of person, fixed in personality and behaviors. She is not codependent, anxious, neurotic, obsessive-compulsive, or any other label to who a person is. She may exhibit behaviors that can be deemed these labels, yet her behavior is changeable. Further, she didn't just view herself as one or more of these traits. It happened through a much larger process where her ideas of the world intermingled with those around her as well as larger societal discourses. As people come together in conversation, they create ideas of what should be. These ideas, such as gender roles, family constitutions, and expectations based on age, change as the social conversation—the larger discourse—changes.

> ## Key Figure
>
> **Kenneth Gergen**
>
> Kenneth Gergen was born on December 9, 1935. His father, John Jay Gergen, served as the Chair of the Mathematics Department at Duke University. After growing up in Durham, North Carolina, Gergen attended Yale University where he earned a Bachelor's degree. He then enrolled in the US Navy and became an officer. Later, he attended Duke University and, under the mentorship of the social psychologist Edward E. Jones, received his Ph.D. in 1962. Gergen is married to Mary M. Gergen, a leading figure in feminist psychology.
>
> In 1967, Gergen became Chair of the Department of Psychology at Swarthmore College. He also served as Assistant Professor in the Department of Social Relations at Harvard University. In his association with the American Psychological Association, he was the President of the Division on Theoretical and Philosophical Psychology as well the Psychology and the Arts. In 1993, Gergen, along with several colleagues, founded the Taos Institute, a non-profit organization that focuses on bridging social constructionism ideas with societal practice.
>
> Gergen has been one of the leaders in the development of social constructionist theory. This view shifts reality from being singular to multiple. He helped to promote a wider shared understanding of science where knowledge is based in communities rather than individuals. He views social constructionism as a meta-theory (which challenges claims of objective knowledge), a social theory, and a societal practice.
>
> Some of Kenneth Gergen's most influential works include his books *Toward Transformation in Social Knowledge* (1982), *The Saturated Self* (1993), *Realities and Relationships: Soundings in Social Construction* (1994), *An Invitation to Social Construction* (2nd ed.) (2009), and *Relational Being: Beyond Self and Community* (2009).

Discourses

From a social constructionist perspective, language is a way of signifying what one is talking about but never is the thing being talked about. Thus, how we use language, how that use of language impacts the meanings being construed, and how people then react to this language changes based on what group is in discourse and how they are using language. This different usage of language configures the world of experience in many ways, which has serious implications for how people make sense of themselves, others, and the situation (Neimeyer, 1998).

Since the language we use is not based on fixed entities, the meaning of the words we use can change over the course of time. This is a benefit for therapists, as we can then enter into a language game with clients to help construct an experience that is more in the direction that the client wants to move. Thus, Xiang's social constructionist therapist will not try to impose how she should be. Instead, the therapist will engage in a therapeutic conversation that attempts to bring forth Xiang's ideas and meanings and see how, through dialogue, they might change.

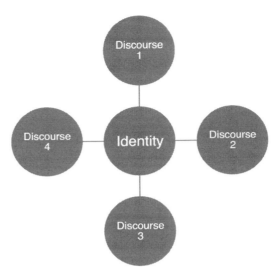

Figure 10.3 The Interaction of Various Discourses on an Individual's Identity.

Social constructionists value **discourses**—conversations between people. These discourses are comprised of verbal, written, and nonverbal communications. The various discourses we come in contact with help construct who we are as we internalize them and then self-police ourselves. These discourses overlap, providing a sense of identity (see Figure 10.3).

Xiang is connected to a multitude of discourses, which impact her sense of self. These include what it means to be 1) Asian, 2) female, 3) Buddhist, 4) divorced, 5) American, 6) a daughter, etc. The more that Xiang internalizes these discourses, which are cultural and time-sensitive (i.e., the discourse surrounding what it means to be a female is quite different when we look at 1918 and 2018), the more limited she will be in how she views herself, others, and possibilities of actions. For instance, if she views herself as an Asian female daughter where that means she is supposed to be loyal to family and sacrifice for them, she is more likely to engage in behaviors that fit this conceptualization. This is what happened for her when she first went to the university; she withdrew in order to help her mother and brother out when her mother and father divorced. This behavior made sense for her, and her family, based on their cultural understandings of familial loyalty. However, the more Xiang becomes Americanized, the more she may choose actions that honor individualism over familialism.

Discourses, as with other social constructionist processes and concepts, are not set and fixed. However, discourses have consequences. In looking at the notion of power, a person, group, or institution does not have inherent power. Rather, it is the process of providing legitimacy to a certain discourse that has some form of power or social control over others (Neimeyer, 1998). For instance, Xiang's workplace may try to assert power over its employees by stipulating working hours, vacation time, and dress codes. These rules and expectations are not inherent in businesses. They were developed by that organization. When everyone follows those rules, they become legitimized. However, as with many organizations, people may challenge the rules so that they change. This has occurred in the United States with ideas such as the amount of hours in a workweek, the age of mandatory retirement, and whether the individual or the company is responsible for covering insurance.

Power

Social discourse, what might be called a **dominant discourse**, holds a lot of power in how people view themselves, others, and subsequently how they behave (see Figure 10.4). Michel Foucault (1980), a postmodern French philosopher/historian, was famous for saying that knowledge is power. When a

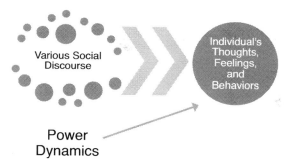

Figure 10.4 Social Discourses Are Related to Power Dynamics, Where People Internalize the Discourse, Which Influences How People Think, Feel, and Behave.

group of people agree on a certain knowledge set, such as psychotherapists' notion that people have mental disorders, this knowledge becomes "truth" and thus has power to influence how people think of themselves or of others. For Xiang, she has internalized the dominant discourse that people can become codependent and that codependency is a bad thing. Based on her belief in the knowledge about codependency, Xiang believes that there is something wrong with her. This leads her to feel bad about herself, that she is inadequate, and that her life cannot be as good as she would like it to be.

What happens is that knowledge of what should be—"truth"—has power in shaping how people understand themselves and how they live. That is, the larger "truths" of who people are become "normalizing" in that they become the expectations for how people should think, feel, and behave (White & Epston, 1990). For Xiang, we can think about how, at 34 years old, she comes to feel bad about herself. She has come in contact with many dominant discourses about how a female should think, feel, and act. How an Asian female should be. What it means to be part of a family. What it says about her that she is divorced. And, among a plethora of other "truths," how she should be in a romantic relationship.

These social discourses are intricately intertwined with power relations. As Drewery and Winslade (1997) explained, "Within human communities, what can be said, and who may speak, are issues of power" (p. 35). As used in this context, power does not mean the ability to physically control another person. Rather, power is about the influence that social practices have in constructing who people are and what they do.

Let's take the discourse of being a woman living in the United States who is in her 30s. Currently, this discourse holds that the woman should have a career as well as a family. For some, taking primary care of the family is considered the woman's career. This discourse has power in that people expect a relationship, likely marriage, to happen by the time a person turns 30 so that they can have children (which is related to the discourse of when it is acceptable—and with who—to have children). Xiang, without even realizing it, has experienced these power dynamics throughout many facets of her life. Perhaps her mother, Chanhira, asked Xiang when she would be having grandchildren. Her first husband, Edward, may have talked with her about whether and when he wanted children. And Xiang likely comes in contact with many media representations, via advertisements in magazines, television shows, commercials, and movies, portraying women in their 30s who are married with children. She then experiences thoughts about herself when she compares herself to the "norm" of other women her age. This may lead her to feel as if she is not adequate enough or is missing out on what other people think is the expected way of being for someone in her position.

Personal Agency

The social discourses that people come in contact with lead to power dynamics where individuals limit and self-police themselves based on the expected norms of the culture, which is articulated through the current social discourse. People are thus living in ways that do not necessarily fit their desired way of

Figure 10.5 The Process of Dominant Discourses Being Internalized by the Individual Who Then Self-Polices Herself, Leading to a Reduction in the Sense of Personal Agency.

being. When they do so, they tend to not exhibit **personal agency**, the process of taking an active stance in living one's desired life. The more that the dominant story takes hold of the person's life, the less sense of choice the person has in her experience. As alternative stories develop and people move away from the subjugating dominant discourse, they experience a heightened sense of personal agency (White & Epston, 1990). White (2007) explained the notion of personal agency:

> Personal agency is the outcome of the development of a sense of self that is associated with the perception that one is able to have some effect on the shape of one's own life; that is, a sense that (1) one is able to intervene in one's own life as an agent of what one gives value to and as an agent of one's own intentions, and (2) the world is at least minimally responsive to the fact of one's existence.
>
> (pp. 78–79)

People coming to therapy usually have a reduced sense of personal agency, as the stories that are dominating their lives tend to be endemic to the culture(s) the person is living in (see Figure 10.5).

Xiang has not been experiencing her life through a sense of personal agency. Rather, she believes she is a victim to her circumstances and personality. She could not help but take the actions she did since she is a codependent person and a loyal family member who had to sacrifice her dreams for the welfare of her family. However, through an alternative understanding of the current story she has about her life, she may see herself in a more heroic way—as being able to accept and hold the values that are important for her.

AUTHENTICITY

As explained in Chapter 8, constructivism holds that there is not an objective truth, but that the individual constructs truth through how she comes in contact with the world and produces meaning. Postmodernism upholds this notion of no objective truth but sees "truth" as being socially constructed. Here, we can switch from a focus on objectivity—an ability to know legitimate truth—to a stance more about authenticity.

Authenticity occurs when people live in accordance with their self-narratives, which is witnessed by themselves and/or others (White, 1993). What is important to note here is that there is not an authentic self, as in that is who the person was, is, and will always be. There is not an essence of us—that this is "who we are." However, there are multiple authenticities based on how we construct our stories to live by. Gergen (1991) described this ever-changing sense of self:

> Critical to my argument is the proposal that social saturation brings with it a general loss in our assumption of true and knowable selves. As we absorb multiple voices, we find that each "truth" is relativized by our simultaneous consciousness of compelling alternatives. We come to be aware that

each truth about ourselves is a construction of the moment, true only for a given time and within certain relationships.

(p. 16)

The authentic self then is temporary, shifting in tune to the meaning that people place on themselves and their lived experience.

Let's take a second to be clear about authenticity. In common parlance, we view and talk as if there is a concrete personhood, "She can't help it. That's just who she is." Social constructionism shifts this view of a person being authentic to their core being (as social constructionism disagrees with this concept), to the view of how the self is constructed through relationships. As Gergen (2006, 2009a) holds, there is a **relational self**. The self is entwined in the various relationships and cultural discourses she is connected to. In this vein, personhood is not about a true self but, rather, a sense of relatedness (Gergen, 1991).

Instead of someone having a "true" self and being the same in all situations, the relationships that people have with one another tend to center around a limited aspect of self. This is what Gergen (1991) describes as a **fractional relationship**. For Xiang, she engages her work colleagues more with her professional self, Ben with her romantic self, Chanhira with her loyal self, and her friends with her silly self. But just a word of caution—people are not as compartmentalized as this. Xiang will be exhibiting a mixture of her various selves with each person she interacts with.

Applying Your Knowledge

What are ten terms you would use to describe your personality? After writing them down, think about three different interpersonal relationships and the contexts in which they are each housed. For each of the ten personality "traits," which are more prevalent in each of the different relationships/contexts? How might a person who "knows" you in one context be shocked by how you act in a different context?

Let's look closer at our client, Xiang, and who she is. Xiang does not have a core self. We cannot know her outside of her context. We might view her as a **multi-being**, where she is able to be many persons (Gergen, 2009a). This is not about split personalities, but that with different people, in different situations, we create who we are in that moment. This then leads us to consider the notion that when we contact someone else, we are not just interacting with that person, but that person as an intersection of multiple relationships. Thus, two multi-beings come together and negotiate a common reality (see Figure 10.6).

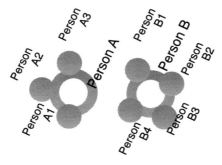

Figure 10.6 The Interaction of Two Multi-Self Individuals.

Reality as Multiverse

As we described, social constructionism is housed within a postmodern epistemology, where there are no absolute truths. Rather, "truth" (or what we might call an agreed upon temporal understanding) occurs through relational interchanges. These exchanges happen through multi-self individuals where the self that is present is created in the moment based on the context—who, what, where, when, and how. Xiang becomes a passive person when in her mother's house with her mother telling her how she should lead her life. However, Xiang becomes a more competent person at work when her colleagues look to her for guidance on a work project. However, she can become different in each of these same contexts given new interchanges that lead to new meanings of self.

From a modernist perspective, there is one truth that can be found. We can look at this as a universe ("uni-" one + "-verse" text = one story). This is a reality in which all people accept the same inherent meaning in that thing. However, social constructionists might understand the process of meaning construction through the notion of a **multiverse** ("multi-" many + "-verse" text = many stories). People do not have to agree with one another but can have differing descriptions and views which, when juxtaposed with one another, provide a more complex understanding (Kassis, 1984).

This notion of not having a truth that people ascribe meaning to goes counter to the famous idiom, "There is his side, her side, and the truth." Constructivists and social constructionists do not believe there is a universe—an event that happens that has its own meaning. Rather, since there is not an ascribed meaning to an event, the event's meaning is contained within all of the meanings that people ascribe to it—the multiverse. In the multiverse, all members can have differing viewpoints, and all members can be right in their viewpoint (Maturana & Poerksen, 2004).

de Shazer (1982, 1991) discussed this concept in terms of a **binocular theory of change** (see Figure 10.7). In therapy, the client comes in with one way of viewing what is happening. The therapist has his own way of viewing. In conversation, these two views (descriptions of understandings) come together to form a new understanding. When there are more than two people engaging in this constructive conversation (i.e., when the therapist is working with a team or there are multiple family members), a process of **polyocularity** occurs.

There have been a seemingly infinite amount of times throughout Xiang's life wherein her interaction and discussion of ideas with others have led both Xiang and the other person to develop new constructions of what is the truth. When Xiang was talking with her good friend and explaining how she was "unlucky in love," her friend had a differing viewpoint—that Xiang was codependent. This conversation provided a new understanding that Xiang was not only codependent, but was entering into relationships that brought

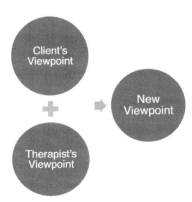

Figure 10.7 The Binocular Theory of Change holds That, When Two People Converse, They Construct a New Combined Understanding.

out her codependency. When Xiang comes to therapy, her current viewpoint, along with the therapist's viewpoint, will likely lead to newer understandings about her life—newer ways of how she is making sense, meaning, and storying her life.

Systems Stories

Most postmodernists, including constructivists and social constructionists, tend to view people's lives through the metaphor of story, where their life is a text. The medium in which this story is told is through language. For the social constructionist therapist, it is in the realm of language where the magic happens (de Shazer, 1994). People's stories are housed within larger discourses—what are called **knowledges**. People usually come to therapy when their self stories are dominated by the dominant discourses that are not in line with their own values and sense of self. Social constructionists tend to deconstruct the **dominant knowledges**—the large scale views of who people are that society tends to promote— and instead highlight the production of **local knowledges**—the individual's viewpoint of who she is (Neimeyer, 1998). This process happens through language.

Language Games

The conversation that happens in the therapy room can be viewed as a **language game** (de Shazer, 1991; de Shazer & Berg, 1992). As de Shazer described, "The therapy system can be seen as a set of 'language games,' a self-contained linguistic system that creates meanings through negotiation between therapist and client" (p. 68). The notion of language games comes from the work of Wittgenstein (1958). In essence, language games occur when people jointly decide what words signify. Xiang engaged in a language game with her best friend when she was describing her behaviors in relationships and they agreed to call those behaviors "codependency." In therapy, Xiang and the therapist may use the word "codependent" yet have it signify something different—perhaps referring to an opportunity for Xiang to assess whether her actions are in line with her values and desires.

The language game that happens in therapy is one where therapist and client develop a linguistic system where they co-construct a form of meaning. Omer (1996) described the process of language games, "It is in the act of conversing about the world that a reality is defined that becomes true to the participants" (p. 319). One way of understanding language games is through the notion of **post-structuralism**, a position that holds that language is reality (de Shazer, 1991, 1994; de Shazer & Berg, 1992). This reality (what something means) is created through language. Thus, if we can language something into existence, we can de-language it. In the context of therapy, this would be the movement of talking about problems to talking about not having the problem/solutions. The social constructionist therapist working with Xiang will view the therapy session as the place where a reality can be constructed, one in which the problems that she has constructed with others are deconstructed via language and then reconstructed via language.

Misunderstandings of Conversations

As we have discussed, we can never know the full meaning of another person's words and language. What we can do is make approximations of our meaning of the other person's meaning. It is impossible for someone to fully convey their meaning to another person, and reciprocally can never receive and understand someone else's meaning fully. What we can do is creatively use the misunderstandings that are inherent in conversations (de Shazer & Berg, 1993).

While this notion may seem paradoxical as therapists attempt to grasp the client's meanings, therapy focuses on engaging in conversations that lead to the client developing alternative meanings. This can come through understanding something differently—or misunderstanding the understanding. de Shazer (1991) explained this dynamic, "Thus, a therapeutic interview is a putting together of various misunderstandings (misreadings) and whatever is meant is a result of how therapist and client agree to misunderstand (or misread) what is said" (pp. 68–69). This goes to the notion of developing new meanings in the therapeutic conversation.

THE STRUCTURE OF NARRATIVES

Postmodernists make a distinction between two modes of thinking: paradigmatic and narrative (Bruner, 1986). The **paradigmatic mode of thinking** is based on a modernist view that functions through logic, mathematics, science, and empiricism. This mode of thinking is the basis for what we know in terms of science—that we can make connections between events in the world and are able to prove these connections. The **narrative mode of thinking** is based on a postmodern view where we attach meaning to action. The constructivist and social constructionist chapters in this book focus, to a large degree, on how therapists utilize a narrative mode of thinking to work with clients to construct new life stories.

Not only do we come to understand ourselves by the stories we write about ourselves, we can also become swept up in other's stories (Rosen, 1996). This was all too clear in an experiment overseen by Rosenhan (1984). He had eight people each present themselves to a different hospital complaining of hearing voices that were unclear but said things such as "empty," "hollow," and "thud." Other than providing a pseudonym and changing their vocation (as several of them were psychologists or psychiatrists), everything else they told the hospital staff was true. Each of the eight people was admitted to the psychiatric ward, whereupon they ceased simulating having any symptoms. They were diagnosed as schizophrenic and were treated as such. Their stays lasted from 7 to 52 days and, upon discharge, were labeled as schizophrenia in remission. These individuals were not viewed as sane, although they never were experiencing schizophrenia.

A person's story is more than a story. Gergen (2009b) explained, "It [a story] is a situated action, a performance that gains its significance through the co-active process" (p. 304). Thus, a story also represents a relationship. It connects and disconnects people, establishing the co-constructed identities that people develop over time. Further, the current story is just one of many possible stories that could have been created. As Gergen stated, we can have "a multiplicity of plausible narratives." Xiang's story of being codependent has influence in her relationships. Even if she does not say it aloud to the other person, her story influences her interactions. With Ben, she may be more vigilant in discerning what he is asking of her as well as her own desires. This leads her to be more hesitant in her interactions with him.

People's narratives—their stories—have two components: a landscape of action and a landscape of consciousness (Bruner, 1986). The **landscape of action** pertains to the events that happen in a certain sequence over time (see Figure 10.8). In the landscape of action, "the constituents are the arguments of

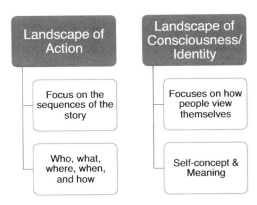

Figure 10.8 The Landscape of Action Describes the "Facts" of the Story While the Landscape of Identity Describes How People View Their Identity Related to the Facts.

action: agent, intention or goal, situation, instrument, something corresponding to a 'story grammar'" (p. 14). The **landscape of consciousness** is how the storyteller and reader each interpret the events of the story. Bruner explained this as "what those involved in the action know, think, or feel, or do not know, think, or feel" (p. 14). White (2007) shifted from calling this notion the landscape of consciousness to referring to it as the **landscape of identity**. This landscape focuses on what people value and how they come to make meaning and know themselves.

All stories have various gaps in both the landscape of action and the landscape of identity. The reader of the story then fills in these gaps. One of the useful functions that gaps in stories have is that these gaps evoke a sense of curiosity in the reader. Here, we can think of the famous *Seinfeld* episode where they introduced the phrase, "Yada yada," such as, "Well, we met, talked for a bit, yada yada, he left in the morning." There is a large gap in the landscape of action. The filling in of the various gaps in this story leads to rich story development that people fill in through their lived experience (White, 2007).

In the landscape of consciousness, there are many consciousnesses that are being referred to (White, 2007). These include the various protagonists of the story, the author of the story, and the reader of the story. Each of them brings implicit meaning to the reading of the text. In therapy, increasing the readship of the text can enhance the landscape of consciousness/identity. That is, not only does the client explore his story, but so do the therapist and anyone else the client thinks is important to bring a larger understanding of what meanings and values the person/client brings to the story. The exploration of how people come to view themselves differently happens through the process of first deconstructing the original landscape of identity and the reconstructing of new meanings of identity.

DECONSTRUCTION AND RECONSTRUCTION

The notion of deconstruction helps therapists and clients to separate themselves from some of the larger cultural and linguistic practices that limit their view of self. It allows the client to revisit the meaning of long-held stories that the client has internalized as fact. For Xiang, these stories may be about what it means to be a heterosexual Asian female living in the United States. There are certain views and expectations that she has internalized—that have become her ways of understanding—without even realizing that she is using them as a guide for her own thoughts and behaviors. These internalizations have become solidified even though Xiang, if taken the time to consider these viewpoints, may not agree with them. Monk, Winslade, Crocket, and Epston (1997) defined deconstruction:

> The process of unpacking the taken-for-granted assumptions and ideas underlying social practices that masquerade as truth or reality. It is achieved by bringing to light the gaps or inconsistencies in a text or discourse or dominant story so that acceptance of the story's message or logic no longer appears inevitable.
>
> (p. 302)

Yet, if one meaning is deconstructed, one or more alternative meanings then need to be developed. This process is called **reconstruction**. Reconstruction helps people to connect with aspects of self that might not have been available or privileged previously (White, 2011).

Deconstruction usually focuses on client stories that have limited them and brought pain and upset into their lives. Unfortunately, these stories have taken on a life of their own and saturated the client's life such that the client is unable to see alternative plotlines. Reconstruction helps to find the unstoried experience of the person, which is usually preferred by the client, because it helps highlight the personal agency of the individual in overcoming the problem and leads to a life that is more desired.

While some therapists discuss how, in therapy, the client authors his own story, this does not take into account the therapist's role in the process. The client might be viewed as the senior author of the story; however, the therapist is the secondary author (Madigan, 1993). In working with Xiang, the therapist might explore with her how, in the past, she lived in ways that fit with her own values and beliefs, rather than those of others. These stories, that were once buried, have the opportunity, through reconstruction, to come to the surface and become the predominant stories that inform Xiang about her own self and experience.

Given that people are interconnected and the stories that we develop about ourselves have been influenced by others, including family, friends, and larger societal discourses, the more people who acknowledge and promote the reconstructed story of the person, the greater chance for that story to take hold. This comes in the form of increasing the readship of the story—that is, by taking what happens in the therapy room to a larger audience.

> ## Applying Your Knowledge
>
> Think about a situation that you recently experienced that you found meaningful. Write down what happened in the landscape of action. Who was present? What happened? Where did this happen? When and how long did it happen? What was the process of the action? Now, shift to the landscape of identity. How did you view yourself that these things happened and you felt a certain way about it? What does it say about you that you acted in the way that you did? When reviewing the landscape of action, what did you notice about what you put value to?

Relational Responsibility

In much of Western thought, we assign responsibility to the individual. "You need to pull yourself up by the bootstraps" and other such phrases are used to highlight how the individual is on his own and expected to help himself. A different way of looking at responsibility is that it is housed in relationships, what McNamee and Gergen (1998) called **relational responsibility**. These authors defined this term:

> We hold relationally responsible actions to be those that sustain and enhance forms of interchange out of which meaningful action itself is made possible. If human meaning is generated through relationship, then to be responsible to relational processes is to favor the possibility of intelligibility itself—of possessing selves, values, and the sense of worth. Isolation represents the negation of humanity.
>
> (pp. 18–19)

Here, we can see that the words we use increase their meaning when housed within the context of interactions with others.

This idea holds that no action in itself has meaning; it is only in connection to another's actions that something has meaning (Gergen, 2009b). For instance, if a person passing you on the street says, "Fine day we are having," what does that mean? Is it a greeting? Is it an intrusion? Is it the ramblings of a disturbed individual? Those words gain meaning when connected to another's actions. You might say, "Yes, it really is." Your words now come into coordination with the other person's words to create a meaningful interchange. Said differently, the context of the interaction is important to understand the meaning of that relationship.

A move from a modernist to postmodernist viewpoint helps us to understand that how people come to make meaning happens in conjunction with others, which happens within a specific context. de Shazer (1994) explained, "The situations in which events occur influence how the participants describe the events to themselves and other people" (p. 245). That is, the context helps people to establish what the meaning is for an event. Let's say you see one person punch another person. We do not know what this definitively means for each person until we have a better sense of the context. If it is two spouses, it might mean the end of their marriage. If it is two kids on a playground, it might mean they are not friends. If it is two people practicing martial arts, it might mean they are learning new skills.

We have been talking about the importance of words and how they are utilized in coordination with others in a specific context to create meaning. However, as we discussed in Chapter 5, communication happens on both the verbal and nonverbal levels. Our body language is also a form of communication that happens in interchange to create meaning. Gergen (2009b) called this process co-action. **Co-action** is the use of our full bodies when we interact—the words we use, how we say them, where we look when we engage someone else, etc.

Let's use an example closer to home to help explain this concept. Think about your family. How is it that your family functions? How does your family come to define itself? You cannot do this on your own. If you say, "We are an extremely close family" but no one in your family calls you, texts you, visits you, or friends you on Facebook, your actions seem very out of place. It is only when other family members engage in actions that support your meaning that there is a co-creation of meaning. When they see you and smile rather than frown, hug you rather than spit on you, and say things related to how family is important to them, in conjunction with you doing the same, we can see how co-action is happening.

Part of relational responsibility is not engaging in mutual blame, where each person views the other as problematic (Gergen, 2009a). This can be done by not attacking the other person, which would lead them to defend themselves. One means of doing this is to talk about their **internal others**. Given that people are the amalgamation of all of their relationships, we might talk about how their current actions are reminiscent of someone else. For instance, Xiang may say to Ben, "Right now, you are sounding like your father." Ben can then think about how he is different than but influenced by his father. He might then engage Xiang in a different manner.

A second means of relational responsibility is focusing on **conjoint relations** (Gergen, 2009a). Here, instead of blaming the other person for whatever went wrong, the communicator can mutualize the situation and explore the impact it is having on the relationship. This shifts the communication from being about individual blame to interdependent relationships. Xiang might say to Ben, "What are we doing to ourselves letting things escalate like this? What can we do differently?" This would allow for a more likely openness between both parties.

A third method of relational responsibility happens when we focus on **group realities** (Gergen, 2009a). This entails exploring how the parties' respective associations with groups and the group differences may be leading to the current difficulties, rather than assessing individual blame for the parties' current difficulties. Xiang could say to Ben,

> It is interesting what is happening in our relationship, and I am wondering how much of that has to do with gender differences. As a female, I am concerned about being marginalized, which I have been feeling recently. What is happening for you as a male?

A fourth means of relational responsibility is the use of the **systemic swim**. This is the broadest view that we can take wherein we contextualize our own behavior and our relational partner's behaviors within the social systems that they occur. While many of the social systems that are in place may bring pain into people's lives, it is difficult to not act in accordance with these social systems, even when we do not like or agree with them. Xiang and Ben may have a conversation about the gendered discrepancies in the United States and how they both sometimes feel limited by the expectations and demands placed upon them.

The more that people engage one another in relationally responsible ways, the more they create a sense of self and a life that lives in accordance with their own values (see Figure 10.9). In essence, they take control of their own story and do not live subjugated by dominant discourses and the power dynamics of social systems.

Relational Responsibility
- Internal Others
- Conjoint Relations
- Group Realities
- The Systemic Swim

Figure 10.9 The Components of Being Relationally Responsible.

Applying Your Knowledge

Think about the relationship that is most important to you. What is the context of that relationship? What are the dominant discourses and social practices that contribute to the norms of how people should think, feel, and act when in this type of relationship? How do you engage in relationally responsible actions? In what ways can you increase your use of internal others, conjoint relations, group realities, and systemic swim?

STRENGTHS RATHER THAN DEFICITS

We end this chapter talking about one of the biggest pushes of the postmodern movement in psychotherapy, especially that of social constructionism—the focus on strengths rather than deficits. The field of mental health has primarily been using a **discourse of deficit** (Gergen, 1994, 2001)—a focus on symptoms, problems, and what is wrong with people. This can be seen in the prevalent use of diagnostic assessments and categories contained in sources such as the DSM and ICD. Managed care companies tend to reimburse only when there is a diagnosis given for a patient. For a traditional psychotherapist, operating from a modernist perspective, Xiang would likely be viewed as a client who is codependent and may be diagnosed, based on the DSM, with Dependent Personality Disorder. While assessments such as a biopsychosocial do have a section on the strengths and resources of the client, this is usually secondary. What is primary for the biopsychosocial is an assessment of what is going wrong and why she is currently having the symptoms/problems she is experiencing.

Applying Your Knowledge

Think about yourself as a person in the widest sense. What are your flaws? Write down your top ten flaws. Now, think about how you view yourself. What seems possible for you? How hopeful are you of being happy? Next, write down your top ten strengths. How do you view yourself now? What seems possible? How hopeful are you of being happy? What differences do you see when you focus on deficits rather than strengths?

Perhaps the biggest change to the field of psychotherapy within the last 20 years is the shift from a focus on deficits to that of strengths. One prime example of this is the advent of the field of positive psychology. While psychologists focused on people's positive aspects and traits long before the field laid

Figure 10.10 The Differences Between a Deficit-Based and Strength-Based Approach.

claim to the term positive psychology, it wasn't until Martin Selgiman, as president of the American Psychological Association, made this term the theme for his presidency that positive psychology took hold and changed the way many psychologists and psychotherapists viewed their role in working with people and clients.

Perhaps one of the first therapists to focus on client strengths and resources was Milton Erickson, the renowned hypnotherapist. Erickson focused on what the client brought with him to therapy that could be utilized to lead them to live a more desirous life. Many social constructionist therapists have utilized this notion of **utilization** that clients bring with them everything they need for change to happen (DeJong & Berg, 2012; O'Hanlon & Weiner-Davis, 1989). Therapy then becomes a language game to access and bring forth the client's strengths and resources, rather than to diagnose and help the client cope with her deficits (see Figure 10.10). This approach focuses on using the positive aspects of how a client thinks, feels, and behaves to help her live the type of life she believes she should have.

Our client, Xiang, is viewing herself and her life through a deficit-based approach. She has conducted an informal assessment of her relationships and her thoughts about herself and others. Based on her informal assessment, she has diagnosed herself as codependent. For her, this disorder requires remediation where she will need a therapist to help cure her of this problem. She believes that she needs to excise this part of herself and insert something new—a person who is more capable. A strength-based therapist would rather explore with Xiang areas of her life where she has acted in ways that she appreciates so she can enhance these ways of being and extrapolate them into other parts of her life. Therapy then becomes the deconstruction of the deficit story and the reconstruction of the strength and resource story.

Questions for Reflection

1. What are the primary discourses that inform therapists as to who they are as professionals? What are the related power dynamics of those discourses?
2. How does viewing the self as relational change how you view the theory of problem formation and problem resolution?
3. What advantages and disadvantages are there to viewing therapy as a language game?
4. What is the relationship between the landscape of action and the landscape of consciousness/identity? How does this help you to understand your clients and what your interactions with them might look like?
5. What benefit is it for the therapist and the client to focus on strengths over deficits?

CHAPTER ELEVEN
Social Construction Pragmatics

Michael D. Reiter

CASE DESCRIPTION

During the first therapy session, the therapist asked Xiang what led her to want to talk to a psychotherapist. She responded:

> For a large part of my life, I have found myself doing for other people. Growing up, both of my parents worked, and I was the oldest child. And I was a female, from an Asian family. It was my job to take care of the house, make sure it was cleaned, and that dinner was ready for everyone when they got home. I also had to look after my brother as well, even though he was only a couple of years younger than me. It took a lot for me to go to school all day, hurry home to make sure it was in shape, be on my brother's back so he kept the house clean, and do his homework. All of this when I didn't get a chance to do my homework. At times it seems I gave up my adolescence for others, as I didn't really get to hang out much with friends. Then, when I got into college, on a full soccer scholarship, which I needed because we didn't have the money for me to go, I had to withdraw because my mother needed my help when my father left. I had to give up my pursuit of a business degree. I got an entry-level job in a company. If that wasn't bad enough, I thought I fell in love, with a guy named Edward. We married, and to make a long story short, I gave up a lot of myself for him. He was emotionally and physically abusive. Needless to say I got a divorce, and it really hurt my self-esteem. Fast-forward to today, and it seems I keep on getting into relationships where I find myself to be codependent. There has to be a time in my life when I actually come first.

In this chapter, we will explore how a social constructionist therapist might work with Xiang. She has come to therapy with a story about herself that is limiting and painful. Therapy will focus on unwrapping her current identity story and co-constructing an alternative story wherein Xiang utilizes her strengths to live a life in line with her values and view of self.

SOCIAL CONSTRUCTIONIST/POSTMODERN THERAPY

Whereas constructivist therapists explore the meaning that the individual creates, constructionists focus more on client and therapist discourse (Gergen, 1994). Regardless of the specific model, constructionists view therapy as co-constructed conversations (Efran & Clarfield, 1992). For postmodernists, psychotherapy tends to be a co-constructing act wherein the focus is helping the client consolidate her preferred view of self.

Postmodern therapists attempt to develop egalitarian relationships with clients in an attempt to reduce the asymmetries of power in the therapeutic encounter (Frosh, 1995). Therapy then becomes a "communal creation of meaning" (Hoffman, 2000). One means of doing this is for the therapist to not take an expert position, such as attempting to assess and diagnose the other person. Instead of viewing people as "schizophrenic," "psychotic," or "anxious," the therapist understands that the labels given to people are based upon social conventions (Gergen, 2009b). Xiang enters therapy labeling herself as codependent. For therapists coming from the substance abuse world, this term is quite familiar. Other therapists might consider assessing her as having a dependent personality disorder. However, for postmodern therapists, Xiang is not codependent, as this would imply that there is an essential self to her, one that is dysfunctional. Instead, the therapist would want to have a conversation with Xiang to unwrap alternative views of who she wants to be. This shifts the notion of problems from being internal to the person to being developed through a collaborative process, but also with additional stakeholders (i.e., family members, friends, legal systems, etc.).

While part of the purpose of the therapeutic conversation is the development of alternative stories, it is really when those new and more identity-affirming stories are enacted outside of the therapy session that they become useful for clients. Given that meanings are socially constructed, having multiple people confirm a construction of new identities and stories becomes quite important. We can speculate on who in Xiang's relational field would be willing to engage in conversations to confirm her preferred identity. These might include her mother, brother, Ben, and other friends or family who she thinks would be important in this process. As we will discuss later in the chapter, some social constructionist therapists try to recruit as many people as possible, both inside and outside of the therapy room, into a discussion about these new identity-affirming stories.

While many modernist therapists take on an expert position, a therapist informed by social constructionism uses skills in *knowing how* rather than *knowing what* (Gergen & Warhus, 2001). Social constructionist therapists believe that it is not the therapist's interventions that make the difference, but how clients make attributions of meaning which lead to them being useful (Fruggeri, 1992). In this view, the therapist's role is as a midwife for these new meanings to be born into the conversation, which leads to clients living a story that is in line with their preferred future (Cantwell & Holmes, 1994). Thus, therapy with Xiang will not focus on what the therapist thinks she should do but, rather, what Xiang wants for herself.

While some therapists who operate from a social constructionist perspective hold that the therapist should not impose himself on the client, this is not quite what being constructionist means. Whatever the therapist does, he realizes that his position is not objective truth and is not legitimate knowledge (Efran & Clarfield, 1992). This leads therapists to understand that they cannot be neutral. They are who they are at that point in time, and who they are influences what happens in the therapy room. Further, who they are influences how they are influenced by the conversation with the client. Given that meanings are co-created, not only in the very local realm of the therapy room, but within communities, therapists operating from social constructionism tend to explore aspects of power, political action, and social responsibility (Moules, 2000). For instance, the therapist working with Xiang might talk about where she learned what it means to be a woman, Asian, an immigrant, a daughter, etc. These conversations would likely explore both the local (Xiang's own views and their relation to her family's views) as well as the dominant discourses (Thai values, American values, as well as other political and social discourses around personhood).

Fruggeri (1992) provided four guidelines for constructionist psychotherapy: "(1) the introduction of differences; (2) the proposal of different descriptions of some event; (3) new ways of connecting behaviors and events; and (4) the introduction of reflexivity" (p. 49). The first guideline might be used to explore the client's understanding of what is happening in her situation to what may be expected from society based on the dominant discourse. For Xiang, this would be in how she views herself as a person in relationship to what is expected of how people should be in relationships. In exploring the second guideline, we can use the term **polyvocality** (Gergen, 2009a). This is the notion that for any idea or event there are a multitude of ways of interpreting that idea or event, which all lead to more possibilities being available than there were previously. The third guideline provides the understanding that the therapeutic conversation becomes a construction. It is not known before therapy begins where it will end; however, it is through the interplay of ideas between therapist and client that new ways of understanding the connection between self, behavior, and events occur. Lastly, the fourth guideline of reflexivity provides the therapist with a reminder that he is an active agent that has viewpoints, influence, power, and responsibilities.

On a micro-level, social constructionist therapy includes **co-reflecting**. This is a form of coordination where each member in a dialogue mirrors, to some degree, the other (Gergen, 2009a). This is not a mirroring of the exact words said:

Xiang: I am very upset with Ben.
Therapist: You are very upset with Ben.

But it is using the other's demeanor and key words to demonstrate a connection between the parties. This may come in the form of talking at the same volume or tone as the other, sitting in a similar position, and talking about the same idea (although an agreement of opinions does not have to occur). Sometimes key words from the client will be used but is not a necessity as alternative words can be used to describe alternative meanings. Gergen (2009a) referred to this as **linguistic shading**: "To shade another's language is to find words that are nearly similar to what the other has said, but slightly change its meaning. Through these slight changes, antagonists can begin to move together" (p. 125).

Xiang: I am very upset with Ben.
Therapist: You find yourself, at times, to be disappointed.

Xiang would then have an opportunity to consider her own meaning and determine whether it helps move her closer to her preferred identity.

Social constructionist therapists view therapy as a co-construction where language is used in a dialogic process. Waters (1994) provided some of the basic tenets of dialogic therapies:

- Shift from therapist as expert to therapy as a mutual process
- Focus on what clients are saying and how this reflects their worldview and meanings
- Belief that changing how people talk about problems changes their relationship to the problem
- A shift away from examining deeper structures, why the problem developed
- Exploration of the future over talk about the past
- Understanding problems as being separate from the person

The rest of this chapter will present techniques, processes, and ways of thinking that fit within postmodern and social constructionist epistemologies.

CLIENT AS EXPERT

For most of the history of psychotherapy, the therapist has been the expert. This comes from the conceptualization of psychotherapy through a medical model where the patient comes to the therapist with a problem and the therapist is the expert on diagnosing and treating that problem. Most laypeople view therapists similar to medical doctors, where the therapist can do a diagnosis/assessment, determine what the pathology is, and then provide some remedy. This is one of the reasons that Dr. Phil is considered to be "America's Therapist." He engages people from an expert position, telling them what they are doing wrong and what they need to do to make things better.

Postmodern therapists have shifted from a therapist *doing-something-to* a patient to a therapist *having a conversation with* a client. As de Shazer (1993) stated, "In fact, I think of clients as experts—they know a lot that I do not know. So, therapeutic conversation is a talking together between or among experts sharing and exchanging ideas and information in language" (p. 88). The therapist is an expert on being able to explore how clients perceive and make meaning in their lives, especially those perceptions that have been potential solutions (DeJong & Berg, 2012).

Given that we cannot know an objective truth, postmodern therapy shifts from trying to find the root of a problem to how people language problems and solutions. The therapist is no longer the purveyor of truth and objectivity, a person with privileged knowledge, but someone who has a viewpoint different to but equal to the other voices present (Gergen, 1994). The therapist throws off the shackles of authority and enters into conversations with people who have unique viewpoints and local knowledge. Therapists can ask clients for an **experience-near description**, where the therapist does not impose an expert position on what is but brings forth the personal knowledge of the client.

One way of inhabiting this stance of the client as expert is when the therapist takes a **not-knowing position** (Anderson & Goolishian, 1992). The therapist does not ask questions he knows the answer to but those that help bring forth the meanings of the client. Thus, the therapist is not an expert, being able to be objective and make a diagnosis, but instead acts from a position of curiosity, needing the client to provide their meanings.

By not trying to impose the therapist's worldview on the client, but instead meeting the client within the client's worldview, the therapist enhances the transformational possibilities of the therapeutic relationship (Short, 2010). DeJong and Berg (2012) provided several basic interviewing skills that therapists can use to maintain a not-knowing position:

- Listening to the client through the client's frame of reference (instead of the therapist's)
- Providing nonverbal behavior that demonstrates the therapist is listening
- Echoing key words
- Using open rather than closed questions
- Summarizing the thoughts, actions, and feelings of the client
- Paraphrasing
- Using silence
- Complimenting the client on their past successes
- Affirming clients' perceptions
- Being empathetic
- Returning the focus to the client (if the client is talking about other people)
- Amplifying solution talk—talk about what the client wants and potential pathways to get there

These actions prioritize the client's worldview while also connecting therapist and client in a two-way conversation that may bring about new meanings and understandings.

Co-Construction

Social constructionism rests on the premise that meanings are generated relationally. We call this process **co-construction**. DeJong, Bavelas, and Korman (2013) defined this process, "In psychotherapy, co-construction refers to the proposal that the therapist and the client(s), in their dialogue, collaboratively create what emerges in their session" (p. 17). From this perspective, we can co-create problems and solutions. Postmodern therapists tend to focus on clients' strengths and resources rather than deficits and problems.

This co-construction is a view of a reality that neither party has yet conceptualized. Gergen (2009a) calls these views **imaginary moments**, which allow participants to form a sense of "us" rather than a "me" and "you." Beyond a creation of imaginary moments between therapist and client, having clients be a significant part of these moments allows them to develop a common cause, where they are not focusing on their differences, but instead on their superordinate goals. Xiang and her therapist will likely have many imaginary moments where they co-construct a vision of what her life may be like. However, what may be even more useful is for Xiang to engage in various imaginary moments with others in her relational field, such as her mother or a significant romantic relationship. The therapist might talk with Xiang, or even ask if it made sense if Chanhira joined them for a conversation on how they are both dealing with the same issue—how to be connected with one another in a way that empowers both of them. This activity is not done through the therapist doing things to the client. Instead, it occurs through language, in a conversation between client and therapist.

RE-AUTHORING CONVERSATIONS

We've discussed the notion that each person is the storyteller of her own story. Some of the stories that people tell of themselves open the space for the person to live a life she wants. Other stories are quite limiting; these tend to lead people to come to therapy. Xiang has developed a story of her life in which she is codependent, leading her to view her relationships with significant others in ways that leave her feeling restricted of choice and options. Further, she has internalized the dominant discourse that it is bad to be codependent and good to be independent. This leaves her feeling bad about herself and her relationships. Given that some story plotlines are restrictive, therapists work with clients in helping re-author their story. This can happen upon subsequent tellings and retellings of the story, as each becomes different than the previously told story (Epston, White, & Murray, 1992).

Re-authoring conversations provide an opportunity for clients to privilege neglected aspects of their stories (and thus their lives). As White (2007) explained,

> Re-authoring conversations invite people to continue to develop and tell stories about their lives, but they also help people to include some of the more neglected but potentially significant events and experiences that are 'out of phase' with their dominant storylines.
>
> (p. 61)

Working with Xiang, the therapist might have a conversation with her about when and how she has been independent in her life and how others have seen her taking more personal agency for her own actions rather than relying on others.

Since people develop a story of their life and provide thick description to it, re-authoring conversations help bring life to unseen aspects of the clients' lives, which are called unique outcomes (White, 2007). **Unique outcomes** are events in people's lives that fall outside of their dominant story (White & Epston, 1990). Xiang has many unique outcomes that she may not have given too much weight to in her examination of her life. These events could be when she quit a job because she did not think she was being treated with respect or when she told her mother that she had other obligations and could not come over when Chanhira wanted her to.

People are able to deconstruct many of the negative identity conclusions they have made about themselves when they are able to highlight their unique outcomes and re-author them into an alternative plotline that counters the inhibiting dominant problem-saturated story (White, 2011). They then shift from being a victim of the situation to having more personal agency in their own identity construction. This leads to a variety of new and different behavioral and emotional experiences.

EXTERNALIZATION

In Chapter 10, we discussed the notion of deconstruction and how this fits within a postmodern perspective. One operational method of enacting deconstruction in therapy comes in the form of externalizing the problem. However, we should first distinguish between the two different uses of the term externalizing that are used by therapists. The first use of externalizing relates to how people exhibit symptoms. This comes from a more modernist perspective, where a person either internalizes or externalizes the symptom. From a traditional therapy perspective, **internalizing behaviors** occur when the person demonstrates symptoms inwardly. This may be when they become depressed, withdrawn, or have suicidal thoughts. **Externalizing behaviors** occur when the person demonstrates symptoms outwardly. Here, the person may get into fights, engage in destruction of property, or other forms of what we might call acting out.

The second type of externalizing comes from family therapy where the symptom is not housed within the person, but within the relationships of people (see Minuchin et al., 2014; White, 2007, 2011; White & Epston, 1990). From this perspective, problems are not the result of deficits or deviancies inside a person. Rather, internal thoughts or problematic behaviors are seen as the outcome of a person's relationship with a wide range of types of ideas that put them at odds with themselves. **Externalizing** is when the therapist helps the client to separate from the effects of the problem. One way to view this is through the slogan: the person is not the problem, the problem is the problem.

Externalizing conversations help people to deconstruct the internalized problem-saturated narratives they've been living by. They help people take a position about their reaction to the problem and its effects; what they might do to keep the problem from taking over their lives; and what cherished values, beliefs, or hopes would strengthen their ability to develop a different relationship with the problem. For Xiang, many things might be externalized but perhaps at the top of her list would be her viewpoint that she is codependent. The social constructionist therapist would not view the problem as Xiang being a codependent person but, rather, that codependency is the problem and is bringing strife to Xiang's life.

Based on an understanding of no objective truth, and people not having problems but being in relationship to problems, therapists can talk about the problem as a distinct entity from the person (see Figure 11.1). This shifts how we language the discussion surrounding what is happening for people. Instead of someone being depressed, we view her as being in relationship to depression. A person is not anxious but oppressed by anxiety. A couple is not conflictual, but conflict has entered and saturated their relationship.

Since problems are created in or by language, the meaning of the problem is determined by every client's unique understanding of the problem, rather than from an objective idea held by the therapist. This then changes the intent of therapy from exorcizing a negative personality trait or mental disorder to talking with the client about what type of relationship she wants to have with the problem.

Externalizing conversations tend to have four parts or what White (2007) calls **categories of inquiry** (see Figure 11.2). First, the therapist helps clients negotiate an *experience-near definition of the problem*. White explained,

> An "experience-near" description of the problem is one that uses the parlance of the people seeking therapy and that is based on their understanding of life (developed in the culture of their family or community and influenced by their immediate history).

(p. 40)

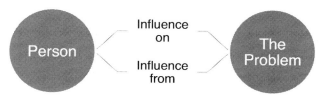

Figure 11.1 The Relationship Between the Person and the Problem.

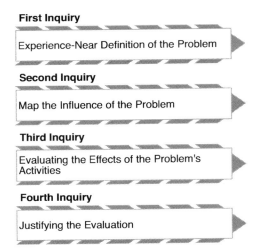

Figure 11.2 The Four Inquiries of an Externalizing Conversation.

With Xiang, the therapist would attempt to get a thick description of her experience with codependency. This would include asking questions about how she comes to know what it is like living with codependency in her life.

The second category of inquiry in externalizing is helping the client to **map the influence of the problem**. This is often called the **statement of position map**. Here, the client is usually asked to name the problem. It could be as simple as "Depression" or "Sadness," or the client could be more poetic and call it, "The big bad blues of sorrow" or "The blanket of despair." The actual name that the client uses to describe the problem is not important. What is important is that the client rather than the therapist introduces the name for the problem. The therapist has a conversation with the client about what the problem has brought into the client's life. The questions asked by the therapist tend to focus on how the problem has impacted the client's behavior, feelings, attitudes, and relationships. In conversation with Xiang, this inquiry may look like the following:

Therapist: Xiang, you have been talking about what it is like for you dealing with this issue. If you were to give a name to the issue, what would you call it?
Xiang: I don't know. Maybe frustration.
Therapist: Frustration would be the best name for it?
Xiang: Ah, maybe not. There definitely is a lot of frustration. But maybe just codependency. It's frustrating being codependent.
Therapist: Okay, so you would call this Codependency. When did Codependency come into your life?

The third inquiry category is **evaluating the effects of the problem's activities**. The therapist helps the client to reflect on how she thinks the problem has impacted her and whether she is okay with it. This is an important step as it is usually other people who have made evaluations of the problem's influence rather than the person herself making them (White, 2007). While helping clients make these evaluations, therapists take a not-knowing attitude and do not assume to know the client's position.

Therapist: Xiang, you have talked about how Codependency has been in your life for a very long time now. How is this for you?

Xiang: I don't like it.
Therapist: You don't like it. Can you say some more about that?
Xiang: I want to do for me rather than always doing for someone else.
Therapist: So right now you are not okay with how Codependency gets you to do for others more than for yourself?
Xiang: That's right.

The fourth inquiry category of externalizing conversations is **justifying the evaluation**. Here, the client is asked why she feels the way she does about her relationship with the problem. These why questions are asked as a way to give voice to people's perspectives. The person may be asked why they are taking their current position and how that may be related to stories in their life that led to this position.

Therapist: What leads you to take this stance regarding Codependency?
Xiang: That I don't really want it in my life anymore?
Therapist: Yes. Why would that be your position?
Xiang: Because I've let it control me and constrict me for too long.
Therapist: You are wanting to be freer and to take more control of your life?
Xiang: Yes. As they say, "I want to do me."

Having an externalizing conversation can lead to the opportunity for unattended stories of personal agency to come forth. These stories can also be connected to cherished beliefs, values, or hopes, leading to stories of when the person had influence over the problem. These are times when the person did not allow the problem to have as much influence as it has had. These times were likely not highlighted in the client's original narrative. As people separate themselves from the problem, they are separating from problem-saturated narratives. When separated in this manner, space is opened to appreciate and give value to previously unexplored stories, which include their preferred narratives (White, 1993).

Externalizing conversations focus on how the problem has influenced the person as well as how the person has influenced the problem. It is in mapping the influence of the person on the life of the problem that new storylines are brought forth that are not part of the problem-saturated description given in the previous component. These new stories include the person's sense of personal agency and the unique outcomes of the dominant subjugating story.

As previously explained, **unique outcomes** are lived experiences that fall outside of the dominant story (White & Epston, 1990). These are times when the client could have experienced the problem but did not or did not experience it to the same level and intensity they had previously experienced it. Unique outcomes also include times that are less behaviorally oriented, such as when clients held onto important beliefs, took a personal stand against injustices or any part of their lives that would not be consistent with the way in which they are often described or think of themselves. The following is a potential of this type of conversation:

Therapist: Xiang, you were talking about wanting control over your own life and "doing you." You just explained to me that, during high school, you tried out for the soccer team, even though you knew that your boyfriend at the time was not fully in favor of that. Could you talk more about that?
Xiang: Well, I love soccer. And I knew soccer was my ticket to college. I needed the athletic scholarship.
Therapist: What does that say about you that you made this choice for yourself?
Xiang: That I have and can choose for me rather than just going along with what someone else wants.
Therapist: And is that knowledge something that you value or don't value?
Xiang: It is definitely something that I value.

> ## Applying Your Knowledge
>
> Change the following therapist statements to an externalizing orientation.
>
> Example: When do you find yourself being angry?
> Externalized: In what situations does Anger come into your life?
>
> 1. How long have you been depressed?
> Externalized:
>
> 2. In what situations do you become anxious?
> Externalized:
>
> 3. What is your ritual when you are anorexic?
> Externalized:
>
> 4. What led you to become not interested in being sexual?
> Externalized:
>
> 5. How do your fights happen?
> Externalized:

Counter Documents

We discussed how social constructionist therapists tend to expand the readship of client's alternative and desired stories. One means of recruiting a wider readership into new identity constructions for clients is through counter documents (White & Epston, 1990). Many individuals who come to therapy have received various documents over the course of their life that have cast them in the light of being problematic. These documents could be court orders, psychological evaluations, police reports, or school sanctions. These various documents help to shape the person's life, usually presenting a story of the person as a problem.

Counter documents present an alternative storyline, casting the person in their preferred identity. Counter documents may be used for the individual client, such as giving a teenager a certificate titled "Fight Fighting Certificate" that commends the teenager for fighting the urge to fight. Another example is giving a child a certificate titled "Escaping From Tantrums Certificate" to acknowledge the child for overcoming his or her tantrums. For children and adolescents, parents would probably be the only people to see these documents. However, the more people who can jump on board and confirm the new preferred story, the more likely it is to hold. White and Epston (1990) stated, "The incorporation of a wider readship and the recruitment of an audience contribute not just to the survival and consolidation of new meanings, but also to a revision of the preexisting meanings" (p. 191).

There are a variety of counter documents that can be introduced into therapy. These include certificates, diplomas, letters, and declarations. **Certificates** tend to represent that a person has achieved a new status, such as a new identity or having a different relationship to the problem. **Diplomas**, similarly, are documents highlighting that the person has developed new conclusions about self contrary to the saturated problem discourse. **Letters** can be written by the therapist, the client, or both with a variety of intended readers. The therapist might write the letter to the client, to the referring agent, or for anyone the client is interested in giving the letter to (given proper release of information). Clients might write a letter to the therapist or to someone they hope will join them in therapy (what is known as a letter of invitation) or a variety of other people they would like to include in the alternative story development.

> **ESCAPE FROM CODEPENDENCY CERTIFICATE**
>
> This certificate is awarded to Xiang in recognition of her victory over Codependency.
>
> For a lot of her life Xiang found that Codependency tried to take over her life, leading to her putting more focus on pleasing others rather than honoring herself. However, Xiang has decided to not be at the beck-and-call of Codependency and instead to engage in interdependent relationships.
>
> This certificate serves as a statement to Xiang, and others, that she has placed Codependency on notice that she will not enable it to blind her from her own views and desires. Instead, she is promoting herself to be respected as a unique person while respecting the uniqueness of others.
>
> Awarded on the 13th day of July, 2019
>
> Signed:

Figure 11.3 The Use of a Certificate as a Counter Document to the Dominant Problem Story.

Declarations are documents that clients sign expressing their movement away from a connection to the problem and toward personal agency. Figure 11.3 presents an example of a certificate that could be used with Xiang.

OUTSIDER WITNESS PRACTICES

Another means of increasing the readship for new stories is to bring additional people into the therapy conversation that can talk about and support the new story and add to the co-created meanings. One means of doing this is through definitional ceremonies. White (2007) developed **definitional ceremonies** wherein clients are able to tell their stories to therapists and in front of **outsider witnesses**—people who have some relation to the problem but likely do not know the client. That is, outsider witnesses tend to be people who have dealt with similar issues/problems as the client.

Definitional ceremonies usually have three components. First, the client tells her story to the therapist. The outsider witnesses may be in the room or perhaps behind a one-way mirror. At a certain point, the outsider witnesses will be invited to retell the client's story (or more accurately, the therapeutic discourse) in the presence of the client. This retelling is the second component of the definitional ceremony and usually entails the outsider witnesses retelling aspects of the story that most resonated for them. They are not there to try to give therapy to the client or tell the client what to do. Rather, the retelling focuses on what the outsider witnesses heard the client holds value to. The third part of the definitional ceremony entails the client retelling the outsider witnesses' retelling of her own story.

A social constructionist therapist working with Xiang might consider using a definitional ceremony that includes outsider witnesses who have some type of relationship with Codependency. The therapist and Xiang would talk about her experience with Codependency and how it has impacted her life as well as how she has, at times in the past, not allowed its influence to be so severe. Then, at some point in that session, Xiang would be asked to sit to the side (or behind a one-way mirror) and either the therapist (or co-therapist) would interview the outsider witnesses as to what in Xiang's story and her relationship to Codependency most stood out for them. Once that conversation ended, the therapist would talk with Xiang about what stood out for her in listening to the outsider witnesses. This definitional ceremony would help substantiate the story that Xiang has personal agency over Codependency and that she is not a "codependent" person.

Reflecting Teams

Similarly to outsider witness practice is the process of reflecting teams, which can be considered to operate from the perspective of polyvocality (Gergen, 2009a). Tom Andersen (1991, 1992, 1993) developed **reflecting teams**: a group of professionals who listen to the discourse between therapist and client and then have their own conversation, in front of the client, of what they heard (see Figure 11.4). These open talks shift the hierarchy of therapist above client to therapist and client as partners in a conversation to open up new distinctions.

Reflecting teams function from a principle of both/and rather than either/or. Instead of the therapist having one viewpoint that counteracts the client's viewpoint (which would be an either/or perspective), the therapist appreciates the client's perspective as well as his own (a both/and position). This entails a shift of *instead of* to *in addition to* (Andersen, 1993). This comes from presenting one's ideas with uncertainty rather from an expert stance. Some therapist phrases that endorse this sentiment include, "Perhaps another way of seeing this . . .,"; "In addition to that, how might . . .,"; and "Maybe this might also be. . . ." This view of *in addition to* is important as the therapist needs to provide a viewpoint that is unusual (different from the client's viewpoint), but not too unusual since the client would not want to continue dialogue with an idea that goes so counter to her own idea (Andersen, 1991). That is, staying in conversation with someone includes the therapist staying close to the client's perspective so that the person can maintain integrity, but not the same as the client so that difference can come into the conversation.

The basic process of a reflecting team is that there is an autonomous group of therapists who are able to watch and listen to a therapist talking with a client; the latter grouping is called the **interviewing system** (Andersen, 1991). The number of people in any of these groups can be altered, from two or more members, but is usually between four and six. Therapists working with reflecting teams can work by themselves or in co-therapy. Clients may be an individual, couple, family, or group. The reflecting team does not define what gets talked about for the interviewing system. While listening to the conversation, each member of the reflecting team has an inner dialogue but does not say anything out loud just yet. This inner dialogue is primarily focused on two questions: "How can the situation or the issue(s) the system presents be described in addition to the presented description? How can the situation or the issue be explained in addition to the presented explanations?" (Andersen, 1991, p. 40). At some point in the conversation, the interviewing system will stop their dialogue, and the reflecting team will then have

Figure 11.4 The Reflecting Team Process.

a dialogue about their ideas and questions while the interviewing system listens. After some time, the interviewing system will talk about their reflections on the reflecting team's conversation.

When members of the reflecting team are providing their ideas and questions in front of the interviewing system, they do so out of a place of curiosity and speculation. While there are usually few rules to the reflecting team, there are a couple of rules of what not to do (Andersen, 1991). First, the members do not reflect on something that was discussed in a different conversation than the interview system had. Second, the members do not provide negative connotations. Thus, the reflecting team is not a group of objective professionals who diagnose the client in front of the client. Rather, the team attempts to support the client and affirm the person's desired identity. However, they must add some type of difference into the conversation. This difference comes in the form of a curiosity into not-yet-seen descriptions and not-yet-thought-of explanations (Andersen, 1991).

One of the intents of the reflecting team is to encourage difference. Andersen (1992) explained, "We hope that thoughts will be shared that might be starting points for new conversations or for finding new descriptions and understandings" (p. 61). Each person on the reflecting team may understand what they heard differently than the others and will then describe their understanding differently. This helps promote the both/and rather than either/or perspective. Clients may then develop additional ways of interpreting their lives and alternative modes of meaning making. These would hopefully be more useful to their subsequent lived experience.

One means of introducing variation into the conversation is to ask questions whose outcome is a double description (Andersen, 1991). **Double descriptions** provide perspective and lead to an exploration of difference. These questions might come in the following forms: in comparison to, in relation to, or different from. "In comparison to" questions explore how the client thought and reacted differently around a situation or how what is being talked about has changed over time:

- Who was the first to attempt something different?
- How have your interactions changed from when this first became an issue?

"In relation to" questions asks about interconnections between people:

- Who are the primary participants in this situation?
- Who is able to not be involved?

"Different from" questions explore how a situation has changed over time:

- When did you notice the situation for the first time?
- How has it gotten worse?
- How has it gotten better?

Applying Your Knowledge

For the following client statements, provide a) an "in comparison to," b) an "in relation to," and c) a "different from" question that could help to bring forth double descriptions in the conversation.

Example: Client: I am so tired of being codependent and taking other people's feelings into consideration before my own.

a. In comparison to: Who would see this different from you?
b. In relation to: Who do you find yourself more wanting to consider their feelings over your own?

> c. Different from: How has your desire to consider others' feelings over your own changed over time?
>
> 1. Client: I am not doing well in school. I think that I may be failing, and I've been a pretty decent student up until now.
>
>   a. In comparison to:
>   b. In relation to:
>   c. Different from:
>
> 2. Client: What can I say? I thought I could control my urges, but I found myself in bed with someone else that was not my partner. I'm a real shit.
>
>   a. In comparison to:
>   b. In relation to:
>   c. Different from:
>
> 3. Client: My mother was just diagnosed with cancer, and I am devastated.
>
>   a. In comparison to:
>   b. In relation to:
>   c. Different from:

PROBLEM TALK VERSUS SOLUTION TALK

As we've explained, social constructionist therapists pay attention to the flow of the therapeutic conversation and how the focus changes based on the back-and-forth development of the dialogue. Movement in therapy is aided when the therapist highlights specific aspects of the client's talk. This can be looked at in terms of what we privilege in conversations.

Usually, when people come to therapy, they expect to talk about what is going wrong in their lives—their problems. The therapist then can hear what it is the client does not want (the problems) or what they do want (the goals). The pathways to clients' goals are solutions. To get there, therapists and clients need to have conversations that move from problem talk to solution talk (de Shazer, 1994).

Problem talk is when conversations focus on what is not going right in a client's life—aspects of what they do not want any more or want less of. Most clients initially come to therapy ready to talk about why they wanted therapy—because there are things they are upset about. de Shazer (1994) explained that problem talk is usually based on people thinking in terms of "truth." In a way, people say, "This is how it is." Those who come to therapy tend to get so caught up in the various facts of the problem talk that they tend not to be able to see how these facts are limiting them to seeing alternatives and possibilities. Further, when therapists engage with clients in talk about the facts of their problems, they jointly construct larger problems (de Shazer & Berg, 1993).

If we go back to the beginning of this chapter, we can look at Xiang's first response to the therapist. Her presentation is similar to many clients, especially at the beginning of a first session. Usually at this point, clients have thought about what they want to say to the therapist about why they are in therapy. Many times, their focus is on what has been going wrong in their lives, aspects that they want to separate from. This presentation of what people do not want obscures talk about how they do want their life to be and aspects of their past or current experience that is in line with this preferred view. Xiang has been experiencing herself and her life as problematic. She can spend many hours discussing the facts of her life that she thinks are problematic and have led to her current identity of being codependent. The more the therapist engages in this conversation, the more these facts concretize, leading Xiang to continue to internalize this limiting view of self. The therapist can help Xiang deconstruct this view of herself by shifting from problem talk to solution talk.

Solution talk is talk between therapist and client that is outside of the problem (de Shazer & Berg, 1993). It is about what clients want in their lives or want more of. This type of conversation moves from the limiting facts of the past to the fantasies, desires, hopes, dreams, and plans of the present and future (de Shazer, 1994). These are the client's solutions, where the more therapist and client talk about solutions, the more each believe in the reality of this conversation.

We can then ask ourselves, where do **solutions** come from? de Shazer (1994) explained, "Thus, a solution is a joint product of therapist and client talking together about whatever it is that the problem/complaint is not" (p. 56). Part of the solution talk conversation is exploring how these fantasies and hopes have occurred in various ways in the client's past.

Being able to shift the conversation from problem talk to solution talk is the craft of therapy. It centers on how therapist and client negotiate the focus of the conversation (Reiter & Chenail, 2016). The therapist follows the client's initial focus, which is usually on problems, and then opens the possibility for the client to then follow in a shift toward solutions. This process is depicted in Figure 11.5.

One means of moving toward solution talk is through asking the **miracle question** (Berg, 1994). The miracle question was developed to help clients move from what was not working in their past and present to how they want things to be in the future. It goes something like:

> Suppose tonight, while you are sleeping, a miracle happens. And the miracle is that all of the things that you were talking about today [the various problems that brought them to therapy] are gone. But when you wake up you didn't know the miracle happened because you were sleeping. What would be the first sign for you that the miracle happened? That something was different?

By languaging this new future, therapist and client are creating the future in the present. This conversation on solutions, rather than problems, becomes a **generative discourse** (Gergen, 2009a), which challenges the traditional ways of viewing (which would be housed within problem talk) and bring forth new possibilities (housed within solution talk).

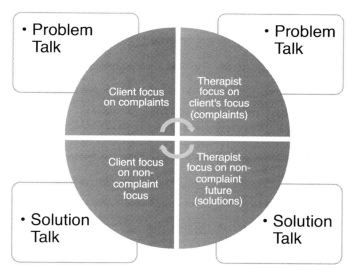

Figure 11.5 The Process of Client and Therapist Shifting From Problem Talk to Solution Talk.

Once the various pieces of the miracle are elaborated upon, the therapist can ask the client about times when these various pieces have already occurred, to some degree, in her life. These times when the problem could have happened but did not or did not occur to the level that the problem is currently at are called **exceptions** (Berg, 1994). A focus on exceptions helps to build hope for the client, as she can see that she has already engaged in beneficial ways of being. When paired with the miracle question, the expansion of exceptions demonstrates that the miracle, to some degree, has already happened. This provides both therapist and client with more expectation that what the client had done to make those exceptions happen can be replicated. These various exceptions, through expansion in the therapeutic conversation, become solutions. The more talk there is about miracles, the more "real" they become (de Shazer, 1994). In working with Xiang, this process may look like the following:

Therapist: [asks the miracle question]
Xiang: I guess I would feel empowered.
Therapist: Okay. So let's suppose you have that feeling. What would you do differently that you didn't do today?
Xiang: I would think about what I wanted rather than what I needed to do for someone else.
Therapist: And when you do that, how would that impact what you would do next?
Xiang: I would probably go to the gym or shopping.
Therapist: When was the last time you woke up and before doing something for someone else, you went to the gym or shopping?
Xiang: I think about three weeks ago. I went to the gym instead of doing some errands my mother wanted me to.
Therapist: Wow. How did you decide to do that?

This conversation builds upon what Xiang is already doing that has worked for her in the past, thus increasing her personal agency to act in ways that are in accordance with how she wants to be.

Most social constructionist therapists explore, through various means, alternatives to the client's problem descriptions. A focus on unique outcomes or exceptions are two pathways to creating alternative understandings for clients. DeJong and Berg (2012) use the acronym **EARS** to help therapists expand client exceptions (see Figure 11.6). The **E** encourages therapists to elicit the exception. The **A** stands for amplifying the exception. This comes by making a distinction between the exception time and the problem time. This will also include amplifying the personal agency the client took in either making the exception happen or allowing it to happen. The **R** relates to the therapist reinforcing the exception,

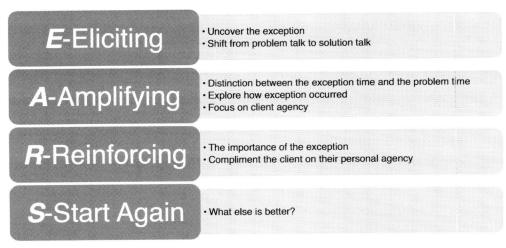

Figure 11.6 The Components of EARS: A Strength-Based Way of Listening to Client Stories.

highlighting the strengths the client used in ensuring the exception happened. These reinforcements of client strengths are called **compliments**. The **S** stands for starting again—asking clients, "What else is better?" The last component of EARS helps to expand the stories of success that are emerging in the therapeutic conversation.

The therapist, listening to Xiang discuss aspects of her life, could use EARS as a means of engaging in conversation to help bring the various exceptions to the forefront of the conversation:

Therapist: Xiang, when you were discussing your relationship with Ben, you mentioned that there were points in the relationship when you felt that it was based on interdependency. What happened during these times?
Xiang: It seemed we were on the same page. That both of our views were respected.
Therapist: How were you able to do that?
Xiang: I'm not sure. It just seemed to happen.
Therapist: But those times were different for you. When you had that experience of interdependency, how were you different?
Xiang: Well, I didn't just give in. I made my position clear and then we negotiated with one another.
Therapist: Wow. Not everyone is able to do that. What let you know you weren't going to just give in? That instead, you were going to be interdependent and negotiate with Ben?
Xiang: I had been frustrated and I wanted things to work out with him.
Therapist: What are some other times where you found that things were more like you wanted them to be?

This conversation helps new constructions of who the client is and what she can do come forth.

Key Figures

Insoo Kim Berg and Steve de Shazer

Insoo Kim Berg and Steve de Shazer co-developed solution-focused brief therapy (SFBT), one of the most popular psychotherapy approaches of the late 20th century and early 21st century. SFBT is predicated on the notion that people have experienced points in their lives where what they were doing was useful for them. Instead of focusing on problems and pathology, SFBT highlights clients' strengths and resources, helping clients to do more of what has worked for them in the past.

Insoo Kim Berg was born July 25, 1934, in Korea. She initially studied pharmacy at Ewha Womans University in Seoul, South Korea. She then moved to the University of Wisconsin-Madison to continue her studies but eventually switched majors to get a Master's degree in social work. In order to get further training, she studied at the Mental Research Institute (MRI) in Palo Alto, California, where John Weakland was her mentor. At the MRI, she met Steve de Shazer.

Steve de Shazer was born on June 25, 1940, in Milwaukee, Wisconsin. He attended the University of Wisconsin-Milwaukee, receiving a Bachelor of Fine Arts and a Master's degree in social work. In his early psychotherapy career, de Shazer utilized hypnotherapeutic ideas of Milton Erickson, cybernetic principles from Gregory Bateson, and therapeutic practice from the MRI brief therapy. John Weakland became a friend and mentor.

Berg and de Shazer married and co-developed the Brief Family Therapy Center (BFTC) in Milwaukee, Wisconsin, in 1978. Originally an off-shoot of the brief therapy of the MRI, the work at the BFTC looked at solutions rather than problems. Berg's writings focused more on the practice of SFBT while de Shazer's writings highlighted the philosophy that formed the foundation.

Steve de Shazer died on September 11, 2005. Insoo Kim Berg died on January 10, 2007.

Either/Or and Both/And

Many clients come to therapy with an **either/or perspective**. Either they are not having arguments with their partner or the relationship is in trouble. Either they are depressed or not depressed. Either they are making progress or they are not making progress. For Xiang, either she is codependent or she is not. This dichotomous thinking leads to a rigidified understanding of the person's situation and what possibilities are available to them.

Those operating from an either/or frame tend to experience themselves as being stuck (Lipchik, 1993). For those in relationships, such as spouses or parent and child, each person thinks that they are right and the other person is wrong. Postmodern therapists tend to privilege increased possibilities, which would entail a deconstruction of the client's more limited viewpoint to an increase in complexity of perspective.

Instead of holding this limiting either/or perspective, therapists can help clients shift to a **both/and perspective**. *Both* they have arguments with their partner *and* the relationship is okay. *Both* they are depressed at times *and* not depressed. *Both* Xiang does for others before herself *and* she does for herself before others. This shift to a both/and perspective helps therapists conceptualize that the client is right and wrong (de Shazer, 1985). This is especially significant when the therapist is working with multiple clients (i.e., couples or families).

When the therapist uses the both/and perspective, he is making overt the implicit resources of the client (see Figure 11.7). Lipchik (1993) explained, "The therapist operates on the assumptions that clients have inherent strengths and resources to find solutions and that, like most things in life, these solutions will be 'both/and,' (somewhere between the worst and the best scenarios) rather than 'either/or'" (p. 26). This entails therapists having conversations with clients as to the advantages and disadvantages of the perceived problem.

A practical way of enacting a both/and perspective is based on how the therapist uses language. Rather than hearing a client and then stating, "Instead of . . ." the therapist can say, "In addition to." (Andersen, 1993). Here are a few examples with our client Xiang:

Xiang: I tried telling Ben that I needed to put myself first.
Therapist: How did you do this?
Xiang: I confronted him that he has too many expectations of me.
Therapist: Did that work?
Xiang: No.
Therapist: Okay. Well, instead of that, why not try this. . . .

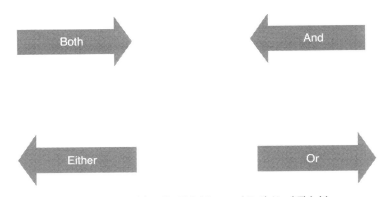

Figure 11.7 The Difference Between Either/Or Thinking and Both/And Thinking.

In this interchange, the therapist is negating the client's position and actions. An alternative way of being that embraces the both/and perspective would be:

Xiang: I tried telling Ben that I needed to put myself first.
Therapist: How did you do this?
Xiang: I confronted him that he has too many expectations of me.
Therapist: Did that work?
Xiang: No.
Therapist: Okay. In addition to what you did, what else do you think would be useful?

In this interchange, the therapist has accepted that what the client tried is a possibility and that there are other possibilities as well.

THERAPY VIA QUESTIONS

While just about every psychotherapy model utilizes questions, postmodern therapists ask questions not to lead clients to a designated location, but to explore how the client comes to understand self and what aspects of self have not yet been explored. This rests upon the therapist's curiosity. Questions that come from a place of curiosity open up new possibilities in the therapy room. Postmodern and constructionist based questions focus on attributed meanings. Strong (2002) explained, "So, their [postmodern therapists'] questions aim to invite clients into constructing effective meanings they prefer. And if those invitations are taken up, our questions can invite clients to *perform* (i.e., experience and enact the implications of) meanings with us" (p. 78, italics in original). These questions focus on client's strengths and resources rather than client's problems and deficits (see Figure 11.8).

Postmodern therapists tend to ask questions with presuppositions of alternatives and possibilities. This comes through in the words and word tenses used. Therapists help make distinctions between the past and present by asking questions that alter the past tense (O'Hanlon & Weiner-Davis, 1989).

Xiang: I have always been somewhat of a codependent person.
Therapist: You experienced yourself as codependent in the past and are now hoping that life will be different?

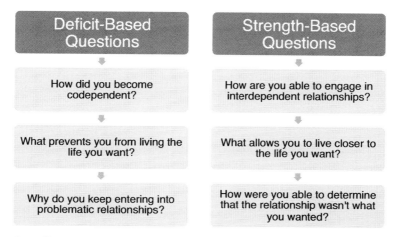

Figure 11.8 The Difference Between Deficit-Based and Strength-Based Questions.

Reiter (2018) discussed this play on past, present, and future as **temporality**. This includes use of phrases such as, "Right now," "At this time," or "In the past." By contextualizing the temporality of the client's experience, a shift from either/or (i.e., "I have been and will always be") to both/and (i.e., "I am upset and I will not be in the future").

Strength-based questions are usually predicated on a sense of being definitive (O'Hanlon & Weiner-Davis, 1989). This is through the use of "will" instead of "would" and "when" instead of "if." When you are talking with someone and use the word "if," it suggests that there is a possibility that something will happen but also the possibility that it will not. For instance, "If you weren't depressed anymore" provides some hope that the person will not be depressed, but it also suggests that maybe they will. Instead, if we asked, "*When* you are not depressed anymore" we are providing an opportunity for a sense of expectation to occur where the person can believe she will no longer be depressed. With Xiang, the therapist would likely ask questions such as:

- When you are having the types of relationships that you want, how will you be different?
- What will be happening when you put yourself first in relationships?
- How will your sense of self be when you are believing more in yourself?

Since these strength-based questions are based on suppositions, O'Hanlon and Weiner-Davis (1989) have called them **presuppositional questions**. These questions help orient clients to aspects of self that are strengths and resources. While the therapist has a general supposition that there are always strengths and resources to be accessed, he does not know the specifics for that client. This is why presuppositional questions are open-ended rather than closed-ended. For instance, instead of asking, "Have you ever been able to have a conversation where you two did not argue?" the therapist would ask, "How was it that you two were able to have a conversation?" Presuppositional questions tend to be asked around exceptions, "What is different when you are doing _____ (the non-complaint behavior)?"

Traditional psychotherapy tended to ask many questions about the past as it was important to try to find out what happened before to understand why someone is like they are in the present. Social constructionist questions tend to be focused more on the present and the future as this is where new meaning is more easily developed. "And thus, to the extent that we engage with others (our clients in this situation) in conversation about the future, we underscore the relational construction of our worlds. We fabricate together what we might live into" (McNamee, 2004, p. 266). One type of future-oriented question is the **fast-forward question** (O'Hanlon & Weiner-Davis, 1989). We have already encountered one example of fast-forward questions, the miracle question. Since some people do not like miracles, this question can be changed so there is a magic wand used to take away the problem or that they were able to live the life they wanted. The therapist could also ask a more straightforward fast-forward question, "When this problem is no longer in your life, what will your life look like?"

RESOURCES

With the switch of therapists' focus being from client deficits to strengths, clients (and all people) can be seen as having competencies rather than deficiencies. Ray and Keeney (1993) call these competencies **resources**. They explained, "By 'resource' is existentially meant *any* experience, belief, understanding, attitude, event, conduct, or interpersonal habit that contributes to the positive contextualization and realization of one's being" (p. 1, italics in original). Clients have a multitude of tapped and untapped resources available for them to shift their context. Therapists also have a multitude of resources available for them in their work with people. Cecchin (1992) explained that the only things therapists have are their resources. Thus, therapy is a medium in which two (or more) resourceful people come together and evoke more out of the other person.

One way of co-creating a resourceful therapeutic experience is for the therapist to be creative, not being held down by a specific model of therapy. Instead, the therapist uses his own resources to help clients express their own resources (Keeney, 1990). This comes in the form of having a mindset of irreverence and an ability in the therapy room to engage in improvisation.

Another way to focus on specific strengths and resources of the client is through **complimenting**. Compliments are when the therapist highlights what the client is doing that is useful for her, which help to enhance the client's personal agency. One of the primary questions to highlight client strengths is, "How did you do that?" (Berg, 1994). With Xiang, a resourceful conversation may be:

Therapist: Xiang, I was very impressed by something you said.
Xiang: What was that?
Therapist: You were saying that although you wanted to just do what Ben wanted, something inside you said, "No" and you didn't compromise yourself. How were you able to do that?

This chapter has presented several applications of social constructionist ideas. These are not all encompassing, and each idea can be provided in more depth. I encourage you to explore these ideas more to see how they might fit within your therapeutic practice.

QUESTIONS FOR REFLECTION

1. How does shifting from an expert position to a "client-as-expert" position change a therapist's engagement with a client? Can the therapist adopt a both/and position and be both expert and non-expert?

2. What is the importance of using counter documents in therapy?

3. How might a focus on solutions, rather than problems, assist clients? How do you respond to a critique of this position that this therapy is just a Band-Aid as it is not getting to the root of the problem?

4. What are the advantages and disadvantages of using a reflecting team with clients?

5. How might externalizing conversations help to empower the client?

References

Andersen, T. (1991). *The reflecting team: Dialogues and dialogues about the dialogues*. New York: W. W. Norton & Company.

Andersen, T. (1992). Reflections on reflecting with families. In S. McNamee & K. J. Gergen (Eds.), *Therapy as social construction* (pp. 54–68). London: Sage.

Andersen, T. (1993). See and hear, and be seen and heard. In S. Friedman (Ed.), *The new language of change* (pp. 303–322). New York: Guilford.

Anderson, H. (1990). Then and now: A journey from "knowing" to "not knowing." *Contemporary Family Therapy*, 12(3), 193–197.

Anderson, H. (1993). On a roller coaster: A collaborative language systems approach to therapy. In S. Friedman (Ed.), *The new language of change* (pp. 323–344). New York: The Guilford Press.

Anderson, H. (1997). *Conversation, language, and possibilities*. New York: Basic Books.

Anderson, H. (2005). Myths about "not-knowing." *Family Process*, 44(4), 497–504.

Anderson, H. (2007a). Dialogue: People creating meaning with each other and finding ways to go on. In H. Anderson & D. Gehart (Eds.), *Collaborative therapy: Relationships and conversations that make a difference* (pp. 33–41). New York: Routledge.

Anderson, H. (2007b). The heart and spirit of collaborative therapy. In H. Anderson & D. Gehart (Eds.), *Collaborative therapy: Relationships and conversations that make a difference* (pp. 43–59). New York: Routledge.

Anderson, H. (2012). Possibilities of the collaborative approach. In T. Malinen, S. J. Cooper, & F. N. Thomas (Eds.), *Masters of narrative and collaborative therapies* (pp. 61–120). New York: Routledge.

Anderson, H., & Goolishian, H. A. (1988). Human systems as linguistic systems: Preliminary and evolving ideas about the implications for clinical theory. *Family Process*, 27(4), 371–393.

Anderson, H., & Goolishian, H. A. (1992). The client is the expert: A not-knowing approach to therapy. In S. McNamee & K. J. Gergen (Eds.), *Therapy as social construction* (pp. 25–39). London: Sage.

Bateson, G. (1936/1958). *Naven* (2nd ed.). Palo Alto, CA: Stanford University Press.

Bateson, G. (1972/2000). *Steps to an ecology of mind*. Chicago, IL: The University of Chicago Press.

Bateson, G. (1979). *Mind and nature: A necessary unity*. New York: Dutton.

Bateson, G. (1987). Information and codification: A philosophical approach. In J. Reusch & G. Bateson (Eds.), *Communication: The social matrix of psychiatry* (pp. 168–211). New York: W. W. Norton & Company.

Bateson, G. (1991). *A sacred unity: Further steps to an ecology of mind*. New York: HarperCollins.

Bateson, G., Jackson, D. D., Haley, J., & Weakland, J. (1956). Toward a theory of schizophrenia. *Behavioral Science*, 1, 251–264.

Berg, I. K. (1994). *Family based services*. New York: W. W. Norton & Company.

Berg, I. K., & de Shazer, S. (1993). Making numbers talk: Language in therapy. In S. Friedman (Ed.), *The new language of change* (pp. 5–24). New York: Guilford.

Berman, P. S. (2010). *Case conceptualization and treatment planning*. Thousand Oaks, CA: Sage.

Bertalanffy, L. V. (1968). *General system theory*. New York: George Grazille.

Boscolo, L., Cecchin, G., Hoffman, L., & Penn, P. (1987). *Milan systemic family therapy*. New York: Basic Books.

Bowen, M. (1994). *Family therapy in clinical practice*. Northvale, NJ: Jason Aronson.

Bridges, S. K., & Raskin, J. D. (2008). Constructivist psychotherapy in the real world. In J. D. Raskin & S. K. Bridges (Eds.), *Studies in meaning 3: Constructivist psychotherapy in the real world* (pp. 1–30). New York: Pace University Press.

REFERENCES

Bronfenbrenner, U., & Morris, P. A. (2006). The bioecological model of human development. In W. Damon & R. M. Lerner (Eds.), *Handbook of child psychology* (pp. 993–1023). New York: John Wiley & Sons.

Bruner, J. (1986). *Actual minds, possible worlds.* Cambridge, MA: Harvard University Press.

Cantwell, P., & Holmes, S. (1994). Social construction: A paradigm shift for systemic therapy and training. *Australian and New Zealand Journal of Family Therapy, 15*(1), 17–26.

Carter, B., & McGoldrick, M. (1999). Overview: The expanded family life cycle. In B. Carter & M. McGoldrick (Eds.), *The expanded family life cycle: Individual, family, and social perspectives* (3rd ed., pp. 1–26). Boston, MA: Allyn & Bacon.

Cecchin, G. (1987). Hypothesizing, circularity, and neutrality revisited: An invitation to curiosity. *Family Process, 26*(4), 405–413.

Cecchin, G. (1992). Constructing therapeutic possibilities. In S. McNamee & K. J. Gergen (Eds.), *Therapy as social construction* (pp. 86–95). London: Sage.

Cecchin, G., Lane, G., & Ray, W. A. (1994). Influence, effect, and emerging systems. *Journal of Systemic Therapies, 13*(4), 13–21.

DeJong, P., Bavelas, J. B., & Korman, H. (2013). An introduction to using microanalysis to observe co-construction in psychotherapy. *Journal of Systemic Therapies, 32*(3), 17–30.

DeJong, P., & Berg, I. K. (2012). *Interviewing for solutions* (4th ed.). Pacific Grove, CA: Brooks/Cole.

de Shazer, S. (1982). *Patterns of brief family therapy.* New York: Guilford.

de Shazer, S. (1985). *Keys to solution in brief therapy.* New York: W. W. Norton & Company.

de Shazer, S. (1991). *Putting difference to work.* New York: W. W. Norton & Company.

de Shazer, S. (1993). Creative misunderstanding: There is no escape from language. In S. Gilligan & R. Price (Eds.), *Therapeutic conversations* (pp. 81–94). New York: W. W. Norton & Company.

de Shazer, S. (1994). *Words were originally magic.* New York: W. W. Norton & Company.

de Shazer, S., & Berg, I. K. (1992). Doing therapy: A post-structural revision. *Journal of Marital and Family Therapy, 18,* 71–81.

de Shazer, S., & Berg, I. K. (1993). Making numbers talk: Language in therapy. In S. Friedman (Ed.), *The new language of change* (pp. 5–24). New York: The Guilford Press.

de Shazer, S., & Molnar, A. (1984). Four useful interventions in brief family therapy. *Journal of Marital and Family Therapy, 10*(3), 297–304.

Drewery, W., & Winslade, J. (1997). The theoretical story of narrative therapy. In G. Monk, J. Winslade, K. Crocket, & D. Epston (Eds.), *Narrative therapy in practice* (pp. 32–52). San Francisco, CA: Jossey-Bass.

Ducommon-Nagy, K., & Reiter, M. D. (2014). Contextual family therapy. In M. D. Reiter (Ed.). *Case conceptualization in family therapy* (pp. 55–81). Upper Saddle River, NJ: Pearson.

Duncan, B. L., Solovey, A. D., & Rusk, G. S. (1992). *Changing the rules: A client-directed approach to therapy.* New York: Guilford.

Efran, J. S., & Clarfield, L. E. (1992). Constructionist therapy: Sense and nonsense. In S. McNamee & K. J. Gergen (Eds.), *Therapy as social construction* (pp. 200–217). London: Sage.

Efran, J. S., & Fauber, R. L. (1995). Radical constructivism: Questions and answers. In R. A. Neimeyer & M. J. Mahoney (Eds.), *Constructivism in psychotherapy* (pp. 275–304). Washington, DC: American Psychological Association.

Efran, J. S., & Greene, M. A. (1996). Psychotherapeutic theory and practice: Contributions from Maturana's structure determinism. In H. Rosen & K. T. Kuehlwein (Eds.), *Constructing realities: Meaning-making perspectives for psychotherapists* (pp. 71–113). San Francisco, CA: Jossey-Bass.

Efran, J. S., Lukens, M. D., & Lukens, R. J. (1990). *Language, structure, and change: Frameworks of meaning in psychotherapy.* New York: W. W. Norton & Company.

Epston, D., White, M., & Murray, K. (1992). A proposal for a re-authoring therapy: Rose's revisioning of her life and a commentary. In S. McNamee & K. J. Gergen (Eds.), *Therapy as social construction* (pp. 96–115). London: Sage.

Ferreira, A. J. (1977). Family myths. In P. Watzlawick & J. H. Weakland (Eds.), *The interactional view* (pp. 49–55). New York: W. W. Norton & Company.

Fisch, R., Weakland, J. H., & Segal, L. (1982). *The tactics of change.* San Francisco, CA: Jossey-Bass.

Flemons, D. G. (1991). *Completing distinctions.* Boston: Shambhala.

Foucault, M. (1980). *Power/knowledge.* New York: Pantheon Books.

Freedman, J., & Combs, G. (1996). *Narrative therapy.* New York: W. W. Norton & Company.

Frosh, S. (1995). Postmodernism versus psychotherapy. Journal of Family Therapy, 17, 175–190.
Fruggeri, L. (1992). Therapeutic process as the social construction of change. In S. McNamee & K. J. Gergen (Eds.), Therapy as social construction (pp. 40–53). London: Sage.
Gelcer, E., McCabe, A. E., & Smith-Resnick, C. (1990). Milan family therapy: Variant and invariant methods. Northvale, NJ: Jason Aronson.
Gergen, K. J. (1982). Toward transformation in social knowledge. New York: Springer-Verlag.
Gergen, K. J. (1985). The social constructionist movement in modern psychology. American Psychologist, 40(3), 266–275.
Gergen, K. J. (1991). The saturated self. New York: Basic Books.
Gergen, K. J. (1994). Realities and relationships: Soundings in social construction. Cambridge, MA: Harvard University Press.
Gergen, K. J. (2001). Social construction in context. London: Sage.
Gergen, K. J. (2006). Therapeutic realities: Collaboration, oppression and relational flow. Chagrin Falls, OH: Taos Institute.
Gergen, K. J. (2009a). An invitation to social construction (2nd ed.). Los Angeles: Sage.
Gergen, K. J. (2009b). Relational being: Beyond self and community. New York: Oxford University Press.
Gergen, K. J., & Warhus, L. (2001). Therapy as social construction. In K. J. Gergen (Ed.), Social construction in context (pp. 96–114). London: Sage.
Gonçalves, Ó. F. (1995). Hermeneutics, constructivism, and cognitive-behavioral therapies: From the object to the project. In R. A. Neimeyer & M. J. Mahony (Eds.), Constructivism in psychotherapy (pp. 195–230). Washington, DC: American Psychological Association.
Goolishian, H. A., & Anderson, H. (1987). Language systems and therapy: An evolving idea. Psychotherapy: Theory, Research, Practice, Training, 24, 529–538.
Goolishian, H. A., & Winderman, L. (1988). Constructivism, autopoiesis and problem determined systems. The Irish Journal of Psychology, 9(1), 130–143.
Guidano, V. F. (1995). Constructivist psychotherapy: A theoretical framework. In R. A. Neimeyer & M. J. Mahony (Eds.), Constructivism in psychotherapy (pp. 93–108). Washington, DC: American Psychological Association.
Haley, J. (1984). Ordeal therapy. San Francisco, CA: Jossey-Bass.
Haley, J. (1987). Problem-solving therapy (2nd ed.). San Francisco, CA: Jossey-Bass.
Hall, C. (1991). The Bowen family theory and its uses. Northvale, NJ: Jason Aronson.
Held, B. S. (1995a). The real meaning of constructivism. Journal of Constructivist Psychology, 8, 305–315.
Held, B. S. (1995b). Back to reality: A critique of postmodern theory in psychotherapy. New York: W. W. Norton & Company.
Herz, F. M., & Rosen, E. J. (1982). Jewish families. In M. McGoldrick, J. K. Pearce, & J. Giordano (Eds.), Ethnicity and family therapy (pp. 364–392). New York: Guilford.
Hines, P. M., Preto, N. G., McGoldrick, M., Almeida, R., & Weltman, S. (1999). Culture and the family life cycle. In B. Carter & M. McGoldrick (Eds.), The expanded family life cycle: Individual, family, and social perspectives (3rd ed., pp. 69–87). Boston, MA: Allyn & Bacon.
Hoffman, L. (1981). Foundations of family therapy. New York: Basic Books.
Hoffman, L. (2000). A communal perspective for relational therapies. Journal of Feminist Family Therapy, 11, (4), 5–17.
Jackson, D. D. (1957). The question of family homeostasis. The Psychiatric Quarterly Supplement, 31, 79–90.
Jackson, D. D. (1965). Family rules: Marital quid pro quo. Archives of General Psychiatry, 12, 589–594.
Jackson, D. D. (1977a). The myth of normality. In P. Watzlawick & J. H. Weakland (Eds.), The interactional view (pp. 157–163). New York: W. W. Norton & Company.
Jackson, D. D. (1977b). The study of the family. In P. Watzlawick & J. H. Weakland (Eds.), The interactional view (pp. 2–20). New York: W. W. Norton & Company.
Kassis, J. P. (1984). A team's development from "Universe to Multiverse." Journal of Strategic and Systemic Therapies, 3(4), 63–72.
Kazdin, A. E. (1986). Comparative outcome studies of psychotherapy: Methodological issues and strategies. Journal of Consulting and Clinical Psychology, 54(1), 95–105.
Keeney, B. P. (1983). Aesthetics of change. New York: Guilford.
Keeney, B. P. (1990). Improvisational therapy. New York: Guilford.
Keeney, B. P., & Ross, J. M. (1983). Learning to learn systemic therapies. Journal of Strategic and Systemic Therapies, 2(2), 22–30.
Keeney, B. P., & Ross, J. M. (1985). Mind in therapy. New York: Basic Books.
Keeney, H., Keeney, B., & Chenail, R. (2015). Recursive frame analysis. Fort Lauderdale, FL: TQR Books.

REFERENCES

Kenny, V. (1989). Life, the multiverse and everything: An introduction to the ideas of Humberto Maturana. In A. L. Goudsmit (Ed.), *Self-Organization in psychotherapy* (pp. 17–47). Berlin: Springer-Verlag.

Kerr, M., & Bowen, M. (1988). *Family evaluation*. New York: Norton.

Korzybski, A. (1933). *Science and sanity*. New York: Institute of General Samamics.

Lax, W. D. (1992). Postmodern thinking in a clinical practice. In S. McNamee & K. J. Gergen (Eds.), *Therapy as social construction* (pp. 69–85). London: Sage.

Lee, J. A., Neimeyer, G. J., & Rice, K. G. (2013). The relationship between therapist epistemology, therapy style, working alliance, and interventions use. *American Journal of Psychotherapy*, 67(4), 323–345.

Leyland, L. M. (1988). An introduction to some of the ideas of Humberto Maturana. *Journal of Family Therapy*, 10(4), 357–374.

Lipchik, E. (1993). "Both/And" solutions. In S. Friedman (Ed.), *The new language of change* (pp. 25–49). New York: The Guilford Press.

Luquet, W. (2007). *Short-term couples therapy* (2nd ed.). New York: Routledge.

Madanes, C. (1981). *Strategic family therapy*. San Francisco, CA: Jossey-Bass.

Madigan, S. P. (1993). Questions about questions: Situating the therapist's curiosity in front of the family. In S. Gilligan & R. Price (Eds.), *Therapeutic conversations* (pp. 219–236). New York: W. W. Norton & Company.

Mahoney, M. J. (1988). Constructive metatheory: II. Implications for psychotherapy. *International Journal of Personal Construct Psychology*, 1, 299–315.

Mahoney, M. J. (1995). Continuing evolution of the cognitive sciences and psychotherapies. In R. A. Neimeyer & M. J. Mahoney (Eds.), *Constructivism in psychotherapy* (pp. 39–67). Washington, DC: American Psychological Association.

Mahoney, M. J. (2003). *Constructive psychotherapy*. New York: Guilford.

Maturana, H. R. (1980). Biology of cognition. In H. R. Maturana & F. J. Varela (Eds.), *Autopoiesis and cognition* (pp. 5–58). Boston, MA: D. Reidel Publishing.

Maturana, H. R. (1988). Reality: The search for objectivity or the quest for a compelling argument. *The Irish Journal of Psychology*, 9(1), 25–82.

Maturana, H. R. (1991). Response to Jim Birch. *Journal of Family Therapy*, 13, 375–393.

Maturana, H. R., & Poerksen, B. (2004). The view of the systemicist: A conversation. *Journal of Constructivist Psychology*, 17, 269–279.

Maturana, H. R., & Varela, F. J. (1980). *Autopoiesis and cognition: The realization of the living*. Boston, MA: D. Reidel Publishing.

Maturana, H. R., & Varela, F. J. (1992). *The tree of knowledge: The biological roots of human understanding* (Revised ed.). Boston, MA: Shambhala.

McGoldrick, M. (1982). Ethnicity and family therapy: An overview. In M. McGoldrick, J. K. Pearce, & J. Giordano (Eds.), *Ethnicity & family therapy* (pp. 3–30). New York: Guilford.

McGoldrick, M., Pearce, J. K., & Giordano, J. (Eds.). (1982). *Ethnicity & family therapy*. New York: Guilford.

McNamee, S. (2004). Therapy as social construction: Back to basics and forward toward challenging issues. In T. Strong & D. Paré (Eds.), *Furthering talk: Advances in the discursive therapies* (pp. 253–270). New York: Kluwer Academic/Plenum Publishers.

McNamee, S., & Gergen, K. J. (1998). *Relational responsibility: Resources for sustainable dialogue*. Thousand Oaks, CA: Sage.

Minuchin, S. (2012). *Families and family therapy*. New York: Routledge. (Original work published 1974).

Minuchin, S., & Fishman, H. C. (1981). *Family therapy techniques*. Cambridge, MA: Harvard University Press.

Minuchin, S., Reiter, M. D., & Borda, C. (2014). *The craft of family therapy*. New York: Routledge.

Monk, G., Winslade, J., Crocket, K., & Epston, D. (1997). *Narrative therapy in practice*. San Francisco, CA: Jossey-Bass.

Moules, N. J. (2000). Postmodernism and the sacred: Reclaiming connection in our greater-than-human worlds. *Journal of Marital and Family Therapy*, 26(2), 229–240.

Neimeyer, G. J. (1995). The challenge of change. In R. A. Neimeyer & M. J. Mahony (Eds.), *Constructivism in psychotherapy* (pp. 111–126). Washington, DC: American Psychological Association.

Neimeyer, G. J., Lee, J., Aksoy-Toska, G., & Phillip, D. (2008). Epistemological commitments among seasoned psychotherapists: Some practical implications of being a constructivist. In J. D. Raskin & S. K. Bridges (Eds.), *Studies in meaning 3: Constructivist psychotherapy in the real world* (pp. 31–54). New York: Pace University Press.

Neimeyer, R. A. (1993). An appraisal of constructivist psychotherapies. *Journal of Consulting and Clinical Psychology*, 61(2), 221–234.

REFERENCES

Neimeyer, R. A. (1995a). An invitation to constructivist psychotherapies. In R. A. Neimeyer & M. J. Mahony (Eds.), *Constructivism in psychotherapy* (pp. 1–8). Washington, DC: American Psychological Association.

Neimeyer, R. A. (1995b). Constructivist psychotherapies: Features, foundations, and future directions. In R. A. Neimeyer & M. J. Mahony (Eds.), *Constructivism in psychotherapy* (pp. 11–38). Washington, DC: American Psychological Association.

Neimeyer, R. A. (1998). Social constructionism in the counseling context. *Counselling Psychology Quarterly*, 11(2), 135–149.

Neimeyer, R. A. (2009). *Constructivist psychotherapy*. New York: Routledge.

Nichols, M. P., & Fellenberg, S. (2000). The effective use of enactments in family therapy: A discovery-oriented process study. *Journal of Marital and Family Therapy*, 26(2), 143–152.

O'Hanlon, B. (1999). *Do one thing different*. New York: William Morrow & Company.

O'Hanlon, W. H., & Weiner-Davis, M. (1989). *In search of solutions*. New York: W. W. Norton & Company.

Omer, H. (1996). Three styles of constructive therapy. In M. F. Hoyt (Ed.), *Constructive therapies: Volume 2* (pp. 319–333). New York: Guilford.

Palazzoli, M. S., Boscolo, L., Cecchin, G., & Prata, G. (1978). A ritualized prescription in family therapy: Odd days and even days. *Journal of Marriage and Family Counseling*, 4, 3–8.

Palazzoli, M. S., Boscolo, L., Cecchin, G., & Prata, G. (1980). Hypothesizing-circularity-neutrality: Three guidelines for the conductor of the session. *Family Process*, 19, 3–12.

Palazzoli, M. S., Boscolo, L., Cecchin, G., & Prata, G. (1981). *Paradox and counterparadox*. New York: Jason Aronson.

Panichelli, C. (2013). Humor, joining, and reframing in psychotherapy: Resolving the auto-double-bind. *The American Journal of Family Therapy*, 41, 437–451.

Papero, D. (1990). *Bowen family systems theory*. Boston, MA: Allyn and Bacon.

Penn, P. (1982). Circular questioning. *Family Process*, 21(3), 267–280.

Penn, P. (1985). Feed forward: Future questions, future maps. *Family Process*, 24, 299–311.

Pilgrim, D. (2000). The real problem for postmodernism. *Journal of Family Therapy*, 22, 6–23.

Piotrkowski, C. S., & Hughes, D. (1993). Dual-earner families in context: Managing family and work systems. In F. Walsh (Ed.), *Normal family processes* (2nd ed., pp. 185–207). New York: Guilford.

Raskin, J. D. (2002). Constructivism in psychology: Personal construct psychology, radical constructivism, and social constructionism. In J. D. Raskin & S. K. Bridges (Eds.), *Studies in meaning: Exploring constructivist psychology* (pp. 1–25). New York: Pace University Press.

Raskin, J. D., & Neimeyer, R. A. (2003). Coherent constructivism: A response to Mackay. *Theory & Psychology*, 13(3), 397–409.

Ray, W. A., & Keeney, B. P. (1993). *Resource focused therapy*. London: Karnac Books.

Ray, W. A., & Simms, M. (2016). Embracing cybernetics: Living legacy of the Bateson research team. *Cybernetics and Human Knowing*, 23(3), 29–57.

Reiter, M. D. (2010). The use of hope and expectancy in solution-focused therapy. *Journal of Family Psychotherapy*, 21, 132–148.

Reiter, M. D. (2014). *Case conceptualization and family therapy*. New York: Pearson.

Reiter, M. D. (2016a). A quick guide to case conceptualization in Structural family therapy. *Journal of Systemic Therapies*, 35(2), 25–37.

Reiter, M. D. (2016b). Solution-focused sculpting. *Journal of Systemic Therapies*, 35(3), 30–41.

Reiter, M. D. (2018). *Family therapy: An introduction to process, practice, and theory*. New York: Routledge.

Reiter, M. D., & Chenail, R. J. (2016). Defining the focus in solution-focused brief therapy. *International Journal of Solution-Focused Practices*, 4(1), 1–9.

Reiter, M. D., & Shilts, L. (1998). Using circular scaling questions to deconstruct depression: A case study. *Crisis Intervention and Time Limited Treatment*, 4, 227–237.

Rogers, C. R. (1961). *On becoming a person*. Boston: Houghton Mifflin.

Rogers, C. R., & Truax, C. B. (1967). The therapeutic conditions antecedent to change: A theoretical view. In C. R. Rogers (Ed.), *The therapeutic relationship and its impact* (pp. 97–108). Westport, CT: Greenwood Press.

Rosen, H. (1996). Meaning-making narratives: Foundations for constructivist and social constructionist psychotherapies. In H. Rosen & K. T. Kuehlwein (Eds.), *Constructing realities: Meaning-making perspectives for psychotherapists* (pp. 1–51). San Francisco, CA: Jossey-Bass.

Rosen, H., & Kuehlwein, K. T. (Eds.). (1996). *Constructing realities: Meaning-making perspectives for psychotherapists*. San Francisco, CA: Jossey-Bass.

REFERENCES

Rosenhan, D. L. (1984). On being sane in insane places. In P. Watzlawick (Ed.), *The invented reality* (pp. 117–144). New York: W. W. Norton & Company.

Satir, V., & Baldwin, M. (1984). *Satir step by step: A guide to creating change in families.* Mountain View, CA: Science and Behavior Books.

Satir, V., Banmen, J., Gerber, J., & Gomori, M. (1991). *The Satir model.* Mountain View, CA: Science and Behavior Books.

Short, D. (2010). *Transformational relationships.* Phoenix, AZ: Zeig, Tucker & Thiesen.

Simon, R. (1985). Structure is destiny: An interview with Humberto Maturana. *Family Therapy Networker, 9*(3), 32–37, 41–43.

Sperry, L., & Sperry, J. (2012). *Case conceptualization: Mastering this competency with ease and confidence.* New York: Routledge.

Strong, T. (2002). Constructive curiosities. *Journal of Systemic Therapies, 21*(1), 77–90.

Thorndike, E. L. (1920). A constant error in psychological ratings. *Journal of Applied Psychology, 4*(1), 25–29.

Titleman, P. (1998). *Clinical applications of Bowen family systems theory.* New York: Haworth.

Titleman, P. (2008). *Triangles: Bowen family systems theory perspectives.* New York: Haworth.

Toman, W. (1961). *The family constellation: Its effects on personality and social behavior.* New York: Springer.

von Foerster, H. (2002). *Understanding: Essays on cybernetics and cognition.* New York: Springer-Verlag.

von Foerster, H. (1984). *Observing systems.* Seaside, CA: Intersystems Publications.

von Glasersfeld, E. (1984). An introduction to radical constructivism. In P. Watzlawick (Ed.), *The invented reality* (pp. 17–40). New York: W. W. Norton & Company.

von Glasersfeld, E. (1995). *Radical constructivism: A way of knowing and learning.* New York: Routledge.

Waters, D. (1994). Prisoners of our metaphors: Do dialogic therapies make other methods obsolete? *Family Therapy Networker,* Nov/Dec, 73–75.

Watzlawick, P. (1976). *How real is real?* New York: Vintage Books.

Watzlawick, P. (1978). *The language of change.* New York: Basic Books.

Watzlawick, P. (1984). Self-fulfilling prophecies. In P. Watzlawick (Ed.), *The invented reality* (pp. 95–116). New York: W. W. Norton & Company.

Watzlawick, P. (1990). *Munchhausen's pigtail.* New York: W. W. Norton & Company.

Watzlawick, P., Bavelas, J. B., & Jackson, D. D. (1967). *Pragmatics of human communication.* New York: W. W. Norton & Company.

Watzlawick, P., Weakland, J., & Fisch, R. (1974). *Change: Principles of problem formation and problem resolution.* New York: W. W. Norton & Company.

Weakland, H. H., Watzlawick, P., & Riskin, J. (1995). Introduction: MRI-A little background music. In J. H. Weakland & W. A. Ray (Eds.), *Propagations: Thirty years of influence from the Mental Research Institute* (pp. 1–15). New York: The Haworth Press.

Weakland, J. H., Fisch, R., Watzlawick, P., & Bodin, A. M. (1974). Brief therapy: Focused problem resolution. *Family Process, 13,* 141–168.

Whitaker, C. A., & Bumberry, W. M. (1988). *Dancing with the family: A symbolic-experiential approach.* New York: Brunner/Mazel.

White, M. (1986). Negative explanation, restraint and double description: A template for family therapy. *Family Process, 25*(2), 169–184.

White, M. (1993). Deconstruction and therapy. In S. Gilligan & R. Price (Eds.), *Therapeutic conversations* (pp. 22–61). New York: W. W. Norton & Company.

White, M. (2007). *Maps of narrative practice.* New York: W. W. Norton & Company.

White, M. (2011). *Narrative practice: Continuing the conversation.* New York: W. W. Norton & Company.

White, M., & Epston, D. (1990). *Narrative means to therapeutic ends.* New York: W. W. Norton & Company.

Whitehead, A. N., & Russell, B. (1910). *Principia mathematica.* Cambridge, MA: Cambridge University Press.

Wiener, N. (1948). *Cybernetics: Or control and communication in the animal and the machine.* Cambridge, MA: MIT Press.

Wiener, N. (1954). *The human use of human beings.* New York: Da Capo.

Wittgenstein, L. (1958). *Philosophical investigations.* New York: Macmillan Publishing.

Worsley, R. (2012). Narratives and lively metaphors: Hermeneutics as a way of listing. *Person-Centered & Experiential Psychotherapies, 11*(4), 304–320.

Index

9-dot problem 93–94, 101

accurate empathic understanding 9, 163
aesthetics: definition 18
Anderson, Harlene 158, 163, 168, 172, 174
anger 1, 26, 39, 41, 50, 109, 134, 139, 206
anxiety 44, 50, 56, 106–110, 113–119, 121–123, 124, 129, 134–136, 138–140, 143, 162–163, 178, 203; acute 107–108; in BFST 104, 107–109; chronic 104, 107–109, 122–123, 140
attributes: external 44; internal 44
attribution theory 156
axioms of communication 81–88, 90–92; Axiom 1 82–83; Axiom 2 83–86; Axiom 3 86–87; Axiom 4 90–91; Axiom 5 91–92

Bateson, Gregory 14–15, 21, 22, 25, 34, 46, 61, 63, 66, 70, 74, 81–82, 90, 92, 96, 145, 147, 151, 213
behavior 40–43; communicational 82–83; consensual 151, 154; depressive 33; externalizing 203; human 74, 81, 105, 111; internalizing 203
behavior theories: classical conditioning 144; operant conditioning 144
benevolent sabotage 95
Berg, Insoo Kim 56, 179, 201, 212–213
binocular theory of change 190
binocular vision *see* double description
biochemical imbalance 5
bioecological model of human development (Bronfenbrenner's) 13–14; chronosystem 14; exosystem 13–14; and macrosystem 13–14; mesosystem 13–14; microsystem 13–14
biopsychosocial assessment 1, 4–5, 174, 196
Boszormenyi-Nagy 177
boundaries 75–76, 79, 100; clear 76–77, 100; diffuse 76–77, 100; enmeshment 78; making 100; rigid 76–77, 100
Bowen, Murray 103–109, 111–114, 116–122, 124, 129, 133–140
Bowen Family Systems approach 103, 109, 134, 141

Bowen Family Systems theory (BFST) 103–105, 107, 111, 136–137, 140
Bowen's Eight Concepts 104–105, 111; differentiation of self 105, 107, 111–113, 117, 129, 134; emotional cutoff 105, 111, 121; emotional triangles 111, 114–116, 123, 132, 134–136, 139; family projection process 105, 111, 119; multigenerational transmission process 105, 111, 120–121; nuclear family emotional process 105, 111, 116–119, 132; sibling position 105, 111, 121–122; societal regression (societal emotional process) 105, 111, 122–123; *see also* Differentiation of Self Scale; illness; marital conflict; relationship anxiety
Bowen Theory Academy 137
Brief Family Therapy Center (BFTC) 213
Bronfenbrenner, U. 13–14

case conceptualization 5–10, 18–19, 50; etiology 6; theory of problem formation 6–7, 10, 18–19, 197; theory of problem resolution 6–7, 10, 18–19, 99, 197; therapeutic pathways 6; treatment plan 5–6, 169; *see also* epistemology
Catholicism 14
cause/effect model 34, 150
change: first order 48–49, 93, 95–96, 98; second order 48–49, 93–96, 98–101
circular questions 55–59; differences in degree 56; differences in temporality 56–57; exception 57, 168, 212–213, 216; future differences ("feed-forward") 58; hypothetical differences 58; triadic (difference in perception) 56; *see also* scaling questions
co-construction 200, 201–202; imaginary moments 201–202
codependency 187, 191, 203–205, 207
cognitive-behavioral model 10
cognitive distortions, language of: catastrophizing 84; overgeneralization 84; personalization 84; polarized thinking 84
communication 15, 26, 41, 43, 46, 74, 83–86, 96, 143, 146, 150, 155, 158, 195; analogic 87, 21; and co-action 195; command level 86–87; digital

INDEX

21, 88; interactional 74, 87; nonverbal 21, 88, 186; paradoxes in/of 15, 61, 92; paradoxical 46; paralingual 87–88; report level 86–87, 96; verbal 21, 87–88, 186; written 186; *see also* axioms of communication; metacommunication
complementarity 37, 40, 48, 52, 68
constructivism 15, 142–145, 151–152, 162, 183, 188; and antirealism 145; radical 74, 145–146; as second order cybernetics 143, 153; *see also* objectivism
constructivist aesthetics 142–161; autopoiesis 150–151; coordination 157–158; hermeneutics 158; meaning 156; observer 147–148; reality 149; structure (determined and coupling) 152–153; *see also* constructivism; deconstruction; discourse; languaging; objectivity; perturbations; postpositivism; realism
constructivist pragmatics 162–180; distinguishing self 176–178; focusing on meanings 164–166; meanings in therapy 166–167; problem-determined and problem-organizing systems 170–175; story/storyteller 167–170; *see also* constructivist psychotherapy; curiosity, therapeutic; enactments; scaling questions
context: client's 10, 19; cultural 182; relational 11, 12, 14, 184; situational 11, 12, 14, 45; social 20, 143; therapist's 10
counterparadox 97
Couples Dialogue 84–85
curiosity, therapeutic 139, 164, 173–174, 176, 193, 201, 209, 215
cybernetics 21, 24–25, 28; definition 21
cybernetics aesthetics 20–38; circularity and recursion 34–38, 40, 49, 56, 63, 176; entropy and negentropy 27–28; history of 21; logical types, theory of 32–34; morphostasis/morphogenesis 31–32; restraint 25–27, 28, 31, 43–44, 47, 49–50, 52, 59, 97–99; tendencies 27; *see also* cybernetics; double description; feedback; homeostasis
cybernetics pragmatics 40–59; stability and change 40; *see also* behavior; circular questions; equifinality; family myths; hypotheses; marital quid pro quo; roles; rules

Darwin, Charles 103–105
deconstruction 159–160, 193–194, 197, 202, 214; text-focused reading 159
definitional ceremonies 207
depression 5–6, 12, 17, 26–28, 33–34, 39, 41, 50, 52, 203–204
Derrida, Jacques 159
Descartes, René 147
de Shazer, Steve 46, 54, 56, 155, 159, 179, 190–191, 194, 200, 210–211, 213
determinism: environmental 144–145; *see also* structural determinism

Diagnostic and Statistical Manual (DSM) 10, 71, 107, 161, 196
Differentiation of Self Scale 112–113
discourse 160–161, 184; of deficit 196; dominant 71, 186–188, 191, 195–196, 199, 202; multiple perspective 161, 176; presupposition 25, 50, 160–161, 215–216; social 182, 186–187, 199; subjectification 161
displays of problems: external 12–13; internal 12–13
dormitive principle 33, 52
double descriptions 37–38, 55, 64, 209

empiricism 148, 182, 192
enactments 89–90, 92; casual 178–180; empty chair technique 178; family sculpting 179; nonverbal 179; therapeutic 89, 178; verbal 178–179; *see also* sculpting
English (language) 3
epistemology 7–10; lineal 10–11, 34, 63; nonlineal 10–11, 13, 34, 36, 63; postmodern 190
equifinality 26, 27, 53–55, 59; do something different task 54–55, 83
Erickson, Milton 15, 99, 197, 213
ethnicity 77–78, 80
evolutionary theory 103, 137
externalization 202–205; externalizing 203; externalizing behaviors 203; *see also* externalizing conversations
externalizing conversations 203, 205, 217; categories of inquiry of 203–205

family: life cycle 78–80; sculpting 179; system 16, 78, 103–107, 109–114, 116–120, 122, 124–126, 128–129, 133–138, 140–141; therapy 15; *see also* family of origin; nuclear family
family diagram *see* genograms
family mapping 76
family myths 49–50, 71; and news 50; and restraints 49–50; *see also* rules
family of origin 17, 30, 79, 106, 116, 121–122, 124–126, 129, 132, 135, 136, 138–140
Family Process journal 46
feedback 21–25; analogic 21; definition 22; digital 21; negative 23–25, 29–30, 32, 38, 96; positive 22–25, 30–32, 96
formula tasks 83; first session 83
Foucault, Michel 186
fractional relationship 189
Freudian theory 103, 104
fundamental attribution error (FAE) 44–45

general systems theory 15, 20–21
genograms 110, 113, 124–133, 139, 140; mechanics of 125–133
genuineness (being public) 163

Gergen, Kenneth 184–185, 188–189, 192, 194–195, 200–201
Gergen, Mary M. 185
Goolishian, Harry 157–158, 170–172

halo effect 156
homeostasis 23, 27–32, 38, 40, 45–46, 49–50, 52, 55, 59, 62, 66, 69, 89, 96–97, 100, 143
horn effect 156
hypotheses 50–51, 59, 115, 148, 176; systemic 50–51

identified patient 36, 41, 52
illness 79; emotional 113, 118; medical 2; mental 103, 111; physical 107, 118; social 107, 118
interactional aesthetics 60–80; difference 61–62; distinctions 62–63; diversity 77–78; ecology 11, 15, 25, 27, 70–71, 74, 77, 153; family life cycle 78–80; information 63; map/territory 69; open and closed systems 74–75; punctuations 63–64; redundancy/pattern 65–66; *see also* boundaries; patterns; systems; whole/part
interactional pragmatics 81–101; boundary making 100; content/process 88–90; first order change 48–49, 93, 95–96, 98; second order change 48–49, 93–96, 98–101; *see also* axioms of communication; communication; counterparadox; enactments; metacommunication; paradox; paradoxes in therapy
interactional presence 158; as I-Thou relationship 158; *see also* love
interactional sequence 64
International Statistical Classification of Diseases and Related Health Problems (ICD) 10, 196

Jackson, Don D. 15, 29, 31, 44, 46, 48, 74, 82

Kerr, Michael 105–106, 109, 117–120, 129, 136–137, 140; unidisease concept of 137
knowledge: constructed 143, 150, 183–184; dominant 191; empirical 182; legitimate 182, 199; local 191, 201; objective 185; personal 201; privileged 201; scientific 15, 104; theory of 146
Korzybski, Alfred 69, 146

language systems 15, 20, 142, 156–157, 171–172, 174, 183
languaging 149, 154–157, 161, 170–172, 211; sharing 155
live goals 169–170
love 2, 11, 64, 73, 86, 103, 109–110, 156–158, 163–164, 178, 190, 198; marriages 184; Maturana's definition of 150–151; true 181

Macy Conferences 15
marital conflict 117–119
marital quid pro quo 48–49; as complementarity 48
Maturana, Humberto 147–153, 157–158, 163, 167; on the autopoitic 152; on love 150, 157–158, 163; Theorem Number One 147–148; on violence 150, 158
Mead, Margaret 14–15, 92
meaning 156; focusing on meanings 164–166; meanings in therapy 166–167
meaningful noise 40
medical model 10, 183, 200
Mental Research Institute (MRI) 15, 46, 61, 74, 82, 92–93, 213; Brief Therapy Center 46, 74, 82, 92
metacommunication 90–92; unbalancing 91–92
Minuchin, Salvador 48–49, 52, 76, 88, 100, 153
modernism 182–183
MRI brief therapy 15, 93, 213
multifinality 26, 27, 53

National Institute of Mental Health (NIMH) 104
natural systems aesthetics 102–123; emotional system 104–107, 109–110, 112–114, 122–123, 124, 128–129, 132–135; individuality and togetherness 78, 104, 109–112, 123; *see also* anxiety; Bowen's Eight Concepts
natural systems pragmatics 124–141; detriangulating 135–139; effectiveness of natural systems theory 139–140; self of the therapist in Bowen Family Systems practice 113, 133–135; therapist as coach 113, 138–139; *see also* genograms
natural systems theory 15, 84, 103, 105, 137, 139–140, 177
Nicaragua 2–3, 14
"not-knowing" 171–176, 180, 201, 204
nuclear family 16, 29, 32, 60, 71–72, 75, 78, 105, 111, 116–120, 132, 138, 147; nuclear family emotional process 105, 111, 116–119, 132

objectivism 143, 161
objectivity 104, 134, 146, 148–149, 152, 182, 184, 188, 201; -in-parentheses 149; -without-parentheses 149
ontic perspective 177; relational dimension 177
orthogonal interaction 154

paradox 32–33, 96–97; in communications 15, 61, 92; *see also* paradoxes in therapy
paradoxes in therapy 97–100; Devil's Pact 100; double bind 15, 46, 96–97; go slow 98; prescribing the symptom 97, 99; pretend technique 99; restraint 25–27, 28, 31, 43–44, 47, 49–50, 52, 59,

97–99; therapeutic 97–98, 100; therapeutic ordeals 99–100
patterns: competitive symmetrical 66–69; complementary 66, 68–69, 79, 91; and redundancy 66; and in relationships 66, 68, 116, 137; submissive symmetrical 66–69; symmetrical 66, 69
personal agency 187–188, 193, 202, 205, 207, 212, 217
personality 13–14, 26, 36, 43–44, 110, 121–122, 144, 176, 182, 184, 188–189, 196, 199, 203
personhood 12, 189, 199
perturbations 63, 150, 152–154, 157–158, 164, 169–170, 174, 178; *see also* orthogonal interaction; structural drift
perturbing the system 63, 154; *see also* peturbations
phenomenology 166
polyocularity 190
positivism 148
postmodernism 182–184, 188
postpositivism 148
post-structuralism 155, 191
pragmatics: definition 18
problem talk 210–213
psychiatry 2, 103, 104, 137
psychodynamic model 10
psychology: analytical 74; feminist 185; positive 196–197; social 44, 156
psychosexual stages of development 10
psychotherapists 18, 27, 82, 95, 104, 152, 159, 165, 181–182, 184, 187, 197, 198; behavioral 69; constructivist 162–166; Gestalt 178; rationalist 165; traditional 196
psychotherapy: behavioral model 69; cognitive model 69; collaborative 158; compassionate relationship as heart of 163; constructivist 144, 162–165, 177; interactional model 61; person-centered 158; social 155; *see also* therapy
psychotropic medication 5, 6

questions: conversational 171, 174–175; fast-forward 198, 216; miracle 211–212, 216; presuppositional 161, 216; right 174; *see also* scaling questions

realism 144–145, 184
reflexivity 177, 199–200
reframing 34, 47, 94–95, 100, 146; positive connotation 95
relational responsibility 194–195; conjoint relations 195–196; group realities 195; internal others 195–196; systemic swim 195; *see also* communication
relationship anxiety 109, 117–119, 135; "overfunctioning" vs. "underfunctioning" partner 118; parental 119

relationships: adult 138–139; egalitarian 198; family 116–117, 119, 124, 129, 133–134, 137, 141; human 21, 104, 109, 111, 114–115, 121, 135–136, 139–140; interactive 183; interdependent 207; interpersonal 39, 50, 189; intimate adult partner 118; as I-Thou 158, 163, 173, 177; marital 5, 117, 119; as patterned interactions 66; person to person 138–139; romantic 7, 28, 48, 72, 109, 121, 134, 160, 177, 181, 187, 202; social 184
research: qualitative 35, 148–149; quantitative 35, 148–149, 152
Rogers, Carl 163–164, 177; core conditions 163–164; *see also* accurate empathic understanding; genuineness; unconditional positive regard
Rogerian model 9–10
roles 51–53; and complementarity 52; as identity 52–53; unwrapping family member identities 52, 59
rules: covert 44, 46–50, 52; of interaction 32, 44, 46, 48, 50, 52–53, 62, 89, 94–95; overt 44, 45–50, 52
Russell, Bertrand 22, 32–33

sandwich generation 78–79
scaling questions 56, 179–180
sculpting 85–86; family 179
second order cybernetics 143, 151, 153
self: authentic 188–189; core 189; -esteem 5, 12, 190; multi- 190; -narrative 165, 188; relational 189
self, sense of 6, 11–12, 178, 186, 188, 191, 195, 216
self, the 12, 43, 101, 133–134, 147, 150, 166, 176, 189–190, 197
Seligman, Martin 197
sexual harassment 48
Silence of the Lambs, The 48
skeleton keys 83; *see also* formula tasks
social construction aesthetics 181–197; authenticity 188–189; deconstruction and reconstruction 193–194; discourses 185–186; language games 191; misunderstandings of conversations 191–192; modernism vs. postmodernism 182–183; personal agency 187–188; power 186–187; reality as multiverse 190–191; strengths rather than deficits 196–197; structure of narratives 192–193; systems stories 191; *see also* deconstruction; postmodernism; relational responsibility; social constructionism
social constructionism 15, 181, 183–185, 189–190, 196, 199, 201
social constructionist theory 185
social construction pragmatics 198–217; client as expert 200–201; counter documents 206–207; either/or and both/and 214–215; outsider witness practices 207; re-authoring conversations 202; reflecting teams 208–209; resources 216–217;

social constructionist/postmodern therapy 198–200; therapy via questions 215–216; *see also* co-construction; externalization; definitional ceremonies; problem talk; solution talk
social ecology 25, 153
solution-focused brief therapy (SFBT) 46, 74, 213
solution talk 201, 210–213; and EARS 212–213; and exceptions 212; as generative discourse 211; miracle question 211–212
South Korea 213
Spanish (language) 3
stories: landscape of action 192–194, 197; landscape of consciousness 192–193, 197; landscape of identity 193–194, 197
storyteller 159, 167–170, 193, 202
structural coupling 152, 157–158
structural determinism 151–152, 179
structural drift 151, 154, 158; co-ontogenic 157
structure coupling 151
structured fight task 46, 83
Sullivan, Harry Stack 46
systems: adaptable 75; closed 27, 74–75, 146, 152; definition 15; functional/dysfunctional assessments of 31; open 27, 74–75; types of 16
systems theory 1, 11–13, 15–18, 69–70, 72, 89, 103–104, 111; family 114, 118; general 15; language 15; *see also* Bowen Family Systems theory (BFST); natural systems theory

Taos Institute 185
Thailand 181
therapeutic alliance 78, 97, 166
therapist: Bowen Family Systems 106, 124–125, 135, 140–141; cognitive 11, 84; epistemology of 7–10; as "information gatekeeper" 9; person-centered 11; psychoanalytic 11; psychodynamic 10; social constructionist 183, 185, 191, 197, 198–200, 203, 206–207, 210, 212; systems 12, 19, 23, 89; therapeutic orientation of 10
therapist maneuverability 84

therapy: cognitive 10; constructivist 162, 170; contextual 177; couples 46; as dialogical process 173; existential 158; family 15, 46, 72, 92, 94, 96, 103–104, 116, 123, 124, 129, 153, 203; interactional 46; as I-Thou relationship 158, 163, 173, 177; marriage 46, 48; Milan systemic family 46, 74; models of 10–11, 46; MRI brief 15, 46, 93, 213; ordeal 99–100; paradoxes in 97–100; person-centered 11, 177; via questions 215–216; social constructionist/postmodern 198–200; strategic family 15, 46; talk 5; working alliance in 165; *see also* solution-focused brief therapy
thick description 166–168, 202, 204
thinking, modes of: narrative 192; paradigmatic 192
Toman, Walter 121–122
truth: absolute 156, 182, 184, 190; objective 143–144, 148, 173, 188, 199, 201, 203; as socially constructed 188; as subjective agreement 184

unconditional positive regard 9, 163
unique outcomes 202, 205, 212
United States 2–3, 14, 15, 22, 71, 137, 181, 186, 187, 192, 195
utilization 84, 197

violence 158; definition of 150; domestic 123; relationship 3
von Foerster, Heinz 147–150; aesthetical imperative 149–150; ethical imperative 150
von Foerster's Corollary Number One 148

Watzlawick, Paul 36, 46–48, 72, 74, 82, 90, 93–94, 98–99
Weakland, John 15, 46, 82, 90, 92–93, 97, 213
Whitehead, A. N. 32–33
whole/part 71–73; nonsummativity 72–73; summativity 72; wholes 72
Wiener, Norbert 21–22
Wittgenstein, L. 155, 191